# THE LANGUAGE QUESTION IN EUROPE AND DIVERSE SOCIETIES

Recent developments in the European integration process have raised, amongst many other things, the issue of linguistic diversity. This is regarded by some as a stumbling block to the creation and sustainability of a European democratic polity and to the fair working of its legal and social institutions. The 'question of language', in this sense, concerns the nature and role of public communication and public discourse, both as sources of information and understanding, and as modes of legitimacy in law and politics. Its solution involves an understanding of the role played by natural languages as the main forms of social communication, and the consequent design of policies and institutional mechanisms which may facilitate interlinguistic and intercultural communication. Put in this way, this is not an exclusively European problem. Nor is it an entirely new problem, for it also presents itself in the form of the relationship between linguistic majorities and minorities within what are traditionally considered as unitary nation-states. However, the effects of globalization and the diffusion of multiculturalism within nation-states have given renewed emphasis to the question of language in diverse societies. Facing the question anew involves a reconsideration of our traditional ideas about social communication and the public sphere, about opinion-formation and diffusion, about the protection of cultural and linguistic minorities, and about the role that language has in the process of formation of political and legal cultures. This volume is intended as a multidisciplinary contribution towards studying and assessing the range of problems that form the 'language question' in Europe and diverse societies.

Oñati International Series in Law and Society

A SERIES PUBLISHED FOR THE OÑATI INSTITUTE FOR THE SOCIOLOGY OF LAW

Titles in this Series

*Social Dynamics of Crime and Control: New Theories for a World in Transition* edited by Susannah Karstedt and Kai Bussmann

*Criminal Policy in Transition* edited by Andrew Rutherford and Penny Green

*Making Law for Families* edited by Mavis Maclean

*Poverty and the Law* edited by Peter Robson and Asbjørn Kjønstad

*Adapting Legal Cultures* edited by Johannes Feest and David Nelken

*Rethinking Law Society and Governance: Foucault's Bequest* edited by Gary Wickham and George Pavlich

*Rules and Networks* edited by Richard Appelbaum, Bill Felstiner and Volkmar Gessner

*Women in the World's Legal Professions* edited by Ulrike Schultz and Gisela Shaw

*Healing the Wounds* edited by Marie-Claire Foblets and Trutz von Trotha

*Imaginary Boundaries of Justice* edited by Ronnie Lippens

*Family Law and Family Values* edited by Mavis Maclean

*Contemporary Issues in the Semiotics of Law* edited by Anne Wagner, Tracey Summerfield, and Farid Benavides Vanegas

*The Geography of Law: Landscapes, Identity and Regulation* edited by Bill Taylor

*Theory and Method in Socio-Legal Research* edited by Reza Banakar and Max Travers

*Luhmann on Law and Politics* edited by Michael King and Chris Thornhill

*Precarious Work, Women and the New Economy: The Challenge to Legal Norms* edited by Judy Fudge and Rosemary Owens

*Juvenile Law Violators, Human Rights, and the Development of New Juvenile Justice Systems* edited by Eric L Jensen and Jørgen Jepsen

# The Language Question in Europe and Diverse Societies

## Political, Legal and Social Perspectives

Edited by

Dario Castiglione and Chris Longman

Oñati International Series in Law and Society

A SERIES PUBLISHED FOR THE OÑATI INSTITUTE FOR THE SOCIOLOGY OF LAW


·HART·
PUBLISHING
OXFORD AND PORTLAND OREGON
2007

Published in North America (US and Canada)
by Hart Publishing
c/o International Specialized Book Services
920 NE 58th Avenue, Suite 300
Portland, OR 97213-3786
USA
Tel: +1 503 287 3093 or toll-free: (1) 800 944 6190
Fax: +1 503 280 8832
Email: orders@isbs.com
Website: www.isbs.com



Hart Publishing, 16c Worcester Place, Oxford, OX1 2JW
Telephone: +44 (0)1865 517530 Fax: +44 (0)1865 510710
Email: mail@hartpub.co.uk
Website: http://www.hartpub.co.uk

British Library Cataloguing in Publication Data
Data Available

ISBN-13: 978-1-84113-667-7 (hardback)
ISBN-10: 1-84113-667-0 (hardback)

ISBN-13: 978-1-84113-668-4 (paperback)
ISBN-10: 1-84113-668-9 (paperback)

Typeset by Compuscript, Shannon
Printed and bound in Great Britain by
Lightning Source UK Ltd

# *Preface*

Recent developments in the European integration process have raised, amongst many other things, the issue of linguistic diversity. This is regarded by some as a stumbling block to the creation and sustainability of a European democratic polity and to the fair working of its legal and social institutions. The 'question of language', in this sense, concerns the nature and role of public communication and public discourse, both as sources of information and understanding, and as modes of legitimacy in law and politics. Its solution involves an understanding of the role played by natural languages as the main forms of social communication, and the consequent design of policies and institutional mechanisms that may facilitate inter-linguistic and intercultural communication. Put in this way, this is not an exclusively European problem. Nor is it an entirely new problem, for it also presents itself in the form of the relationship between linguistic majorities and minorities within what are traditionally considered as unitary nation-states. However, the effects of globalisation and the diffusion of multiculturalism within nation-states have given renewed emphasis to the question of language in diverse societies. Facing the question anew involves a reconsideration of our traditional ideas about social communication and the public sphere, about opinion-formation and diffusion, about the protection of cultural and linguistic minorities, and about the role that language has in the process of formation of political and legal cultures. This volume is intended as a contribution, from a variety of perspectives, to studying and assessing the range of problems that form the 'language question' as here specified.

The volume originated from a Workshop on 'The Public Discourse of Law and Politics in Multilingual Societies' that we organised in Oñati (Gipuzkoa, Spain) several years ago, under the sponsorship and with the support of the International Institute for the Sociology of Law (IISL). The workshop's location in Oñati was not without significance, given the topicality that the issue of linguistic and cultural diversity has in the Basque context. The workshop—like, ultimately, the volume—had to face the issue of the language in which to conduct its business. English was the obvious choice, for practical reasons. But the choice itself highlights some of the problems facing the construction of common political and legal institutions across Europe (or in other multilingual societies). The dominance of English as the de facto lingua franca in so many fields of civic engagement and professional life confronts the EU with the seeming paradox of, on the one hand, defending the doctrine of *de jure* multilingualism as the basis for equality of its citizens, and, on the other, having perhaps to accept the imperatives of communicative needs in order to establish the status of citizenship itself. This is the conundrum from which this volume starts and to whose resolution it aims to contribute.

In the process of preparing and writing this book we have become indebted to many people and colleagues for their intellectual and material support. We gladly acknowledge, first of all, the financial support and generous hospitality of the IISL, which made possible (and indeed pleasurable) the original workshop. In particular, the two Directors at the time, Professor Manuel Calvo García and Bill Felstiner, and Ms Malen Gordoa Mendizabal were instrumental in providing the perfect conditions for a successful workshop. We also thank those participants in the workshop (Urko Aiartza, Miriam Aziz, Richard Bellamy, Idil Boran and Roberto Toniatti) who are not represented in the volume, but whose contributions to the lively and intense discussions were of great help in shaping the volume in its current form. Equally decisive was the input of the two anonymous referees for the Series in which the volume appears, and of Professor Johannes Feest, one of the Series directors, during the phase in which the chapters comprising this volume were written and revised, and the volume as a whole took shape. We are particularly indebted to one of the anonymous readers for having suggested ways in which to present this volume and its findings. The editors also acknowledge the financial support of the European Commission, since their work towards this volume benefited greatly from their participation in the CIDEL FP5 Integrated Project. Castiglione is indebted to the British Academy for a personal travel grant towards his participation in the Oñati Workshop. For assistance in the preparation of the manuscript, the editors are grateful to Rob Lamb. Our final thanks go to the other contributors to this volume for the patience that they showed while waiting for the project to come to fruition. As an old Italian saying has it: 'Col tempo e con la paglia si maturano le sorbe.' Hopefully, some of the ideas put forward in this volume are ripe for public consumption.

DC
CL

# *Contents*

# *Contributors*

**Dario Castiglione** teaches Political Theory at the University of Exeter. His main research interests lie in the history and theory of political thought and European constitutionalism. His publications comprise co-edited volumes on *The Constitution in Transformation* (Blackwell, 1996), *The History of Political Thought in National Context* (CUP, 2001), *The Culture of Toleration in Diverse Societies* (Manchester UP, 2003) and *Making European Citizens* (Palgrave, 2006). He is currently working on a book on European constitutional politics.

**Peter A Kraus** holds the Chair of Ethnic Relations at the University of Helsinki. He previously was Associate Professor (Privatdozent) of political science at Humboldt University in Berlin. He has published widely and in several languages on problems of democratic transition and consolidation, politics in Southern Europe, cultural diversity and identity politics, and the present dilemmas of European integration. His most recent work is on the implications of cultural pluralism and multilingualism for European polity-building. His recent publications include *Europäische Öffentlichkeit und Sprachpolitik. Integration durch Anerkennung* (Campus, 2004); an English edition of this title is in preparation.

**Chris Longman** is Deputy Director of the Centre for European Studies at the University of Exeter. His research interests include: the politics of cultural diversity in Europe; the construction of European identity; language and politics in the European Union; European political integration; multi-level governance; and regionalism and sub-state nationalism in Europe. He is currently co-authoring a book on European constitutional politics: *Constitutional Politics in the EU: The Convention Moment and its Aftermath* (Palgrave, 2007).

**Philippe Van Parijs** directs the Hoover Chair of Economic and Social Ethics at the Université catholique de Louvain (Belgium). He is the author of *Evolutionary Explanation in the Social Sciences* (Rowman & Littlefield, 1981), *Marxism Recycled* (CUP, 1993), *Real Freedom for All* (OUP, 1995), *What's Wrong with a Free Lunch?* (Beacon Press, 2001) and the editor of *Cultural Diversity versus Economic Solidarity* (De Boeck Université, 2004).

**Alan Patten** is Associate Professor of Politics at Princeton University. He is the author of *Hegel's Idea of Freedom* (OUP, 1999) and co-editor, with Will Kymlicka, of *Language Rights and Political Theory* (OUP, 2003). His articles include 'Political Theory and Language Policy', *Political Theory* (2001), 'Democratic Secession from a Multinational State', *Ethics* (2002), and 'Liberal Neutrality and Language Policy', *Philosophy & Public Affairs* (2003). He is currently writing a book on political theory and language politics.

**Omid A Payrow Shabani** is Assistant Professor of Philosophy at the University of Guelph, Canada. He is the author of *Democracy, Power and Legitimacy: Critical Theory of Jürgen Habermas* (Toronto UP, 2003) and 'Who is Afraid of Constitutional Patriotism?', *Social Theory and Practice* (2002). He is currently working on bridging the gap between the theoretical work of critical theorists and multiculturalists in order to be able to address concrete questions of policy making from the normative perspective of Habermasian constitutional patriotism.

**Philip Schlesinger** is Professor of Cultural Policy at the University of Glasgow and Academic Director of the Centre for Cultural Policy Research. He is currently working on cultural creativity in the film and television industries, on communicative spaces in Europe, and also on ethnography and exile. Amongst his most recent co-authored books are *Open Scotland?* (Polygon, 2001), and *Mediated Access* (Luton UP, 2003). His most recent co-edited books are *The SAGE Handbook of Media Studies* (SAGE, 2004) and *The European Union and Public Sphere* (Routledge, 2007).

**Niamh Nic Shuibhne** is a Reader in EC Law at the University of Edinburgh. She has also lectured in Constitutional Law and Jurisprudence at the National University of Ireland, Galway. Her monograph, *EC Law and Minority Language Policy: Culture, Citizenship and Fundamental Rights*, was published by Kluwer Law in 2002. She has published widely on the legal status of the Irish language and on minority rights generally, and on substantive EC law. She is currently engaged in work on EU citizenship and freedom of movement.

**Miquel Strubell,** MA (Oxon) MSc (Lond) specialised in the Psychology of Education and then in bilingualism, language status planning and minority language policies in Europe. After working for the government of Catalonia on the promotion of Catalan, he is now employed by the Open University of Catalonia (www.uoc.edu). He has been a consultant for the OSCE and the Council of Europe, and has co-ordinated several European research projects and policy reports.

**Reetta Toivanen** is in charge of the interdisciplinary research project 'Teaching Human Rights in Europe' in the Department for European Ethnology at the Humboldt University in Berlin where she also teaches anthropology. She is also affiliated Senior Research Fellow at the Institute for Human Rights at the Åbo Akademi University in Finland. Her publications include Minderheitenrechte als Identitätsressource? (Lit Verlag, 2001), 'Saami and the Nordic Civil Societies' in N Götz and J Heckmann (eds), Civil Society in the Baltic Sea Region (Ashgate, 2003), and more recently Rethinking Non-discrimination and Minority Rights, edited with M Scheinin (Åbo Akademi University, 2004).

**Sue Wright** is Professor of Language and Politics at Portsmouth University, UK. She has written extensively on the subject of language in governance and political associations, including two monographs: *Community and Communication: The Role of Language in Nation Building and European Integration* (Multilingual Matters, 2000) and *Language Policy and Language Planning: From Nationalism to Globalisation* (Palgrave-Macmillan, 2004).

# 1

# *Introduction: Negotiating Language Regimes*

DARIO CASTIGLIONE

IS THERE A language question in 'diverse societies'? This book suggests that there may be more than one, and that the nature of the questions raised by language use in such societies is both complex and multi-faceted. The particular angle from which we look at these questions is one that tends to emphasise the role of language in a political community. This is a perspective that has become more salient as modern societies have become both more porous in their relations with each other and more internally differentiated. In the recent past, the political role of language appeared to be less problematic; for language was meant to be, on the one hand, an important element of distinction between different political communities, and, on the other, one of the main instruments for binding the members of the community together. Both these functions have been weakened as the combined effects of globalisation and multiculturalism have impacted on the internal and external dynamics of the political community. This is particularly evident in the European Union, where questions about the political role of language are mostly avoided, due to what is generally considered to be the intractable nature of its multilingual regime. But avoiding the problem does not solve it. Moreover, the avoidance strategy tends to obscure the nature of the questions posed by multilingualism in modern societies, and consequently the variety of measures and solutions that these may require. This volume is meant to raise precisely such questions, thus contributing, if not to their solution, at least to identifying the problems and engaging in a discussion of the possible solutions.

Although the more theoretical and normative contributions to this volume apply to diverse societies at large, the majority of its chapters take the European experience, and the EU in particular, as their main focus of analysis. This, of course, narrows the range of problems and experiences encompassing the language question, but, at the same time, offers a sustained analysis of how this question applies to the European case, at least in its transnational (rather than sub-national) dimension. The other common feature of the contributions to this volume, their already-mentioned focus on the political dimension of language, is enriched by the diversity of approaches characterising the various chapters, thus providing some basis for a dialogue between disciplines: from politics to socio-linguistics, from law to anthropology, from political sociology to normative theory. Part of the aim of this volume is to suggest that only by entering into such a dialogue and by developing a sustained exchange of insights may it be possible to give a satisfactory account of the language question in diverse societies. Indeed, such an interdisciplinary approach has played an important role in the emergence of socio-linguistics during the last 50 years, a discipline whose main scope is to study from both a micro- and a macro-perspective the interactions between language and society (Coulmas, 1997: 1–3). Nonetheless, the more specific question of how to deal with multi-lingualism in diverse societies has tended to be framed in mainly political and legal terms. Bringing in the knowledge of sociologists, linguists, anthropologists, educationalists, and indeed sociolinguists is meant to broaden the framework, offering a richer account of what language and communication both entail and mean for individuals, groups, and societies at large.

## THE NATURE OF DIVERSITY

Having outlined the general scope and intent of the chapters comprising this volume, the rest of this introduction aims to offer a context within which to place them. It does so first by providing a few considerations on the nature of diversity, secondly by offering a summary account of the questions raised by multilingualism, followed by a discussion of how to deal with it politically, and finally by giving a brief overview of the topics covered by the individual contributors to this volume and of some of the lines of research that may follow from their analysis. The idea of diverse societies is one where 'diversity' is given a prominent role, not just as a descriptor, but also—albeit often implicitly—as a norm: as the recognition that 'diversity' has a particular meaning and/or value for the society in question. This is evident in the way in which the EU, for instance, describes itself as a community 'united in diversity', which is, after all, the way in which its linguistic regime is also characterised. But the idea of 'unity in diversity' poses a series of complex challenges. As Europe, for instance, becomes a more integrated area of economic production and exchange, there are greater opportunities for both development and co-ordination between sectors, activities and institutions that have similar problems and interests. This provides a definite push towards unity, while narrowing the range of diversities. And yet, it may also increase the degree of inter- and intra-territorial difference (at European, national and sub-national levels), making social cohesion more problematic. Moreover, the integration process needs to come to terms with the sheer variety of national and sub-national situations, as they are determined by social and demographic factors, by particular cultural and institutional histories, and by the political composition and the kind of life-styles and aspirations diffused in each country or region of Europe. This variety has recently increased, both quantitatively and so to speak qualitatively, as the result of enlargement, making this aspect of diversity more problematic, as attested by the number of languages that are now officially recognised in the institutions of the EU. The socio-cultural diversity of the EU is further complicated by the presence of large minorities that are the product of recent and not so recent immigration waves. In Europe, in contrast to the American experience, such minorities have been assimilated to only a limited degree, and in so far as their values and life-styles are not supported by a separate territorial authority, their 'diversity' poses yet another challenge.

But diversity is not just a *condition* of the European society. As I have already hinted at, due to several ideal and material processes, it has become a *value* of the European experience of integration (the purpose of the integration *process* being 'an ever closer union of the *peoples* of Europe'). This is a point worth considering, since the dominant perspective has been to treat diversity as a *problem* that needs to be either accommodated or overcome. By contrast, in both the EU's official communications and the self-consciousness of many of its citizens, diversity has a *constitutive* role (the EU as a 'Union of *peoples*'), which has important implications for both its identity and its evolving structure of governance. Furthermore, there may be different forms and ideas of diversity, some more backward-looking, emphasising belonging, others forward-looking, emphasising hybridity. The role of language, for instance, can be characterised in either way, as the accretion of past experiences, or as the malleable instrument for engaging with people in a fast changing world. But, in general, there are at least five kinds of inter-related diversity that one may want to consider in describing the range of differences present in modern diverse societies.

1) There are differences that have a national and cultural dimension (including minority nations), most of which may also manifest themselves as linguistic differences.
2) There are differences produced by the existence of legal and political regimes at state, regional, supranational and international levels. Although, on the face of it, these are organisational differences that can be altered at will and with a certain facility, they tend to assume a more cultural and entrenched nature as time passes, so that they are often hardly distinguishable from the more specific national and cultural differences.
3) There are ethnic and religious differences, which in themselves are distinct, but which can also be overlapping. Although in theory the former are ascriptive, while the latter are voluntary, religion itself is rarely a matter of choice in the lives of individuals.

4) There are social and economic differences that are associated with the modern economy and the processes of globalisation. These are differences of income, class and status that overlap and often tend to reinforce each other. They may also result in cultural differences, or, increasingly, in a process of individuation.
5) Finally, there is a complex group of differences based on gender, life-styles and needs, often made more relevant and entrenched by the kind of socio-economic processes mentioned under (4) above.

These types of diversity are not exclusively European, but common to all advanced economies in which the division of labour has led to differentiated spheres of economic and social life. What is distinctive of modern diverse societies is their appreciation that the social pluralism that comes from such diversities is considered a 'fact' with an important normative component, determining the way in which we ought to interact with each other. This appreciation and consequent attitude is also the product of a post-colonial view of race and a post-feminist view of gender. All together, they have produced a new positive attitude towards diversity and the propagation of discourses of recognition. The discourse of multiculturalism in Europe, as in other parts of the world, has tried to capture such a new attitude of respect for and recognition of diversity. But multicultural policies, as many critics are only too ready to point out, present modern democratic societies with problems of formulation, instrumentation and implementation if the recognition of deep diversity is to be combined with the equal treatment of citizens. Language is one prominent area of debate about the opportunities and shortcomings of multicultural policies.

In the EU, however, contemporary diversity and its discourses have been grafted onto the particular historical experience of a plurality of nations and peoples with their respective institutions, social arrangements, cultures, habits, traditions and, of course, languages. At the same time, the process of Europeanisation has created supranational and postnational structures and arrangements with the overlapping of cultural, political, legal and social spaces—all of which require more intense forms of exchange and communication. These developments have produced a complex pattern of diversity, with demands for recognition and difference sometimes competing with demands for efficiency, justice, equality and social cohesion.

From these considerations it follows that one of the fundamental criteria for the development of a European form of governance is that of *governing diversity by valuing diversity*. In truth, this is not always possible, nor is it right in all circumstances, since there are also elements of diversity that are negative and that may be the source of intractable conflicts. Moreover, conflict management through bargaining, compromise and consensus-building is a difficult art, which can be achieved only through various institutional devices cutting across law, politics and education. In the case of linguistic differences, particularly when they are both widespread and entrenched as in the European case, finding both the instruments and the guiding principles for a policy that governs diversity by *valuing* it, would seem an impossible task. To face such a task requires, first of all, identifying the particular questions posed by multilingualism in diverse societies.

## THE CHALLENGES OF MULTILINGUALISM

In a most obvious sense, (natural) languages function as an instrument of communication between people, but also as a social bond. Whichever side one takes on the origins of languages, as nature or convention, it is apparent that a language is not simply an abstract means of communication between different people, but—like all other such social 'institutions'—it binds them together, while offering them a ground for identification and belonging. Besides, as a means of social exchange, it offers opportunities for power politics and social domination. Thus, communication, identity and power are all processes in which language matters.

On the face of it, the first challenge posed by multilingualism is that there is more than one currency in which communication, identity and power relationships can take place in society. This poses obvious problems of efficiency, complicating all three sets of social relationship, thus endangering the unity of the society in question. Economically, transaction costs are greater, particularly if exchanges take place between people who speak different languages. Politically, people may find it more difficult to come to an agreement, since besides all other barriers, they also need to overcome the one posed by the difficulty in communicating and finding a way of understanding each other. Moreover, linguistic differences are, more often than not, part of a broader pattern of cultural differences due to different historical traditions and experiences developing in different parts of the world across time. But it is perhaps less remarked, at least in a political context, that multilingualism poses not simply the problem of 'conflict' between different systems of communication, but also that of 'communication' between these very systems (Laponce, 2002: 587). In other words, two languages that come to share part or the whole of the social space in which they operate enter into some relationship with each other, either as systems of communication, which are subject to transformation by the very fact of coming into contact with each other, or as alternative systems of communication for individuals who happen to operate in a social environment where two or more systems of communication apply equally. The crucial point is that both 'conflict' and 'communication' affect languages and the relationship of the community of speakers (as a whole or as individuals) with a language (their own or any other that is available to them within the same social space).

In other words, in a bilingual or multilingual environment, there are two sets of linguistic effects, which derive from the particular way in which two or more languages either enter into conflict or communicate. These effects impact on the languages themselves as systems of communication, but also on the community of speakers who predominantly identify with one language or another, and on the individuals whose interests and identity are variously related to language use and intra-group communication. This complex set of relationships is already evident in the context of social and personal bilingualism that may arise from inter-linguistic marriages, or from the close proximity of different linguistic communities. It acquires a more pregnant meaning, however, when bilingualism takes the form of diglossia, ie in those contexts where the languages available are not used interchangeably across all roles and levels of social discourse, but contextually, according to specific rules and conventions differentiating the use of one language from the other. There are cases in which diglossia may be regarded as merely functional, as when there may be a more or less tacit agreement between members of a community (or family) to speak one language privately (or at home) and another in public (which is often the case with dialects). There are other cases in which diglossia serves to separate the sacred from the profane, thus establishing a linguistic hierarchy and reinforcing a separation of roles, as when, for instance, it was the practice in the Catholic Church to use Latin in religious services (indeed, remnants of this system are still in place). But when diglossia applies to the political sphere, the functional reasons take on a more direct and divisive meaning, establishing a hierarchy of status and power. In such a case, the variety of relationships that diglossia establishes between languages, groups and individuals become more contested and the direct object, not only of personal psychology, but of political struggle. One of the issues raised by multilingualism in politics is whether there is any alternative to political diglossia (ie where one language is selected as the language of the political sphere), and whether any other arrangement is stable enough to guarantee effectiveness of communication while ostensibly offering equality of treatment and dignity to all linguistic groups comprising the political community.

## LANGUAGE AS A POLITICAL PROBLEM

Until recently, the subject of multilingualism in political societies was only perfunctorily addressed, for it was often assumed that the legal and political systems of modern nation states required a common language in order to function. The question of the diversity of languages was seen as operating at the margin of the nation state: either as part of the assimilation process of migrant communities, or as part of the accommodation of relatively small, but concentrated, linguistic minorities. On the rare occasions that language emerged as a *political* issue, it was either as part of a discourse about national character or as a challenge to the supposed unity of the political 'nation', rather than to its monolingualism. The other political contexts in which multilingualism mattered were, of course, those of direct domination through either imperial or colonial power.

Lately the issue has acquired a new salience, due mainly to the new sensitivity towards diversity and recognition discussed above. Issues of language diffusion and language use have become part of a moral and political discourse meant to address questions of rightful entitlements and policy programmes, beside the more traditional issues of political domination. In their comprehensive introduction to a volume on *Political Theory and Language Rights* (2003), Will Kymlicka and Alan Patten have identified two series of issues, one concerned with practical and the other with theoretical questions, which have contributed to raising the awareness that language matters politically. Their list of practical problems comprises ethno-linguistic conflicts (in Eastern and Central Europe), sub-national linguistic demands (in Western Europe), immigrants' linguistic enclaves (eg, Hispanics in the US), transnational political contexts (the European Union), and the protection of 'bio-diversity' (protection of small minority languages). In different ways these developments have contributed to put linguistic diversity onto the political and legal maps. Kymlicka and Patten also list two broad theoretical developments, namely the debate on multiculturalism and that on the deliberative features of democracy, as factors contributing to the new awareness of the importance of language issues, in so far as these are considered to be relevant to the definition of visions of politics and society that engage with the broader questions of social and political co-operation in diverse societies.

In fact, and looking at these developments from a broader perspective, it may be argued that the new literature on language has grown around the cluster of practical and theoretical issues, such as those identified by Kymlicka and Patten, which have to do with the perceived crisis of the modern nation state as the main locus of legitimate political action both internally and at the international level. Interest in linguistic issues has therefore emerged at the intersection of three main debates, which are of both practical and theoretical relevance, and which have characterised recent work in the social sciences, and in particular in politics, law and sociology. Multiculturalism, globalisation and post-colonial discourses of cultural diversity are such debates, providing the background against which the issue of multilingualism has acquired both new meaning and political urgency.

Most of the practical developments listed by Kymlicka and Patten are determined and/or characterised by the interaction between these three main processes. In the case of the ethno-linguistic and the sub-national conflicts that have emerged across Europe, these are only superficially the expression of a return to past nationalist feelings. For multiculturalism, globalisation and post-colonialism are radically changing the model of statehood in which nationalism thrived in the 19th and 20th centuries. As we have already seen, the questions of identity and diversity, which are posed by new forms of migration, by the emergence of transnational political action and communication, and by the diffusion of new ecological sensibilities, are shaped in intricate ways by the combined effects of multiculturalism and globalisation, and given a different value in our post-colonial cultures.

When we move to the context provided by theoretical developments, the multicultural and deliberative debates singled out by Kymlicka and Patten can similarly be deconstructed along the three lines here suggested. The recent debate about multiculturalism obviously involves a re-definition of the relationship between particularity and universality, and between the individual and the community (or communities) that is determined as much by the internal differentiation of the political body as by the increasing porousness of national legal and political systems to global forces and influences. The emergence of a more global dimension, however, has its problems, for it has become increasingly difficult and contested to advance universal claims from within any single belief system.

The issue of deliberation would seem to be distinct from those of multiculturalism, globalisation and post-colonialism. And indeed, there are internal developments of democratic theory that make this debate independent from those other issues. However, it is true that one of the reasons for the growing attention given to deliberative processes in relation to the legitimation of legal and political decision making is due to the fact that these have been partly de-personalised, while becoming less dependent on a hierarchy of norms and institutions within which the modern constitutional state tends to frame both law and politics. The crisis of sovereignty affecting the nation state encourages the re-discovery of the intrinsic discursive elements of law and politics, making the legitimacy of the institutions depend not on superior norms and authority, but on how people reason, negotiate and communicate with each other.

Now, in different ways, multiculturalism, globalisation and post-colonialism have re-introduced *culture*, and the attitude one has towards other people's culture, as a political issue. Linguistic diversity is part of this general problem. But the politics of language, as an aspect of the politics of culture, is both simpler and more complex. It is simpler, in so far as it offers a relatively easy test for the identification of issues of cultural identity and for the elaboration of cultural (ie linguistic) policies. In this respect, language is a good example of why and in what sense culture matters in politics and law. It is also simpler because language is a paradigmatic example of the relationship between universalism and particularism and of that between the individual and the community. Indeed, language is something that only comes in a particular form and can only exist as the product of social and interpersonal interaction. And yet, language—in the abstract—is one of the fundamental and universal human capacities. Moreover, individuals can grow up as bilingual or can learn another language with relative ease. In certain conditions, they can make a second language their own, using it to their own advantage, and without this causing them any problem in terms of their personality or detracting from their sense of identity.

But the politics of language present some difficulties, for the way in which language conjugates universalism and particularism, individual and collective expression, often complicates issues of identity, while rendering political choices starker, since the more traditional strategies of toleration, indifference, side-to-side cohabitation, and separate flourishing cannot easily apply in the case of language as they might more readily to other aspects of culture or to religion.

For all the reasons mentioned above, language has become a new political issue. Multilingualism, in particular, poses a political problem in two different contexts. One consists of those situations in which there are minorities whose main language of social communication is different from that of the majority (this poses more a problem of social bilingualism). The other context is when there are many languages of social communication, and the question is whether or not to give privileged status to one of them within the legal-political system (this poses the problem of political diglossia as defined above). Some recent political and socio-legal literature on language has mainly addressed issues linked to minority languages, but with the solidification of the political and legal structure of the European Union, the question of a truly plurilingual polity has also become a specific theme for reflection—even though other cases such as India already existed.

Although at a more abstract level the two contexts may pose similar questions, it is apparent that there are important differences between them, both in relation to the kind of arguments that one may wish to use in support of multilingualism, and in relation to the policies to be adopted for such recognition and/or maintenance of languages. It is also debatable whether the two contexts—one characterised by the presence of one or more linguistic minorities, and the other by plurilingual political communication—can each be treated consistently, abstracting from the assessment of the precise form that multilingualism takes in particular circumstances. For example, with respect to minority languages, does the size of the population of speakers and its territorial concentration make a difference to the kinds of demands that the speakers of that minority language can make on the majority speakers? And with respect to multilingual communication, should arrangements for public communication be sensitive to historical circumstances and take on board general issues of economic and ideological domination?

Without entering into the details of these two contexts, it is here possible to assume that they pose relatively different problems and theoretical questions. Indeed, the suggestion advanced earlier on, that multilingualism poses both conflict and communication issues, and that these apply to languages, groups and individuals, suggests that there are some distinctive differences between tackling the issue of language in one context or the other, since the dynamics of conflict and communication between languages may apply differently in situations characterised by the presence of minority languages from those of plurilingualism. Moreover, different aspects of language planning would seem to be relevant to either of these contexts. Traditionally, language planning has been concerned with policies aimed at different features of a language: its 'corpus', its 'status', or its 'use'. Social bilingualism and political diglossia may affect differently the body and standards of a language, and may have different effects on the 'corpus' of either the 'dominant' or the 'weak' language in a social community. The level of protection (or promotion) that a language needs from (or towards) its own speakers is something that is difficult to determine, and for which there may not be a general abstract solution that applies indifferently to both de-territorialised linguistic minorities and linguistic groups within more or less defined borders and with institutions of their own. The issue of 'status' has immediate and diffuse relevance for political diglossia, particularly if the language of the public sphere has strong historical and/or cultural connotations, which makes it difficult for other linguistic groups to accept its privileged status without reservations. But it is also relevant in situations of social bilingualism, where there are large enough communities which for some reason tend to preserve and transmit their language of origin. Finally, the issue of 'use' is directly linked to that of 'status', and it may indeed be even more relevant to devising different policies for language planning.

However, most of the recent literature on the protection of language status and on the political and legal implications of language use has tended to gloss over such distinctions, while dividing on three broad theoretical and ideological approaches. In different fashions, they insist on different ways of looking at the relationship between speakers and their own language, or between speakers of different languages who may need to communicate with each other in a socio-political context. A first approach concentrates on the kinds of entitlement that a speaker (or a community of speakers) acquires in relation to their own language, producing a series of perfect and imperfect obligations in other speakers. A second approach focuses on the way in which language is inextricably linked to the speaker's identity—or to the collective identity of a community of speakers. This approach may result in an entitlement-based theory, but it can also be used to support a more republican view of how the political community shapes and assimilates individuals through language acquisition. Finally, a third approach makes use of the broadly liberal vocabulary of justice and fairness in order to evaluate issues of equality and the relative costs and benefits that speakers of different languages may accrue in their exchanges through some common medium. These three approaches tend to produce different political theories of language and different policy proposals. But it remains to be seen whether they are flexible enough to apply to different multilingual contexts, and whether their principles are mutually exclusive, or instead can be combined in some coherent fashion.

## THIS VOLUME'S CONTRIBUTION

The chapters comprising this volume reflect some of the issues raised in the previous discussion. Some of them illustrate the theoretical approaches just outlined, but none of them takes a straightforward entitlement-based position. Although language rights are an easy way in which to formulate the issue of language protection, besides establishing minimum standards for citizens' access to public provisions, none of the contributions to this volume sets out a complete theory of language rights. Alan Patten, for instance, is interested in the more general formulation of a political theory of language based on justice and fairness. In doing so, he considers what he calls the 'triangle' of language policies (recognition, harmonisation and maintenance) in terms of the different ideas of equality supporting them. Shabani, on his part, emphasises the importance of identity, but he does so from the perspective of constitutional patriotism, which, in his view, considers language in its 'communicative' function, so that this should not be regarded as a natural aspect of the identity of a people, but a factor actively contributing to the formation and transformation of their political identity. Kraus underscores the importance of a policy of recognition of linguistic and cultural diversity as part of a dynamic process involving at the same time the formation of a common identity and the formation of a common space for communication. The latter, however, will need to rely on the reflexive capacity to acknowledge that such a commonality rests on a diversity of identities and languages.

The following three chapters focus on the status of minority languages from a variety of disciplinary perspectives: historico-linguistic, anthropological, and legal. Wright and Toivanen raise a number of questions on the way in which language relates to group identity. This complicates issues of language rights, for it makes it more difficult to assimilate a particular language to a particular group identity. Shuibhne turns to the legal dimension of language use, analysing both the direct and indirect influence of EC directives and case-law jurisprudence on language issues. She suggests that the EC's piecemeal legal intervention is filling the gap left open by the lack of a general and coherent EU policy. Moreover, she suggests that although there is no specific European competence on language, the integration process is changing the European linguistic map, so that some form of intervention may in fact be required.

The remaining four chapters carry on the discussion of language in the European Union by partly returning to some of the theoretical problems raised in the opening chapters, but also dealing with multilingualism intended as the context for plurilingual political communication. Strubell analyses the official documents and the official rhetoric of language diversity at the European level, which is generally considered to be the cornerstone of the EU language policy. As he and Longman demonstrate, however, this policy operates at a very superficial level, hiding a series of linguistic practices and language regimes at the institutional and semi-institutional levels that go against the high-minded but often impractical pronouncements behind the official support for linguistic diversity. Moreover, as Longman illustrates and Van Parijs further discusses, the European language regime operates within a more general context in which English is progressively becoming a lingua franca. Neither of them considers this to be necessarily in antagonism with language pluralism and with policies supporting some form of it. Indeed, Van Parijs suggests that there are powerful reasons that militate in favour of promoting the generalised use of English as a lingua franca in Europe, but at the same time that a number of corrective strategies need to be pursued in order to reduce the linguistic unfairness and disadvantages that come with the dominance of one natural language over others. Finally, Schlesinger raises the issue of language diversity and the formation of a European public sphere. He returns to some of the issues of identity and communication raised by Shabani, emphasising that, for a European space of communication to emerge, a common language is not sufficient. Linguistic dynamics within Europe should therefore be seen as part of a more general process of communication dynamics and identity construction.

## CONCLUSION: THE LANGUAGE QUESTION AND LANGUAGE REGIMES IN EUROPE

When taken together, the essays of this collection seem to widen the scope of the more recent political literature on language rights. Indeed, as noticed in the previous section, most of the contributors seem to pursue a line of enquiry that bypasses or goes beyond the strictly entitlement-based approach of much of the literature on language protection and linguistic minorities. Language rights may be necessary as an instrument of defence against political and cultural oppression. They may have a role in those cases where the viability of minority cultures and the self-determination of certain communities are under threat (Patten and Kymlicka, 2003: 32–37; Skutnabb-Kangas and Phillipson, 1995). But language rights cannot be the beginning and the end of a politics of language in democratic societies. This should be obvious from the discussion above of the complex way in which multilingualism is based on both conflictual and communicative relationships involving different agents. But there are also other reasons. An obvious one is that the internal development of both language and language communities cannot be fixed, since they depend on the complex relationships between innovation and tradition, and between individual choices and collective constraints. Another reason is that a situation of multilingual communication requires an intricate web of negotiations through which different people and groups may come to recognise each other and understand each other's needs, and these are unlikely to be regulated simply by legal rights. Moreover, as I have hinted at by distinguishing the context of social bilingualism from that of political diglossia, the issue of multilingualism in diverse societies has many aspects which touch on different levels of interaction, from the social to the political, from the legal to the cultural.

For instance, if we take the case of the European polity, the language issue has relevance in five interrelated areas:

1. As the instrument of public debate within the political institutions (its use in Parliament and the other main institutions, such as the European Court of Justice, the Commission, the Council).
2. As the instrument of intra-institutional communication within the administrative machinery of the EU and between civil servants and experts in the conduct of normal administrative business.
3. As the instrument of communication between the citizen and the administration (rights of enquiry, petition, political pressure and lobbying, etc).
4. As the main vehicle for the formation and diffusion of public debate and opinions (the general public sphere, and the way in which different specialised publics interact within the public sphere, and how this feeds in, controls and influences institutional deliberation and decision making).
5. Finally, as a general instrument of social communication.

In each of these areas different considerations about rights and power need to be made in order to find a system that reflects the demands of both cultural diversity and political and economic co-operation and solidarity.

In this respect, the problem of multilingualism in a democratic society may turn out to be a 'constellation' of problems, which may need addressing from a variety of theoretical and normative perspectives and with a variety of policies, leading to overlapping linguistic regimes, rather than depending on the application of a single principle or by the listing of general linguistic rights. The strategy of 'negotiation', therefore, may apply particularly well to an issue that, as it was suggested towards the beginning of this introduction, may need policies for the governance of diversity, not by suppressing it, but by highlighting its relative value in different situations and circumstances. This strategy is particularly appropriate to the governance of linguistic diversity in society, given that this is what we often do in intra-linguistic communication when translating from one linguistic code to another. As Umberto Eco remarks: 'translation is based on negotiation, this being a process according to which, in order to obtain something, we need to renounce something else—and by the end the players should come out with a sense of reasonable and reciprocal satisfaction, in accordance with the golden principle that one cannot have everything' (2003: 18, my translation).

In conclusion, one particular line of enquiry that I think may follow from the variety of contributions comprising this volume is that the governance of linguistic diversity may require, in the first instance, the negotiation of different linguistic regimes across society and politics. The particular normative principles and institutional arrangements that may apply to each regime, and how they can be made to work together, is however an open question to which the present volume attempts to make a contribution.

## References

Coulmas, F (1997) 'Introduction' in Coulmas, F (ed), *The Handbook of Sociologuistics* (Oxford, Blackwell), pp 1–11.

Eco, U (2003) *Dire quasi la stessa cosa. Esperienze di tracduzione* (Milan, Bombiani).

Laponce, JA (2002) 'Language and Politics' in Hawkesworth, M and Kogan, M (eds), *Encyclopedia of Government and Politics*, vol 1, 2nd edn (London and New York, Routledge), pp 587–602.

Patten, A and Kymlicka, W (2003) 'Introduction: Language Rights and Political Theory: Contexts, Issues and Approaches' in Kymlicka, W and Patten, A (eds), *Political Theory and Language Rights* (Oxford, Oxford University Press), pp 1–51.

Skutnabb-Kangas, T and Phillipson, R (1995) *Linguistic Human Rights: Overcoming Linguistic Discrimination*, in collaboration with M Rannut (Berlin and New York, Mouton de Gruyter).

# 2

# *Theoretical Foundations of European Language Debates*

ALAN PATTEN*

LINGUISTIC DIVERSITY IS among the most exciting—and most challenging—features of the new Europe. The fifteen member states of the EU prior to the 2004 enlargement together contributed eleven 'national' or majority languages to this diversity as well as numerous regional or minority languages and many non-territorial or 'immigrant' languages. Prior to 2004, twelve of the EU's territorial languages were spoken by five million or more people and several dozen counted 100,000 or more speakers.[1] The 2004 enlargement introduces nine new majority languages and important new minority languages.

The fact of linguistic diversity poses two broad questions for those engaged in thinking about European citizenship. The first relates to the design of European institutions themselves: in what language, or languages, should European institutions conduct business and offer services? What should be the 'official' and 'working' languages of European institutions? The second question concerns the language policy of European institutions with respect to all other domains of language use. Having determined their own official and working languages, what additional measures, if any, should European institutions take to shape or alter patterns of language-use by Europeans? Should there be, for example, a Europe-wide policy on second-language teaching or a charter regulating how national governments relate to their linguistic minorities?

To a considerable extent these questions have already been answered in practice.[2] Pre-enlargement EU institutions recognised all eleven national languages as official and working and accorded a number of linguistic rights on this basis. These included: the rights of individuals (regardless of

* A first draft of this chapter was presented in November 1998 at a conference in Braga, Portugal, and has been heavily revised since as my work on language has developed in a series of papers. I am grateful to a great many colleagues for both their critical comments and their encouragement along the way, and especially to participants at the Oñati conference where I presented some of the central themes of the paper.

country of residence) and national governments to communicate with the Commission in any of the official languages; the right that European law, and policy documents and public information released by the Commission, be published in all of the eleven languages; and the right to use any of the official languages in the European Parliament and to have speeches and parliamentary documents given in other languages translated into one's own. With the 2004 enlargement, the EU recognised all twenty national languages as official and working.

In the area of second-language teaching, EU governments have co-ordinated their policies, and agreed upon various standards and requirements, since 1976, and in 1990 inaugurated the ambitious LINGUA program to encourage citizens to acquire a second European language. During the same period, the European Parliament and the Council of Europe have been active in the area of minority language protection. The European Charter for Regional or Minority Languages, which guarantees a number of rights to linguistic minorities that are claimable against national governments, was opened for signature in 1992 and has since been ratified by a number of European governments.

These various language policies certainly do not reflect a European consensus on language questions, however, nor does it seem likely that a consensus will be achieved any time soon—as Europe both deepens and enlarges, as regional linguistic minorities continue to make claims for recognition against both national and European institutions, and as unease spreads about the growing international hegemony of English. The current policy regime is challenged from at least three different directions. One challenge comes from speakers of regional and minority languages, such as Catalan, Galician, Basque, Welsh, Irish, Occitan, Breton, and so on. They criticise European institutions for failing to recognise their languages and seek more assistance from European institutions in demanding recognition in national and regional institutions from their own national governments.

A second challenge to the current European language regime emphasises many of the advantages of convergence or harmonisation. Adopting a restricted number of official and working languages—in the limit, perhaps, just English—according to this argument would have one or more advantages: it could help to forge a common European identity, improve democratic deliberation at the European level, enhance the social mobility of all Europeans, and make European institutions more efficient and cost-effective.

Finally, a third challenge maintains that the current regime of (limited) official multilingualism facilitates the de facto hegemony of English and threatens the long-term viability of other European languages. Critics of this kind tend to advocate more active measures designed to promote European languages other than English. Some argue, for example, in favour of a significant reduction in the number of working/official languages with a view to giving at least some languages other than English an enhanced public role (an approach that is already practised with respect to language use in the internal workings of the European bureaucracy). For similar reasons, others maintain that the European language policy framework should tilt more decisively in the direction of what is sometimes called the 'territoriality principle': according to this principle, Europe should be divided, as far as is feasible, into a patchwork of linguistic regions in which institutions at all levels would operate exclusively in the locally dominant language.[3]

Visually, it is helpful to think of the European language debate in terms of a triangle. At one corner of the triangle is the principle that all European languages should be recognised equally. European institutions should conduct business, and offer services, in all major European languages and should promote the recognition of all languages by national and regional institutions. At a second corner is the idea of language harmonisation. Inspired by the European 'nation-state' tradition, this view emphasises the various advantages that would ensue if European institutions were to promote convergence on a single public language. Finally, at the third corner is the principle of language maintenance. Here the fear is that Europe's linguistic diversity will be swallowed up by the inexorably rising tide of English and the claim is that European institutions should promote the maintenance of European languages other than English. At present, European policy is probably closest to the equal recognition corner, although a number of regional and minority languages are not fully recognised in regional, national and European institutions. The main question facing Europeans is whether, and to what extent, their common institutions should move away from this corner of the triangle in the direction of either the harmonisation or the maintenance corners.

The aim of the present chapter is less to defend a particular answer to this question than to explore some of the issues in political theory that lie behind the policy choices facing Europeans. What values and principles can proponents of the different positions appeal to and with what degree of plausibility? Are these values and principles fundamentally different and incommensurable from one another, or can they be lined up on a common terrain of ideas and thereby made amenable to reasoned discussion and deliberation? And what theoretical puzzles remain regarding the different values and principles that are in play in this debate?

In his 1990 textbook, *Contemporary Political Philosophy*, Will Kymlicka proposes that the leading political theories of the day can be laid out beside one another on an 'egalitarian plateau'. They all accept, explicitly or implicitly, the minimal idea that persons should be treated with equal concern and respect. Where they differ from each other is in the concrete interpretation of this abstract ideal of equality and, in particular, about what it is that should be distributed equally in order to remain faithful to the idea of equality. Lining up the various positions in this way puts them into dialogue with one another and may even lead to the resolution of certain theoretical disagreements.

Inspired by Kymlicka's suggestion, I will pursue a similar strategy in this paper with respect to the three competing positions on European language questions. I shall endeavour to show how each involves a distinctive view of how people with different linguistic capacities and different language-related identities and attachments can be treated as equals by a European language regime. By setting out the debate in this way, it should be simpler to assess the relative merits of the different positions and to identify what remains puzzling or unsatisfactory about particular views.

I begin by developing in more detail the idea of equal recognition and connecting it with the abstract idea that European institutions should be designed in such a way as to treat all citizens with equal concern and respect. I then sketch out the language harmonisation and language maintenance perspectives as possible challenges to equal recognition and connect them with the same abstract egalitarian idea. In each case, I try to bring out the strength of the challenge but also some of the limitations and puzzles.

## EQUALITY OF RECOGNITION

According to the first view I shall consider, it is *recognition* that should be distributed equally amongst the speakers of Europe's different languages in order to satisfy the abstract requirement that speakers of Europe's different languages be treated with equal concern and respect. To explain and motivate this view I will use this section to answer three questions: What is recognition? Why is recognition valuable? Why should recognition be distributed equally?

A language is recognised in public life, according to my terminology, when, as a matter of policy or right, public services are offered and public business can be conducted in that language. The Swedish language enjoys public recognition in Finland, for instance, to the extent that there are public schools and universities operating in Swedish, health care services available in Swedish, and public business such as court proceedings, making a speech in the legislature, or dealing with a public official, can all be transacted in Swedish. In the context of European institutions, the recognition of Swedish would involve a right on the part of citizens, national governments and regional governments to communicate with those institutions in Swedish, a right to use Swedish in public meetings of those institutions (eg the European Parliament, the European Court of Justice), and a right to have laws and official policy documents published in that language.

It is possible to distinguish two basic goods that an individual can enjoy through recognition of her language. One such good, which can be labeled 'public access', is concerned with the communication that takes place between members of the public and the public institutions that apply to them. The interest in public access is the interest that people have in being able to access public services and participate in the conduct of public business. Since the ability to access public institutions depends on the ability to communicate in the context of those institutions, this interest is clearly relevant to language policy.

The connection is rooted in the fact that people have different language capabilities. Some people speak two or more languages fluently and seem capable of learning additional languages almost effortlessly. Others, perhaps because they do not begin at an early enough age, find it difficult to achieve competence in a second language even when they make very great efforts to do so. The interest in public access is advanced by the recognition of some language *L* when this recognition works to accommodate the linguistic needs of *L*-speakers who lack fluency in other publicly used languages. Obviously, this consideration applies with particular force to people having little or no facility in any of the other publicly recognised languages, but in certain contexts it is important even for people who have achieved a reasonable degree of competence in the other languages. In highly stressful contexts, such as hospitals or courts of law, or in contexts involving a particularly technical vocabulary, such as filling out one's tax return, even a quite fluently bilingual person can find it easier to communicate in her own language. Recognition serves the good of public access, then, in the straightforward sense that it facilitates understanding and communication on the part of people who have limited fluency in other public languages.

Important as the good of public access is, it ends up providing a rather limited basis on which to defend the recognition of any particular language. The main reason for this is that people have a capacity to learn new languages. In the long run, Swedish-speakers in Finland do not depend on the recognition of Swedish to ensure access to Finland's public institutions. Members of the Swedish language community who do not already speak the majority language can be assisted to do so through an intensive programme of language training and education. To the extent that this programme is successful, even members of the Swedish language minority will be able to access public institutions: they will be able to do so in Finnish. It is true that it is difficult for adults to learn new languages and thus some transitional accommodations might be necessary for unilingual Swedish-speakers. But children, on the other hand, are typically very good at learning new languages and so a 'Finnishisation' policy could be aimed especially at them and have a reasonable likelihood of success.

To make a stronger case for the value of public recognition to the speaker of some language, a second kind of good needs to be introduced, one that goes beyond the communicative considerations emphasised by the good of public access. This good might loosely be called 'identity'. People often have fairly strong attitudes, preferences and attachments relating to their language use and language community. An individual may self-identify with the (local) community of speakers of her language. She may be proud of the language and the cultural achievements that have been expressed through it. She may take pleasure in using the language and encountering others who are willing to use it. She may enjoy experimenting with the language and discussing its intricacies and subtleties with co-linguists. She may hope that the language community will survive and flourish into the indefinite future. And so on. In some contexts, she may feel respected and affirmed when others address her in her language and denigrated when others impose their linguistic preferences on her.

The good that I am terming 'identity' is realised for individuals with attitudes such as these when their languages are treated with respect by public institutions and, beyond that, when their language communities survive and flourish. The recognition of a particular language means that services are offered in that language and public business can be conducted in it, and this for many people is a sign of consideration and respect. Recognition also contributes to the goal of language survival and vitality and thus promotes aspects of an individual's identity that rely on the flourishing of her linguistic community. All else being equal, people are more likely to make the decisions about language use that contribute to the maintenance of the group—eg the decision to raise or educate their children in the language of the group—to the extent that there are meaningful public activities taking place in that language. Of course the language of public institutions is only one aspect of a complex calculation and other considerations, such as language use in the economy and in civil society, may well be of greater importance. But the use of the language in public institutions helps to signal that the language is a going concern and that committing oneself or one's children to the group will not be futile or disadvantageous.

Different languages—for instance, French, German and Dutch—enjoy equal recognition when public institutions are able to offer comparable services and conduct business of equal importance in each of those languages. French-, German- and Dutch-speakers are treated with equal concern and respect when their respective languages enjoy equal recognition. On the view being proposed, to recognise French and German, but not Dutch, would be to fail to treat Dutch-speakers with equal concern and respect. It would be to give to French- and German-speakers a basis for the accommodation of their linguistic needs, and the affirmation and promotion of their linguistic identities, but to deny the same treatment to Dutch-speakers.

Equality, on this view, is a matter of achieving a certain distribution of institutional space and capacity. Whether or not French- and German-speakers are equal in the stipulated sense depends on whether comparable public services are offered, and comparable public business can be transacted, in each of the two languages. It does not depend on whether the overall linguistic needs of French- and German-speakers are equally accommodated, their self-respect equally enhanced, or their language-based identity equally promoted.

Why should we care about equality of recognition? It is possible to anticipate two important challenges to the view that we should. The first challenge notes that the good of public access can be met through learning the majority or dominant language and asserts that other non-language-related goods should be prioritised over the good of identity. The second challenge accepts the importance of both public access and identity but then questions whether it follows that recognition is the best metric of equality in this area. If we care about recognition because recognition serves the goods of public access and identity, then perhaps it is *these* goods that should be distributed equally?

It turns out that these challenges are associated with the language harmonisation and language maintenance alternatives to equal recognition respectively. I will consider them in more detail later in the paper. For now, let me try to articulate the ideal behind the equal recognition proposal.[4]

The language harmonisation and language maintenance views share a commitment to what can be called 'language planning'. The policy-maker, or institutional designer, identifies some desirable outcome—a common language, or the survival and flourishing of many languages—and then determines how public institutions can best allocate language rights to realise these outcomes.[5] The distinctive feature of the equal recognition approach is its rejection of language planning. The task of language policy is not to realise some specific linguistic outcome but to establish fair background conditions under which speakers of different languages can strive for the survival and success of their respective language communities.

The simple proposal behind equal recognition is that fairness with respect to different languages and language-based identities is established through a policy of equal treatment.[6] If a policy is fair between languages *P* and *Q*, then the same public rights and benefits that are extended to *P* are also extended to *Q*. Within the space left to them by this framework, individuals will develop their linguistic identities and make choices about language use. Some languages will flourish under such conditions; it is likely that others will not. But nobody will be able to say that they did not have a fair opportunity to realise the language-related identity commitments that they hold dear.

The normative logic here is quite analogous to the logic behind standard liberal responses to religious diversity. For most liberals, the state should be neutral with respect to religion, in the sense that it should avoid 'religious planning'. The state should not take a stand on the desirability of certain religious outcomes and arrange institutions and allocate rights with a view to bringing about these outcomes. Instead, it should strive to establish 'a just basic structure within which permissible forms of life have a fair opportunity to maintain themselves and to gain adherents over time' (Rawls,

1993). Some ways of life will succeed under such 'fair background conditions' and others will not (there is no social world in which every way of life flourishes) (*ibid*). But again the significant point is that, even for those ways of life that do not succeed to the degree that their followers would like, those followers cannot reasonably complain of unfair treatment.

In the area of religion, fair background conditions might take the form of disestablishment or, perhaps, an attempt to establish positively and even-handedly a variety of different religions and ways of life (eg through the design of the school curriculum, the designation of public religious holidays, and so on). For language, disestablishment is obviously not an option, and so equal recognition seems the most obvious way of realising fairness.

The underlying idea, then, is that we sometimes show equal concern and respect for people by striving to treat them fairly. As proponents of various forms of resource egalitarianism have long argued, in a range of situations fair treatment is best understood as requiring the devotion of the same amount of resources or attention to each individual, *even though* it is foreseeable that different individuals will have varying degrees of success at translating resources or attention into something of ultimate importance to them (eg their 'identity').[7] It is this fundamental idea that finds expression in equality of recognition: public institutions show equal concern and respect for speakers of different languages by devoting the same space and capacity to each of their languages.

## LANGUAGE HARMONISATION

Imagine that European institutions came fully to respect the idea of equal linguistic recognition. They established comparable institutional space and capacity for each of the languages used by Europeans such that public business could be transacted, and public services accessed, in each of those languages. In addition, they worked to promote equality of recognition within national and regional jurisdictions through a Charter of Minority Linguistic Rights and other policy instruments. Such a language regime could conceivably contribute to two broad kinds of outcome. One possibility is that it could contribute to the maintenance of a number of different languages in regular use by Europeans. A second possibility is that it would not be able to prevent a shift away from some languages and a convergence on some dominant or hegemonic language.

These two possible outcomes give rise to the two different challenges to equality of recognition mentioned earlier. The first challenge criticises equal recognition by appealing to some of the advantages of linguistic convergence or harmonisation. Equality of recognition is defective from the point of view of this objection because it does too much to encourage linguistic diversity and not enough to encourage harmonisation. The second challenge spotlights the second kind of outcome and makes essentially the opposite objection. It appeals to the idea that an important responsibility of public institutions is to promote the maintenance and success of endangered languages. Equality of recognition is objectionable from the point of view of this idea because it does not do enough to ensure the survival and flourishing of vulnerable languages and is too tolerant of social forces that lead to linguistic convergence. I will consider the first of these challenges in the present section and the second in the next section. In each case, the emphasis will be on bringing out the intuitive force of the challenge and also on identifying some of the limitations and puzzles that are connected with it.

The first challenge worries, in effect, that equal recognition will be successful at fostering linguistic diversity. Rather than converging on some hegemonic public language, individuals will maintain language repertoires that keep alive over time a plurality of different languages. This is problematic, so the objection goes, because of the numerous advantages associated with linguistic convergence. Once these advantages are taken into consideration, the case for equal recognition of Europe's various languages is weakened and the policy priority becomes the promotion of language harmonisation. Such a policy, it is important to emphasise, need not be coercive in character. The decision that European institutions will not recognise certain languages, together with an aggressive policy of second-language teaching in a designated, widely spoken language, could conceivably have the desired effect. Moreover, the argument need not imply that *no* public recognition be given to certain languages, since the argument for accommodating linguistic diversity will be extremely compelling in some contexts of language use (eg translations will presumably be needed where European law overrides national law). It does mean to imply that steps should be taken to promote convergence on a privileged language or group of languages, by limiting recognition in some spheres of language use and perhaps denying it altogether in others.

Four different advantages of linguistic convergence deserve to be highlighted.[8] Linguistic convergence can (i) enhance social mobility, (ii) facilitate democratic deliberation, (iii) encourage the formation of a common political identity, and (iv) increase the efficiency of public institutions. Let us look at each of these advantages more closely.

*Social mobility*. Smaller language communities can easily become ghettoised when their members are unable or unwilling to master other, more widely spoken languages. The economic opportunities of those citizens will be limited by the work available in their own language and they will have trouble accessing the culture of the larger society or participating meaningfully in its political life. A policy promoting the integration of members of smaller language communities into a larger language community could in the long run, according to this argument, expand the choices and opportunities available to members of the minority community and in this way promote equality of opportunity. The relevance of this consideration to the European case should be apparent. One of the central goals of European integration has been the elimination of internal barriers to the free movement of goods, persons and capital. Language differences remain a significant barrier to the free movement of persons and, to this extent, to the equalisation of opportunities for all Europeans.

*Democratic deliberation*. The challenge of democratising European institutions is faced not just at the formal institutional level but also in the informal sphere of public discussion and civil society. Democratic decision-making presupposes an informal process of deliberation and discussion in which free and equal citizens exchange reasons and are sometimes moved by them to change their opinions and preferences. Linguistic diversity can be a serious barrier to the full flourishing of this informal dimension of democracy. If citizens cannot understand one another, or if they seek only to communicate with co-linguists, then the exchange of reasons and the transformation of outlook that one expects of democratic politics will inevitably be compromised. To the extent that fully effective democratic institutions are a component and condition of any egalitarian social order, language harmonisation helps to facilitate equality.

*Common identity*. Fellow citizens must be willing to tolerate and trust, to defer to the requirements of public reason, and to accept certain burdens and sacrifices for the sake of the common good. If Europeans cannot develop a common sense of citizenship, or shared political identity, then these virtues and dispositions are likely to be absent or weakened at the European level. Legitimate goals of European institutions, including the pursuit of greater equality, cannot be achieved when the community is fragmented into identity groups that do not share any of the bonds of citizenship and which view co-operation with one another solely as an instrument of mutual advantage. With linguistic convergence, language no longer serves to separate citizens into distinct and often mutually antagonistic groups but can become one of the defining bonds of a common identity. Linguistic harmonisation can thus facilitate the creation of one of the essential conditions for a successful egalitarian order.

*Efficiency*. Perhaps the most obvious advantage of linguistic convergence is its cost-effectiveness. When all the citizens of a community converge on the use of one language, public (and non-public) institutions can make numerous savings. It is no longer necessary to spend as much money on translating written documents or on simultaneous translation in the conduct of official business. Meetings, and the policy-making process more generally, can be conducted more quickly, without the need to be constantly pausing for translations. And public institutions need not go to the additional expense of finding or training multilingual staff or of setting up parallel institutions in various languages. In Europe, the financial cost of multilingualism is one of the most commented upon features of the current language regime. According to one estimate, as much as 40 per cent of the EU's administrative budget is connected with its official multilingualism and approximately 14 per cent of the Commission's staff members work for the translation and interpretation services (Coulmas, 1991b: 23).[9]

All of these considerations suggest an alternative to the view that equal concern and respect implies equality of recognition. Whereas the equal recognition perspective associates equality with devoting equal amounts of institutional space and capacity to the different languages used by Europeans, the language harmonisation perspective sees convergence on a common European language as one of the pre-conditions for making Europe a fully democratic and egalitarian community. Harmonisation can enhance equality of opportunity and reduce social exclusion; facilitate discussion between all citizens and make democracy more responsive to deliberation; encourage a shared political identity that fosters virtues and dispositions hospitable to the creation of an egalitarian society; and make for a more efficient public sector, one which frees up time and resources for allocation to other priorities.

So how damaging is the language harmonisation challenge to the view that all of Europe's languages should be equally recognised? An initial observation is that, at best, the challenge shows there to be a trade-off between two different dimensions of equality. According to the equal recognition perspective, alternative language regimes themselves constitute ways in which people are made more or less equal. A decision to recognise French and German but not Dutch, for instance, compromises the equality of Dutch-speakers quite independently of any further consequences that this decision might have. And the language harmonisation perspective does not take issue with the claim that non-recognition constitutes an inequality. Instead, it anticipates a broader state of social equality that may be realised in the future if some degree of language inequality is enforced in the present. The best we can say for the harmonisation challenge, therefore, is that it highlights the fact that we may have to choose between respecting equality now and promoting social equality in the future.

There is a puzzle here regarding which of these forms of equality should be prioritised when they are in conflict. It is not clear that everything I described under the heading of 'social equality' should necessarily be prioritised over equality of recognition. Most people do not, for instance, think that *every* possible measure reducing the cost of public administration should for that reason be implemented. In many areas of public administration, people are willing to tolerate costly or time-consuming procedures aimed at enhancing equality or fairness. The same goes for measures designed to promote a stronger sense of common identity. It is conceivable that a religiously homogeneous society would have a stronger sense of common identity than a heterogeneous society. But, even if this were the case, most liberals at least would still oppose a policy of state preference for the majority religion designed to bring about greater homogeneity. On the other hand, many people would regard the identity considerations I sketched in the previous section as being of secondary importance. If promoting those considerations, through equal recognition, implied a high enough cost in terms of social equality, they would not hesitate to prioritise the latter form of equality.

The language harmonisation alternative to equal recognition also raises a series of empirical questions. Assuming for the sake of argument that the advantages associated with language harmonisation do take priority over the considerations embodied in equal language recognition, the language harmonisation challenge makes three significant empirical assumptions that should be explored:

(1) *Significant linguistic convergence will not be achieved under a policy of equal language recognition.* This assumption ignores the fact that people frequently learn more than one language. Despite the equal recognition of its various languages, second-language acquisition may mean that one or several European languages emerge that are common to all or most people. According to recent estimates, about half of Europeans are able to speak a second European language and this figure goes up to 77 per cent for students. A majority of young Europeans are adding English to their linguistic repertoires.[10]

This de facto convergence on a common (second) language presents a significant problem for those who advocate abandoning equal recognition in order to secure the advantages of linguistic convergence. It means that many members of smaller language groups are able, if they wish, to pursue opportunities in larger language communities and, to this extent, are not ghettoised by their linguistic capabilities. For these people, it cannot be argued that social mobility considerations support the abandonment of equal recognition. The same is true to a significant degree for the problem of democratic deliberation. People will naturally conduct certain political discussions in their own language but many will also be able to follow and participate in political deliberations conducted in at least one other European language. For this reason, it is important not to exaggerate the extent to which the maintenance of linguistic diversity through a policy of equal recognition impedes the process of democratic deliberation.

Of course it might be wondered why Europe should bother with equal recognition at all if so many people can get along in a small subset of Europe's languages. 'They all speak *X* anyway' is a common complaint of *X*-speakers against extending language rights to other languages. The argument so far suggests a paradox: the more some linguistic group is able to speak another language, the stronger its case to have its own language recognised. This paradox should not alarm us, however, for the value of recognition only partially depends on assumptions about linguistic capabilities. As we saw earlier, public access is one good provided by recognition, but recognition also serves the good of identity. Moreover, access considerations can still be important for people who have achieved a reasonable level of competence in another public language, for instance in stressful or technical contexts of language use, where they will often find it easier to function in their own language.

(2) *Significant linguistic convergence is necessary to secure goods such as social mobility, democratic deliberation, a common identity, and efficiency.* This assumption can be partially countered in some cases, arguably including the European one. It is not clear, for instance, how much commonality of language deliberative democracy actually requires. If deliberative democracy entails that every citizen should be able to communicate directly with every other citizen, then the absence of a common language would indeed be a problem. But for reasons having to do with scale, and with the limited amount of leisure time that citizens have for deliberation, most deliberative democrats would not advocate such a demanding ideal of citizen deliberation. Citizens can exchange reasons through mediators and go-betweens (the media, elites, and so on), and thus it is not necessary for them literally to be able to speak with every fellow citizen. So long as these mediators and go-betweens are able, through personal bilingualism, or reliance on translators and interpreters, to bridge any linguistic divides that they encounter, a common public language is not necessary for deliberative democracy.

A common identity of some form may be a crucial condition of the success of the European project but it is not clear that it depends on convergence around a single European language. An alternative is that such an identity might coalesce around an acknowledgement and affirmation of difference (eg linguistic diversity and official multilingualism become sources of pride and identity). Social scientists do not yet have a definitive account of when to opt for unity in difference and when for unity in commonality.

Finally, the argument from social mobility is also difficult to read. So long as the diverse languages of Europe each enjoy relative institutional completeness, the speakers of those languages have *adequate* opportunity and choice within their own language community and do not seem to need fluency in other European languages. This condition of adequate opportunity seems to be met for many of Europe's languages, including smaller ones such as Portuguese, Danish, Finish, and so on. On the other hand, we also know that all over Europe competence in English is becoming an increasingly important pre-condition of access to higher-status jobs in business and government. To promote equal opportunity, it may soon be important, if it is not already, to reinforce efforts to diffuse knowledge of English across all European citizens.

(3) *The advantages of language harmonisation can be secured through a policy of withholding recognition of certain European languages.* For the sake of argument let us grant the first two assumptions and suppose both that significant convergence will not take place under a regime of equal recognition and that the goods associated with convergence cannot be achieved in the absence of convergence. It might still be questioned whether the goods of convergence *can* be achieved through a policy of unequal recognition. In certain respects, in fact, such a policy might make things worse not better.

Consider first the goal of forging a common European identity that could underpin more specific dispositions and solidarities operating at the European level. Why should we think that denying recognition to some particular language would encourage rather than discourage speakers of that language to adopt a European identity defined (partly) in terms of some shared public European language? The argument, presumably, is that non-recognition would lead eventually to a shift towards the public language and an identity would form around it. Allowing for the sake of argument that such a shift would occur, this argument ignores the fact that identity differences often survive, and can even be magnified by, linguistic or other forms of cultural convergence. To cite just one example, the gradual shift away from the Irish language—partly encouraged by a long period in which Irish was not officially recognised— has not been accompanied by the formation of any kind of pan-British Isles identity. Far from leading to a common European identity, there is some reason to believe that a European policy of withholding recognition from certain language groups would only lead to a sense of betrayal and alienation from the whole European project. If there is a future for a shared sense of European citizenship, it seems much more likely that it will be grounded in an acknowledgement and affirmation of multilingualism rather than in any deliberate campaign of language harmonisation.[11]

The claim that a policy of non-recognition would eventually enhance social mobility might also be questioned. Imagine that such a policy did encourage convergence on some common European language or group of languages. Speakers who manage to learn the common language as a second language might encounter a degree of discrimination on the basis of their language capabilities. Language capabilities are relatively visible (or audible) characteristics around which support for discriminatory policies can easily be mobilised. Meanwhile the effect of non-recognition may be to undermine to some extent the work and business opportunities in the speaker's original language—thus leaving them no better off in terms of European social mobility and less mobile in local institutions.

All these different considerations together raise a number of puzzles and questions about the language harmonisation approach and suggest that that approach inflicts only limited damage on the case for equal recognition of Europe's languages. Even if we accept all the assumptions underlying the language harmonisation challenge, the argument still only establishes that there is a trade-off between respecting present language equality and promoting future social equality. This is not necessarily a trade-off that should always be decided in favour of future social equality. Moreover, at least three of the empirical assumptions underpinning the challenge are difficult to assess. It might be questioned whether equal recognition really would prevent wide-scale convergence on some shared European language; whether actual harmonisation really is necessary to achieve the advantages associated with harmonisation; and whether a policy of withholding recognition from certain European languages would be any better a strategy for securing those advantages.

## LANGUAGE MAINTENANCE

I turn now to the second alternative to equality of language recognition, which I term 'language maintenance'. This approach starts from the observation that the equal public recognition of several languages does not guarantee that they will be equally successful or even that they will all survive. Even though public services are offered, and public business can be transacted, in some language, this does not ensure the health or vitality of that language. It does not guarantee that the number of speakers of the language will not decline or even that the language will not disappear entirely.

Public recognition is but one among a number of determinants of language success. The birth-rate within the language community, the language that parents choose to raise and educate their children in, and the language repertoires and choices of newcomers each affect the size and vitality of a language community. Even though a language is publicly recognised, it may not be the principal language of work, business, or even much internal communication within public institutions; some other language may be the de facto medium of economic opportunity and social interaction. In this context, it may be rational for adults to invest heavily in acquiring the more widely-used language and for parents to educate their children in, and newcomers to integrate into, this language as well. Where these choices to adopt another, economically more powerful language become widespread, even a publicly recognised language may have difficulty surviving. Such a trend is only made worse by a low birth-rate within the vulnerable language community and by the myriad daily choices concerning media and culture made by members of the community.

Irish is a textbook example of a language that enjoys significant forms of public recognition but can hardly be called a success story. The immense economic and cultural power of English means that very few Irish people avail themselves of the Irish-language opportunities offered by public institutions. It is much more attractive for adults seeking economic opportunity, parents making decisions on behalf of their children, and immigrants to Ireland, to orient themselves to the English-speaking society than it is to opt for Irish, however much people may regret the loss of a part of the Irish heritage.

Some Europeans worry that, in the long run, other, currently more widely-spoken languages will face the same kind of crisis as Irish. In business dealings, in the work-place, and in informal meetings between public officials there is immense utility in being able to co-ordinate on the use of a single language. With its tremendous international economic and cultural power, that lingua franca would certainly be English. Even a European regime of equal recognition may be powerless to prevent the gradual marginalisation of other European languages. English is already the language of much European communication and, as we saw earlier, there is considerable evidence that Europeans—particularly younger ones—are adding English to their language repertoires.

These observations and conjectures lead to the objection that equality of recognition is much too formal an interpretation of equal concern and respect when it comes to language policy. Equality of language recognition in effect advocates giving the same treatment to all even though it is predictable that some will race ahead and others lag behind. By treating all languages the same, very unequal outcomes result. An alternative way of understanding equality in connection to language would focus on the outcomes themselves. On such a view, we treat speakers of different languages with equal concern and respect when we ensure that the various languages they speak are equally successful—where success is a function of, for instance, the number of speakers, the range of activities that can be conducted in the language, and so on.

Although the policy implications of an equality of language success perspective are rather hard to make out at the European level, it seems clear that they could diverge from the ones associated with equal recognition. One possibility is that the recognition of English in European institutions could be limited or curtailed in some way as a means of raising the profile of other European languages. It seems extremely unlikely, however, that such a policy would be much of an obstacle to the growing hegemony of English, even if the policy could be defended against various other objections. A different idea might be to limit recognition of all but a handful of European languages, with the aim of enhancing the public status of major European languages other than English. A Europe with five official languages—say English, French, German, Spanish and Italian—might stand a better chance of maintaining at least some languages other than English than a Europe with twenty or more official languages.[12] The idea would be that no language could possibly compete with English unless a few are singled out and given a special public role.

A different proposal has been urged by Philippe Van Parijs in a series of papers (Van Parijs, 2000; Aziz and Van Parijs, forthcoming; and Van Parijs, this volume). According to him, English is all but certain to become the lingua franca of transnational government and business in Europe and beyond. Instead of putting up futile resistance to this outcome, a European language regime should work even harder (eg by banning dubbing) to ensure that English is evenly diffused through the whole European population, so that the shift of elite-level communications to English does not result in a loss of equal opportunities for large sections of the European population. At the same time, Van Parijs worries that the shift to English will mean the weakening or even disappearance of other European languages. To avert this outcome he recommends that Europe follow the principle of territoriality. Europe should be divided, as far as is feasible, into a patchwork of linguistic regions in which institutions at all levels would operate exclusively in the locally dominant language. Migrants from other parts of Europe or the world, and other 'internal' minorities, would have to adopt the local dominant language or move somewhere else. Only at the highest levels of government and business communication would English be allowed to supersede the local language (Patten, 2003b).

As I have already suggested, the language maintenance alternative to equal recognition rests on a distinctive idea of equality. Whereas the equal recognition perspective associates equality with devoting equal amounts of institutional space and capacity to the different languages used by Europeans, and the language harmonisation perspective sees convergence on a common European language as one of the pre-conditions for making Europe a fully democratic and egalitarian community, the language maintenance perspective identifies equality with the actual success of different European languages.

But why should we care about equality of success rather than equality of recognition or facilitating future social equality? To evaluate the language maintenance challenge we need to step back and ask why it might be important to ensure the success of various languages. Policies of the kind mentioned above involve withholding recognition from certain European languages and would thus be disadvantageous to some of the speakers of those languages. Under the territoriality principle, for instance, speakers of internal minority languages (eg Spanish-speakers in Catalonia, French-speakers in Flanders, English-speakers in the Welsh-speaking areas of Wales) would find their enjoyment of the goods of public access and identity curtailed. In light of these costs, it is important to know what the justification of such policies might be and why we should care about the underlying ideal of equality of success (Patten, 2005).

I mentioned one possible answer to this question earlier in the paper. One reason for caring about the success of different languages is that language success is connected with the extent to which people actually enjoy the goods of public access and identity. The intuition underpinning equality of success is that it is better to equalise the degree to which people actually enjoy these goods than it is to equalise recognition, which, in any case, is only valuable because of its contribution to the enjoyment of these goods. As I will now argue, however, this argument has significant limitations and gives rise to difficult puzzles.

Consider first the good of public access. It is hard to see why it would be necessary to opt for language maintenance rather than equal recognition in order to promote this good. Arguably, the opposite is true. If language maintenance means, for instance, that only Catalan is recognised in Catalonia, then unilingual Spanish-speakers of the region will find it difficult to access regional public institutions. By contrast, under equal recognition, public business could be conducted in either language.

The good of public access is connected with a larger good, however, which is the good of being able to communicate with others around us. Communication in public institutions is just one form of important communication that a language policy should consider; there is also communication in work, business, civil society, and so forth. Perhaps the argument for language maintenance is on stronger grounds if the focus is shifted to communication in this broader context?

The argument here would focus on the communicative possibilities that people are left with when their language goes into decline. As a language deteriorates, a monolingual speaker of that language may eventually find her options becoming restricted. She may face difficulties finding a job, transacting business, making friends, practising her religion, participating in the informal public life of her community, and so on. To borrow a term from Will Kymlicka, her 'context of choice' may shrink and to this extent she will be less free or autonomous than she was before (Kymlicka, 1989: chs 7–9; Kymlicka, 1995: ch 5). One reason why language maintenance might matter, then, is that individual autonomy matters: we want to avoid situations in which citizens face the possible loss of their context of choice.

To illustrate, imagine that under a regime of equal recognition Catalan would gradually be pushed out of key domains of language use (eg white-collar employment) in favour of Spanish or even English. If that were to happen, Catalan-speakers who lacked fluency in the high-status language would face a significant restriction on their choices. One solution might be to intensify the teaching of the high-status language amongst Catalan-speakers (most Catalan-speakers are, in any case, proficient in Spanish). But it is conceivable that this solution may not be practical in some cases. It is not normally straightforward to get a whole population to acquire a second language and there may, in particular, be great class and regional variations in success that are of concern from an egalitarian perspective.

This is an important argument on behalf of the language maintenance approach, but it is important to note its limited empirical applicability. For the argument to go through, three key conditions would have to be met: (1) the equal recognition alternative would have to make a crucial difference in tipping people away from the local majority language towards some other language in key domains of communication; (2) this shift would have to strand certain unilinguals, shrinking their life opportunities; and (3) these stranded unilinguals would have to be unresponsive to language training in the emerging, high-status language.

Can an appeal to the good of identity offer a less limited set of grounds for endorsing the language maintenance approach? Even if the demanding empirical conditions set out above are not satisfied in some particular language community, people might still feel very strongly about the health and vitality of their language and its relative place in the world. They might derive part of their self-esteem from the fact of speaking a language that is shared by millions of people or that serves as a vehicle of international communication. The flourishing of their language—that a constant or increasing number of people should continue to use it in a wide variety of domains—might be an important part of their identity. Perhaps the importance of ensuring equal language success derives simply from the good of identity?

There is a puzzle, however, regarding how equality of language success could be considered an attractive ideal when it appeals to identity in this way. The idea that social and political institutions ought to be designed in order to equalise everyone's sense of self-esteem, or the promotion of everyone's identity, leads to absurd implications. People report a drop in self-esteem in response to all kinds of social and political arrangements but this does not always imply that those arrangements are objectionable. Likewise, different people define their identities in a huge variety of different ways. For some ethnic identity is central; for others, religious, sexual, local or professional identities are more dominant, and so on. We presumably do not think that social and political arrangements ought to be designed in such as way as to promote as equally as possible all these different identities.

To see these points more concretely, consider an analogy to the language maintenance challenge, which we might call the 'religion maintenance challenge'. It is possible that a state's policy of equally recognising different organised religions (or its decision not to recognise any religion) could be powerless to prevent very different degrees of success amongst the different religions. For any number of possible reasons, some religions might be relatively successful (their number of adherents is increasing, their role in the lives of their adherents is enlarged, and so on) whereas others decline in importance. For members of the less successful religions, the plight of their religion might conceivably contribute to a diminished sense of self-esteem and a feeling that a cause that is central to their identity is not faring very well. But we surely do not think that *these* are good reasons for abandoning the policy of equal recognition (or universal non-recognition). To some extent, at least, any plausible view of equality has to hold people responsible for the esteem- and identity-commitments that they have and not seek to compensate whenever projects they attach importance to do not turn out as well as they would like (Dworkin, 1981).

In fact, the idea of equalising everybody's success at realising their language-related identity may not even be a coherent one. The basic problem is that there is no reason to think that all of the languages and identities that are found in a particular community can flourish or even survive at the same time. To some degree, languages and identities compete with one another for a fixed amount of social space. A flourishing language is one that gets used in a variety of high-status contexts, such as white-collar employment, popular culture, politics, formal social occasions, and so on; a language's survival is in peril when it is completely shut out of all such domains of language use. Since there are a limited number of languages that can be used in high status language domains, it follows that any goal of promoting the survival and flourishing of all languages is likely to be unachievable. There is no way of arranging social and political institutions to protect every language, and thus the mere fact that under some institutional arrangement a particular group's language is not doing well is not sufficient to warrant the conclusion that members of the group are not being treated with equal concern and respect. Indeed it is precisely this problem that motivated the earlier argument that equal recognition (and its idea of fair treatment rather than equal success) may be the best way of doing justice to the abstract egalitarian ideal.

## CONCLUSION

In this paper, I have considered various perspectives in political theory on the European language question. According to one view, the basic theoretical commitment should be to equal recognition: equal amounts of public institutional space and capacity ought to be devoted to the different languages used by Europeans. When this ideal is realised, speakers of different European languages can reasonably feel that their public institutions are treating them with equal concern and respect.

Equal recognition faces important challenges from two alternative views, each of which offers a distinctive interpretation of what equality means in connection with language. The language harmonisation approach sees convergence on a common European language as one of the pre-conditions for making Europe a fully democratic and egalitarian community. The language maintenance perspective claims that equality entails the equal success of different languages used by Europeans. Rather than seeking to refute these challenges, I noted various limitations in their underlying arguments and identified certain puzzles that supporters of these approaches would have to consider.

## Notes

[1] Estimates of the number of speakers of different European languages and dialects can be found at http://www.ethnologue.com/country_index.asp?place=Europe (accessed 31 August 2006).

[2] A number of the papers in Coulmas, 1991a discuss aspects of Europe's language regime.

[3] In his contribution to the present volume, Philippe Van Parijs challenges the current European linguistic order from both the second and third perspectives. He urges a rapid and fairly ruthless move to English as a lingua franca of European institutions *and* a move towards greater adoption of the territoriality principle for all domains of public language use in which a common European lingua franca is not necessary. I return to Van Parijs and the territoriality principle later in this paper.

[4] The next few paragraphs sketch in compressed form an argument I develop in Patten, 2003a.

[5] Sociolinguists often use the term *language planning* in a somewhat broader sense, to denote 'organised efforts to find solutions to societal language problems'. See Fishman, 1972*:* 186.

[6] I qualify this proposal in various ways in Patten, 2003a, especially p 371 fn 29.

[7] For a sophisticated discussion of equality along these lines see Dworkin, 1981. Dworkin's argument has been challenged and qualified in various ways since its publication, but almost nobody defends a simple-minded equality-of-success alternative.

[8] The discussion that follows draws heavily on an earlier paper: Patten, 2001.

[9] Coulmas' figures are from his 1991 paper. More recently, Miriam Aziz and Van Parijs (forthcoming) estimate that the Commission spends approximately EUR 800 m on translation and interpretation.

[10] These figures are reported in *The Economist*, 25 October 1997 and were drawn from Eurobarometer. For further evidence of the growing de facto importance of English to European communication see Laitin, 1997: 287–9.

[11] I discuss the idea of an identity defined (partly) in terms of the acknowledgement and affirmation of difference, in Patten, 2000.

[12] A proposal of this kind was made by French Minister of European Affairs, M. Lamassoure, in December 1994 at the European Parliament.

## References

Aziz, M and Van Parijs, P (forthcoming) 'Linguistic Legislation for XXIst Century Europe' in B De Witte (ed), *European Law and Linguistic Diversity* (Oxford, Oxford University Press).

Coulmas, F (ed) (1991a) *A Language Policy for the European Community* (Berlin, Mouton de Gruyter).

Coulmas, F (1991b) 'European Integration and the Idea of the National Language' in F Coulmas (ed), *A Language Policy for the European Community* (Berlin, Mouton de Gruyter).

Dworkin, R (1981) 'What is Equality? Part I: Equality of Welfare', and 'What is Equality? Part II: Equality of Resources' *Philosophy and Public Affairs* 10(3): 185–246 and 10(4): 283–345.

Fishman, J (1972) *The Sociology of Language* (Rowley, MA, Newbury House).

Kymlicka, W (1989) *Liberalism, Community, and Culture* (Oxford, Oxford University Press).

Kymlicka, W (1995) *Multicultural Citizenship: A Liberal Theory of Minority Rights* (Oxford, Oxford University Press).

Laitin, D (1997) 'The Cultural Identities of a European State' *Politics & Society* 25(3): 277–302.

Mc Kinnon, C and Hampsher-Monk, I (2000) *The Demands of Citizenship* (London, Continuum).

Patten, A (2000) 'Equality of Recognition and the Liberal Theory of Citizenship' in C McKinnon and I Hampsher-Monk (eds), *The Demands of Citizenship* (London, Continuum).

Patten, A (2001) 'Political Theory and Language Policy' *Political Theory* 29(5): 683–707.

Patten, A (2003a) 'Liberal Neutrality and Language Policy' *Philosophy & Public Affairs* (Fall 2003): 356–86.

Patten, A (2003b) 'What Kind of Bilingualism?' in W Kymlicka and A Patten (eds), *Political Theory and Language Rights* (Oxford, Oxford University Press).

Patten, A (2005) 'The Rights of Internal Linguistic Minorities' in A Eisenberg and J Spinner-Halev (eds), *Minorities Within Minorities* (Cambridge, Cambridge University Press).

Rawls, J (1993) *Political Liberalism* (New York, Columbia University Press).

Van Parijs, P (2000) 'Must Europe be Belgian? On Democratic Citizenship and Multilingual Polities' in C McKinnon and I Hampsher-Monk (eds), *The Demands of Citizenship* (London, Continuum).

# 3

# *Language Policy of a Civic Nation-State: Constitutional Patriotism and Minority Language Rights*

OMID A PAYROW SHABANI

HITHERTO THERE HAS been relatively little work done on the question of minority language rights. A recent collection of essays, *Language Rights and Political Theory*, goes some way to redressing this (Kymlicka and Patten, 2003). Despite a variety of normative approaches in the volume, however, none of the papers approaches the issue of language rights from a critical theory perspective of constitutional patriotism (see Coulombe, 2000). This paper is an attempt to fill that gap. A commonplace criticism of constitutional patriotism, as a model of political association where the criterion of membership is the shared practice of law-making, is that such a model cannot cultivate the strong feelings of allegiance necessary to hold the political community together. I have dealt with this criticism in detail elsewhere.[1] Here, I would like to turn my attention to a different criticism of constitutional patriotism: namely, the charge of insensitivity to diverse groups' demands for recognition. For example, a common objection raised by liberal culturalists is that constitutional patriotism is incapable of accommodating minority language rights as a result of its abstract and universalistic thrust (Tamir, 1993; Miller, 1995; Canovan, 1996; Margalit and Raz, 1990; Canovan, 2000). I do not take this criticism to mean that in a pluralist society every language spoken by some members of the society should be recognised publicly for institutional use. My effort here will rather be focused on explaining which languages are selected for public use and why.

Thus, the aim of the paper is to examine the conditions surrounding the question of minority language rights from the normative perspective of constitutional patriotism. In doing so, I will begin by giving a brief outline of three main versions of intrinsic/instrumental argument for the relation of language and the political community, revealing the essentialist underpinning of this relation. I will then outline the architectonic of constitutional patriotism as a normative model of political association sensitive to diversities found in multicultural nation-states. Next, I argue that the language policy of a civic nation-state should be devised so as to be pragmatically aimed at operationalising the constitutive effect of language with its communicative power. That is to say, the traditional intrinsic/instrumental dichotomy is too restrictive for the purpose of policy-making and has to be overcome by a communicative view of language as the context of mutual understanding between political subjects. Finally, through a discussion of the Official Languages Act in Canada I will show how this communicative approach is sensitive to, and constrained by, the political culture of the community, its historical contingencies, and practical feasibility. In conclusion I reiterate my argument that the increasing diversity in liberal-democratic societies requires us to rethink our approach to the problem of political association along the lines of constitutional patriotism.

## THREE MODELS OF LANGUAGE POLICY-MAKING

In a general sense, there are two main orientations in approaching the role and significance of language within the political domain: (1) an instrumental argument which views language as a *medium* or *tool* that facilitates socio-political life; (2) an intrinsic argument for language that perceives it as a primary good (in the Rawlsian sense), which itself has two versions: (a) an intrinsic argument based on the desire to *use* one's own language in conducting one's life where the usefulness of language is bound closely to one's idea of the good life; and (b) an intrinsic argument which views language as a *human accomplishment*, a good in itself. For my purposes here, these arguments should be spelled out a bit further:

1. In living one's life in a democratic society the individual is supposed to take part in the political life of the community and be able to plan her life as a free and equal agent. According to this view participation and self-directed life are democratic ends in themselves. In other words, democratic citizenship is valued not because it leads to some further goods but because, as an expression of freedom and belonging, it is good in itself. Liberal culturalists have taken this to mean that culture possesses inherent worth because it is the context within which the individual interacts with others and makes life choices. Thus, the cultural context of choice and liberty is as intrinsically valuable as the freedom and life that it grounds. It is further argued that an important aspect of culture is language, which is a necessary condition for the planning of a life. *Language in this sense is not any particular language but language in general.* In this general sense, language is good only in so far as it is an instrument of cultural interaction and political

participation. According to this view, then, language is valued as a medium of interaction among members of a culture.

The language policy that this view normatively grounds is that of *linguistic convergence*. The interest in language as a means of communication requires promoting convergence on a privileged public language(s) because it is conducive to greater communication, mobility, efficiency, and common identity. Thus, to view language instrumentally dictates a language policy that aims to make various languages converge onto the most privileged one in order to promote a greater democracy. An example of such a language policy would be the status and use of French in France and English in the United States.[3] The notion of citizenship that accompanies this view of language and language policy is a liberal view where all individuals are to be treated equally before the law as equal members of the political community.

2.(a) A second conception of language takes the instrumental character of language and argues that in so far as we talk about language in general and not about any particular language it is difficult to recognise its value in terms of its use for other ends. And in so far as we look at particular languages we realise how their value is tied to the value of the ends for which they are used. In other words, we will see that those ends are meaningful only through the language in which they are pursued. Given this connection and the inherent values of democratic life, the medium of living such a life—ie language—is intrinsically valuable too. On this view one's language is an integral part of one's life.

The language policy that this view of language proposes, therefore, would be a sort of *multilingualism* where any language or languages used by the political community is granted the same official recognition. The multilingual policy, in turn, is said to accommodate various aspects of the diverse citizenry's need for communication, identity formation and recognition. As such, the policy of multilingualism aims to balance the interests of diverse linguistic communities. On this account, treating languages equally is not to treat them equally with respect to a privileged language but to treat them equally by way of equal recognition. We see this language policy at work in countries like Belgium and Switzerland. The corresponding view of citizenship to this language policy is one based on an historical contract between the founding communities of the nation-state—French, Flemish and German communities in Belgium; and French, German, Italian and Rhaeto-Roman communities in Switzerland. The criteria of membership, thus, are defined along the lines of values found in the traditional culture of the founding communities.

2.(b) Given increasing multilingualism, however, it has been argued that the intrinsic argument for language can no longer be developed solely by way of an appeal to the intrinsic value of one's life plans; rather, it needs to be developed by way of understanding the intrinsic value of language itself as a human achievement. On this view any language is good in itself, independent of what it is used for. Language is valued as an instance of human creativity along with culture, which is viewed as being involved in the process of identity-constitution of the members of a cultural group. It is argued that this constitutive aspect of language, as an inherent good, is not captured by instrumental views of language. To view language in this way is to treat language rights as a category of human rights.

Hence, the corresponding language policy to this view is a *protectionist* policy. Advocates of this policy argue that equal recognition of different languages does not necessarily entail their equal success and survival. Therefore, the goal here is not equal treatment but equal success of languages. Since language is a good in itself, language policy should require protection and maintenance of the language(s) that will guarantee their flourishing. India perhaps comes closest to this model of language policy: in 1956 it redrew the boundaries of its states along linguistic lines in order to accommodate people's linguistic identity.[4] The accompanying citizenship view is defined along natural ties of kinship (religious, cultural, linguistic, etc).

The above sketch is not meant to be a comprehensive account of arguments for language policy. Rather it is meant to provide an overview of the main positions on policy options. Despite their differences, the common thread that runs through these arguments is the belief that culture, language and political identity are intricately connected. Now, with respect to the question of policy-making, what matters most is whether this connection is understood and theorised in essentialist terms or in constructivist and more adaptable terms. For, when the question of identity is posed in a multicultural context, the model of political association requires a more inclusive underpinning identity than that of ethnic or cultural identity. Justice requires that the problem of differentiated identity in such a context be approached and contextualised in terms of concrete social and political questions of law and policy-making within a constitutional framework that allows for deliberative negotiation based on mutual recognition. To this end, I would like to show in the following section how constitutional patriotism could present an outline of such an auspicious model of political association for differentiated rights, including minority language rights.

## THE INCLUSIVENESS OF CONSTITUTIONAL PATRIOTISM

The demands of culture have increasingly forced political philosophers to rethink the boundaries and architectonic of the nation-state. For them, the historical formula of ethnonationalism has repeatedly proven incompatible with prevalent currents of multiculturalism and globalisation. Among these theorists, Jürgen Habermas has forcefully argued for replacing ethnonationalism with a form of civic nationalism that he calls constitutional patriotism. Constitutional patriotism is a *normative* doctrine that draws on the civic tradition of founding a constitutional republic in Europe. The political project of modernity, namely the nation building project, was first constructed by way of the projection of a nation onto the founding act of constitution-making (eg France). Later in the course of nineteenth century, however, this project was pursued predominantly along the lines of ethnonationalism, which stemmed from an imaginary organicity of a nation that was prior to any constitution. According to this later model, the criterion of belonging was 'defined by "the nation" as the expression of a *Volk*, a people with a pre-political, organic form of shared identity rooted in place, descent, and language' (Pensky, 2001: xv). Laws that resulted from the constitution of such an ethnic nation bestowed a citizenship privilege only upon those who identified with national culture as its natural members. From this perspective, political association was legitimate only in so far as constitutional laws drew their binding force from the consent of its co-nationals who felt tied to the political community by virtue of kinship. This identification and sense of allegiance, in turn, provided the system with the solidarity and cohesion necessary for political unity. In this model of nation-building, the constitution formalised the supposed homogeneity that grounded national identity.

Moreover, the modern conception of nation marked a transformation from a nation of the nobility into a nation of people. This transformation, in turn, resulted in a further renovation of the early modern state into a democratic republic. The subjects of the newly formed nation-state became citizens of a polity connected by a feeling of solidarity that arose from a sense of belonging to the nation as the pre-political people. 'Thus the achievement of the nation-state consisted in solving two problems at once: it made possible a new *mode of legitimation* based on a new, more abstract form of *social integration*' (Habermas, 1998: 111). This meant that the problem of political authority, which used to be legitimated by appeal to God or Nature as grounding divine rights, was then justified by an appeal to the democratic institutions of the secularised state. Popular sovereignty and human rights were the two ways of satisfying the condition of the legitimacy of the modern nation-state. 'However, political philosophy has never really been able to strike a balance between popular sovereignty and human rights, or between the "freedom of the ancient" and the "freedom of the moderns"' (Habermas, 2001: 116). This is so because, on the one hand, according to the classical model of the constitutional nation-state of the late eighteenth century citizens come together as free and equal agents to grant one another a system of basic rights in the form of a constitution that would govern their common life, while on the other hand, the nation-state model of the nineteenth century contains a view of popular sovereignty that presupposes a nation that is prior to the constitution. On the first model human rights are institutionalised through positive law while on the second model positive law is subordinated to popular sovereignty (Habermas, 1998: 133). For Habermas both accounts are inadequate.

Habermas contends that today the increasing diversity demands

> the end of the symbiosis between the constitutional state and 'the nation' as a community of shared descent, and a renewal of a more abstract form of civil solidarity in the sense of a universalism sensitive to difference. (Habermas, 2001: 84)

First, and in order to avoid liberals' and republicans' one-sided emphasis, either on human rights or on popular sovereignty, Habermas envisions co-originality between the two ideas. He suggests that the practice of constitution-making be treated as a discursive situation where private rights are justified and legitimised through democratic discourses of public deliberation (Habermas, 2001: 117). Neither public nor private autonomy is given priority over the other so as to ensure that the ideals of stability and legitimacy, facticity and validity are brought into a working balance. The complementarity of sovereignty and individual rights, in turn, reveals an internal connection between democracy and the rule of law (Habermas, 2001: 115–18; Habermas, 1996: 449–50). The advantage of this view is that 'once we take this internal connection between democracy and the constitutional state seriously, it becomes clear that the system of rights is blind neither to unequal social conditions nor to cultural differences' (Habermas, 1998: 208).

Secondly, modern law is viewed as a set of abstract norms that are comprised of a system of rights recognised by all citizens in the form of a constitution. Such a construct of law, while it is produced through the procedures of democratic will-formation—as the only source of postmetaphysical legitimacy—itself generates solidarity as a form of social integration. The democratic process of discursive deliberation and negotiation fosters a sense of solidarity among its participants without requiring an appeal to a unifying *ethnos*. Within a constitution, the abstract laws are not envisioned in order to homogenise different social groups and violate their autonomy. Rather, they are formulated in order to facilitate the coexistence of differences within a political community by making further negotiation possible and by endorsing individual autonomy. Accordingly, Habermas' model of constitutional patriotism is made so that the constitution reflects diversity. To this end, the practice of constitution-making aims to protect diversity through rights.

The aim of starting from abstract principles in constitutional patriotism is to enable the unitary demand of the majority culture to be separated from the demands of minority cultures for recognition by fostering a political culture that includes both. Habermas explains this as follows:

> The majority culture, supposing itself to be identical with the national cultures as such, has to free itself from its historical identification with a general political culture, if all citizens are to be able to identify on equal terms with the political culture of their own country. To the degree that this decoupling of political culture from majority culture succeeds, the solidarity of citizens is shifted onto the more abstract foundation of a 'constitutional patriotism'. (Habermas, 2001: 74)

This uncoupling takes the form of an open-ended process of discursive procedures, in which political actors deliberate in light of their concrete histories. The result is a civic patriotism where political values such as stability and political legitimacy emerge from citizens' communicative understanding of a shared polity as opposed to a shared national identity. The communicative practices of political deliberation are open to citizens of all backgrounds, without enclosing them within the uniformity of a homogeneous community. The open-ended and inclusive character of such a civic bond transforms diverse feelings of individual identity into a sense of solidarity among co-patriots without erasing the diversity. Thus, a political culture fostered along the lines of constitutional patriotism can accommodate the inclusion of the other and the freedom of the difference.

## CONSTITUTIONAL PATRIOTISM AND LANGUAGE POLICY

Habermas' concept of political culture here is analogous to Kymlicka's notion of 'societal culture'.[2] In so far as it similarly involves a common language and social institutions, rather than common religion beliefs, family customs, or personal lifestyles (Kymlicka, 2001: 164). *Contra* traditional groundings of national consciousness, such an understanding of political culture allows for greater inclusion and elasticity.[5]

For Kymlicka, however, the sufficient condition for political unity and social cohesion is a shared sense of national identity, which is owed to citizens' shared history and a common language (Kymlicka, 2001: 311–13; Kymlicka, 1995: ch 5). According to him, citizens' conflicting interests can be adjudicated only if these commonalities are present. In this way, Kymlicka distinguishes his view from civic patriotism when he insists that mere shared principles are not enough to hold members of a political community together. However, such a commonplace criticism (see Canovan, 2000; Yack, 1996; Mertens, 1996; Böckenförd, 1995; Scruton, 1990) of civic patriotism is mistaken since it ignores the binding power of common practices of law-making.

As I suggested earlier, we need to contextualise the question of identity and solidarity according to specific questions of political association and policy-making. And if we do that, we realise that a common political bond can be obtained and then maintained when the cohabitants of the political community recognise each other as sharing a political life through participation, deliberation and law-making. That should simply suffice because citizenship is increasingly about what one does and not who one is (Benhabib, 2002: 170). It used to be that the cohabitants of a homogeneous society were joined through many natural ties. Today's increasing diversity, hybridity and pace has weakened and in some places dissolved those close ties. Hence, in order to identify with a person or a group as one's compatriots one ought not need to feel a strong sense of love or intimacy characteristic of general kinship ties in a family or a clan. In fact, one does not necessarily need a common history (as the average of 200,000 newcomers to Canada every year seems to show). Rather, one needs to identify with the particular political negotiation in which one is engaged. Of course, if there is love, friendship, common history and homogeneity, so much the better. But under the condition of diversity the minimum requirement is the recognition of the fact that we live together, and as such have the status of free and equal partners in governing our common life. Hence, the trust needed for this negotiation to succeed is the trust between free and equal partners and not the trust of lovers, best friends, or family members.

> A free and democratic society will be legitimate even though its rules of recognition harbor elements of injustice and non-consensus if the citizens are always free to enter into processes of contestation and negotiation of the rules of recognition. (Tully, 2000b: 477)

Here, a sense of belonging arises out of identifying with a set of institutions and practices as a reference point that expresses the polity of the original law, which reflects the will of citizens as its authors. And it is within this framework that issues of public policy, including language policy, need to be addressed.

The model relies on public deliberation and negotiation among the citizens of the political community that is not bound by any *a priori* and fixed notion of identity and rights. Citizens or their representatives make laws and policies that in turn govern and affect them. This construct of law and policy-making is equipped with the procedural openness to allow for differentiated rights based on changing and criss-crossing identities. In this way, laws and policies can reflect differentiated rights that encompass a variety of rights, from special representation rights to self-government rights, including language rights. The realisation of differentiated identity rights based on an overarching principle of association in constitutional law would imply that policies concerning linguistic rights of national minorities and immigrant groups cannot and should not be decided based on a unitary view of the dominant language.

Instead, such policies should be approached pragmatically with respect to a specific set of political problems that they are trying to address.

On this model, language is the communicative medium of deliberation, which entails that a common language is important because it can facilitate political interaction and deliberation among the political actors for the purpose of their common life. Thus, the political happens through language. While from various perspectives language may be viewed as a good in itself, from the political perspective it is good for something else, namely, allowing political actors to take part in common practices of communication, deliberation and law-making. Intrinsic arguments for the value of a language are tenable only from the internal standpoint of the culture hosting the language. And since that would be the case for people belonging to different cultural groups in all multicultural and multilingual societies, the question of official language cannot be decided by way of appeal to intrinsic arguments for a language.

Thus, the communicative view of language is not based on pure intrinsic arguments relating to human achievement. However, this should not be seen as endorsing the instrumental approach either, not because it doesn't value language as a means of communication among citizens to their political end, *but because unlike instrumental actions the guiding principle here is understanding and not success or domination.* Language is the context of reaching mutual understanding with others. This communicative sense of language is qualitatively different from the instrumental sense of language. Hence from the viewpoint of constitutional patriotism, the argument for language policy is neither instrumental nor intrinsic. It is rather a communicative or pragmatic argument. The adjective 'pragmatic' should not be understood in its general political sense here. Rather, the pragmatic character of the communicative view of language refers to Habermas' 'transcendental pragmatic argument', which uncovers the presuppositions of rules of argumentation at the rhetorical level of process that is capable of hosting an ethical content: 'In argumentative speech we see the structures of speech situation immune to *repression* and *inequality* in a particular way: it presents itself as a form of communication that adequately approximates ideal conditions' (Habermas, 1990: 88; emphasis added). This point needs to be accompanied with a second clarification about what kinds of rights are language rights.

As mentioned in the first section of this paper, some liberal nationalists argue for the intrinsic value of language, demanding full recognition and protection of the language (Réaume, 2000). When it comes down to deciding what language(s) is to be granted official status, however, they argue that only those languages of considerable size and vitality are to be recognised. This seems to indicate a reversal in their reasoning. For, while the size and vitality of linguistic community is very important with respect to the status of a language, they plainly contradict the intrinsic thrust of the argument. That is to say, if something is inherently good, then, philosophically speaking, its size or any other empirical consideration should not matter. Conversely, if contingent and empirical elements are a part of the argument, then the argument cannot be an intrinsic one.

Hence, it looks as if what these theorists have in mind might be a *political* understanding of the intrinsic argument, which would imply that, as a good, language is to be regarded as a collective practice and not an individual activity—a view similar to the communicative argument for language. In this sense, then, language, as a constitutive element of people's identity, requires a certain size and vitality to satisfy the symbolic needs and expectations of the community's members. But it is exactly in this sense that language rights are not a type of human rights. This is so because while torturing an individual would amount to a violation of that individual's human rights, not offering Japanese language services to Japanese tourists in Canada is not a violation of their human rights (MacMillan, 1990: 10–22). 'Language rights, to be human rights, must be universal or else they are not rights at all' (*ibid*: 105). But this should not be taken to mean that language rights are an entirely different species of rights. As long as constitutional patriotism entails a universalistic understanding of the rule of law and democracy that allows us to normatively separate unjust language rights from just ones, language rights too have some universalist strands in them. This clarification suggests that language rights are a sub-species of human rights that require different treatment.

So far we have established that from the viewpoint of constitutional patriotism the role of language should be viewed pragmatically as a communicative medium aimed at mutual understanding between political actors, and that language rights are not pure human rights. Now, as for the way in which this insight is supposed to guide the processes of opinion and will-formation in the deliberative democracy model with respect to minority rights in general and language right is particular, we have to emphasise not only the *inclusive* character of this model, which 'makes it particularly attractive to the concerns of excluded minorities' (Benhabib, 2002: 134), but also its *empowering* character that results from insistence on the consent of all those affected by the acquired laws as the ground of its legitimacy. The discourse principle, as the consensus of all those affected by the discursive norm, has been criticised for being overly ambitious and exclusive. But as James Bohman and Jorge Valadez have argued, this principle need not be seen as requiring identical reasons for the agreed upon norms but rather as what entails 'moral compromise' where:

> the parties do not modify the framework to achieve unanimity, although they may when conflicts are not so deep. Rather, they modify their conflicting interpretations of the framework so that each can recognize the other's moral values and standards as part of it. (Bohman, 1996: 91; Valadez, 2001: 59–66)

The practice of law-making, then, results from the process of discursive public deliberation whose outcome in a multicultural context is characterised by moral compromise. Or 'As the Supreme Court of Canada has put it, a free and democratic society rests not on a set of rules immune to criticism but on a "continuous process of discussion" involving the right of dissent, the duty to acknowledge dissenting voices, and the corresponding amendments of the rules of the democracy over time' (Tully, 2000: 474). This attitude is most consonant with the spirit of constitutional patriotism, which is why I will take Canada as a model for constitutional patriotism in the next section. This convergence, however, is not to suggest that the politicians and policy-makers in Canada adopted and employed this theoretical model but to find the ideas and practices that I describe here at work in the Canadian system. Indeed, the Constitution of 1982 along with the Charter of Rights and provisions of bilingualism and multiculturalism aimed at governing a diverse society based on liberal democratic values anticipated the theoretical articulation of this model by Habermas.

In such a context language policy is open and inclusive; and as a compromise it is constrained by (1) values of a liberal *political culture*—that includes civility, mutual recognition, equal respect, tolerance, etc, (2.a) *historical contingencies* such as the historical role of the founding communities, and (2.b) *practical feasibilities* such as the size and vitality of contending languages. The first criterion of political culture has priority over the next two since it is the precondition for any liberal-democratic contestation. The next two criteria are on a par and neither has priority over the other. This is important since it implies that the language policy drawn from these criteria is not static and remains open to change based on future changes in practical feasibility such as size and vitality. As for the justification for the importance of these criteria, the democratic values of a liberal political culture is the precondition upon which any genuine contestation and negotiation can take place. Historical contingencies are normatively important since they separate the claims of the founding communities in terms of specific historical development, a criterion that, for example, separates the linguistic demands of Anglophone, Francophone and Aboriginal people in Canada, as founding communities, from those of the Italian immigrant community in Toronto or the Ukrainian immigrant community in Alberta. The reason for the normative weight of these kinds of claims is that 'they are claims to nationhood based on historical priority, on the fact that they were present at the creation of the state, and that the state's very legitimacy on their collective consent' (Ignatieff, 2001: 67). Finally, practical feasibilities matter since policy-making is always constrained by limited resources, which, in turn, make considerations of size, viability, vitality, efficiency, etc very relevant.

Here, one might ask: if language policy is guided by these three criteria, then in what way is understanding language communicatively important to policy-making practices? It is important in the following way. To understand language as a medium of communicative action allows us to escape a Scylla of instrumentalist views and a Charybdis of intrinsic views with their respective policies of convergence and protection in favour of a multilingual policy of recognition. One might point out that the first version of the intrinsic argument too results in multilingual policy based on recognition. As discussed above, the advantage is that while this view suffers from an internal tension when their advocates emphasise the importance of such factors as size and vitality of language, these considerations are consistent with the pragmatic character of the communicative view. Moreover, the communicative view would allow for a finer distinction that would separate language rights from human rights as their sub-species.

In a multicultural and constitutional state there will not be as many official languages as there are diverse groups, but a language or small number of languages, together with a shared practice of political participation, would ensure that no citizen is left out of the democratic process of law-making as a result of a lack of knowledge of an official language. Now, depending on whether one or more languages in a specific context performs that service, the question of official language needs to be decided differently. Its should be clear, hence, that the aim of a normative language policy, with respect to accommodating the democratic ideal of transparency, is not to promote linguistic homogeneity but to serve the communicative goal of political deliberation.

## CANADA AND THE NORMATIVE MODEL OF LANGUAGE POLICY

In this section I would like to show how Canada's practice of law- and policy-making with respect to the question of official language policy approximates the normative model of constitutional patriotism, which I have been advancing here. From this perspective Canada's language policy can be seen as a civic achievement that involves a deliberative compromise between two (of the three) founding nations of Canada (I will address the absence of the Aboriginal People from this negotiation later).

Recalling the above-mentioned criterion for devising a language policy, we can say that, with respect to principle (1), Canada's political culture of liberal democracy is the matrix upon which the discursive deliberation concerning official language(s) has taken place. The Official Languages Act in Canada is set to deal with the obligations of federal institutions regarding service to the public and language of work, and sets out the government's commitments in the area of equitable participation of its citizens.[6] Regarding condition (2.a), the Act is divided into two parts: Official Languages and Minority Language Educational Rights, as reflected in sections 16 and 23 of the Charter of Rights respectively.[7] The first part, reflecting the founding role of the English and French national minorities as the original settler groups—the contingent element of the Canadian history—states that 'English and French are the official languages of Canada and have equality of status and equal rights and privileges as to their use in all institutions of the Parliament and Government of Canada'.[8] This suggests that not any minority group can have a claim to official language status for their language, which means that only national minorities, as groups historically grounded in the political community, can make that claim. 'Since immigrant groups are not national minorities, they are not accorded similar language rights' (Kymlicka, 1995: 46). The historical role of language communities makes the language rights in Canada 'compromise rights of fundamental sort' (Green, 1987: 669) The second part of the Act, reflecting the condition of practical feasibilities (2.b) based on population concentration, geography, resources, etc, states that Canadians who constitute a linguistic minority—either French or English—in their province are entitled to 'have their children receive primary and secondary school instruction in that language in that province' (*ibid*). The spirit of these three criteria is captured in a statement made by the Human Rights Commission of Prince Edward Island, during a meeting of the Task Force on Canadian Unity:

> Language and language-of-education rights should be protected, not because they are "basic or fundamental human rights" but because they have acquired a "special and powerful status" in the life of the country, and because they "may be integral to the existence or survival of a culture, which some citizens may regard as tied to the existence or survival of a culture, which some citizens may regard as tied to their own identity." In that context they would be "constitutional rights" only.[9]

The Canadian official-language regime includes the use of either official language—English or French—in the federal courts, by federal legislators, in the publication of statutes, in communicating with federal government agencies, and in minority-language education. The official bilingualism policy took the historical founding role of the English and French people seriously in adopting both languages as official languages of Canada. Yet, since after the original settler groups more peoples have been involved in building this nation, further elaboration of this historical compromise was required. Hence, shortly after bilingualism policy, the official policy of multiculturalism[10] was adopted as an attempt to acknowledge the significance of the role and contribution of the other ethnic groups in constituting Canada.

While at first glance there might seem to be a tension in introducing a policy of multiculturalism into a bilingual framework, a closer look would reveal a political insight that can accommodate greater diversity and enhanced inclusion. In *Finding Our Way* (Kymlicka, 1998), Will Kymlicka makes the point that the policy of multiculturalism within a bilingual framework has served to separate language from lifestyle and ethnic descent. He argues that to acknowledge two public languages because of their historical role over other languages is not the same as valuing English and French lifestyles and ethnic interests over others:

> In other words, the promotion of English and French as dominant languages need no longer be associated with the promotion of the lifestyles of citizens of English and French descent. Multiculturalism is thus seen as a means of integrating immigrants into one of the two societal cultures in Canada: francophone or anglophone. Each is characterized by its language and social institutions, but neither of them imposes common religious beliefs and specific lifestyle. (Coulombe, 2000: 286)

A language policy devised along these lines reflects a civic commitment to ideals of justice and inclusion, which are pursued by the constitutional norms aimed at accommodating cultural diversity. James Tully calls these norms constitutional conventions of mutual recognition, consent and continuity (Tully, 1995). Such forms of law-making are the result of the recognition of the fact that:

> The individual's existential dependence on intersubjectively shared traditions and identity-forming communities [which] explains why the integrity of the legal person cannot be secured without equal cultural rights in culturally differentiated societies. (Habermas, 2001: 74).

In Canada legal recognition of the individual's cultural rights has proceeded in the form of continuous negotiation marked by a bargaining character necessitated by the deep diversity of Canadian society. Indeed, the jurisprudence of the Canadian Supreme Court has viewed the official language rights as a political compromise between the two founding nations of French and English Canadians. This can be seen in the court's ruling in *MacDonald v City of Montreal* and *La Société des Acadiens du Nouveau Brunswick v Minority Language School Board.*[11] In the first case MacDonald claimed that under section 133 he had the right to be served a traffic offence summons in the official language of his choice. The court ruled that the right in section 133 of the Constitution Act 1867 was that of speakers and not of addressees of the communication, meaning that the government official could use her own language regardless of whether that was the same as the language of MacDonald's choice or not.[12] Similarly in hearing the case of La Société des Acadiens du Nouveau Brunswick where the appellant claimed that they were entitled under section 19 of the Charter of Rights to a judge capable of understanding their official language, the court ruled that the right was to be understood as a negative liberty of the speaker and was not meant to impose any positive obligation on the recipient of the speech.[13] In both cases the court characterised its decision as being 'based on a political compromise rather than on principle'.[14]

The position of the court was widely criticised as being too instrumentalistic, failing to see the intrinsic value of using one's own language. Given the court's tendency to apply a restrictive interpretation of the right to use French or English in courts, in 1987 Bill C-72 was introduced as a revision to the Official Language Act.[15] Prior to the Bill the Commissioner of Official Languages had recommended to the Parliament that the language rights be *personalised* with respect to one's 'right to be served in either language that would complement the existing institutional obligation to provide the service', and with respect to 'the formal recognition of the right of federal employees to carry out their duties in official language of their choice, subject to certain conditions'.[16] The recommendations were incorporated into the Bill:

> These provisions significantly expanded the scope of the meaning of a right to a trial in either official language. They also specifically corrected the restrictive interpretation of language rights in courts as developed by the Supreme Court ... The individual to a proceeding became the holders of the right and controlled the decision regarding the language of court proceeding. (MacMillan, 1998: 83)

Consequently, the revisions allowed the court to revisit the issue and confront this criticism in 1999 in the case of *R v Beaulac*.[17] The appellant, Jean Victor Beaulac, charged with first degree murder, requested a 'trial before a judge and jury who speak both official languages of Canada pursuant to s 530 of the *Criminal Code*'.[18] The court ruled in favour of the appellant, arguing that 'Language rights must in all cases be interpreted purposively, in a manner consistent with the preservation and development of official language communities in Canada'. And referring to the previous ruling it stated that 'To the extent that *Société des Acadiens* stands for a restrictive interpretation of language rights, it is to be rejected'. Despite this revision, however, the court's characterisation of the interpretation as 'purposive' suggests that 'language rights be interpreted as a fundamental tool for the preservation and development of official language communities'. That is because, the court argued, 'Language rights are a particular kind of right, distinct from the principles of fundamental justice'.[19]

The court, through its ruling, indeed upheld a distinction between constitutional rights grounded in principle and language rights based on the political history of the two founding national groups. This distinction mirrors the subtle distinction between human rights and language rights that was pointed out earlier. Language policy in the context of deep diversity of the founding groups is marked by a normative negotiation aimed at obtaining a workable compromise. Of course, arriving at such compromise in the constitution still leaves the question of the language used for constitutional deliberation untouched. However, recognition of the differences and the need for coexistence among the diverse groups compels their elites who are usually bilingual or multilingual to carry out the negotiation. Such negotiation in turn impregnates the constitutional law regarding language rights with the practical impression of the society's bilingual or multilingual makeup. The allegiance to such a law would be guaranteed since the citizens see the signature of their character imprinted on the law.

The discussion of the Canadian case would not be complete without saying something about the question of Aboriginal claims for linguistic equality. Advocates of these claims express their demand by appealing to various forms of intrinsic argument for the value of language. They argue that the threat of extinction of Aboriginal languages that results from lack of recognition is a source of social inequality. Kymlicka voices this worry in the following way:

> Aboriginal fears about the fate of their cultural structure, however, are not paranoia—there are real threats. The English and French in Canada rarely have to worry about the fate of their cultural structure. They get for free what Aboriginal people have to pay for: secure cultural membership. This is an important inequality, and if it is ignored, it becomes an important injustice. (Kymlicka, 1989: 190)

How can such claims for equality of status and demands for recognition be assessed? To apply the three guiding principles of values of political culture, the significance of the historical role of Aboriginal peoples, and the consideration of practical feasibility to these claims would reveal a tentative answer.

So far as the liberal values of tolerance, recognition, equality of treatment and respect go, some form of recognition should be granted to Aboriginal languages. This recognition is buttressed by the historical role of Aboriginal communities as one of the founding peoples in Canada. However, it is with respect to the third principle that Aboriginal demands for linguistic equality are challenged. According to censuses of 1981 and 1991 the size of the Aboriginal community of languages collectively adds up to 0.5 per cent of the population. This small population is scattered across the country without a sizable concentration. Furthermore, this small percentage of the population represents the speakers of, not one native language, but multiple languages, each spoken by a small number of people. More importantly still, these languages are not widely used in those communities. Given these factual considerations, the demand for equal status of Aboriginal languages with the official languages of Canada is not justifiable.

This conclusion, however, should not mean that there should be no recognition for these languages. The demand for recognition can be accommodated by addressing the Aboriginals' more fundamental demand for self-government and local levels of regional or provincial policy-making. For instance, in 1988 the Northwest Territories Official Languages Act was amended to include Chipewyan, Cree, Dogrib, Gwich'in, Inuktitut, and Slavey as official languages of the region along with English and French. Similarly, the Quebec government's language law known as Bill 101 exempts Cree, Inuktitut and Naskapi from its application in Aboriginal communities. In these communities the right of people to use their languages and of their school boards to educate Aboriginal children in these languages is recognised by law.

## CONCLUSION

Our contemporary world confronts us with an unprecedented degree of diversity, hybridity and pace. These changes require that we rethink our approach to the problem of political association. Questions of membership, belonging and recognition of diversity can no longer be answered from an ethnonational view but have to be addressed based on a common practice of democratic law-making crystallised in a constitution. The procedural character of this practice, while beginning from abstract principles of human rights, democracy and justice, are further filled in by the specific content of a political culture of a concrete country. Policy questions, such as language policy, in diverse societies are best approached from this flexible model of constitutional patriotism where allegiances are formed around the democratic practice of law-making.

In conclusion, I would hope that my discussion of such difference-sensitive law-making and policy-making has demonstrated the capacity of the normative framework of constitutional patriotism to approach the goals of justice and inclusion with a degree of procedural flexibility and open-endedness appropriate for democracies that exhibit deep diversity.

## Notes

1 Briefly, I first argue that this criticism unnecessarily overburdens the goal of solidarity with the inflated language of 'love', 'friendship', 'intimacy', etc. In other words, for the citizens of a constitutional state to feel connected to each other they do not need to feel like lovers or best friends, but rather it will suffice for them to feel mutual trust and respect as free and equal partners. Secondly, the criticism confuses the normative and sociological aspects of the debate. It repeatedly emphasises the empirical fact of a pre-political 'we' as the ground of

political association which requires a normative valuation. However, the critical and reflective characteristics of the citizens of postconventional democracies enable them to go beyond the tradition by criticising, revising and modifying what has been the case in favour of what should be the case. (See Shabani, 2002.)

[2] In his words societal culture 'provides its members with meaningful ways of life across the full range of human activities, including social, educational, religious, recreational, and economic life encompassing both public and private spheres. These cultures tend to be territorially concentrated and based on a shared language.' (See Kymlicka, 1995: 76.)

[3] The United States has no official language in the sense that there is no such clause in the constitution or other such documents. But English is its 'official' language since a minimum competence in English is a condition of eligibility for citizenship. The 'Naturalization Requirement Document' published by INS states: 'Applicants for naturalization must be able to read, write, speak and understand words in ordinary usage in the English language' (http://www.usains.org/citizenship_prep.htm).

[4] This redrawing was repeated in 1960—to separate people who spoke Gujarati and those who spoke Marathi—in the State of Bombay and in 1966—to separate Punjabi speakers and Haryanvi speakers—in the State of Punjab. Despite this, India also has pursued a convergence policy around the Hindi language which is spoken by more than a third of the population.

[5] Kymlicka states that the governments of liberal democratic states in their project of 'nation-building' may promote two or more societal cultures (see Kymlicka, 2001: 165).

[6] Government of Canada, Official Languages Act, http://laws.justice.gc.ca/en/charter/index.html

[7] See the Charter at http://laws.justice.gc.ca/en/charter/index.html.

[8] *Ibid.*

[9] Task Force on Canadian Unity, *A Time to Speak: The Views of the Public* (Hull, Minister of Supply and Services, 1979), 265.

[10] Canada adopted its multiculturalism policy in 1971, and in 1988 formally enshrined the policy in legislation with the Canadian Multiculturalism Act, which reads in part as follows: '3.(1) It is hereby declared to be the policy of the Government of Canada to (a) recognize and promote the understanding that multiculturalism reflects the cultural and racial diversity of Canadian society and acknowledges the freedom of all members of Canadian society to preserve, enhance and share their cultural heritage; (b) recognize and promote the understanding that multiculturalism is a fundamental characteristic of the Canadian heritage and identity and that it provides an invaluable resource in the shaping of Canada's future; (c) promote the full and equitable participation of individuals and communities of all origins in the continuing evolution and shaping of all aspects of Canadian society and assist them in the elimination of any barrier to that participation' (http://www.multiculturalism.pch.gc.ca).

[11] Supreme Court of Canada, *McDonald v City of Montreal*, 1986 at http://scc.lexum.umontreal.ca/en/1986/1986rcs1-460/1986rcs1-460.html; *La Société des Acadiens de Nouveau Brunswick v Minority Language School Board*, No 50, 1986 at http://scc.lexum.umontreal.ca/en/1986/1986rcs1-549/1986rcs1-549.html.

[12] Section 133 reads: 'Either the English or the French language may be used by any person in the debates of the House of the Parliament of Canada and of the Houses of Legislature of Quebec; and both those Languages shall be used in the respective Records and Journals of those Houses; and either language may be used by any person or in any pleading or process in or issuing from any courts of Canada established under this act, and in or from all or any of the courts of Quebec' (http://laws.justice.gc.ca/en/const/c1867_e.html).

[13] Section 19 of the Charter reads: 'Either English or French may be used by any person in, or in any pleading in or process issuing from, any court of New Brunswick' (www.patrimoinecanadien.gc.ca/charter-anniversary/section-16-22_e.cfm).

[14] Supreme Court of Canada, *McDonald v City of Montreal*, 1986, pp 500–1.

[15] House of Commons, Bill C-72, An Act Respecting the Status and Use of the Official Languages of Canada, 2nd session, 33rd Parliament (first reading 25 June 1987, passed 7 July 1988).

[16] Commissioner of Official Languages, News Release (11 February 1986).

[17] *R v Beaulac* at http://scc.lexum.umontreal.ca/en/1999/1999rcs1-768/1999rcs1-768.html.

[18] *Ibid.*

[19] *Ibid.*

**References**

Alonso, W and Starr, P (eds) (1987) *The Politics of Numbers* (New York, Russell Sage Foundation).
Anderson, M and Fienberg, SE (1999) *Who Counts? The Politics of Census-Taking in Contemporary America* (New York, Russell Sage Foundation).
Arato, A (1994) 'Constitution and Continuity in the East European Transitions' *Constellations* 1: 92–112.
Arato, A (1996) 'Slouching Toward Philadelphia?' *Constellations* 3: 225–47.
Bader, V (1995) 'Citizenship and Exclusion: Radical Democracy, Community, and Justice. Or, What is Wrong with Communitarianism?' *Political Theory* 23: 211–46.
Baker, J (ed) (1994) *Group Rights* (Toronto, University of Toronto Press).
Balibar, E (1996) 'Is European Citizenship Possible?' *Public Culture* 8: 355–76.
Barbour, T and Carmichael, C (eds) (2000) *Language and Nationalism in Europe* (Oxford, Oxford University Press).
Bellamy, R and Warleigh, A (1998) 'From an Ethics of Integration to an Ethics of Participation: Citizenship and the Future of the European Union' *Millennium* 27: 447–68.
Benhabib, S (2002) *The Claims of Culture: Equality and Diversity in the Global Era* (Princeton, NJ, Princeton University Press).
Böckenförd, W (1995) 'Die Nation' *FranhfurterAllegmeine Zeitung*, 30 September.
Bohman, J (1994) 'Complexity, Pluralism, and the Constitutional State: On Habermas' *Faktizität und Geltung*' *Law and Society Review* 28: 897–929.
Bohman, J (1996) *Public Deliberation: Pluralism, Complexity and Democracy* (Cambridge, MA, MIT Press).
Bohman, J (1999) 'Citizenship and Norms of Publicity: Wide Public Reason in Cosmopolitan Societies' *Political Theory* 27: 176–202.
Bohman, J and Lutz-Bachmann, M (eds) (1997) *Perpetual Peace* (Cambridge, MA, MIT Press).
Bohman, J and Rehg, W (eds) (1997) *Deliberative Democracy: Essays on Reason and Politics* (Cambridge, MA, MIT Press).
Booth, J (1999) 'Communities of Memory: On Identity, Memory, and Debt' *American Political Science Review* 93: 249–63.
Bourdieu, P (1991) *Language and Symbolic Power* (Cambridge, MA, Harvard University Press).
Boyd, M (1999) 'Canadian eh? Ethnic Origin Shifts in the Canadian Census' *Canadian Ethnic Studies* 31: 1–19.
Brown, W (1998) 'Democracy's Lack' *Public Culture* 10: 425–9.
Canovan, M (1996), *Nationhood and Political Theory*, Cheltenham: Edward Elgar.

______ (2000) 'Patriotism is Not Enough' *British Journal of Political Science* 30: 413–32.

Carens, J (ed) (1995) *Is Quebec Nationalism Just? Perspective From Anglophone Canada* (Montreal and Kingston, McGill–Queens University Press).

Connor, W (1972) 'Nation Building or Nation Destroying?' *World Politics* 24.

Coulombe: P. A. Coulombe (2000) 'Citizenship and Official Bilingualism in Canada', in Kymlicka, W and Norman, W (2000), pp 273-93

Derrida, J (1986) 'Declaration of Independence' *New Political Science* 7–15.

Famia, J (1996) 'Complexity and Deliberative Democracy' *Inquiry* 39: 357–97.

Gaffield, C (2000) 'Linearity, Nonlinearity, and the Competing Constructions of Social Hierarchy in Early Twentieth-Century Canada' *Historical Methods* 33: 255–64.

Gaffield, C (2002) 'Language, Ancestry and the Competing Constructions of Identity in Turn-of-the-Century Canada' (Ottawa, Institute for Canadian Studies, University of Ottawa) (unpublished manuscript).

Godway, EM and Finn, G (eds) (1994) *Who is This We?* (Montreal, Black Rose Book).

Goldberg, D (1997) *Racial Subjects: Writing on Race in America* (New York, Routledge).

Government of Canada (1900) House of Commons Debates, 16 July, Vol 3, 10334.

Government of Canada (1901) *Fourth Census of Canada: Instructions to Officers* (Ottawa, Department of Agriculture).

Government of Canada (1956) Dominion Bureau of Statistics, *Ninth Census of Canada, 1951* (Ottawa, The Queen's Printer).

Government of Canada (1979) Task Force on Canadian Unity, *A Time to Speak: The Views of the Public* (Hull, Minister of Supply and Services).

Green, L (1987) 'Are Language Rights Fundamental?' *Osgoode Hall Law Journal* 25: 639–69.

Habermas, J (1990) *New Conservatism: Cultural Criticism and the Historian Debate* (tr SW Nicholsen) (Cambridge, MA, MIT Press).

Habermas, J (1996) *Between Facts and Norms* (tr W Rehg) (Cambridge, MA, MIT Press).

Habermas, J (1997) *A Berlin Republic: Writing on Germany* (tr S Rendall) (Lincoln, NE, University of Nebraska Press).

Habermas, J (1998) *The Inclusion of the Other* (tr C Cronin and P De Greiff) (Cambridge, MA, MIT Press).

Habermas, J (2001) *Postnational Constellation* (Cambridge, MA, MIT Press).

Halli, S, Trovato, F and Driedger, L (eds) (1990) *Ethnic Demography, Canadian Immigrant, Racial and Cultural Variations* (Ottawa, Carleton University Press).

Honig, B (1996) 'Difference, Dilemmas, and the Politics of Home' in S Benhabib (ed) *Democracy and Difference* (Princeton, NJ, Princeton University Press).
Honig, B (1998) 'Immigrant America? How Foreigness "Solves" Democracy's Problems' *Social Text* 56: 1–28.
Kertzer, DI and Arel, D (2002) *Census and Identity: The Politics of Race, Ethnicity, and Language in National Censuses* (Cambridge, Cambridge University Press).
Kymlicka, W (1989) *Liberalism, Community and Culture* (Oxford, Oxford University Press).
Kymlicka, W (1991) 'The Ethics of Inarticulacy' *Inquiry* 34: 155–82.
Kymlicka, W (1995) *Multicultural Citizenship: A Liberal Theory of Minority Rights* (Oxford, Oxford University Press).
Kymlicka, W (1998) *Finding Our Way: Rethinking Ethnocultural Relations in Canada* (Toronto, Oxford University Press).
Kymlicka, W (2001) *Politics in the Vernacular: Nationalism, Multiculturalism, and Citizenship* (New York, Oxford University Press).
Kymlicka, W and Norman, W (2000) *Citizenship in Diverse Societies* (New York, Oxford University Press).
Kymlicka, W and Patten, A (eds) (2003) *Language Rights and Political Theory: Context, Issues, and Approaches* (New York, Oxford University Press).
Ignatieff, M (2000) *Right Revolution* (The Canadian Broadcasting Corporation).
Ignatieff, M. (2001) *Human Rights as Politics and Idolatry*, Princeton University Press.
Ignatieff, M (2002) *Human Rights* (Princeton, NJ, Princeton University Press).
Ingram, A (1996) 'Constitutional Patriotism' *Philosophy and Social Criticism* 22: 1–18.
La Silva, S (1996) *The Moral Foundation of Canadian Federalism* (Kingston and Montreal, Queens–McGill University Press).
Laforest, G (ed) (1993) *Reconciling the Solitudes: Essays on Canadian Federalism and Nationalism* (Montreal and Kingston, McGill–Queens University Press).
Laforest, G (1995) *Trudeau and the End of A Canadian Dream* (Kingston and Montreal, Queens–McGill University Press).
Macedo, S (1999) *Deliberative Politics: Essays on Democracy and Disagreement* (New York, Oxford University Press).
MacMillan, M (1998) *The Practice of Language Rights in Canada* (Toronto, University of Toronto Press).
Manin, B (1987) 'On Legitimacy and Political Deliberation' *Political Theory* 15: 338–68.

Mansbridge, J (1994) 'Using Power/Fighting Power' *Constellations* 1: 53–73.
Margalit, A & Raz, J (1990) 'National Self-Determination'. *The Journal of Philosophy*, 87:99, 439–61.
Markell, P (1997) 'Contesting Consensus: Rereading Habermas on the Public Sphere' *Constellations* 3: 377–400.
Mason, A (1999) 'Political Community, Liberal-Nationalism, and the Ethics of Assimilation' *Ethics* 109: 261–86.
McCarthy, T (1994) 'Kantian Constructivism and Reconstructivism: Rawls and Habermas in Dialogue' *Ethics* 105: 44–63.
McCarthy, T (1999) 'On Reconciling Cosmopolitan Unity and National Diversity' *Public Culture* 11: 175–209.
MacMillan, C. Michael. 1998, *The Practice of Language Rights in Canada.* Toronto: University of Toronto Press
Mertens, T (1996) 'Cosmopolitanism and Citizenship: Kant Against Habermas' *European Journal of Philosophy* 4: 328–47.
Miller, D (1995) *On Nationality* (Oxford, Oxford University Press).
Nussbaum, M (1996) *For Love of Country: Debating the Limits of Patriotism* (ed Joshua Cohen) (Boston, Beacon Press).
Omid A. Payrow Shabani (2002) 'Who's Afraid of Constitutional Patriotism? the Binding Source of Citizenship in Constitutional States', *Social Theory and Practice*, Vol. 28:3, pp. 419–43.
Parekh, B (2000) *Rethinking Multiculturalism: Cultural Diversity and Political Theory* (London, Macmillan).
Patten, A (2001) 'Political Theory and Language Policy' *Political Theory* 29: 691–715.
Pensky: Introduction to J. Habermas, (2001) *The Postnational Constellation: Political Essays*, ed. and trans. by Max Pensky, Cambridge, MA: MIT Press
Philips, A (1994) 'Dealing with Difference: A Politics of Ideas or a Politics of Presence?' *Constellations* 1: 74–91.
Post, RC (1990) 'The Constitutional Concept of Public Discourse' *Harvard Law Review* 103: 603–86.
Preuss, U (1996) 'Prospect of a Constitution for Europe' *Constellations* 3: 207–24.
Prewitt, K 'The Census Counts, the Census Classifies', in Nancy Foner and George M. Fredrickson (eds.), *Not Just Black and White: Historical and Contemporary Perspectives on Immigration, Race, and Ethnicity in the United States*. New York: The Russell-Sage Foundation, 2004. pp. 145–64.
Putnam, H (1983) *Realism and Reason: Philosophical Papers*, Vol 3 (Cambridge, Cambridge University Press).
Réaume, DG 'Official-Language Rights: Intrinsic Value and the Protection of Difference', in Kymlicka, W and Norman, W (2000), pp. 245–73.

Schiffman, HR (1996) *Linguistic Culture and Language Policy* (London, Routledge).
Scruton, R (1990) 'In Defense of Nation' in JCD Clark (ed), *Ideas and Politics in Modern Britain* (London, Macmillan).
Tamir, Y (1993) *Liberal Nationalism,* Princeton: Princeton UP.
Taylor, C (1994) *Multiculturalism and the Politics of Recognition* (ed A Gutmann) (Princeton, NJ, Princeton University Press).
Taylor, C (1995) 'Cross-purposes: The Liberal Communitarian Debate' in *Philosophical Argument* (Cambridge, MA, Harvard University Press).
Taylor, C (1996) 'Why Democracy Needs Patriotism?' in J Cohen (ed), *For the Love of Country: Debating the Limits of Patriotism* (Boston, Beacon).
Taylor, C (1997) 'Nationalism and Modernity' in R McKim and J McMahan (eds), *The Morality of Nationalism* (Oxford, Oxford University Press).
Trudeau, PE (1986) *Federalism and the French Canadians* (Toronto, Macmillan).
Trudeau, PE (1990) *Towards a Just Society* (Kingston and Montreal, Queens–McGill University Press).
Tully, J (1995) *Strange Multiplicity: Constitutionalism in an Age of Diversity* (Cambridge, Cambridge University Press).
Tully, J (2000a) 'Aboriginal Peoples: Negotiating Reconciliation' in J Bickerton and A-G Gagnon (eds), *Canadian Politics*, 3rd edn (Peterborough, ON, Broadview Press).
Tully, J (2000b) 'Struggle over Recognition and Distribution' *Constellations* 7:4, 469–82.
Tully, J (2002) 'Caricatures of Multiculturalism' *Ethnicities* 2: 273–7.
Valadez, JM (2001) *Deliberative Democracy, Political Legitimacy, and Self-Determination in Multicultural Societies* (Boulder, CO, Westview Press).
Viroli, M (1998) 'On Civic Republicanism: Reply to Xenos and Yack' *Critical Review* 12: 187–98.
Walzer, M (1990) 'What Does it Mean to be an "American"?' *Social Research* 57: 591–614.
Wolin, S (1994a) 'Norm and Form: The Constitutionalization of Democracy' in JP Euben, JR Wallach and J Ober (eds), *Athenian Political Thought and the Reconstruction of American Democracy* (Ithaca, NY, Cornell University Press). Wolin, S (1994b) 'Fugitive Democracy' *Constellations* 1: 11–25.
Xenos, N (1998) 'Questioning Patriotism' *Critical Review* 12: 197–201.
Yack, B (1996) 'The Myth of Civic Nation' *Critical Review* 10: 193–211.
Yack, B (1998) 'Can Patriotism Save Us from Nationalism: A Rejoinder to Viroli' *Critical Review* 12: 203–6.
Young, I (1997) 'Asymmetrical Reciprocity: On Moral Respect, Wonder, and Enlarged Thought' *Constellations* 3: 340–63.

# 4

# *Intercultural Recognition and Linguistic Diversity in Europe*

PETER A KRAUS

THE TREATY ESTABLISHING a Constitution for Europe, signed by Heads of State and Government in October 2004 (though yet to be ratified by all Member States), confirms the central normative status assigned to diversity in the political integration of the Continent. Thus, to offer only one example, Article 3 of the Constitution, listing the objectives of the European Union (EU), includes the following paragraph: '[The Union] shall respect its rich cultural and linguistic diversity, and shall ensure that Europe's cultural heritage is safeguarded and enhanced.'[1] The constitutional text contains several additional mentions of the Union's commitment to the protection of cultural diversity.

When it comes to giving a concrete meaning to a general norm, cultural diversity, taken in general terms, may appear to be an evasive concept. Nevertheless, hardly anybody would deny that linguistic differentiation is a fairly uncontroversial candidate when we look for salient manifestations of diversity in the political realm of the EU. In an enlarged Union, 27 member states make for 23 official languages (ie state languages). By being official at the member state level, these languages automatically become official languages of the Union as well. Moreover, there are a considerable number of languages that have an official or semi-official status in different regional or subnational contexts, eg Welsh, Saami and Catalan. Finally, we must not forget the linguistic communities formed by immigrants from such areas as North Africa or Asia Minor: in several West European countries, there are large groups of people whose mother tongue is Arabic, Turkish or Kurdish. Accordingly, it should be easy to concede that cultural diversity in Europe is, first and foremost, linguistic diversity.

What are the implications of Europe's pronounced multilingualism regarding the process of creating a public sphere that could support an emerging transnational polity? When raising such a question, we should keep in mind that European nation-states typically established a close connection between linguistic standardisation and political communication. Both democratic theory and democratic practice tend to conceive the modern political public as a linguistically integrated public. Does the multiplicity of languages linked to specific political cultures entail barriers that limit the options for democratising the EU? To a considerable extent, the language issue reflects the challenges involved in the process of developing a legitimate framework for Europe's transnational order. In this context, the politics of language seem to be inextricably intermingled with the politics of European identity. On the following pages, I do not pretend to give a systematic account of the complex relationship of linguistic and political identities in Europe. My main concern is to shed some light on the impact that linguistic differentiation has on structuring a transnational communicative space in the EU. The approach I adopt will combine normative considerations with a political sociology perspective. My first step sketches out the ways in which a political theory of language can contribute to our understanding of the impact of multilingualism on transnational communication in Europe. The thesis put forward is that, beyond all instrumental considerations, the expressive dimension of language has a special relevance for political communication. In multilingual settings, the recognition of linguistic diversity pays tribute to this relevance. Second, I argue that when confronting situations of linguistic pluralism, the politics of recognition usually aim at compensating the effects of diglossia. Third, I maintain that the logics of recognition in the EU are hampered by the lack of a coherent language policy. This exacerbates the negative consequences that the imperatives of communicative efficiency have anyway for the institutional articulation of diversity in Europe. As the last section of the paper tries to show, the perspective of a democratic interculturalism may help to reduce the tensions between diversity and communicative integration in an institutional framework that links recognition and reflexivity.

## LANGUAGE AS A POLITICAL BOND

Modern societies are societies built upon complex communication. Functional differentiation and the division of labour led to an enormous increase in routinised large-scale interaction. Such interaction usually required people to communicate in a shared and standardised language. At the same time, by connecting structural social transformations to specific communicative requisites, modernisation generally implied that culture, as the resource sustaining comprehensive social communication, became politicised.[2] The revolution in the field of information technologies that we are experiencing at present seems to give additional relevance to the role of cultural identity in processes of social and political integration.[3]

Under functional aspects, language has to be considered an absolutely central element of a common culture. The infrastructure of industrial and postindustrial societies can't work properly without a lingua franca. The functional perspective highlights the *instrumental* dimension of language. Accordingly, language is primarily seen as a medium that designates things and facts. By using language, people are able to communicate in order to achieve specific purposes. The instrumental component of linguistic communication becomes patent in virtually all social domains. To have the possibility to communicate instrumentally can be a matter of life or death, as extreme examples prove. In March 2001, several people died in a train collision in Belgium. The accident happened in an area close to the linguistic border that separates the country's Flemish and Francophone territories. Apparently, one of the reasons why last minute attempts to avoid the tragedy failed was that the two railway employees in charge of controlling the points in the two stations located on each side of the border were each fluent in only French and Dutch, respectively, and thus not able to communicate with each other on the telephone in an effective way.[4] The example is certainly not fully representative of everyday communication routines, yet it shows the extent to which information systems in our societies depend on securing a quick understanding based on a shared linguistic repertoire.

Language, however, cannot be reduced to its instrumental side. Language also has an *expressive* dimension that goes beyond the mere designating of objects and facts.[5] Many things only come into existence when we move within the expressive dimension of language. In this sense, language makes a central contribution to how we gain our conception of ourselves and frame our way of life (Taylor, 1985: 10). Expressive meaning can never be completely detached from its linguistic medium, as it only becomes patent in the reflexive use we make of this medium. Finding an appropriate approach to the expressive dimension of language not only has far-reaching implications for our understanding of language use; it also bears substantially on our understanding of the subject of language. In this context, Taylor (1985: 232–4) emphasises the seminal contribution of Johann Gottfried Herder and Wilhelm von Humboldt in pointing out the links between language and expressivity. The two representatives of an intellectual current blending Enlightenment concerns with Romantic sensitivities shared the view that language is created and changed by human communication, by speech. To the extent that language is to be conceived as an activity, the primary locus for this activity is conversation. Accordingly, language develops in a *linguistic community*; it can be considered a paramount example of a good that is irreducibly social (Taylor, 1995: 135). Both Herder and Humboldt highlight the social component of the expressive dimension of language. On the one hand, language is seen as a resource that is constitutive of human autonomy and freedom. On the other hand, this autonomy is socially embedded and relates to the collective practices of a language community. From this angle, language creates an elemental social bond. Thus, in a certain sense, individual speech acts always refer to a speech community. At the same time, it is ultimately language itself that defines and sustains the speech community. Humboldt uses the image of a web (*Gewebe*) to describe how language simultaneously shapes and is shaped by human communication. The web frames our communicative repertoire: we cannot speak outside language. Yet, by relying on the structure of language, we find the freedom to articulate ourselves.[6]

The political relevance of the instrumental dimension of language is obvious: in all kinds of everyday contexts, we have to be able to employ language in conformity with the specific functional requirements of different situations. How we realise our life chances depends to a considerable extent on our linguistic competence. As learning languages involves costs, the right to use our mother tongue in a multitude of social domains has an instrumental character. It is the expressive dimension, however, that gives language its particular political salience, a salience frequently intermingled with claims for 'recognition' (Taylor, 1992). Language is a resource we need for individual communication. By acquiring this resource, we are attached to a specific, culturally defined community. If a language, as a line of reasoning running from Herder and Humboldt to Taylor holds, forms an irreducible social web, securing potentials for individual development and freedom becomes a matter of a collective support that, in modern polities, translates into institutional provisions sustaining this web. Moreover, if the dignity of individuals is to be respected, the linguistic and cultural identity of their communities of origin must be recognised to a satisfactory extent. When the cultural bases that underlie our personal development and that we regard as authentic are institutionally ignored, negated or even repressed, our self-esteem, which is an asset of great significance in the process of building up and protecting our individual autonomy, will be severely hampered.

The importance it has as a social bond is one of the main causes that has made language a recurrent point of reference in nationalist mobilisations since the 19th century. In some cases, language and nation became virtually interchangeable concepts. As the great sociolinguist Joshua Fishman (1973: 82–85) argues, one need not be sympathetic to nationalist approaches to language in order to still understand their deep-rootedness in social reality, which gives them a force that should be taken seriously. Writing three decades before the new 'global' millennium, Fishman anticipated that, in the realm of culture, the proliferation of all kinds of international and transnational linkages would entail a successive political activation of particular identities all over the world. In his view, the striving for authenticity has hardly lost the impetus it has had since the dawn of the age of nationalism; therefore, social scientists would make a big mistake if they underplayed the impetus or limited their analytic efforts to offering a derogatory assessment of its foundations. Fishman (1973: 83) writes:

> The need for identity, for community, to make modernity sufferable, is greater than it was and will become greater yet, and woe to the elites—in universities,

governments, and industries—who do not recognize this or, even worse, who consider it to be only a vestigial remnant of nineteenth century thinking.

Against this background, it is to be stressed that there is nothing anachronistic or 'primordial' in this quest for authenticity and in the claims for having this authenticity recognised in the political realm. The wish to be authentic is an important element in the motivational configuration of our *modern* selves (Taylor, 1989). Accordingly, the quest for *linguistic authenticity* must not be misinterpreted as a longing for perennial and supposedly 'organic' identity patterns. In modern societies, linguistic identities can certainly not be considered an outcome of 'natural' processes of evolution. On the contrary, they reflect the dynamics of processes of political integration. There is plenty of evidence that linguistic identities can be transformed, both at the individual and at the collective level, at least within certain limits. That linguistic identities are—relatively—mouldable, however, does not reduce the political relevance of the expressive dimension of language. That a person is understood in a context of linguistic communication does not automatically mean that her linguistic identity is recognised. In a certain sense, what makes for a good part of the political salience of linguistic identities is their very malleability. The weight of expressivity is typically highlighted in multilingual settings, where claims for the recognition of collective identities that are felt as authentic and related to specific linguistic communities generally go hand in hand with claims for the recognition of an autonomous institutional frame of political and cultural relations. From this perspective, linguistic and political culture cannot be separated from each other.

## RECOGNITION AND DIGLOSSIA

In a still highly recommendable comparative study dealing with the causes and political implications of the 'ethnic revival' in modern, industrialised West European societies, the Finnish social scientist Erik Allardt (1979: 43–47), after analysing a broad sample of empirical cases, maintains that the mobilisation of territorial linguistic minorities in the developed West can generally not—or, at any rate, not anymore—be properly interpreted as a reaction against types of discrimination that are based upon social exclusion and bear negative material consequences. In contrast with, for instance, the ethnic groups formed by immigrants, Europe's 'autochthonous' linguistic minorities, in most cases, do not struggle in order to overcome a subordination that could be measured in social and economic terms. They rather struggle for recognition, as Allardt (1979: 44) literally put it in the late 1970s. From Allardt's viewpoint, by making such claims for recognition, their primary goal is that their self-categorisation is accepted by the majorities.

For the bulk of the minority groups in question, this self-categorisation is not so much related to a socio-economic background; ultimately, its core consists in a distinctive cultural identity whose principal symbol is language. In particular, those groups with a high mobilisation capacity, such as the Tyroleans in Italy, the Basques and Catalans in Spain, the Walloons and Flemings in Belgium or the Swedish-speaking Finns, cannot be adequately characterised by attributing to them a subordinate position in a system of cultural division of labour. What they have been striving for are political and institutional provisions that allow them to reproduce a collective identity which they consider to be specific.[7] Simplifying things, we can draw the conclusion that the major issues on Europe's current language policy agenda are less related to questions of material status than to questions of self-respect and 'honour'.

For the approach adopted here, recapitulating Allardt's account of the mobilisation of linguistic minorities in Western Europe seems a helpful exercise if we want to tackle some important political issues raised by cultural and linguistic diversity in the European Union. An important additional step that we should be prepared to take in order to gain a comprehensive understanding of the conflict structures that are characteristic of multilingual contexts consists of establishing a connection between the role of recognition in language policy and a prominent research tradition in sociolinguistics that has focused on the study of diglossia. The concept of diglossia refers to linguistic situations in which two or more languages occupy clearly separate functional domains within the same society. Moreover, this functional separation generally denotes a social hierarchy. Typically, a 'high' language, that is used in the realms of education, administration, finances and the media, can be distinguished from a 'low' language.[8] As Fishman (1971: 286–8) points out, there are different combinations of societal bilingualism and diglossia. Shifts in the relationship between different languages and between speech communities indicate the dynamics of political and cultural change at work in a country. In the case of France, for example, French had attained an exclusive role as the functionally 'high' language well before Jules Ferry's educational reforms brought about its sweeping implantation across the whole country in the late 19th century. However, according to the historical account of how 'peasants' were turned into 'Frenchmen' presented by Eugen Weber (1976), around 1850 it was still common for the rural population in the peripheries to be fluent only in the regional *patois*. Thus, a peasant in Brittany would only speak Breton. To the extent that there was no encompassing language community (based on the use of French), the situation was characterised by diglossia without bilingualism. Today, in contrast, we will observe a co-occurrence of diglossia with (limited) bilingualism in those areas of France with surviving regional languages. The Breton peasant may still speak Breton, but he has certainly acquired a solid knowledge of French as well. The subordinate status of the regional languages has remained unchanged. Yet, in the meantime, everybody is able to communicate in the 'high' language.

From the angle of theories of recognition, the concept of diglossia can make an important contribution to our understanding of linguistic conflict in Western democracies. In the terrain of language policy, claims for recognition are, to a significant extent, claims made in order to attenuate, or sometimes even to overcome, the effects of diglossia. The members of the groups exposed to diglossic institutional settings want to expand the range of social and functional domains in which they have the possibility of using their vernacular language. Linguistic recognition thus implies that individuals who belong to a minority have the option to live an everyday life that is not too far away from the communicative 'normality' that the members of the dominant culture are used to. It must be considered remarkable that bilingualism is experienced as particularly problematic within groups whose members experience diglossic situations as situations of status inconsistency. In the recent past, examples such as the Québécois in Canada, the Catalans in Spain and the Flemings in Belgium exhibit this pattern. In such cases, the discontent caused by the functional subordination of the 'own' language regarding the dominant language (English, Spanish and French, respectively) fuelled demands for full political and cultural equality. The linguistic mobilisation of the three groups gained significantly in strength after they had gone through periods of intense modernisation, which were accompanied by the formation of a new middle class characterised by a great concern for questions of cultural status.

The Breton peasant who is not proficient in the dominant language belongs to a distant past. Nowadays, the members of Western Europe's linguistic minorities are generally bilingual. Often, their knowledge of the majority language tends to be even better than their competence in the mother tongue. At the same time, however, they are frequently quite determined not to give up their vernacular and to resist complete linguistic assimilation. As the public support for a policy upholding official bilingualism (Irish and English) in Ireland demonstrates, the allegiance to the 'own' language even reaches well into the large segments of the population who were assimilated generations ago. For many people, language is a key to the realm of authenticity, a symbol of collective identity that must not be renounced. In consequence, in sociocultural contexts characterised by diglossia, struggles over recognition often involve conflicts about the status of languages.

As has been argued so far, relating the issue of recognition to the phenomenon of diglossia will help us to develop a better understanding of identity conflicts that revolve around language. At the same time, however, it should be clear that establishing this link will not lead us to an institutional standard formula for addressing the political challenges of multilingualism. If our aim is to find a normatively sound balance between the imperatives of instrumental communication and the commitment to protecting diverse linguistic identities in multilingual settings, we will have to put forward a political analysis that allows for thick sociolinguistic evidence. When we move into the field of recognition, it becomes patent that designing an adequate institutional response to the challenges of diversity requires a careful appreciation of context, a context that will vary from case to case. Language policies are no exception in this regard. Bringing diglossia into focus may still help us to grasp the contextual factors that make for the specific configuration of conflicts over linguistic recognition. Accordingly, the interplay of recognition and the (latent) problems of diglossia may be an important aspect of the politics of language in the European Union.

## THE CHALLENGE OF LINGUISTIC PLURALISM IN THE EUROPEAN UNION

Cultural and linguistic diversity can be considered to be one of the key elements in the multinational space constituted by the European Union and its institutions. The commitment to protecting diversity not only corresponds to a broadly shared normative orientation. The blunt empirical fact is that the member states of the EU would hardly give any support to an integration agenda threatening their specific political and cultural identity patterns. Accordingly, European institutions operate under the premise of respecting and fostering (cultural) diversity while trying to work towards 'an ever closer Union'.

The great institutional relevance that a politics of mutual recognition has in the EU assigns multilingualism an important symbolic role. This is underpinned in the Union's 'linguistic constitution', if we are prepared to use such an expression for a rather rudimentary set of rules. Since the ratification of the Treaty of Rome, in which the language issue is mentioned almost in passing, as a matter to be regulated by the Council, and the ensuing directive adopted by the Council in 1958 in order to sketch out the basic features of the European language regime, an intergovernmental consensus has been the basis of European language policy. It has materialised in the official guideline to respect the pluralism and the equality of the member states' languages within European institutions. In principle, the 'linguistic constitution' of the European Union does not differentiate between official languages and working languages in Community organs. All state languages are both official and working languages. Up to now, the admission of new members has not led to a modification of the principle of formal equality of all state languages. Thus in the 2004 Eastern enlargement of the EU, the number of official languages[9] increased from 11 (15 member states) to 20 (25 member states). This number will increase further in the next few years due to the successive entry of new members from Eastern Europe, and the change in status of Irish from January 2007. In view of its official language regime, the EU constitutes an institutional domain in which an unrestricted and 'integral' multilingualism applies.[10]

To some extent, the obligation to protect linguistic and cultural diversity in the EU responds to a situation marked by a tactical sense of reciprocity, in which the member states acknowledge to themselves that their particular identities have to play a determining role in the political development of the Union. The language policy officially adopted by the EU reflects a multinational constellation that is characterised by continuous efforts to maintain a basis for intergovernmental compromises. In this context, the politics of recognition are imbued with a statist bias, as the recognition of linguistic diversity must be primarily interpreted as a concession to the importance of the tradition of national languages in Europe, all of which turn out to be the languages of nation-*states*. By conferring the same official status on all state languages, the fragile principles of a shared political culture of integration were to be protected against nationalist setbacks caused by an issue that was taken to be symbolically very sensitive. The political elites willing to pass the first critical thresholds in the uniting of Europe shared the belief that the construction of a common institutional frame should not be endangered by risking the question of language becoming politicised (Coulmas, 1991).

In the meantime, however, the language policy guidelines set up to regulate institutional communication in the EU seem to have brought about a specific dynamic going beyond the tactical considerations that sustain intergovernmental bargains. In the corresponding approach to linguistic pluralism, normative aspects must not be discounted. In a compact form, the importance of such aspects is highlighted in an information leaflet provided by the Joint Interpreting and Conference Service of the European Commission. Under the suggestive title 'Multilingualism: The Key to Success', the 'philosophy' of European multilingualism is explained in succinct terms.[11] The information offered deserves to be quoted extensively:

> Language is one of the most obvious... signs of diversity, which characterise mankind. The global society in which we live is moving more and more towards the three major economic poles, Europe, the United States and Japan, Europe being the continent of greatest diversity and, by the same token, the one with the greatest need for a language policy in its common endeavour.
>
> The European Union wants to preserve, defend and foster language diversity and has realised that a desire for political unity is not enough to bind together heterogeneous peoples. The best way to bring people together is to respect their differences rather than to coerce them into unity.

> This is the sign of real respect for multilingualism in the EU: more than a legal imperative, it is a reflection of the whole philosophy of the European idea....
>
> The European Union's sense of cultural diversity is one of its strong points and one which will help to move it towards a greater interdependence or globalisation whilst safeguarding its differences. Anyone who feels that his or her cultural identity, and that means primarily language, is protected, will not feel that identity threatened. Such a threat would have been an anathema to the founding fathers of the European Union.

The document from which the quoted paragraphs are taken establishes an interesting synthesis between the functional imperative 'to bind together heterogeneous peoples' and normative postulates. On the normative side, the respect for diversity, which is basically understood as linguistic diversity, is assigned an absolutely central place. Recognising different cultural identities, as they become manifest in the pluralism of languages in Europe, will facilitate an articulation of difference that avoids conflicts and does not hamper political integration. In addition to its significance for Europe's 'internal' affairs, the intercultural sensitivity shown in the area of linguistic diversity is taken to be an advantage that the Union has over other regional poles of integration in the global context.

The approach towards multilingualism adopted by the EU's Joint Interpreting Service has a normative basis that, all in all, does not seem to be too distant from the view on language and recognition sketched out in the first sections of this contribution. It is obvious, however, that adhering to this approach involves a significant political challenge, a challenge that has not really been addressed by the Union so far. Since John Stuart Mill, theories of liberal democracy have generally held that a democratic public sphere must be a linguistically integrated public sphere. From this perspective, which has reappeared in the debate on Europe's constitutional future and, for instance, is a key aspect in the lines of argumentation put forward by Dieter Grimm and Jürgen Habermas, processes of political communication that are to meet democratic standards require the vehicle of a shared lingua franca.[12] If the point is taken seriously, it implies a major political dilemma for the EU: seen from a Millian angle, a context of communication as pronouncedly multilingual as the European context represents a barrier to political integration that cannot be ignored. Thus, the EU has to confront a complicated situation: to the extent that it promotes multilingualism in order to protect cultural diversity, it may be reducing the possibilities of creating an integrated transnational space of political communication.

In reality, the problem appears to be even more intricate, for the EU's institutional routines respond to the official multilingual creed in only a fairly limited way. In the realm of *internal communication*, the status equality of all official languages turns out to be a *de jure* provision with modest consequences. The truth is that French and English have a clear leading role as working languages in the EU, and there are increasing signs that English has recently become more and more dominant at the expenses of French (Schloßmacher, 1994; de Swaan, 2001). In terms of efficiency, such a drastic reduction in the number of languages used in the Union's internal communication processes seems unavoidable. Nonetheless, it is normatively problematic that the distinction between a *de jure* and a *de facto* language regime is not made within a clearly defined political frame. This has negative repercussions for the credibility of the major programmatic guidelines of Europe's 'linguistic constitution'. Moreover, as the silent substitution of integral multilingualism by a language regime that, in the end, is rather selective takes place in a normative grey area, there is much potential for conflict regarding the Union's internal linguistic functioning. The increase in institutional tensions relating to issues of language policy during the last years indicates the resilience of this conflict potential.

From a recognition perspective, the sphere of *external communication* is even more important than the language policies the EU applies internally. Here, the first major issue is how the communication processes between European institutions and the emerging European civil society are organised. Moreover, in the same context, it has to be asked what underlying communicative bases exist for the making of a transnational public sphere within the Union. The dynamics of integration are fostering the development of new spaces of communication in Europe. So far, however, their capacity to enhance democratic participation seems to be relatively limited. Data provided by Eurobarometer reports show that the levels of knowledge on the EU are highest among managers and people with an educational background that is well above the average; in contrast, the levels of information are particularly low among women and the unemployed.[13] It is obviously no coincidence that the *Financial Times Europe* is considered to be the only newspaper targeting a genuinely European public, to be found predominantly in the circles of political and economic elites. Generally speaking, the structure of political communication via mass media channels that cover the EU as a whole is characterised by segments of a transnational public operating in the communicative spaces shaped by the interactions of functionally specialised elites. These elites typically use English as their lingua franca (Schlesinger, 1999: 271, 276).

Against this background, it is striking that the White Paper on European Governance, presented by the Commission of the European Communities in 2001, deals extensively with the question of communication in the European Union, but mentions the language issue only in passing. One section of the document (European Commission, 2001: 11) emphasises that both the institutions and the member states of the EU have to 'communicate more actively with the general public on European issues'. This call for broadening the public channels for political communication in Europe touches indeed upon the linguistic dimension, as is admitted in the document: 'Information should be presented in a way adapted to local needs and concerns, and be available in all official languages if the Union is not to exclude a vast proportion of its population—a challenge which will become more acute in the context of enlargement.' In their practice, however, European institutions often lag far behind this objective. The Commission, for instance, has made major efforts to establish the Internet as a major tool for facilitating access to information on the EU. Yet documents placed on the Commission's website are often available only in English, French and, sometimes, German. Obviously, the capacities of the translation services in Brussels are limited, so that the number of languages used in the European Union's external communication cannot easily be maximised in order to meet the standards of linguistic equality. It is nonetheless difficult to understand why, to give just one example, information about an EU project targeting homeless children in Palermo is only available in English on the EU's official website.[14] This is not simply anecdotal evidence, as a significant amount of web documents in which European institutions explain their activities to the European public can only be downloaded in English or French. Therefore, it seems doubtful that groups specifically affected by EU policies do always have direct access to the information on the programmes that are of immediate concern to them. If we take into account what we know about the distribution of language skills within the European population, the institutional channels of political communication in the EU remain fairly selective.

Linguistic barriers remain an important element in Europe's emerging communicative space. When we summarise the main findings of a special Eurobarometer report on Europeans and languages (Eurobarometer, 2001b), it becomes patent that foreign language skills in the European Union are distributed very unevenly, in both social and geographical terms. Thus, EU citizens reaching levels of foreign language competence that would enable them to take an active part in transnational public debates belong predominantly to the upper strata of society. Moreover, up to now, English, as Europe's leading lingua franca, is apparently much more extended in the Northern and Central regions of the Continent than in the South. According to the empirical indicators listed in the special Eurobarometer report on language, the hegemonic position of English as the first foreign language in Europe can hardly be questioned. Nevertheless, there are also factors that qualify this general assessment. Not even half (46.5%) of the 41% of EU citizens who declare to have a knowledge of English as a foreign language consider this knowledge to be 'good' or 'very good'. Such an appreciation puts limits on the lingua franca potential of English. We may speculate that for many Europeans English serves as a helpful basic asset for communication when they travel abroad. This does not imply, however, that it constitutes a linguistic bond uniting the EU as a transnational political community. In a nutshell, the conclusion is that English clearly holds the position of Europe's first second language today. Yet such a position does not mean that it will easily become a 'second first language' for the bulk of European citizens, as observers such as Jürgen Habermas (2001: 122) would have it.

As soon as we turn to empirical indicators, it is evident that the problems associated with the weak communicative bases of a European civil society cannot really be separated from the question of how language skills are distributed among European citizens. In the present context of transnational political communication, a substantial number of Europeans have only limited access to information that is potentially relevant to their concerns, due to the great variation in linguistic repertoires within the Union. Such a narrowing of communicative spaces accentuates tendencies towards elitism and technocratic rule that have often been criticised as being inherent to European politics (Featherstone, 1994).

In the end, the ongoing debate on the perspectives for building a European public sphere points at a more fundamental problem. This problem appears recurrently when the relationship between politics and communication is brought into focus in modern democratic theory. In analyses of democratic processes and institutions, language is typically regarded as a factor that is exogenous to the proper domain of politics. Yet, in contrast to such an approach, language should be seen as a central element of political life. In intercultural settings, defining the linguistic modalities of political communication is a salient political issue. From a normative point of view, building the structures of a public sphere that offers a discursive frame contributing to the formation and consolidation of a common political identity and, at the same time, remains respectful of linguistic and cultural diversity, is an ambitious and innovative project. Under present circumstances, however, the EU runs the risk that its public sphere will shift vertically into discrete loci of specialised discussion, without being sustained by a horizontal dynamics of political communication as well. For many citizens, a realm of political deliberation dominated by circles of experts and elites will remain inaccessible. If the tendency prevails, it may render transnational decision-making more efficient. Such gains in efficiency, however, will only be reached at the expense of the European project's normative attractiveness.

In order to avoid an open outbreak of linguistic conflict, the main institutional players in the EU have so far refrained from entering into a political debate on the language issue. Ultimately, to adopt the strategy of circumventing conflict means to bring about a situation in which the dynamics of negative integration spill over from the domain of the common market and permeate transnational political culture, too. On the one hand, it is obvious that there is a growing need to overcome communicative obstacles in the European political space. On the other hand, the diffuseness of institutional criteria regulating the protection of diversity and the weakness of genuinely European structures of political decision-making interact in a way that leads to the marginalisation of politics by the logics of the market in the development of an encompassing frame of communication in the Union. It is obvious that *European English*, as the Continental variant of *global English*, has attained a quasi monopolistic position in the Union's linguistic market. To deny the advantages that this position entails for confronting the complex communicative challenges in the process of transnational integration would be pointless. Therefore, it will be impossible to adopt a pragmatic approach towards the language issue in the EU without taking into account the particular role of English.[15] Yet the political foundations of a European public sphere must not be based on instrumental considerations alone. At the top level of European institutions, the inclination to avoid politicisation of the language issue seems to prevail. The underlying expectation would be that a shared communicative space will form in quasi 'spontaneous' ways, as a result of the interplay of market-like mechanisms. From such an angle, the political discourse of diversity would eventually have to be taken as lip service without any serious consequences when it comes to counterbalancing the 'tough' functional imperatives of transnational communication. The alternative strategy consists in stressing that the language issue is an eminently political issue and has to be confronted accordingly. Hence, the regulation of multilingualism needs to be included as a pressing topic in the constitutional politics of the European Union.

## THE ROLE OF DEMOCRATIC INTERCULTURALISM IN EUROPEAN INTEGRATION

Democratic rule is based upon the principle of citizenship. Citizens are the key element of any political order that aims at meeting democratic standards (Schmitter, 2000: 5). To a large extent, citizenship is defined by legal aspects. Yet the citizenship status cannot be reduced to its legal components, however important these may be. If citizens are to exert their rights in a meaningful way, they have to rely on cognitive resources. In order to act as free and autonomous individuals, the members of a democratic political community must have the chance to acquire 'enlightened understanding' (Dahl, 1989: 111). In the context of modern, representative democracy, the very idea of self-government implies the existence of emancipated citizens who have attained a level of communicative competence that allows them to develop and to sustain a qualified and critical notion of politics. In consequence, the status of democratic citizenship is the result of far-reaching processes of political and cultural socialisation. In the course of these processes, educational institutions are of the utmost significance for transmitting a basic cognitive repertoire that gives the members of a society the capacity to act as autonomous subjects (Callan, 1997; March and Olsen, 2000). Such a basic repertoire typically includes a minimum of linguistic competence, which adds to the other parts of a general curriculum the content of which will vary with the overall political constellation. The chances to provide the structures of public communication with a broad democratic base sink to the extent that the cognitive component of the citizenship status is neglected. It is in this very respect that some of the European Union's political legitimation problems are most palpable at present. For the same reason, it seems difficult to imagine how further advances in the political integration of Europe can be made without raising the issue of communication and language. 'Grand' constitutional politics, as practised by the Convention, will hardly have the effect of counterbalancing the deficiencies at the 'micro-level' of democratic integration, that is at the level at which democratic subjects are constituted.

By serving as the media of public communication, languages combine cultural and political elements in specific ways. Therefore, in modern societies, linguistic culture and political culture tend to be closely interrelated. The creation of the communicative space of a European civil society must be considered a highly significant task when it comes to setting the Union's constitutional foundations; to confront this task obviously implies dealing with the issue of the linguistic integration of a European public sphere. Linguistic integration, however, should not be automatically equated to integration in *one* language. The diversity of the cultural patterns of identification that represent the specific collective experiences of the different political communities composing the Union must have a palpable presence in the transnational discourses led by the emerging European public. On the one hand, this is a normative requisite that can be derived from the principal European treaties, and that has been included in the Treaty establishing a Constitution for Europe as well. On the other hand, the commitment to protecting cultural and linguistic diversity responds to functional imperatives that have deep roots in the world of European politics. It will be all but impossible to give the project of political integration a stable basis if the demands raised in order to secure the protection of particular identities, demands which are characteristic of the multinational constellation shaping the EU's political development, are not taken into account. What could a language policy that aims at finding a balance between communication and diversity in the making of a European public look like, in the light of the analysis offered so far?[16]

A converging multilingualism that would be more or less selective depending on the communicative levels and institutional domains concerned might be the option for those areas that are most immediately relevant for the political structuring of a European public sphere, such as the external communication of EU organs or the communicative logistics of a transnational civil society. *European English* is certainly bound to be a substantial component of this option. Yet the English language should not be granted an unquestionable monopoly status in the processes of transnational political communication in Europe. The EU has rather to look for ways to support multilingual structures that comprise different languages in response to varying sociocultural situations. The European framework of public communication would thus be split up according to both functional and territorial criteria in order to promote the use of more than one lingua franca, securing operative niches for languages such as French or German. Finally, it would also be highly important to find some place, if only at the symbolic level, for the so-called 'smaller' languages—including regional and minority languages—in the European space of political communication.

The concrete regulation and implementation of the option of a converging multilingualism is an issue that is deliberately left open here. It has already been said that the option is supposed to sustain a flexible approach to the challenges of linguistic pluralism in the European polity. What is to be stressed at the same time, however, is that the option pursues one main goal: its intention is to contribute to formulating a deliberately *political* answer to the questions raised by the interplay of language and politics in Europe's communicative space. The constitutional path followed by the Union commits European institutions to protecting the diversity of cultures and languages. It is hardly an exaggeration to speak of a historically novel undertaking when such a commitment is linked to the making of an integrated institutional framework in the realms of the economy and of politics. Moreover, as the language example shows, the undertaking is difficult and involves great conflict potential. Which kind of normative perspective may allow us to tackle the issue of linguistic pluralism in the process of European polity-building in a constructive way?

From the angle adopted in this contribution, the framework of public communication in the EU should be based upon the principles of an institutionally differentiated and democratic interculturalism. In the first place, such a model implies the continuation of the premise of democratic integration. Thus, one of the principal objectives of transnational political communication in the context of the Union would be to contribute to the definition of a European 'common good'. In this respect, the concept of *inter*culturalism departs intentionally from a tendency observable in some *multi*cultural approaches, in which collectivities are conceived as the carriers of discrete cultural identities in a given political setting and juxtaposed to each other in a static or even essentialising fashion. To a large extent, the patterns of collective belonging that constitute cultural identities can be changed by political means and become a matter for self-determination. Yet, in the very same context, it has to be emphasised that a normatively meaningful understanding of the concept of interculturalism implies the recognition of the political weight of these identities in processes establishing a constitutional association marked by diversity.[17] Seen from such an angle, the respect for linguistic diversity is to be taken as a central element in a transnational political ethos inspired by intercultural motives. Europe will increasingly be in need of such an ethos, should it really strive for an 'ever closer Union' of its peoples. If the EU is to become a political community relying on an institutional order that is prepared to deal with identity conflicts, intercultural competence at the level of civil society must be considered a highly valuable political resource. As it is likely to foster the development of intercultural competence in the transnational public space, the promotion of multilingualism, even when operating on a differentiated and flexible basis, may well make a substantial contribution to the creation of a political framework that offers appropriate responses to Europe's diversity.

In culturally diverse political settings, recognition becomes a crucial factor in ensuring that group relations are permeated with reflexivity. Even if conceived of as freedom in a transnational political space, the freedom of European citizens continues to be a situated freedom. Accordingly, Europe's intricate constitutional process requires all parties involved to understand that the sociocultural dimension of political integration is a fundamental aspect of the transformations we are going through. In the end, the politics of recognition make it evident that the citizens themselves cannot be considered to be a 'given', exogenous factor in the fabric of democracy. Citizenization[18] and its institutional regulation must instead be regarded as elementary ingredients of democratic politics. From this viewpoint, recognition is not a mechanism supposed to support a static politics of 'being'; it rather paves the way for a reflexive politics of 'becoming'. Recognition thus implies a focus on identities that carries a transformative potential.[19] In this sense, recognition appears to be a normative pillar for those forces who want to link the transnationalisation of the public sphere with democratic politics. In a European Union committed to the respect of diversity, recognition is a requirement for making the impact of diglossia more acceptable to the groups who have to make major concessions, in terms of their cultural status, because of the dynamics of linguistic integration. For the members of other groups, it offers a key they absolutely need if they want to see their own identity in a reflexive way, in a way that remains aware of the existence of different identities.

## Notes

1 Draft Treaty establishing a Constitution for Europe, as submitted to the President of the European Council in Rome on 18 July 2003: http://www.europarl.org.uk/constitution/ConstitutionSingleMain.htm.

2 The intertwining of social, economic and cultural mobilisation in the process of modernisation is a topic dealt with extensively in classic approaches to nationalism, such as Deutsch (1966) or Gellner (1983). Benedict Anderson (1991) emphasises the importance of

'print capitalism' for the making of 'imagined communities' that were to become the typical manifestations of modern collective identity.

3 This is one of the main theses advanced by Manuel Castells (1996, 1997, 1998) in his thorough interpretation of the coming 'information age'.

4 The case is taken from an article published in the newspaper *El País* on 31 March 2001.

5 In distinguishing an instrumental and an expressive dimension of language I follow Taylor (1985: 9–11, 218–19; 1995: 101–3); cf also Réaume (1991: 45).

6 The corresponding views are outlined in Herder (2001 [1772]: 80–95) and Humboldt (1963 [1830]: 414–39).

7 For general overviews of Western Europe's new regionalism and peripheral nationalism focusing on their political goals cf also Puhle (1995) and Tiryakian and Rogowski (1985).

8 When Ferguson (1959) introduced the concept of diglossia, his purpose was to designate a 'high variety' and a 'low variety' of the same language (among the examples he mentioned were classic vs popular Arabic and High German vs Swiss German). The concept was given a broader meaning by Fishman (1967), who used it to analyse situations in which the functions of the higher and the lower code in intrasocietal communication correspond to different languages (Spanish and Guaraní in Paraguay, for instance).

9 It should be noted that Irish and Luxembourgian have had a special status in this respect, as they are not considered regular official languages at the Union's institutional level. The two member states concerned endorsed this special arrangement at the time of their accession. However, Irish becomes an official language from January 2007.

10 A more detailed analysis of the EU's institutional language regime can be found in Kraus, 2000 and 2004.

11 European Commission, Joint Interpreting and Conference Service, 1995–2002: *Multilingualism*. The passages quoted are from the version found on the internet on 18 February 2002.

12 See Mill (1972 [1861]: 392) as the classic reference. Although Grimm (1995) and Habermas (2001) do not agree on Europe's constitutional prospects, they do have similar opinions as to the importance of linguistic integration for European polity-building.

13 See the data in Eurobarometer 55 (Eurobarometer, 2001a).

14 See *Frankfurter Rundschau*, 6 June 2001 ('Englisch bevorzugt').

15 Contrasting assessments of the expansion of *global English* in Europe can be found in Phillipson and Skutnabb-Kangas (1994) and de Swaan (2001).

16 A detailed discussion of this question is given in Kraus (2004).

17 Tully (1995) persuasively shows how important recognition is for the shaping of an innovative intercultural approach to contemporary constitutional politics.

18 The concept is taken from Tully (2001: 25).

19 The significance of recognition in determining the normative grounds of an emancipatory politics is discussed systematically in Honneth (2003).

## References


Allardt, E (1979) *Implications of the Ethnic Revival in Modern, Industrialized Society. A Comparative Study of the Linguistic Minorities in Western Europe* (Helsinki, Societas Scientiarum Fennica (*Commentationes Scientiarum Socialium* 12)).

Anderson, B (1991) *Imagined Communities, Reflections on the Origin and Spread of Nationalism* (London, Verso).

Callan, E (1997) *Creating Citizens. Political Education and Liberal Democracy* (Oxford, Oxford University Press).

Castells, M (1996) *The Rise of the Network Society* (Oxford, Blackwell).

Castells, M (1997) *The Power of Identity* (Oxford, Blackwell).

Castells, M (1998) *End of Millennium* (Oxford, Blackwell).

Coulmas, F (1991) 'European Integration and the Idea of the National Language. Ideological Roots and Economic Consequences' in F Coulmas (ed), *A Language Policy for the European Community. Prospects and Quandaries* (Berlin, Mouton de Gruyter).
Dahl, RA (1989) *Democracy and its Critics* (New Haven, CT, Yale University Press).
Deutsch, KW (1966) *Nationalism and Social Communication* (Cambridge, MA, MIT Press).
Eurobarometer (2001a) Standard Eurobarometer Report Number 55 (Directorate-general Press and Communication), Brussels, October 2001.
Eurobarometer (2001b) Special Report Number 54, 'Europeans and Languages' (Education and Culture Directorate-General, Centre for the citizen—Analysis of public opinion), Brussels, February 2001.
European Commission (2001) White Paper on European Governance, Brussels.
Featherstone, K (1994) 'Jean Monnet and the "Democratic Deficit" in the European Union' *Journal of Common Market Studies* 32: 149–70.
Ferguson, CA (1959) 'Diglossia' *Word* 15: 325–40.
Fishman, JA (1967) 'Bilingualism With and Without Diglossia; Diglossia With and Without Bilingualism' *Journal of Social Issues* 23(2): 29–38.
Fishman, JA (1971) 'The Sociology of Language, An Interdisciplinary Social Science Approach to Language in Society' in JA Fishman (ed), *Advances in the Sociology of Language*, Vol I (Den Haag, Mouton), 217–404.
Fishman, JA (1973) *Language and Nationalism* (Rowley, MA, Newbury House).
Gellner, E (1983) *Nations and Nationalism* (London, Blackwell).
Grimm, D (1995) *Braucht Europa eine Verfassung?* (Munich, Carl Friedrich von Siemens Stiftung).
Habermas, J (2001) *Zeit der Übergänge* (Frankfurt am Main, Suhrkamp).
Herder, JG (2001) [1772] *Abhandlung über den Ursprung der Sprache* (Stuttgart, Philipp Reclam jun).
Honneth, A (2003) 'Umverteilung als Anerkennung. Eine Erwiderung auf Nancy Fraser' in Nancy Fraser and Axel Honneth (eds), *Umverteilung oder Anerkennung?* (Frankfurt am Main, Suhrkamp).
Humboldt, W (1963) [1830–5] 'Ueber die Verschiedenheit des menschlichen Sprachbaues und ihren Einfluss auf die geistige Entwicklung des Menschengeschlechts' in W von Humboldt, *Werke in fünf Bänden, III, Schriften zur Sprachphilosophie* (Berlin, Rütten & Loening).
Kraus, PA (2000) 'Political Unity and Linguistic Diversity in Europe' *Archives Européennes de Sociologie/European Journal of Sociology*, XLI, 1, 138–63.
Kraus, PA (2004) *Europäische Öffentlichkeit und Sprachpolitik. Integration durch Anerkennung* (Frankfurt am Main, Campus).

March, JG and Olsen, JP (2000) 'Democracy and Schooling, An Institutional Perspective' in LM McDonnell, PM Timpane and R Benjamin (eds), *Rediscovering the Democratic Purposes of Education* (Lawrence, University Press of Kansas).

Mill, JS (1972) [1861] 'Considerations on Representative Government' in JS Mill, *Utilitarianism, Liberty, Representative Government* (London, Dent).

Phillipson, R and Skutnabb-Kangas, T (1994) 'English, Panacea or Pandemic' *Sociolinguistica* 8: 73–87.

Puhle, H-J (1995) *Staaten, Nationen und Regionen in Europa* (Vienna, Picus).

Réaume, D (1991) 'The Constitutional Protection of Language, Survival or Security?' in D Schneiderman (ed), *Language and the State. The Law and Politics of Identity* (Cowansville, Éditions Yvon Blais).

Schlesinger, P (1999) 'Changing Spaces of Political Communication, The Case of the European Union' *Political Communication* 16: 263–79.

Schloßmacher, M (1994) 'Die Arbeitssprachen in den Organen der Europäischen Gemeinschaft. Methoden und Ergebnisse einer empirischen Untersuchung' *Sociolinguistica* 8: 101–22.

Schmitter, PC (2000) *How to Democratize the European Union ... And Why Bother?* (Lanham, MD, Rowman & Littlefield).

Swaan, A de (2001) *Words of the World. The Global Language System* (Cambridge, Polity Press).

Taylor, C (1985) *Human Agency and Language. Philosophical Papers I* (Cambridge, Cambridge University Press).

Taylor, C (1989) *Sources of the Self* (Cambridge, Cambridge University Press).

Taylor, C (1992) *Multiculturalism and 'The Politics of Recognition'* (Princeton, NJ, Princeton University Press).

Taylor, C (1995) *Philosophical Arguments* (Cambridge, MA, Harvard University Press).

Tiryakian, EA and Rogowski, R (eds) (1985) *New Nationalisms of the Developed West* (Boston, Allen & Unwin).

Tully, J (1995) *Strange Multiplicity. Constitutionalism in an Age of Diversity* (Cambridge, Cambridge University Press).

Tully, J (2001) 'Introduction' in A-G Gagnon and J Tully (eds), *Multinational Democracies* (Cambridge, Cambridge University Press).

Weber, E (1976) *Peasants into Frenchmen* (Stanford, CA, Stanford University Press).

# 5

# *What is a Language? The Difficulties Inherent in Language Rights*

SUE WRIGHT

GENERAL ACCEPTANCE THAT the right to speak a language should be a legal right is a relatively new phenomenon. Until the end of the 20th century, the right to use one's language in the public space depended almost entirely on the political muscle of the language community to which one belonged or the tolerance of the dominant groups among which one lived. Those in power might make it possible to use another language in the institutions and forums of public life, but such use was not universally accepted as a right. Moreover, where a 'minority' language was employed, the purpose was often to maintain difference and to exclude members of that linguistic community from the exercise of power. Even when international bodies finally enshrined in declarations the concept that individuals should have the fundamental right to speak their language of choice, the intention was that speakers would be protected from persecution or unequal treatment. There was no explicit commitment, or even implicit intention, to use the language in the public space. Positive, rather than negative, rights did not develop until late in the 20th century. Only then did the human rights movement come to a consensus that the languages of minority groups should be promoted and protected as well as tolerated.

According universal language rights has not proved unproblematic, for a number of reasons. The first, and perhaps the most potent, is that language use is a good barometer of power. To relinquish use of one's own language to make space for the language of another group is almost always indicative of a shift in power relations. Language renaissance is rarely neutral but is usually a harbinger or reflection of power shifts. It will thus be resisted by those who could expect to lose by any change.

The second reason for the problematic nature of language rights is that positive language rights are *de facto* group rights, even if they are presented *de jure* as individual rights. Where governments accede to demands from minority groups for educational provision in their language, for access to government and the legal process in their language, they usually cater for the group as a whole. When this happens, it is difficult for an individual to opt out. Institutions function in a language and the choice of language to be used is usually a zero sum process. Once one language is adopted, it ousts the others. Even in systems where languages are made co-official, only one is in the prime position and the others are relegated to secondary positions in what necessarily becomes a hierarchical arrangement. Decision making takes place in one language, leaving the speakers of the others at a disadvantage, dependent on interpretation and translation, with all the delay and distortion that may accompany the process. Thus, in effect, individual language rights mean little because of the difficulties of implementation. Kymlicka (2001) has demonstrated clearly how this is the case for minority groups faced with the dominant language of the state. It is also the case for minority groups within minority groups when a minority language is adopted for use in educational, legal, bureaucratic or governmental settings. As Bourhis (2001) has remarked, there is a Russian doll aspect to language: in each linguistic territory there is always another language or dialect that speakers wish to have acknowledged.

This brings us to the third problematic aspect of language rights, which has to do with the nature of language itself and what it is we mean when we say that an individual speaks a certain language. To defend the right to use a language means that we must be in accord on the object of that defence. Defining what is a discrete language is a political rather than linguistic exercise. There are few *Abstand* languages (Kloss, 1967) clearly differentiated from the languages of neighbouring groups. More are *Ausbau*, related to adjacent varieties on the dialect continuum, but diverging over time and space by the patterns of association and loyalties of their speakers. In the context of language rights, the question to be posed is whether the group to be accorded rights is the group which all the individuals concerned by linguistic change would identity with, and give loyalty and allegiance to. If it is necessary to accept a measure of linguistic assimilation in order to become a member of an enfranchised minority group, do the individuals concerned accept that assimilation?

The arithmetic of the situation makes it clear that not all those who see themselves as members of discrete language groups will be able to use their own language in state institutions. At the moment the imbalance is extreme. Of the 6,000 or so languages presently spoken in the world, only 4% have an official status in governance (Romaine, 2002). Given these figures, it is difficult to see how this inequality could ever be wholly expunged.

Furthermore, to exercise one's right to use one's language in the public space, for example as the language of record in bureaucracy or as the medium of education, requires that the language has a written form, accepted by all the speakers it serves. In other words it must be codified and standardised, and this may be problematic.

It is these last dilemmas that I want to explore in this paper. This is not to say that the other two points are not important, but I have discussed them at length elsewhere (Wright, 2000a; 2004). The thesis of this paper is twofold. Firstly, I want to argue that how we conceive language will determine whether we feel that it is necessary to protect individual languages. Secondly, I want to discuss how problematic the concept of standard language can be. Finally I want to demonstrate with three case studies that when we set out to promote language rights, we are largely in agreement on what we mean by rights, but far less sure about the language that we aim to protect.

## WHAT DO WE UNDERSTAND BY LANGUAGE?

There are two recurrent themes in the debate in Western Linguistics and Western Philosophy on the nature of language, which have influenced our perception of what language is and which subtly colour how we approach the issue of language rights. The first theme is the belief in the monogenetic nature of language and in its essentially universalist character. The second theme is the reification of language as a scientific object of study.

### Universalism

The claim that human languages stem from a single source is recurrent throughout history. Many cultures have a myth to explain the multiplicity of languages, where the division of humanity into groups that cannot understand each other is usually presented as a punishment (Steiner, 1975). In the Judaeo-Christian tradition, for example, the story of the Tower of Babel recounts how language diversity was the penalty for human hubris. These myths imply that the ideal state would be one in which all human beings could communicate with each other without hindrance. Many European medieval scholars devoted their life's work to recovering the lost language, which would bring back this state (Eco, 1995). Being the 'perfect', God-given language, it would also restore channels of communication to the deity. Muslims believed that they already possessed such a language since the Qu'ran was the word of God verbatim and the 'pure and uncontaminated form of Arabic' (Suleiman, 1995) in which it had been revealed necessarily perfect and God-given.

The search for the perfect language faded in Europe as the paradigms of Renaissance and then Enlightenment thinking eclipsed the mysticism on which it was founded. However, the desire of Renaissance and Enlightenment scholars to establish universal values often extended to a desire to uncover a universal medium for them. The Modistae of the 13th and 14th centuries believed that there was 'a single, underlying grammar which was realised independently in different languages' (Wheeler, 1995: 169). This theory was later taken up by the Port-Royalists in France and by Leibniz in Germany. Alongside the research into extant languages, there were numerous practical attempts to create a universal language from scratch. Seventeenth century Oxford was one centre which spawned a number of works, including the tellingly titled *Groundwork of a New Perfect Language* (Francis Lodowyck, 1652). Thus, even as the search for the perfect sacred language faded, the humanist desire for the perfect means of expression for all humanity was developing.

In the 19th century, empirical work by scholars of Historical and Comparative Linguistics revealed regular patterns of similarity among many Asian and European languages. Europeans in the Indian sub-continent noted the remarkable affinities of Sanskrit, Greek and Latin. Sir William Jones, a scholar of Persian and judge in Calcutta, is credited with suggesting in 1786 that such similarities existed because these languages derived from a proto Indo-European parent language. This was totally in keeping with the monogeneticism of European thought in Jones' day and consistent with the contemporary belief in a 'cradle of civilisation' (Rocher, 1995).

In the 20th century, studies in Cognitive Psychology contributed to the universalist tradition. Scholars in this tradition argued the existence of a universal language facility (rather than of a universal language). Chomsky (1972) contended that humans are born with an innate mechanism for acquiring and understanding language. This consists of a universal grammar, which establishes the set of possible forms that language can take, and a language acquisition device, which allows individuals to select a particular grammar from that set, based on the limited data that comes to them as language learners in a particular community. Following Chomsky, one branch of 20th century Linguistics attempts to understand innate, universal grammar and the workings of the language acquisition device and to account for the diversity of languages that people can speak.

This brief overview of the universalist/monogenetic strands of scholarship is adequate to demonstrate that one significant strand in Linguistics is likely to contribute little to valuing diversity. Medieval religious beliefs led their proponents to see multilingualism as a punishment; the scholars of the Enlightenment favoured universalism over difference; Historical linguists believed that they would find the original language; Cognitive scientists argue for a strongly universalising and innatist theory of grammar, seeing language as wired in the brain. These influential traditions in Western thinking have nurtured the position that *languages* must be studied as manifestations of language, 'a biological adaptation to communicate information' (Pinker, 1994: 19) rather than as the 'ineffable essence of human uniqueness' (*ibid*).

This opinion remains prevalent in many Linguistics departments. I recently worked with colleagues who challenged the differentiation that I was making between language as faculty and language as practice! Once you begin to look at language not as one of the signs of group identity and community but as an instinct by which humans seek to gain their ends in the most rational and economic way possible, the need to defend any one particular expression of the phenomenon fades rapidly.

So to conclude this section, if we see languages as related manifestations of a universal instinct, we will not approach language rights in the same way as those who take the relativist approach and believe that thought is moulded by languages, that each discrete language is an irreplaceable human treasure and that the survival of discrete cultural groups depends entirely on the maintenance of language diversity.

**Language as System**

The second theme in Western Linguistics and Philosophy which is germane to the rights issue is the fundamental question: 'What is a language?' When we say that we will protect a language, are we talking about an object or a subjective practice? 'Does a language exist as an ideal system outside the speaker?'

There are two traditions which take opposing views. One is the scientific tradition which holds that there is a real world 'out there' that can be understood and described in language and which found expression in Positivism in the 19th century and in some forms of Structuralism in the 20th. The other is the belief that the speaker/writer is an autonomous subject who, through free will, determines what will be said and meant. Words mean what the subject intends them to mean. From Humanist and Romantic thinkers of the 19th century to some Postmodern theorists of the late 20th century, there is a current that holds that individuals created language from their own individual experiences and for their personal communication needs and that each set of language practices frames reality for those who use them. These two traditions have led to contradictory conceptions of language, which are at the heart of the conflict over the nature of language and essential to understand for any work on language rights. For whether we conceive of language as an autonomous system or as individual creativity profoundly affects what we mean by language rights and how we act to defend them or implement policy to promote them.

It seems justifiable to start the review of the debate with de Saussure, widely recognised as the originator of Structuralism and the father of modern Linguistics. De Saussure (1857–1913) directed attention to the discrepancies between language systems in their formal description and what people actually say and write. He conceived of language as *langue* and *parole*, where the latter is the performance of individual speakers with all the idiosyncracies of their idiolects and is an imperfect and incomplete reflection of the former, which is the ideal system. De Saussure did not go so far as to conceive language as a system with *a life of its own*, but he did claim that *langue* is not completely present in any speaker, but *exists perfectly only within a collectivity* (de Saussure, 1916: 14). So, although in his conception, language should not be reified and seen as existing independently of speakers, it can be an imagined system which represents the totality of what all its speakers do. De Saussure was concerned to promote Linguistics as a science, and for this purpose, advised study of the ideal, normative structure that could be dealt with as an abstraction, rather than the nebulous and changing idiolects of individuals. He is famously reported to have said, 'Language is speech less speaking' (*ibid*: 77).

De Saussure's normative structure derived not from absolutes, but from a system of regular distinctions. For example, we cannot understand the concept of 'brown' in isolation, by simply attaching the label to a thing or concept. We can only begin to comprehend brown if we compare it with red, yellow, grey, tan or black. Brown is what it is not, and it is only by seeing the relations between it and other colours that we begin to grasp the idea of brownness. It follows that, in order for a language to be effective for communication, its speakers must have essentially identical systems of distinctions in their minds. There are thus in de Saussure's legacy two distinct strands: the first focuses on the social nature of *langue* and the second on the mental and abstract nature of *langue* (Joseph, 1995).

The idea of an abstract, self-contained conceptual system—a system of incontestable, normatively identical forms—was very attractive to those engaged in nationalist language planning. Nation builders needed the single standard language that could be employed, taught and acquired throughout the national space and which would build the national community of communication felt to be key for the creation of a homogenous national group (Wright, 2000a; May, 2001). Nationalist language planning entailed the imposition of language sometimes from outside and always from above and nationalist language planners were thus at ease with the concept of language as system, although the subtlety of de Saussure's reasoning was often lost among those it influenced.

The idea of an abstract, self-contained conceptual system that could be isolated and examined was also very attractive to all those who followed de Saussure in wanting to promote Linguistics as a science. Louis Hjelmslev and the Danish school of Glossematics 'took the Saussurean dictum that *langue* is form not substance to its logical conclusion' (Harris, 2001: 128) and worked in the sphere of possible and ideal systems rather than the realisation of actually present expression systems. Even though those who followed the Structuralist paradigm based their research on empirical data, they concentrated on form over meaning and saw abstract levels of analysis as more 'fundamental, more deep-seated—in a word more real—than concrete ones' (Joseph, 1995: 225). The last phase in the Structuralist tradition is arguably Chomskyan generative linguistics which deals with the mental and abstract nature of *langue* and is concerned with the ideal speaker rather than actual practice.

The Saussurean approach resonated with those who sought to counter the Romantic/Humanist view that language is an activity performed by the autonomous human subject who articulates internal thought processes. Heidegger argued that language users are just that: they do not create language; they acquire a structure that they then use. 'We do not speak language, language speaks us.' As we acquire language we acquire an independent system of differentiations. Speakers merely inhabit pre-existing structures (*langue*) that enable them to make any particular sentence (*parole*). Language use is not original but merely the recombination of some of the elements in the pre-existing system. Hence every new sentence we speak or write is made up of the 'already spoken', every new text of the 'already written'. Again, such beliefs were coherent with nationalism, particularly essentialist nationalism. We are the national group we are because we inhabit the national language, which makes us speak and think as we do.

The concept of language as system has been challenged by all those who see the human language facility as essentially creative, and therefore divergent and heterogeneous. The Russian linguists, Medvedev, Voloshinov and Bakhtin, refuted any objective ontological status for language and pointed out that a view of language that stressed structure and system to the detriment of creativity and evaluation of meaning did not reflect how language actually works. Voloshinov framed the argument in the following way:

> The basic task of understanding does not at all amount to recognizing the linguistic form used by the speaker as the familiar, 'that very same', form, the way we distinctly recognize for instance, a signal that we have not quite become used to or a form in a language that we do not know very well. No, the task of understanding does not basically amount to recognizing the form used, but rather to understanding it in a particular, concrete context, to understanding its meaning in a particular utterance, ie it amounts to *understanding its novelty and not to recognizing its identity.*[1]

Medvedev, Bakhtin and Voloshinov insist upon the social aspect of language, the need to consider the essentially dialogic nature of language. All utterances are in accordance with or in response to what has been said or written before. All utterances are dependent on the context in which they are uttered. All utterances are evaluated and interpreted by their recipients. Thus every utterance becomes 'a responsive link in the continuous chain of other utterances which, in effect, constitute the continuity of human consciousness' (Morris, 1994: 5).

On this interpretation language can only exist in performance, and it survives by being taken up and reiterated in subsequent performance. The continuous chain of utterances that results in effect constitutes ongoing human consciousness, with meaning being created and recreated in every dialogic event.

> In other words, the understander, belonging to the same language community, is attuned to the linguistic form not as a fixed, self-identical signal, but as a changeable and adaptable sign[2]

Language thus becomes an ongoing dialogue, learnt by being understood in context and subtly changed in an active and responsive context. Thus to speak a language means to be part of a community and language behaviour cannot easily be imposed from outside or above, in the ways that language planning sometimes attempts.

In Western scholarship a parallel tradition of linguistic philosophy drew on Wittgenstein and his view that there is no fixed meaning associated with linguistic forms. The most that a linguist can do is situate the expression within its context. The Constructivist tradition elaborated the idea that meaning is social and dependent almost entirely on the meanings constructed in interaction. Discourse theorists made the radical claim that the realities we take to define our social circumstances and our selves within them are to a large extent socially constructed and that everything derives from discursive construction of the real:

> Important aspects of our social lives are constructed in and through language whether in the moment-to-moment social interchanges of everyday talk or in the beliefs, understandings and principles that structure our lives.[3]

To hold that language exists outside its speakers is now a minority position in the academic community, although Poststructuralist and Postmodern thinkers such as Lacan, Foucault, Derrida and Kristeva take a complex position on the dichotomy of language as independent system and language as performance. They challenge the idea that fundamental deep structures underpin forms in an external world but also posit impersonal forces in discursive texts (Barthes, 1968; Foucault, 1984). Thus they admit the existence of language outside performance and acknowledge that the text acts as a store of cultural meaning that escapes its originator. Foucault speaks of stepping into the flow of meaning, Lacan of our entering, through language, into the 'Law of the Father', the systems which govern conceptions in our culture. Derrida argues that texts have meanings that we can sensitise and attune ourselves to but never fully determine or control. Derrida returns to de Saussure, propelling his ideas in new directions and coining the term *différance*, to introduce a dynamic dimension into the idea. 'An element functions or signifies ... only by referring to another past or future element' (Derrida, 1981: 28–29). In this way the 'system' can only be studied in use, as it is constantly renegotiated.

The focus in much recent linguistic theory has been on the ideological dimension of language. In this view, the way we use language is constrained by the power structures and systems of the societies in which we live. Julia Kristeva explains that there is far more to understanding language than understanding the system or the practice; there are also, crucially, constrictions in the environment. She argues that

> Semiotics must not be allowed to be a mere application to signifying practices of the linguistic model—or any other model, for that matter. Its raison d'être, if it is to have one, must consist in its identifying the systematic constraints within each signifying practice.[4]

Language is *parole* and highly individual but subject to systematic constraints. However, these constraints are profoundly different from the closed rules of structural linguistics. Where the latter can judge every sentence to be grammatical or ungrammatical, and *as having some agreed meaning*, the former reveals the constant tension between the agreed symbolic and the changing semiotic (Kristeva, 1986). Thus, like Bakhtin and Voloshinov, Kristeva recognises that language is contextually unique, related to the particular view of the world that comes from acquiring and using it in particular dialogic situations and particular settings; in other words, it is ideologically anchored.

Although the debate among linguists on the ontological nature of language may at present be veering towards the idea that language is practice, the position is not necessarily accepted by the wider public. Governments and their policy makers often reify language and act as if it were a free-standing discrete system, because it is difficult to manage anything but standard language in schools, the courts and state bureaucracy. It is clear, however, that how we deal with language rights will be profoundly affected by whether we see language as an ideal system or as contextually bound performance and ideologically grounded practice.

In the final part of the paper, I shall discuss how these warring visions play out in the renaissance of Arbresh, Ladin and Occitan—three European languages which are termed 'lesser used' or 'minority' in the states in which they are spoken—and show how linguistic theory is very relevant for language rights.

## ITALY

Some regions with large ethnic groups whose language and culture differ from those of the Italian population as a whole have enjoyed special forms of legislative and administrative autonomy within the Italian state for some decades. Before 1999, the regions with a special statute were Sicily, Sardinia, Trentino-Alto Adige, Friuli-Venezia Giulia and Valle d'Aosta.

Other ethnic and linguistic minority groups received less protection because of their smaller size; teaching of their language and culture was organised at the local community level (for example: the Greek-Albanian communities in Calabria, Sicily, etc) (Eurydice, 1998). In 1999, Law No 482 Regulations regarding the protection of historic language minorities introduced a new framework law and gave greater recognition to the latter group.

### Arbresh

Piana Arbresh is a dialect of the variety of Albanian currently spoken in five communities in Sicily. The Arbresh speaking population in Piana degli Albanesi numbers about 7,000 (Derhemi, 2002). Arbresh has been the language of the community for the past 500 years—since the Albanians came to settle in Sicily.

In a recent study of Arbresh speakers, Eda Derhemi suggests that the survival of the language derives in part from the fact that the Albanians were Orthodox Christians within a Catholic population. They maintained their religion and practised endogamy, which kept them a separate and cohesive group. Other factors encouraging maintenance included the relative prosperity of the group, which made the issue of status work for the minority rather than against it, since the Albanians were rather contemptuous of the rural Sicilian majority and dissociated themselves from the surrounding population. The prosperity and confidence of the Piana degli Albanesi group contributed to the survival of Albanian in the town and may be the significant variable missing in the other centres where Albanians settled, but which have not remained Arbresh-speaking into the 21st century.

Derhemi presents Arbresh as a language with some vitality. Despite their centuries-long contact with Italian/Sicilian speakers, Arbresh speakers have conserved their language and maintained stable diglossia. The 1999 law gives them legal instruments to strengthen their position and puts them in a position to promote Arbresh in new settings. In particular, the legislation makes it possible to use Arbresh in education, in public office, in local government, in the judicial system and in the mass media, and allows for the reinstatement of place and personal names. The status and prestige of the language thus appear to be strengthened.

Derhemi reports, however, a general perception in Piana degli Albanesi that the use of Arbresh is declining, both in the number of domains in which it is used and among younger speakers. Having witnessed 'the semi-speakers or non-proficient Arbresh speakers' in other communities, community leaders have expressed their determination to work to stem attrition in Piana itself (Derhemi, 2002).

The principal course of action in the language maintenance and revitalisation programme was to be courses in and using Arbresh in schools.

This received the support of the majority of parents according to a survey conducted in 2001 (Derhemi, 2002). Arbresh would be used in the earliest years of primary education as the language of school socialisation, which would formalise a practice that already existed, as teachers habitually provided a bilingual bridge for Arbresh-speaking children. In addition, older students would be able to acquire literacy in Arbresh in more advanced classes.

However, since Arbresh had never been a language of institutions or of governance, it had not been developed as a written language and there is no standard. The educational initiatives could not proceed until the form of the literacy to be promoted was agreed. Obtaining agreement proved immensely difficult. There were two camps among the supporters of Arbresh: those who believed that a standard should be developed for the 7,000 Arbresh speakers in Sicily, and those who argued that it made more sense to adopt the written standard of Albanian, which already existed and which gave access to wider sources and contacts, and an extensive literature.

The ready-made standard is exterior and slightly alien. Those opposed to its adoption reason that there is little point in struggling to conserve a language if what is conserved is not the group's language but another, which, although close in many ways, is alien in others. Importing standard Albanian introduces another idiom and adopting it would create a situation of double diglossia for Arbresh speakers.

The alternative solution for codifying and standardising Arbresh also proved problematic. The difficulty arose because the project was eventually assigned to a small group of scholars and poets and they subsequently failed to consult widely (my own fieldwork in Italy, 2002). The result is a highly literary standard that needs to be introduced top down to speakers. The few school texts produced so far have been badly received. Teachers report that their pupils found the language difficult to understand and did not relate it to what they actually spoke (Derhemi, 2002; my own fieldwork in Italy 2002). The controversy and the subsequent slow rate of progress in producing texts is a key reason for the slow implementation of the educational initiative.

In Sicily, the planners encountered the fundamental problem of language planning. Planners need to deal with language as system in order to introduce Arbresh into institutions and promote its acquisition in education. Thus, it was language as system (*langue*), not language as practice and ongoing dialogue (*parole*) that was protected and promoted in these initiatives. However, this was not what Arbresh speakers had hoped for. They were demanding a language renaissance so that their practice could be enshrined as a language of power. The imposition of a norm, even slightly different from practice, was experienced as alienating by individual speakers.

## Ladin

Ladin speakers live principally in five valleys of the Dolomite Alps in the north of Italy. There are approximately 30,000 members of the Ladin-speaking community[5] who speak six (according to some, seven) distinct varieties of the language (Schmid, 1998). The area has only recently acquired effective communication systems and the relative isolation of the communities in separate valleys has enabled the different varieties to develop and continue.

Since 1989 Ladin has been an official language in Bolzano/Bosen province, alongside standard Italian and standard German. In 2001, Ladin speakers' new rights were implemented in Trento province following the 1999 legislation. Only in Belluno province are Ladin speakers unable to use their language extensively in the public domain. Pressure for a standard language has come from the provincial authorities who, in a multilingual situation, have seen no good reason to accept variety in Ladin, when both Italian and German dialect speakers of the Trentino-Alto-Adige and Bolzano/Bosen provinces accept the standard languages in their contacts with local government (Schmid, 1998).

Heinrich Schmid recounts the debates that have taken place in the pursuit of an acceptable standard. As the differences among the dialects are quite significant in both written and spoken forms of the language, extensive accommodation is necessary if there is to be interdialectal comprehension. He argues that since Ladin competes in the local public space with two major European languages, which both have accepted written standards, it would be unlikely that Ladin could survive in this role without some agreement as to variety. He suggests that the solution could be a *Dachsprache*, a variety which could exist alongside the different dialects as a koiné. He argues that the *Dachsprache* cannot be one of the varieties, even that of the most numerous groups, since it would be rejected by the others. It cannot be a *Mischsprache* (a mixture of terms from all the varieties) since this would cause dissension at the micro level of choice and decision rather than at the macro level. Furthermore, he notes that the Ladin speaking area is extremely difficult to delimit, since, as in all dialect continua, the various particularities of the dialects are not regular and congruent and many 'Ladin' features appear in neighbouring Venetian and Lombard dialects.

Schmid, a German-speaking linguist, well known for his work promoting Romansh, a language also very close to Ladin on the continuum, suggests that the experience of the German-speaking world permits optimism. The German standard (*Hochdeutsch*) is accepted across the German dialect continuum as the acceptable written form of spoken forms that differ widely. Schmid himself has produced a *Dachsprache* with as much 'elemental' Ladin in it as possible so that all speakers should be able to see how it relates to their own version. To do this he has returned to the Latin roots of the language and based his choices on historical linguistics as well as present usage. This is, of course, the ultimate perfect system. An outsider, a professional linguist, constructs a language that no one actually speaks by adjudicating among dialectal choices and with reference to Latin roots.

Whether or not the Ladin standard will be widely used remains to be seen. It is logical and it is 'fair' as far as that is possible, but it is not part of 'the continuous chain of other utterances which, in effect, constitute the continuity of human consciousness' and which is what is treasured by speakers.

The Ladin example illustrates how renaissance may be brought about from outside the group. This is the case in many settings of language renaissance. Language revitalisation sometimes originates among activists who come from outside the group of current speakers, usually from communities where the language is part of the heritage but where its use has disappeared. The two groups involved in the process are thus the current speakers and the aspirational speakers, who acquire the language as a second language. The former are (stereo)typically rural, poor and old. The latter are (stereo)typically young, educated and politically literate. Where revitalisation includes insertion of the language into education, law and governance, there is a need for a written form of the language. Where this does not already exist, it is likely that the intellectual activists—the educated urban speakers—undertake this work. This often leaves the rural speakers at the periphery of language practice once again, stigmatised by the association of their version of the language with poverty and powerlessness. Hoffmann (1996) and Green (1994) have described this process as one which puts minority speakers in a situation of double jeopardy.

## FRANCE

France differs from Italy in that it has a history of muscular centralisation and the institutions of the state have made rigorous attempts to mould citizens into a linguistically and culturally homogenous group. The dominant discourse about language rights in France is still highly republican and nationalist, as the debates in 1999 over France's ratification of the Charter for Regional and Minority Languages and in 2001–2 over the state funding of Diwan schools testify.

### Occitan

The result of this muscular centralism is that the situation of minority language speakers differs radically from the position of minorities in

France's neighbouring countries. The first and most important difference derives from the lack of state support for Occitan. The second is the comparative lack of interest for the language among those whose ancestors were speakers, and who could claim it as their heritage. The third is that this lack of interest exists despite an extensive literature and an imposing heritage. If Occitan speakers want to celebrate their linguistic and cultural specificity there is an enormous fund of historical material on which to draw.

This lack of interest is a manifestation of how successful the French Republic has been in its nation building. The cohesion of the French state and the tendency of the French to identify with the state rather than with their regions is remarkable. Even though much of the Midi was incorporated by force into the French state and at times has been neglected in terms of economic development and infrastructure by central government, there has been relatively little popular interest in or widespread argument for any political autonomy. Elsewhere similar experiences have fuelled independence movements.

Only a very small minority of the southern French has been interested in regionalism, regional particularity and heritage, and an even tinier proportion has been interested in making common cause across the various dialects in the continuum. The appellation 'Occitan' would not be recognised by most Occitan speakers. They describe themselves as speakers of Languedocien, Gascon, Provençal, Limousin, Vivaro-Alpin or Auvergnat. Occitania is not and never has been a linguistic space with a recognised centre. Occitan is largely a scholarly term, employed to describe part of the Romance dialect continuum, bounded by Catalan and Aranese in the west and Piemontese in the east. Occitan is thus a set of related dialects, and, unsurprisingly, has no single agreed standard.

There is, however, a major difference between this case and many others, in that Occitan has existed as a written language and a language for literary production for one thousand years. Poets in the various dialects of Occitan from the 11th century provide some of the earliest examples of European vernacular literature.[6] Occitan continued as a European language of literature to the 13th century with an audience well outside its homeland. After the incorporation of the various kingdoms of the south into the French state, however, the language disappeared from public domains and there was a move to French in the towns and among the elite, and Occitan literature waned.

In the 19th century, at the height of interest in ethnic origins and national particularity, there was a revivalist movement. The Félibrige, led by Frédéric Mistral, differed, however, from most nationalist movements in having no political agenda. They were interested only in the cultural revival of the written language. For this they promoted an orthographical system based on that of French, adapted to the distinctive Provençal of Arles and Avignon

(Davies, 2000). Their position was elitist and they had no programme for the promotion of standard Provençal among its speakers, who at the time were still numerous. Unsurprisingly, there was a considerable gap between the scholarly and literary Provençal in which they wrote and the various spoken practices of the Occitan area as a whole.

In reaction to the elitist and regionalist position of the Félibrige, groups of activists in Limousin and western Languedoc advocated the adoption of a koiné, usable throughout the area. Interestingly, although their motivation was more inclusive, their decision to return to the medieval language for their standard actually meant that the written language they promoted was in some ways even less accessible than Mistralien Provençal.

The division between the two movements continued into the 20th century and it was only in the very recent past that a rapprochement came about. However, it is really only the leaders of the two groups who are collaborating and they report continuing hostility towards the other standard among their members (my own fieldwork, 2003 and 2004). Unsurprisingly, the consequence of the lack of interest in regional activism among the majority of the population and of a long running feud among the activists has been a continuing decline in interest in maintaining Occitan.

Although this state of affairs seems fairly negative for the continued existence of the Occitan dialect continuum, there is actually a positive consequence. The fractured situation has allowed all those who wish to maintain their language to maintain the language they actually speak. There is widespread acceptance among language activists (Wright, 2000b) that the various varieties of Occitan will be maintained and learnt as heritage languages on a par with dance, music and traditions. As there is no general support for the adoption of Occitan in institutions, in governance and as a medium of education, this has allowed the Occitanists to sidestep the difficulties encountered by the Ladin and Arbresh speakers. Since there is no need for a standard written language for use in such forums, the different forms of Occitan can be tolerated. Language variety can be catered for in the few settings where Occitan is employed. For example, the daily newspaper *La Marseillaise* prints a weekly page in Provençal and mentions in footnotes where practice is divergent for Languedocien and Gascon speakers. The weekly news magazine *La Setmana* prints articles in any and all of the varieties. Where students opt to study Occitan as a subject in secondary schools, the programme can accommodate difference and some textbooks (eg *Òc-ben!*) are adapted to the language practice of the region. Most interestingly, email and internet communication seems to be written in any and every variety, with some texts exhibiting features of more than one form. There is also evidence that Occitan is sometimes used in email, chatroom communications and even on websites according to French orthographic rules, presumably by those who have not acquired literacy in formal settings (Wright, 2006).

The trade-off seems clear. Where a language becomes a language of power of any kind (the language used in interaction in democratic institutions and in bureaucracies and the language spread through a state-run education system), the cost is acceptance of that language as system—a codified, stable written standard that may not entirely reflect the practice of those designated as its speakers. However, where the speakers of a language have minimal linguistic rights (ie the right to maintenance in private, as an expression of cultural heritage) there may be greater likelihood that the differing practices of speakers will be recognised and preserved. This, of course, is cold comfort if there is a gradual language shift because the language does not represent cultural capital, in the sense of being of economic value or of conferring political advantage.

## CONCLUSION

It seems reasonable to argue that, because of this tension, language rights are always going to be problematic. A constant conflict exists between acceptance of the heterogeneity of practice and the necessity of fixing a set of forms that will remain invariant across all contexts. In the past, this tension was resolved in the context of nation building and its homogenising processes. Where a group accepted the assimilatory imperative within that ideology, they accepted language as system and converged linguistically. In the present contexts of lesser used languages and the desire of their speakers to have their idiom recognised, this ideological framework is often missing.

The case studies clearly illustrate different aspects of the problem. Firstly, in a fairly small group such as the Arbresh, it might seem eminently sensible to use the ready-made standard of Albanian, which will save money and give speakers and readers access to a larger community of communication. However, if the desire of the Arbresh is to use their language to underpin the homogeneity of their own small group and be a vehicle for its distinctive history and culture, then trying to impose an external standard is pointless. A language similar to one's own but with distinctions that make it appear alien may not be any more acceptable than a language that is radically different. Whether one takes the view that centuries of meaning making within a particular context give a language its particular system of differentiation and relationships or whether one believes that all utterances derive from the context in which they are uttered, it is clear that if a group is concerned to defend its own language, it can only do this from within.

Secondly, in a situation where there is great intra-language diversity, there is a need for convergence among dialects to achieve easy communication and comprehensibility. The need for a widely accepted written standard where the language is used in governance, in education and in intergroup communication may mean that some groups on the periphery need to accept linguistic assimilation. Now, if one is going to assimilate, one may prefer to assimilate to the national language rather than to the standard of a neighbour. However, if there is no agreement on or acceptance of a standard and no recognition of a community of communication, then it is hard to see how the language can play a role in institutions. The impossibility of any legal use is just one difficulty that springs to mind.

Thirdly, where the solution to diversity has been a standard written language that has been devised by scholars and intellectuals, there may also be problems. Where there has been a return to forms of the past either for orthography or for items of lexis, a diglossic situation may arise, as is already happening in Galicia (Hoffmann, 1996) and which may develop in the Dolomites.

The rights movement derived from the desire of groups to express the identity implicit in their language on a larger stage. Given the difficulty of deciding what is to be protected even in small, demographically concentrated groups, it remains to be seen how the right to maintain one's own language, now framed in international law, will be exercised in practice. Do language rights depend on the acceptance of standardisation and the concept of language as ideal system in the mould of nationalist linguistics or is there a way to manage diversity of practice? And, of course, those who agree with the universalists and see language as a human instinct which simply has different manifestations may feel that the loss of some of those manifestations is inevitable and not a cause of great worry.

## Notes

1 Voloshinov, 1994: 33, emphasis added.
2 *Ibid.*
3 Voloshinov, 1994: 33.
4 Coupland and Jaworski, 2001: 134.
5 Kristeva, 1986: 26.
6 Only Bolzano province has a language census. The figures are taken from estimations in Schmid (1998) and Beninca (2000).
7 Guilhem de Poitier, Jaufre Rudel, Marcabrun, Bernard de Ventadour, Bertrand de Born, Arnaud Daniel, Guiraut de Borneil, Peire Vidal,Raimbaud d'Orange, Arnaud de Mareuil, etc (Dupuy, 1972).

## References

Barthes, R (1968) *The Elements of Semiology* (New York, Hill and Wang).
Beninca, P (1998) 'Dolomitic Ladin' in G Price (ed), *The Encyclopedia of the Languages of Europe* (Oxford, Blackwell).
Bourhis, R (2001) 'Acculturation, Language Maintenance and Language Shift' in J Klatter-Holmer and P van Avermaet (eds), *Theories on Maintenance and Loss of Minority Languages* (Munster,Waxmann).

Chomsky, N (1972) *Language and Mind* (New York, Harcourt).
Coupland, N and Jaworski, A (2001) 'Discourse' in P Cobley (ed), *Semiotics and Linguistics* (London, Routledge), 134–48.
Culler, J (1976) *Ferdinand de Saussure* (London, Fontana).
Davies, P. (2000) 'Occitan' in G. Price (ed.) Encyclopedia of the Languages of Europe, Oxford, Blackwell (pp 343–348).
Derhemi, E (2002) 'The Endangered Arbresh Language and the Importance of Standardised Writing for its Survival. The Case of Piana degli Albanesi, Sicily' *MOST Journal on Multicultural Societies* 4(2).
Derrida, J (1981) *Positions* (trans A Bass) (London, Continuum).
Dupuy, A (1972) *Petite encyclopédie occitane* (Montpellier, Saber).
Eco, U (1995) *The Search for the Perfect Language* (Oxford, Blackwell).
Eurydice (1998) *The Italian Education System* (Biblioteca di documentazione pedagogica, Unità italiana di Eurydice/European Commission).
Foucault, M (1966) *Les mots et les choses. Une archéologie des sciences humaines* (Paris, Bibliothèque des sciences humaines).
Foucault, M (1972) *The Archeology of Knowledge and Discourse on Language* (trans S Smith) (New York, Pantheon).
Foucault, M (1984) *The Foucault Reader* (P Rabinow (ed)) (Harmondsworth, Penguin).
Green, J (1994) 'Language Status and Political Aspirations, the Case of Northern Spain' in M Parry *et al* (eds), *The Changing Voices of Europe* (Cardiff, University of Wales Press).
Harris, R (2001) 'Linguistics after Saussure' in P Cobley (ed), *Semiotics and Linguistics* (London, Routledge), 118–33.
Hoffmann, C (1996) 'Twenty Years of Language Planning in Contemporary Spain' in S Wright (ed), *Monolingualism and Bilingualism: Lessons from Canada and Spain* (Clevedon, Multilingual Matters), 59–91.
Joseph, J (1995) 'Saussurean Tradition in Linguistics' in E Koerner and R Asher (eds), *Concise History of the Language Sciences* (Oxford, Elsevier and Pergamon), 233–9.
Kloss, H (1967) '*Abstand* Languages and *Ausbau* Languages' *Anthropological Linguistics* 9: 29–41.
Kristeva, J (1986) *The Kristeva Reader* (ed T Moi) (New York, Columbia University Press).
Kymlicka, W (2001) *Politics in the Vernacular* (Oxford, Oxford University Press).
May, S (2001) *Language and Minority Rights: Ethnicity, Nationalism and the Politics of Language* (Harlow, Longman).
Morris, P (ed) (1994) *The Bakhtin Reader* (London, Edward Arnold).
Morson, G and Emerson, C (1990) *Mikhail Bakhtin: Creation of a Prosaics,* (Stanford, CA, Stanford University Press).
Mühlhäusler, P (2001) 'Babel Revisited' in A Fill and P Mühlhäusler (eds), *The Ecolinguistics Reader: Language, Ecology and Environment* (London, Continuum), 159–64.

Pinker, S (1994) *The Language Instinct* (Harmondsworth, Penguin).
Rocher, R (1995) 'Discovery of Sanskrit by Europeans' in E Koerner and R Asher (eds), *Concise History of the Language Sciences* (Oxford, Elsevier and Pergamon), 188–95.
Romaine, S (2002) 'The Impact of Language Policy on Endangered Languages' *MOST Journal on Multicultural Societies* 4(2).
Saussure, F de (1916) *Cours de linguistique générale* (Paris, Payot).
Schmid, H (1998) *Wegleitung für den Aufbau einer gemeinsamen Schriftsprache der Dolomitenladiner* (Istitut Cultural Ladin).
Steiner, G (1975) *After Babel. Aspects of Language and Translation* (Oxford, Oxford University Press).
Strubell, M (2001) 'Catalan a Decade Later' in J Fishman (ed), *Can Threatened Languages be Saved?* (Clevedon, Multilingual Matters), 260–83.
Suleiman, Y (1995) 'Arabic Linguistic Tradition' in E Koerner and R Asher (eds), *Concise History of the Language Sciences* (Oxford, Elsevier and Pergamon), 28–41.
Voloshinov, V (1994) 'Marxism and the Philosophy of Language' in P Morris (ed), *The Bakhtin Reader* (London, Edward Arnold).
Wheeler, G (1995) 'Port-Royal Tradition of General Grammar' in E Koerner and R Asher (eds), *Concise History of the Language Sciences* (Oxford, Elsevier and Pergamon), 169–74.
Wierzbicka, A (2003) 'Empirically Established Universals of Language and their Importance for Cognitive Science', paper given at the Joint International Conference on Cognitive Science, Sydney, Australia, 13–17 July.
Wright, S (2000a) *Community and Communication: The Role of Language in Nation State Building and European Integration* (Clevedon, Multilingual Matters).
Wright S (2000b) 'Jacobins, Regionalists and the Council of Europe's Charter for Regional and Minority Languages' *Journal of Multilingual and Multicultural Development* 21(5): 414–25.
Wright, S (2004) *Language Policy and Language Planning: From Nationalism to Globalisation* (London and New York, Palgrave Macmillan).
Wright, S (2006) 'Regional or Minority Languages on the WWW' Journal of Language and Politics 5(2), 189–217.

# 6

# *Linguistic Diversity and the Paradox of Rights Discourse*[1]

REETTA TOIVANEN

LANGUAGE IS OFTEN considered to be a neutral element, which helps to distinguish between different groups of people; whereas other characteristics, such as ethnicity and culture, have been regarded as unfitting as the basis of distinctions among people and groups within a liberal order (Dworkin, 1974; Barry, 2002). Even though there is not much case law on linguistic minorities (Spiliopoulou Åkermark, 2002), all minority treaties of the United Nations and the Council of Europe pay extensive attention to language rights.[2] Similarly, many other international and European recommendations appeal to some form of worldwide consensus on the importance of language protection and language rights.[3] The problem with which this chapter is concerned is whether language rights presuppose a *fixed* conception of such rights, applying to potentially homogeneous and static groups, whose 'genuine' language needs protection. Upon examination of some empirical cases, it becomes apparent that many of the groups treated as 'language minorities' are actually seeking official recognition of either their cultural distinctiveness or their difference, while language is only one element—often of varying importance—of their group identity.

In fact, minority groups do not necessarily speak one single language; one can find many languages and/or dialects within them. It may also be the case that members of these minorities have already switched to the majority language(s) in the course of previous generations, due to long lasting assimilation policies. If language is seen as the ultimate sign of minority status, people seeking political recognition as being separate from, or different to, the majority population in a state, have to prove that they have one traditional language that needs to be protected. Through language protection the group, then, may become eligible for other kinds of minority culture protection and promotion. If the group is unable to establish one language as the genuine one, there is a concrete danger that all rights claims of that group may fall outside international legal protection.

In the first part of this chapter, I offer a brief introduction to legal anthropological perspectives on rights research. I then work through a number of empirical cases involving two national minorities in Europe (Sorbs in Germany and Sámi in Scandinavia). These exemplify the problems that many 'minorities' encounter in constructing one single natural mother tongue. I conclude with some conceptual observations and an empirical analysis of codified minority rights, focusing on the question of who (or what) is actually covered by minority protection in the European context. The Finnish Advisory Board for Ethnic Relations will exemplify the problems that may arise if language is treated as though it is a neutral and natural element of group identification and how this treatment makes language an effective vehicle of struggle for political resources.

## ANTHROPOLOGY AND RIGHTS

Anthropologists have long been interested in the relationship between society and law as well as that between culture and rights (Nader, 1997 [1969]; Moore, 1978; Wilson, 1997). Classic studies document how legislation and rule producing have always been motivated and informed by power relations within society (Hoebel, 1954; Llewellyn and Hoebel, 1941; Gluckman, 1956, 1963). In earlier studies, the role that rights play in forming culture and setting up either preconditions or requirements for cultures to be considered authentic was ignored. Sally Falk Moore lists three prototypical ways in which the relationship between culture and rights has been particularly interesting for anthropologists: rights versus culture, the right to culture, and rights as culture (Moore, 1978; see also Dembour, 2001; Merry, 2001). The earlier anthropologists stressed the importance of respecting the legal culture of every human community and warned about transposing ideas of Western law into other cultures. The cultures that anthropologists were interested in were mostly interpreted as tradition-driven societies without any law in the modern (Western) sense. Rights and culture were understood as standing opposed to one another.

The decolonisation process forced a change of perspective. Suddenly it became obvious that non-Western societies were not, as it was often supposed, tradition-driven and without laws in the Western sense, but that they themselves had law-like features, also influenced by their relationship with Western societies. It became an important aspect of anthropologists' work to engage with the decolonisation process and argue that, in the wording of the United Nations Universal Declaration of 1948, every human being has the right to culture. Culture was conceived of as an object of rights claims. Culture is here understood as a unique setting of practices and meanings. It is a 'thing' we are entitled to 'have' and 'enjoy'.

Anthropologists were then eagerly helping people to establish cultural distinctiveness claims. Some anthropologists' research actively contributed to making rights claims possible for certain disadvantaged peoples.[4] In the second half of the 20th century, there was a growing interest among anthropologists in the study of the right to culture, ie culture as something to which people were entitled. Many studies were rather uncritical, underestimating the malleability of both the concept of 'right' and that of 'culture'. It is now recognised that many anthropologists contributed to a reified and essentialist understanding of both group identities and group boundaries. By treating groups as natural intrinsic entities, these researchers 'fabricated' the objects of their own study. Today, several anthropologists look at rights as something which *an sich* would constitute culture (see eg Cowan, Dembour and Wilson, 2001). Clifford Geertz and Laura Nader are often considered as the initiators of this third paradigm in anthropological studies, which considers 'rights as culture'. According to them, law is conceived as a world-view, or structuring discourse, which shapes how the world is apprehended (see Nader, 1990; Geertz, 1983). This means that there is no legal evidence 'out there' to be discovered by lawyers; everything is socially constructed through rules of evidence, legal conventions, and the rhetoric of legal actors. In many societies, it is argued, legal reasoning has become one of the most important ways in which people try to make sense of their own world. Human rights, and also more recently (and increasingly) minority rights, are a core aspect of modernity, an active part of global and transnational culture. International declarations, conventions and agreements which are negotiated, implemented and monitored by national, international and transnational institutions, form a structuring discourse with forceful influence on our societies and especially on how we perceive our societies. My own approach follows a similar line by looking at minority rights as culture, as a part of a transnational and global human culture. It will be shown that minority rights as a discourse and as a legal reality not only give rights to people who feel different. Minority rights also form and constitute the minority groups and co-determine what kinds of groups can claim to be authentic minorities. Language is not just a natural feature of minority groups, it is also a way in which environmental expectations contribute to form a group's identity; as in the case, for instance, in which minorities are expected to speak an 'ancient' mother tongue, which they wish to preserve for future generations.

## SHIFTING LANGUAGES

During one trip to Bautzen, I attended a party at the Sorbian Institute.[5] At the table next to me were some older Sorbian activists sitting together with one young man whom I knew had been born in West Germany and who had no Sorbian ancestors. He had learned many languages and also spoke fluent Upper Sorbian. Upper Sorbian and Lower Sorbian are the two official Sorbian languages.[6] The whole table spoke in Upper Sorbian until the young man temporarily left the room. From that moment, the group of activists carried on their conversation in German, until, that is, the young man re-entered the room, when the conversation shifted back to Upper Sorbian. At the time, I was puzzled by this. Were the old activists putting up a show for the young man? Were they afraid to either disappoint or disillusion him? The answer lies in the harsh assimilation policies that existed during the National Socialist period, and in the relatively more benign ones implemented by the East German regime. Such policies had turned previous generations of Sorbians into a mainly German-speaking community. Thus old Sorbians live in the continuous dilemma of which language to communicate in, since they are more fluent in German, but need the Sorbian languages to support their claims as a separate and authentic group in the German context. They fear that by admitting that they speak better German than Sorbian, their minority status will be engendered. The young Sorbian-speaking German told me that although the Sorbian activists were very appreciative of his engagement in their cause, they did not consider him to be one of them.[7] Since he had no Sorbian ancestors, he was thought to be unable to understand the 'real' Sorbian identity.

During my fieldwork in Germany as well as in Lapland,[8] I often observed language shifting depending on the situation, and on who was listening at the time. People with no Sámi or Sorbian origins were, to some extent, considered as outsiders, even though they were fluent language speakers. Others, with a much reduced understanding of the language, but who had at least one Sorbian (or Sámi) parent or even grandparent, were more readily recognised by the activists to be natural members of the 'community', as some kind of lost members who were now reunited with them. This is no isolated phenomenon, but applies more generally to national minorities, many of whose members may not speak the minority's original language, either because of past assimilation policies, or lack of educational opportunities, or discrimination.

In many cases, members of a minority may speak a variety of significantly different minority languages, so that it may be difficult to establish 'the' one and only minority language of the community. For example, the Sámi people in the North of Europe speak nine different languages; many of them differ radically from each other. An Inari Sámi speaker (Inari belonging to the most vulnerable of Sámi languages[9]) may opt to speak Finnish rather than learn Northern Sámi, though this is the most diffuse language amongst the whole of the Sámi population. Such a choice can be interpreted in two ways. On the one hand, the speaker may find it easier and less costly to learn the majority state language than one of the other languages spoken in the minority group. In fact, such a choice increases the likely circle of people with whom she can communicate, since other Sámi people speak Finnish or—if they are outside Finland—Scandinavian.[10] On the other hand, and additionally, she may decide that Northern Sámi speakers have already gained lots of political power and that language is about politics and politics is about power. In the case of Sámi, as with many other minorities, language is about power of certain families. She may decide not to support the language group that is negatively affecting the power of her family and consider the state majority's language(s) as a more neutral means of communication.

In Finland, language legislation was amended in 1990 to create better chances for Sámi to learn their languages in schools.[11] Before the 1990s, many Sámi people could not learn the language they nevertheless considered to be their (political) mother tongue (Svonni, 1996; Rosjo, 1997: 6). The number of Sámi speakers is no longer declining rapidly, although for most Sámi languages the legislation came too late. Nevertheless, the number of pupils learning Northern Sámi is increasing steadily as parents become educated and informed about the importance of minority language teaching. Of course, the whole concept of a mother tongue is a difficult one in the context of many minority languages, because mothers (and fathers) seldom use the minority languages as their first or best language, for obvious reasons. It still seems to be important for the activists to play down the fact that the number of people using the minority language, at home is low. As we have seen, it is felt that such a type of admission may risk weakening identity claims.

It remains true that language is an extremely important identity symbol, though this needs important qualification. As I wish to show, language is an instrumental symbol, which can easily be put to serve some of the political purposes of the minority, relying on the generalised belief diffuse in our societies that language, as one's mother tongue, is a natural sign of one's ethnic identity. At the same time, one does not need to speak the language that is classified as one's mother tongue. Nor does one need to be interested in learning it; as long as one goes along with the ideological belief that one nation speaks one language. The members (or potential members) need to acknowledge the power of language as 'the' marker of the minority nation. This is no coincidence, for all documents on minority rights define minorities as having a genuine language and culture to protect.

## WHAT NEEDS TO BE PROTECTED? SOME CONCEPTUAL REMARKS

Before we look at minority rights documents, we should clarify some conceptual issues. The minority rights treaties contain terms such as 'minority', 'identity', 'culture' and 'mother tongue'. These are seen as the essential attributes or elements of the identity of a person belonging to a minority.

However, it remains unclear what the drafters had in mind when using such concepts. The United Nations twice tried to define the concept of 'minority': first in 1977, with the Capotorti report, and 10 years later with the Deschênes report, which broadly agreed with the previous report's main findings (Capotorti, 1977; Deschênes, 1985). Nevertheless, both reports left the definition of a minority open. The Travaux Préparatoires of the European Convention for the Protection of Human Rights and Fundamental Freedoms (ECHR) give the impression that, to a certain extent, during its preparation there was a more sustained attempt to give a more concrete meaning to the use of the concept (see Spiliopoulou Åkermark, 2002).

The concepts 'majority' and 'minority' are relational categories and mediate political values which should not be adopted without recognising the dynamic relationship between dominant and subordinate groups, or without being aware of the continuously varying power circumstances among or within the groups (Kraus, 1997). Khleif (1993) introduced the concept of 'minoritised', which acknowledges the reality of the life circumstances of people who are labelled as being part of a minority community. Khleif emphasises that 'minoritised' groups do not voluntarily assume a position in which they have less power and fewer economic advantages. He remarks that most such groups are trying hard to escape from their state of subordination. Berry (1992) uses the notion of an 'acculturating group' for similar reasons, illustrating the process-like nature of belonging to groups defined as minorities. The fundamental difference between majority and minority groups seems to be in their unequal access to economic, social and their so-called 'own' cultural resources. Peoples who have access to such resources through the mediation of another group can be classified as minorities (see also Toivanen, 2001b).

Identity is not about free choice, but neither is it a marker with which we are damned. It is certainly an ongoing process rather than a set of fixed characteristics. Whenever we talk about groups, like the Sámi or the Sorbs, or the Frisians or the Ladins, we strive for one construct. We try to talk about a group as though it was a simple and easy task to set the borders of this identity definition. But even though it might often seem to us that the minority groups are stable and their identity characteristics almost timeless, such an opinion does not stand up to critical inspection. We need to take the personal and social context of identification seriously and respect the identities that people wish to present. Maybe it would be wise to move from debating the 'politics of identity' to discussing the politics of identity representation.

Language boundaries, real or imagined, can easily become exploited politically. In his thought-provoking book, *Language and Symbolic Power* (1992), Pierre Bourdieu discussed the phenomenon of the performative character typical of ethno-political entrepreneurs, who may live 'off' as well as 'for' ethnicity. By invoking groups, they seek to evoke them, summon them, call them into being. By reifying groups, ethno-political entrepreneurs may, as Bourdieu notes, 'contribute to producing what they apparently describe or designate' (Bourdieu, 1992: 220). Why is it, then, that ethno-political entrepreneurs consider it to be a useful tactic to essentialise the groups they wish to represent and create an image of a compact, homogenous group, whose common history and destiny is demarcated by a common culture and, above all, by a common language? Many researchers, myself included, have conducted a vast number of interviews with these 'ethno-political entrepreneurs' as a basis for their work and therefore similar images often get represented in the scientific literature on minorities. At the same time, we have learned to understand that a certain kind of 'identity talk' by activists is part of a survival strategy. The activists have to choose their arguments carefully and fit them within the political context in which the identity claim is made. There is no free choice of representation of an identity. Hence one of the most important questions in this field of social science is why such ethno-political entrepreneurs choose to represent the group in a certain manner. The report on the situation of Sorbian culture published in 1994 (*Bericht zur Lage sorbischer Kultur*) concluded that: 'Since there is neither a closed territory nor a homogenous language or any other unambiguous criteria of belonging for the Sorbs, at least some of the functions which create unity and a common will have to be realised by certain institutions.'[12] It is from such a perspective that one may look at linguistic rights.

## INTERNATIONAL LANGUAGE RIGHTS

Minority rights are sometimes perceived as 'fourth generation' rights, and constitute rights that are both vague and difficult to enforce. De Varennes (2001: 1) stresses that minority rights are an integral part of basic human rights. Language rights should not be seen as an additional layers of rights, for in his view, they enable the people whose mother tongue is not the state's official language(s) to enjoy the same rights as everyone else. In this sense, minority rights are a precondition for universal rights (Scheinin, 2003: 495).

The argument put forth here is that many of the existing minority rights consisting of language protection provisions treat minority groups as homogenous and static groups carrying a distinct and genuine language as a permanent feature. The International Covenant on Civil and Political Rights (1966) was designed to specify the contents of the Universal Declaration of Human Rights of 1948. In Article 27 it states: '[I]n those states in which ethnic, religious or linguistic minorities exist, persons belonging to such minorities shall not be denied the right, in community with other members of their group to ... use their own language.' In 1994, the Human Rights

Committee gave a General Comment on this article in which it clarified the scope of the minority rights (UN, 1994). Even though in the article itself, the term 'persons belonging to ... minorities' is used, the General Comment refers to groups by maintaining that, '[a]lthough the rights protected under article 27 are individual rights, they depend in turn on the ability of the minority group to maintain its culture, language or religion' (UN, 1994: para 6.2). The singular form 'language' and 'culture' of the minority is repeatedly used, giving the impression that minority groups are normally characterised by a single, unique and compact culture and one genuine language.

For a very long time, this was as close as international law came to issuing a legal codification of language rights. The more recent United Nation Minority Rights Declaration offers a positive, but non-legally binding, formulation.[13] When reading through the 'concluding observations' of the six Human Rights treaty bodies,[14] the right to use, to be educated, and to have access to important information in one's mother tongue is given extensive attention—more, for instance, than religion or other cultural aspects. The authors of the 'concluding observations' give the impression that they regard language as something that one can more easily identify as a marker, while other aspects of minority status may be more difficult to assess. As a consequence, it would seem that they assume that there are clear-cut groups with no internal conflicts, which have one language they wish to preserve, and for which they need protection from 'their' states. The fact that language issues are almost never so simple, even inside the language speaker's community itself, is not addressed at all.[15]

The European Human Rights Convention does not contain any minority protection provision (Council of Europe, 1950).[16] At least partly because of this lack of legal basis, the European Court of Human Rights has not been very sensitive to linguistic, cultural and ethnic minorities (Spiliopoulou Åkermark, 2002). Still, there are a great number of cases under the ECHR that have dealt with linguistic rights. The Strasbourg institutions have, however, consistently held that there is no right to use a particular language in one's dealings with government authorities.[17] The use of a minority language in the private sphere is protected as a right to freedom of expression under Article 10, but there is no right to a mother tongue education under the ECHR.[18] Freedom of religion is guaranteed under Article 9, which includes the right to manifest that religion, though the state may limit certain manifestations of a minority's religion for reasonable and objective reasons. According to the Court, 'a minority group is in principle entitled to claim the right to respect for the particular lifestyle it may lead as being "private life" or "home"' under article 8 of the Convention. Several cases involving the Roma and the indigenous peoples of northern Europe have sought to raise such a claim, although without success.[19]

In 1992, the Council of Europe adopted the legally binding menu type Charter for Regional or Minority Languages (Council of Europe 1992, ETS 148). This Charter protects national and traditional minority languages spoken by the citizens of the signatory states, though it does not include dialects and languages of migrants (Article 1). The charter's overriding purpose is cultural. It is designed to protect and promote autochthonous regional or minority languages as a threatened aspect of Europe's cultural heritage. The Explanatory Report to the Charter (Council of Europe, 1992) states that:

> [f]or this reason it not only contains a non-discrimination clause concerning the use of these languages but also provides for measures offering active support for them. The aim is to ensure, as far as reasonably possible, the use of regional or minority languages in education and the media and to permit their use in judicial and administrative settings, economic and social life and cultural activities. Only in this way can such languages be compensated, where necessary, for unfavourable conditions in the past and preserved and developed as a living facet of Europe's cultural identity.

Paragraph 17 continues, 'the charter is able to refrain from defining the concept of linguistic minorities, since its aim is not to stipulate the rights of ethnic and/or cultural minority groups, but to protect and promote regional or minority languages as such'.[20] Although I do not wish to dismiss the Charter's achievements in promoting minority rights in Europe, it is only fair to point out that the Charter relates mainly to those language groups whose protection and promotion may contribute to the furthering of democracy in Europe, without however jeopardising national sovereignty and territorial integrity (see the text's Preamble).

Two years later, the Framework Convention on the Protection of National Minorities (Council of Europe, 1995, ETS 157) was adopted. To a large extent, it transforms the political commitments of the OSCE[21] Copenhagen Document of 1990 into legal obligations. Article 5(1) is worth citing in full: 'The parties [to the covenant] undertake to promote the conditions for persons belonging to national minorities to maintain their culture, and preserve the essential elements of their identity, namely religion, language, traditions and cultural heritage.'[22] This formulation reveals a vision of groups of people carrying these essential elements of their identity with them. Many of its articles deal with language protection: the right to use a minority language (Articles 10 and 11); the official recognition of names in the minority language (Article 11); the onus on signatory states to 'endeavour to ensure' the use of the minority language before the authorities (Article 10); the right to display bilingual signs in the areas inhabited by national minorities 'traditionally' or 'in substantive numbers' (Articles 10 and 11); and educational rights in the minority language (Articles 13 and 14). A nation, even one in a minority position, speaks one language; that is the impression one has after reading the whole Convention.

In Article 1 of a Resolution on linguistic and cultural minorities in the European Community (EU, 1994), the European Parliament stresses 'the need for Member States to recognise their linguistic minorities and to make the necessary legal and administrative provisions for them to create the basic conditions for preservation and development of these languages'. Even though the resolution is on linguistic *and* cultural minorities, the document gives the impression that all cultural minorities have a genuine language to be preserved and developed. The Resolution on cultural co-operation in the EU underlines that 'one of Europe's distinctive cultural features is its unity in diversity' and that 'European cultural policy by no way seeks uniformity' (EU, 2002). In both the Treaty of Maastricht (1992) and the Treaty of Amsterdam (1997), the European Union has expressed its willingness to support cultural diversity. Article 151(1) of the Treaty of Amsterdam states that '[t]he Community shall contribute to the flowering of the cultures of the member states while respecting their national and regional diversity and at same time bringing the common cultural heritage to the fore' (EU, 1997). The right not to be discriminated against as a member of a specific (national, ethnic, linguistic, religious) group is established in many European documents, such as the Treaty of Amsterdam, Article 13 (Nowak, 2002: 255). However, the EU itself has no minority policy. The need for such a policy, as proposed by the European Parliament, was not even considered worthy of discussion in the Council (De Witte, 1993: 179). By and large, the European Council follows the political line created by interstate organisations such as the Organisation for Security and Co-operation in Europe (OSCE) and the Council of Europe (CoE). These standards have been created to secure stability and peace in post-socialist Europe (Hughes and Sasse, 2003), not to strengthen minorities as such.

But how do such treaties and charters influence the identity politics of minority members and especially activists? All national minorities stress the importance of maintaining 'their own minority language'. The word 'language' is in most cases used in the singular. The fact that most minorities have two or more languages[23] to preserve is seldom addressed publicly. How much is this behaviour influenced by the minority rights documents which only protect minority groups who have 'a distinctive, traditional language' (in the singular)? The image of the group that is projected to the majority society as well as to potential members of the minority is influenced by the minority rights provisions, and the definition of the group itself seems to get transformed to fit the minority protection treaties accordingly. The overall impression given by these documents is that minorities have a different culture and a specific mother tongue that they want to preserve.

## LANGUAGE AS A NEUTRAL GROUP BOUNDARY?

Two examples from the Finnish context[24] may serve to illustrate the general assumptions emerging from the minority rights international legal provisions. These take language as a neutral marker of identity and a natural characteristic of minority groups.

In Finland an Advisory Board for Ethnic Relations (ETNO) was founded in 1998.[25] Its aim was to gather representatives of all minorities living in Finland. For the ETNO the main goal was to recruit half of the Board members from immigrant groups and so called 'old minorities'.[26] The other half of the Board consisted of representatives of relevant ministries and organisations.[27] Even though the name of the organisation refers to 'ethnic relations' and its statute speaks about linguistic and cultural minorities (Asetus 1391, 1991: 3§), the representatives chosen to sit on the body do not represent 'cultures' or 'ethnic groups', but rather languages: English speakers, Somali speakers, Arab speakers, Vietnamese speakers and 'Yugoslavians'. Yugoslavians form in many ways an interesting 'group' since there is no such language and the speakers of the Serbian and Croatian languages living in Finland do not agree upon that label.

This raises a number of interesting questions. How might we define the representation of interest of a language speaker? How, and on what basis, can one assume that a Canadian English speaker will be able to represent the interests of a Jamaican person, or a person from Cameroon the interests of a French citizen? Hence, the Finnish ETNO has been criticised for its oversimplified view of languages and language boundaries (Lepola and Suurpää, 2003). In fact, it was a conscious decision not to choose representatives directly from immigrant associations, because they were too numerous, and because the problematic political situation in their 'home countries' made it difficult to avoid internal disagreements (Lepola and Suurpää, 2003: 7).[28] The organisations were defined as too political. Although common sense and often participants' own arguments attribute coherence, identity, interest and especially agency to ethnic groups, these attributes are actually characteristics of organisations (Brubaker, 2002). As Brubaker shows, the relationship between organisations and the groups they claim to represent is often deeply ambiguous. Seemingly, the Finnish government decided to avoid some of the problems supposed to reside in the organisations run by foreigners and assumed that language-based representatives would be less politically motivated, something they wanted to avoid. ETNO also comprised religious groups, but not in the sense that one Muslim group would be representative of all Muslims. Islam entered the picture only through the long established Muslim Tartar group (all members of which are Finnish citizens), which had for many years avoided direct contact with other (immigrant) Muslim groups in Finland.[29]

The emphasis on languages may be partly explained by the fact that Finland is a bilingual country. The Swedish speaking group has an equal footing in the Finnish constitutional system even though fewer than 6 per cent of inhabitants belong to it (STM, 2001). When Sámi and Roma rights began to receive more attention in the mid-1980s, Finland was already on its way to becoming a country of immigration rather than emigration. Mother tongue teaching for refugees, asylum seekers and immigrant children was seen as the best method of integrating them into Finnish society (Opetusministeriö, 1987). When educational experts began to stress the importance of the mother tongue for refugee children, attention was paid to the fact that Sámi[30] and Roma children with a long history in Finland (with citizenship rights in Finland) did not enjoy any specific rights for their own cultures and languages. Against this historical background, language was seen as the key to open the 'closet' of culture. Teaching of the mother tongue would give them access to their 'own' culture, and that of Finnish to the 'national, Finnish' culture (Toivanen, 1995).

New legal initiatives were quickly created to address this problem. Two hours of 'own mother tongue' teaching per week was introduced for all cultural minorities. The reason for adopting the expression 'own mother tongue' was partly related to the difficulties encountered in Sweden with the use of the concept of '*hemspråk*', which means 'home language'. For it soon became apparent that in many immigrant homes the national majority language was used in preference to the original mother tongue of the parents. The expression 'mother tongue' was also excluded in consideration of the fact that Roma and Sámi parents did not learn these languages as their 'first' language, due to previous repressive and assimilative state policies. In the circumstances, 'own mother tongue' was considered to have a more neutral ring to it (Toivanen, 1995). But this was not the end of the story. The Finnish authorities did not anticipate that the concept of 'own mother tongue' itself raised political sensitivities. For instance, the Kurdish community of refugees, despite sharing the same language, were profoundly divided politically. Hence some parents would forbid their children to attend language lessons taught by a teacher who did not share their political allegiances. A similar issue applied to the Vietnamese community, whilst amongst the Somali, tribal relationships were often considered to have much greater weight than language bonds. Speaking the same language was only incidental to group identification, so that all these experiences tended to confirm that language groups are not co-extensive with ethnic and/or cultural groups. Finnish educational experts, however, played down these socio-emotional aspects, sticking instead to a neutral vision of language-based identification. This resulted in many families from the minority communities opting out of the 'own mother tongue' teaching system. The authorities often interpreted this as a lack of interest and ambition on the part of poorly educated parents. They refused to see the political aspect of such choices, reproducing the kind of attitude that was behind the way in which ETNO's membership was established in the first place (see Lepola and Suurpää, 2003).

This situation is not unique to Finland, even though other countries offer language support programmes different from 'own language' teaching for school-age children. Invariably, all those support programmes are well-meaning, aiming to offer services to immigrants and refugee communities in a language that they are supposed to know well and feel confident with. The problems are however almost always similar to those experienced in Finland. Sometimes people choose to use another language as their own in order to avoid some other political or cultural barriers that the speakers of the same or similar languages have. The refusal to identify themselves with a language group puts some individuals in an awkward position; they become complete outsiders, whose claims for other kinds of minority rights become more difficult to sustain.

## LANGUAGE IDENTITY AS A VEHICLE FOR POLITICAL STRUGGLE

Many of the groups treated as 'language minorities' in Europe, such as Sámi, Sorbian, Frisian and Ladin, are seeking official recognition for their cultural distinctiveness and difference. In the same way, migrant groups are often treated as language groups (on the assumption, for instance, that all Turks speak Turkish, and people from Morocco speak Arabic, etc). But language is only one element of group identity. The question of what language a minority speaks is never easy to answer. For various reasons, mostly due to past assimilation policies, a minority may speak the majority language more fluently than their 'own' mother tongue, as is the case for Roma people in Scandinavia. Although, *prima facie*, the right to difference is clearly established in international, and especially European, legal documents, this right is subject to a number of constraints. In short, one could say that one's right to have a different identity is dependent on the way in which such difference is accepted and recognised by either states or inter-state organisations. It is such recognition that makes minority identity congruent with the rights agreed upon by state and international institutions. The concepts of difference employed in the international minority rights documents reflect a vision and understanding of what cultural or ethnic minorities should look like. Moreover, these documents give the state authorities a wide margin of interpretation regarding the provisions that will be offered to minorities. In this way, the rights discourse both enables and constrains. Minority rights discourse *enables* in so far as it encourages policy supporting equality and fairness. This is its greatest achievement, forcing states to commit themselves to the recognition of difference, and to establishing both protection provisions and promotion programmes for minorities. However, minority rights discourse also *constrains*, for it establishes a narrow path along which minorities can have their right to difference recognised. Political optimists may object that, by paying attention to such complex mechanisms of inclusion and exclusion, we have moved somewhat towards the amelioration of a minority's rights and opportunities; and that in order to find remedies to the unintended effects of legislation, we need strong co-operation between law and the social sciences.

For their part, anthropologists have abandoned the closed concept of culture, now tending to emphasise the shifts, transformations, multiple influences, and commitments that people make. Cultures are no longer considered to be distinct entities—they are seen as related phenomena (Appiah, 1992). The context of, and the reasons for, postulating a specific culture or identity are today considered as being critical to the analysis of cultural phenomena.[31] More attention is paid to the context in which a specific culture or identity is being claimed. In the debates on cultural rights, the right to language is used as the main argument, as though language constitutes the ultimate feature of culture.

Minority activists have come to share this way of representing their group. As a consequence, a strong tendency has developed in favour of a specific way of formulating identity claims. Such claims are based on elements emphasising tradition, folklore and ancient forms of culture, for these very features are more easily recognised by the external world, and therefore give a more realistic chance of 'survival' to minorities in the present world. Minority activists, who portray their minority language (in the singular) as proof of a specific identity, are fully aware of the strategic value of the kinds of discourse and arguments they employ. It is part of their job, as activists, to be alert to the kinds of claims and arguments that may more easily capture the imagination in public debates, whilst at the same time identifying the kinds of arguments that may harm the process of negotiation with states and other power structures. Those minorities which are able to support their claims to be considered as a nation, based on a common history stretching 'beyond mankind's memory', with one 'common' language distinct from others, with a territory where their ancestors have 'always' lived, and with a distinctive genetic make up, will undoubtedly stand a better chance of being recognised and securing 'cultural survival'.[32] Minority groups stressing these factors in their self-definition (or politics of identity) are accepted as authentic minorities and 'real' peoples by both the international community and state administrations.

In the future, we should move from research on the politics of recognition to research on the politics of identity representation. Looking at the politics of representation would allow us to make a deeper analysis of the power relationships determining cultural definition and survival. We should pay more attention to the way in which states (and inter-state organisations) influence societies by the use of legal means that apportion 'rights'. An analysis of the politics of representation would allow us to concentrate on how rights discourses influence the political agendas of people and how people make use of the rhetoric of rights. Here I have tried to argue that that type of rights discourse that emphasises the neutrality and the constituent character of language identity has heavily influenced the way in which minorities make political use of identity arguments, in order to lay claim to the status of being 'authentic' minorities, entitled to state recognition, protection and promotion.

## Notes

[1] My gratitude for financial support goes to the Finnish Science Academy Syreeni programme on Marginalisation, Inequality and Ethnic Relations in Finland.

[2] See eg the United Nations Declaration on the Rights of Ethnic, National or Religious Minorities, 1995; ILO Convention No 169 on the Rights of Indigenous and Tribal Peoples, 1989; European Charter for Regional and Minority languages ETS 148 (Council of Europe, 1992); Framework Convention on National Minorities ETS 157 (Council of Europe, 1995).

[3] See Recommendations and Opinions by the Advisory Committee on the Framework Convention on National Minorities and Reports by the European Committee Against Racism (ECRI). See for Advisory Committee http://www.coe.int/T/E/human_rights/minorities and for ECRI http://www.coe.int/T/E/human_rights/Ecri/.

[4] A classic study was conducted by Eugeen Roosens with Huron Indians in the late 1960s. See Roosens, 1989.

[5] The Sorbian community is rather small—with ca 60,000 members and about 15,000 speakers. It is located in the eastern part of Germany, in Lausitz, between the two Bundesländer of Brandenburg and Saxonia. The capital of this officially recognised national minority is the city of Bautzen in Saxonia. Sorbian sources emphasise that the Sorbs are the first inhabitants of what they consider their homelands, and should be seen as aborigines of this area (Mahling, 1991: 7). Even in Lausitz, however, the group is a minority (Oschlies, 1990).

[6] The language spoken in Brandenburg is more closely related to Polish, and is called Lower Sorbian. The other language, spoken in Saxony, is related to the Czech language and called Upper Sorbian. All Sorbs speak German (Elle, 1995a, 1995b; Spieß, 1995).

[7] It should be added that the Saxonian as well as the Brandenburg constitutions state that 'membership in the Sorbian minority is free'. See Verfassung des Freistaates Sachsen, 1992 and Verfassung des Landes Brandenburg, 1992.

[8] I am here referring to the fieldwork I did in 1995–7 for my dissertation and to a number of follow-up studies since. The results of these studies were published in Toivanen, 2001a and 2001b. The Sámi people enjoy the status of the aborigines of Scandinavia and Finland. Today, Sámi people live in four different states: Norway, Sweden, Russia and Finland. Altogether, there are estimated to be about 70,000 Sámi. About 6,500 Sámi live in Finland (Lehtola, 1997). There are nine to eleven different Sámi languages and even more dialects. Three of the languages, Northern, Inari and Skolt Sámi, are spoken in Finland. The Sámi organisations are the heart of the minority's existence. The Sámi Council (before 1992, the Nordic Sámi Council) was founded in 1956 to further cross-border co-operation among Sámi. In 1996, the Finnish Sámi were granted cultural autonomy in their home area in Lapland (Government Act 974/95).

[9] A Report from the Finnish Sámi Parliament (1997) concludes that 'The speakers of Inari Sámi and Skolt Sámi both number 400 to 500 persons. These languages are dying out in Finland and in the world'.

[10] Scandinavian is an artificial language generally used for Northern co-operation, mixing Danish, Norwegian and Swedish. Swedish is one of the official languages in Finland. In Lapland

people have extensive contacts with Norway and Sweden and tend to use two to four different languages at a conversational level.

[11] L 25.1.1991/171. Finnish Law on changing School legislation (Laki peruskoululain muuttamisesta).

[12] In the original: 'Da es für die Sorben weder ein abgeschlossenes Territorium noch eine homogene Sprache oder andere eindeutige Zugehörigkeitskriterien gibt, müssen einheitsstiftende und willensbildende Funktionen nicht zuletzt über bestimmte Institutionen realisiert werden.'

[13] According to Article 1(1), '[s]tates shall protect the existence and the national, cultural, religious and linguistic identity of minorities within their respective territories, and shall encourage conditions for the promotion of that identity.' 'Persons belonging to [...] minorities have the right to [...] use their own language' (UN, 1992: Art 2(1)).

[14] The six treaty bodies are the Committee against Torture (CAT), the Committee on the Elimination of Discrimination (CERD), the Human Rights Committee (CCPR), the Committee on the Elimination of Discrimination against Women (CEDAW), the Committee on Economic, Social and Cultural Rights (CESCR) and the Committee on the Rights of the Child (CRC).

[15] http://www.bayefsky.com offers easy access to all the Concluding Observations of all the six treaty bodies.

[16] The prohibition of discrimination in Article 14 can be used in conjunction with a violation of another substantive provision as the basis for minority protection (see Spiliopoulou Åkermark, 2002: 2).

[17] Under Article 5.2 everyone has the right to be informed, in a language he/she understands, of the reasons for arrest. In Article 6.3.a everyone has the right to be informed of the nature of any criminal charges and there is a right to a free interpreter if a defendant cannot speak then language of the court (Article 6.3.e). See Council of Europe, 1950.

[18] Unless the right previously existed and the state then tries to withdraw it.

[19] The UN Guide for Minorities, Pamphlet No 7, 4. See for the texts of the Court's jurisprudence www.echr.coe.int.

[20] In para 23, it is added that 'it will be left to the authorities concerned within each state, in accordance with its own democratic processes, to determine at what point a form of expression constitutes a separate language'.

[21] Organisation on Security and Co-operation in Europe, previously CSCE.

[22] The Explanatory Report to the Framework conventions comments on Article 5, para 1 as follows: 'This provision does not imply that all ethnic, cultural, linguistic or religious differences necessarily lead to the creation of national minorities.'

[23] In some cases, two or more dialects of a language with no standardised form, for example Sardu in Sardinia.

[24] Finland was until the beginning of the 1990s an emigration country and has now gradually become an immigration country. However the number of minorities remains very low, ca 2%. (http://www.uvi.fi/englanti/oleskelu.html).

[25] This Board was actually a direct continuation of the previous Advisory Board for Refugee and Immigrants Matters (PAKSI) that worked in 1992–7. ETNO was established under the same government regulation A1319/1991 with which PAKSI had been founded.

[26] The following groups qualify as old minorities: Indigenous Sámi people, Roma people, Jewish, Tatar and an old Russian minority (Työministeriö, 2001: 1).

[27] The ministry officials were the same persons who had also worked in PAKSI. These two groups are called the two wings of the Board: the 'officials wing' and 'minority wing' (Lepola and Suurpää, 2003: 2).

[28] Some refugee groups such as the Vietnamese and Somalis left their homes because of problems created by deep ethnic divisions and political conflicts. These very same problems normally reoccur in the countries of settlement.

[29] Finnish immigrant and other Muslim groups are in the process of establishing an umbrella Muslim organisation, the Muslim Federation, which may speak for all the Finnish Muslims. Their common language is, of course, Finnish. (Helsingin Sanomat, 2002).

[30] Sámi are now recognised as the only indigenous people in Finno-Scandinavia.

[31] In his book *Modernity at Large* (1996), Arjun Appadurai uses the term 'cultural phenomenon' instead of 'culture' to provide more space for the shifting and ambiguous nature of the concept.

[32] It may be that during the process of negotiation, some members will step back from the group and say that the identity icon produced by the activists does not resemble what they feel is important for them.

## References

### *Primary Sources*

Asetus etnisten suhteiden neuvottelukunnasta A1319/1991. Government regulation concerning the Advisory Board on Ethnic Relations.

Council of Europe (1950) Convention for the Protection of Human Rights and Fundamental Freedoms as amended by Protocol 11, http://conventions.coe.int/treaty/EN/Treaties/html/005.htm.

Council of Europe (1992) ETS 148, European Charter for Regional or Minority Languages in European Treaty Series 148, http://conventions.coe.int/Treaty/en/Treaties/Html/148.htm.

Council of Europe (1992) Explanatory Report to the Charter, http://conventions.coe.int/Treaty/en/Reports/Html/148.htm

Council of Europe (1995) ETS 157, Framework Convention for the Protection of National Minorities, http://conventions.coe.int/Treaty/en/Treaties/Html/157.htm

EU (1994) Resolution on linguistic and cultural minorities in the European Community. A30042/94, OJ C 61, 29/2/1994, 110–13.

EU (1997) Treaty of Amsterdam, http://www.europarl.eu.int/topics/treaty/pdf/amst-en.pdf.

EU (2002) European Parliament Resolution on Cultural Co-operation, 2000/2323(INI), A50281/2001, OJ C 72E, 142–6.

Finnish Law on changing the School legislation (Laki peruskoululain muuttamisesta), L25.1.1991/171.

Finnish Saami Parliament (1997) 'Land Rights, Linguistic Rights, and Cultural Autonomy for the Finnish Saami People', *Indigenous Affairs*, No 33/34, July–December, http://arcticcircle.uconn.edu/SEEJ/sami1.html

Government Act 1995. Laki Saamelaiskäräjistä. N:o 974: 1–45§. Vom 17.7.1995. Suomen säädöskokoelma 1995. N:o 969–80, 2340–6.

Organisation for Security and Cooperation in Europe 1990, Document of the Copenhagen meeting of the Conference on the Human Dimension of the CSCE, http://www.osce.org/documents/odihr/1990/06/13992_en.pdf

STM (2001) Omakielisten palvelujen turvaaminen sosiaali- ja terveydenhuollossa. Sosiaali- jaterveysministeriön julkaisuja: 1.

Työministeriö (2001) Kohti etnistä yhdenvertaisuutta ja monimuotoisuutta. Hallituksen etnisen syrjinnän ja rasismin vastainen toimintaohjelma. Työhallinnon julkaisuja 284. Helsinki.

UN (1976) International Covenant on Civil and Political Rights.
UN (1992) Declaration on the Rights of Persons Belonging to National or Ethnic, Religious or Linguistic Minorities. Adopted 18/12/1992.
UN (1994) United Nations Human Rights Committee, The rights of minorities (Article 27): 08/04/94. CCPR General Comment 23.
UN Guide for Minorities, Pamphlet No 7: Minority Rights under the European Convention on Human Rights.

*Secondary Sources*

Appadurai, A (1996) *Modernity at Large: Cultural Dimensions of Globalization* (Minneapolis, University of Minnesota Press).
Appiah, A (1992) 'Identity, Authenticity, Survival: Multicultural Societies and Social Reproduction' in A Gutman (ed), *The Politics of Recognition* (Princeton, NJ, Princeton University Press).
Barry, B (2002) *Culture & Equality: An Egalitarian Critique of Multiculturalism* (Cambridge, MA, Harvard University Press).
Bericht zur Lage der sorbischen Kultur (1994) *Langsam wirds Zeit* (Bautzen, Domowina-Verlag).
Berry, JW (1992) *Cross-cultural Psychology: Research and Applications* (Cambridge, Cambridge University Press).
Bordieu, P (1992) *Language and Symbolic Power* (Cambridge, MA, Harvard University Press).
Brubaker, R (2002) 'Ethnicity without Groups' *Archives européennes de sociologie* XLIII: 163–89.
Calhoun, C (1994) 'Social Theory and the Politics of Identity' in C Calhoun (ed), *Social Theory and the Politics of Identity* (Cambridge, MA, Blackwell).
Capotorti, F (1977) 'Study on Rights of Persons belonging to Ethnic, Religious and Linguistic Minorities' UN Doc E/CN.4/Sub.2/384.
Cowan, J, Dembour, M-B and Wilson, RA (eds) (2001) *Culture and Rights: Anthropological Perspectives* (Cambridge, Cambridge University Press).
De Witte, B (1993) 'The European Community and its Minorities' in C Brölmann, R Lefeber and M Zieck (eds), *Peoples and Minorities in International Law* (Dordrecht, Martinus Nijhoff).
Dembour, M-B (2001) 'Following the Movement of a Pendulum: Between Universalism and Relativism' in J Cowan, M-B Dembour and RA Wilson (eds), *Culture and Rights: Anthropological Perspectives* (Cambridge, Cambridge University Press).
Deschênes, Jules (1985) 'Deschenes Report' § 181, UN Doc E /CN.4/ Sub.2/1985/31.
Dworkin, G (1974) 'Non-Neutral Principles' *Journal of Philosophy* 71: 491–506.

Elle, L (1995a) 'Die sorbische Minderheit' in C Schmalz-Jacobsen and G Hansen (eds), *Ethnische Minderheiten in der BundesrepublikDeutschlan d: ein Lexikon* (Munich, Beck).
Elle, L (1995b) *Sprachenpolitik in der Lausitz. Eine Dokumentation 1949 bis 1989* (Bautzen, Domowina-Verlag).
Geertz, C (1983) *Local Knowledge: Further Essays in Interpretative Anthropology* (New York, Basic Books).
Gluckman, M (1956) 'The Technical Vocabulary of Barontse Jurisprudence' *American Anthropologist* 61: 743–59.
Gluckman, M (1963) *Order and Rebellion in Tribal Africa* (London, Cohen and West).
Helsingin Sanomat (2002) Heidi Korva: Tapasimme Yasin Arasen—Nokian insinööri yhdistää muslimeja, A16.
Hoebel, AE (1954) *The Law of Primitive Man* (Cambridge, MA, Harvard University Press).
Hughes, J and Sasse, G (2003) 'Monitoring the Monitors: The EU Enlargement Conditionality and Minority Protection in the CEECs' *JEMIE* 1.
Khleif, BB (1993) 'Minoritization of Languages in their Traditional Historical Territories: Issues of Autonomy and Identity in the Nation-State' *Sociologia Internationalis* 31: 159–78.
Kraus, PA (1997) 'Minderheiten' in D Nohlen, P Waldmann and K Ziemer (eds), *Lexikon der Politik, Band 4 die östlichen und südlichen Länder* (Munich, Beck).
Kymlicka, W (1998) 'Ethnic Relations and Western Political Theory' in M Opalski (ed), *Managing Diversity in Plural Societies: Minorities, Migration and Nation-Building in Post Communist Europe* (Ottawa, Forum Eastern Europe).
Lehtola, V-P (1997) *Saamelaiset. Historia, yhteiskunta, taide* (Jyväskylä, Kustannus-Punsi).
Lepola, O and Suurpää, L (2003) *Vallan syrjässä? Tutkimus etnisten suhteiden neuvottelukunnan toiminnasta* (Työministeriö).
Llewellyn, K and Hoebel, AE (1941) *The Cheyenne Way* (Norman, University of Oklahoma Press).
Mahling, J (1991) 'Zur politischen und kulturellen Geschichte der Sorben' in J Mahling and M Völkel (eds), *Die Sorben in Deutschland* (Bautzen, Domowina-Verlag).
Merry, SE (2001) 'Changing Rights, Changing Culture' in J Cowan, M-B Dembour and RA Wilson (eds), *Culture and Rights: Anthropological Perspectives* (Cambridge, Cambridge University Press).
Moore, SF (1978) *Law as Process: An Anthropological Approach* (London, Routledge and Kegan Paul).
Nader, L (1990) *Harmony Ideology: Justice and Control in a Zapotec Mountain Village* (Stanford, CA, Stanford University Press).

Nader, L (ed) (1997) (1st edn 1969) *Law in Culture and Society* (Berkeley, University of California Press).

Nowak, M (2002) *Einführung in das internationale Menschenrechtssystem* (Vienna, Neuer Wissenschaftlicher Verlag).

Opetusministeriö (1987) Vieraskielisten lasten äidinkielen opetuksen työryhmän muistio. Opetusministeriön työryhmän muistioita: 19 (Helsinki).

Oschlies, W (1990) *Die Sorben—Slawisches Volk im Osten Deutschlands. Forum Deutsche Einheit Nr 4* (Bonn, Friedrich-Ebert-Stiftung).

Roosens, E (1989) *Creating Ethnicity* (London, Sage).

Rosjo, B (1997) 'Engineering a Cultural Comeback. Tell Us', Research Council of Norway, 4–7.

Scheinin, M (2003) 'Minority Rights: Additional Rights or Added Protection?' in M Bergsmo (ed), *Human Rights and Criminal Justice for the Downtrodden: Essays in Honour of Asbjørn Eide* (Leiden/Boston, Martinus Nijhoff).

Smith, A (1986) *The Ethnic Origins of Nations* (Oxford, Basil Blackwell).

Spieß, G (1995) 'Die sprachliche Situation bei den Sorben in der Niederlausitz. Zur Motivation, Zielsetzung und Durchführung einer soziolinguistischen Untersuchung', Letopis 42, Sonderheft, 59–62.

Spiliopoulou Åkermark, S (2002) 'The Limits of Pluralism—Recent Jurisprudence of the European Court of Human Rights with Regard to Minorities: Does the Prohibition of Discrimination Add Anything?' *JEMIE* 3.

Sunstein, C (2000) 'Rights and their Critics', 70(727) *Notre Dame Law Review*.

Svonni, M (1996) 'Sámi Language as a Marker of Ethnic Identity among the Sámi' in I Seurujärvi-Kari and U-M Kulonen (eds), *Essays on Indigenous Identity and Rights* (Helsinki, Yliopistopaino).

Toggenburg, GN (2003) 'The Race Directive: A New Dimension in the Fight Against Ethnic Discrimination in Europe' in A Bloed ua (Hrsg), *European Yearbook of Minority Issues, Vol l, 2001/2*, 231–44.

Toivanen, R (1995) 'Kieli on avain ja lukko' (The language is a key and the lock), Helsingin yliopisto. Unpublished licenciate's thesis.

Toivanen, R (2001a) *Minderheitenrechte als Identitätsressource? Die Sorben in Deutschland und die Saamen in Finnland* (Münster, Lit Verlag).

Toivanen, R (2001b) 'Minority Rights and Minority Identities—Sámi in Finland and Sorbs in Germany' *Yearbook of Population Research in Finland* XXXVII: 83–102.

Toivanen, R (2003) 'Saami People and Northern Civil Societies' in N Götz and J Heckmann (eds), *Civil Society in the Baltic Sea Region* (Aldershot, Ashgate).

Varennes, F de (2001) 'Language Rights as an Integral Part of Human Rights' *MOST Journal of Multicultural Societies* 3(1).
Verfassung des Freistaates Sachsen (1992) vom 27 Mai 1992. Sächsisches Gesetz- und Verordnungsblatt Nr 20/92.
Verfassung des Landes Brandenburg 1992 vom 22 April 1992.
Wilson, RA (ed) (1997) *Human Rights, Culture and Context: Anthropological Perspectives* (London, Pluto Press).

# 7

# *Minority Languages, Law and Politics: Tracing EC Action*

NIAMH NIC SHUIBHNE

THE EUROPEAN COMMUNITY (EC) offers the ultimate project for the language policy-maker, representing a unique multilingual setting. In addition to enabling the machinery of EC administration and EU-Member state relations to function effectively in such a multilingual context, tasks also faced by other international organisations, an EC language policy will have to facilitate the extent to which Community law pierces domestic legal systems and, moreover, confers an array of rights and obligations directly on natural and legal persons. And yet, a readily discernible EC 'language policy' simply doesn't exist. Instead, we must plough through the linguistic aspects of EC competence in culture, the institutional (administrative) language rules and the impact of substantive Community law more generally on Member State language policies. On the one hand, in so doing, we can point to the EC as a locus of governance which has considerable influence—both directly and indirectly—on the language practices, and thus the language patterns, of its Member States (and of the various sub-state regions and/or authorities therein, where relevant). But very particular rules and requirements govern EC law-making of any kind, since it constitutes a very particular kind of governing polity. And so, the legal capacity of the Community to act in the linguistic (as in any) domain must be clearly established. In other words, it must be flagged at the outset that, in terms of advancing an EC language policy, there is likely to be a considerable difference between what *might* be possible (theoretically) and what *is* actually possible (legally).

The balancing act introduced above is complicated further still by zooming in more acutely on EC action in respect of minority languages. There is no clear Treaty mandate for the EC to act in respect of languages of *any* status beyond the most basic competence to regulate institutional administration. More specifically, there is certainly no explicit competence for the EC to act in the field of minority rights. Because of this, the extent to which a minority language 'policy' can be cobbled together from other strands of

Treaty interest will need to be outlined briefly; not surprisingly, justification of an EC action will depend in large part on the attribution of breadth and a certain elasticity in respect of more 'traditional' competences. But it will become clear that the EC is not an altogether successful actor, especially when its achievements are gauged against the requirements and expectations of minority language speakers.

The limitations and restrictions identified must be further contemplated against the backdrop of supranational governance. Even if the realisation of minority language policy is accepted as a responsibility of 'government', to what extent is it a responsibility of *supranational* government? By siting this analysis almost entirely in a relatively sheltered discourse of law, it runs somewhat contrary to the contemporary tide of European studies, which encourages more lateral and interdisciplinary thinking. But if reform is exposed as a necessary ambition for EC minority language policy, a clear understanding of the current legal position marks an essential starting point.

## THE ROOTS OF EC (MINORITY) LANGUAGE POLICY

When conceiving a language policy at the domestic level, several questions fall to be determined. For example, which languages should be included, and to what extent? Can languages spoken within a state be legitimately excluded and, if so, why? This debate becomes all the more complex when transposed to the supranational stage. The EC Treaty provisions especially relevant to EC (minority) language policy are collected together at the end of this chapter. The absence of *directly* relevant Treaty provisions might not seem problematic on one view since language policy measures cannot be confined discretely in terms of subject matter; and so, it might be felt that the absence of an empowering linguistic planning provision is actually better than the presence of an overly restrictive one. Moreover, it will be shown below that the legal (Treaty) basis deficiency did not exactly deter the institutions from acting in the minority language sphere anyway, at least initially.

Before getting into a discussion of derived competence, however, and aside from the expected difficulties that will be identified in this regard—eg lack of coherence, certainty and direction—a more basic and increasingly damaging drawback must be explored: essentially, there is no recognition of linguistic diversity as a principle that can underpin EC action in any 'constitutional' sense. So not only is the execution of minority language policy itself haphazard, the foundations upon which it had been assumed to rest are proving largely fictitious.

Every Member State is presently 'represented' in the EC language scheme by at least one of its domestic official languages, a settlement derived from

Article 314 of the EC Treaty. This means that there are (for now) twenty working and official languages of the EC (and, it is presumed, the EU): Czech, Danish, Dutch, English, Estonian, Finnish, French, German, Greek, Hungarian, Italian, Latvian, Lithuanian, Maltese, Polish, Portuguese, Slovak, Slovenian, Spanish and Swedish.[1] Crucially, all of the twenty languages are generally considered to be equally authentic in a *legal* sense, a position derived from but going somewhat further than Article 314 EC (which merely provides for the equality of all language versions of the Treaty itself).[2]

The very first piece of legislation enacted by the (then) EEC institutions, Regulation 1/58, sets out guidelines for communications between Member States and the EC institutions, and for the language practices to be followed by the institutions in a general sense.[3] While there is no formalised distinction between the 'working' and 'official' functions of the EC languages, the institutions do, in reality, work through a reduced number for purposes of internal administration (typically, through French, English and, to a lesser but apparently growing extent, German) while generally respecting the equality of 'the eleven' for communications that involve Member States and/or natural and legal persons. Notwithstanding internal cuts, there are considerable implications for translation and interpretation resources which in turn generate cost and delay; this practical dimension has taken on even more urgency in light of EU enlargement. The Intergovernmental Conference (IGC) held in 2000 and the resulting Treaty of Nice did not grapple with the 'language question'; but it is difficult to see how serious evaluation of both present arrangements and the need for reform can be postponed for much longer.

If, as had been generally assumed, the above language practices generated a *constitutional* principle of linguistic equality, it might well have accommodated the development of minority language policy. But this notion was recently dispelled by the Court of First Instance (CFI) in *Kik*,[4] a stance affirmed, on appeal, by the Court of Justice.[5] The CFI judgment represents the defining chapter in the long-running *Kik* narrative, the applicant having initiated her original challenge against the language rules in question almost a decade ago.[6] The Office for Harmonisation in the Internal Market (OHIM) deals *inter alia* with applications for Community trade marks. It is an EC 'body' rather than a fully-fledged institution and has, in relative terms, a much more restrictive language regime: only English, French, German, Italian and Spanish are recognised as its working languages. An application for a Community trade mark may be filed in any of the (twenty) official EC languages, but applicants must specify a second language—which must be a working language of OHIM—in which OHIM may send written communications. Furthermore, the applicant is deemed to accept this second language as the language of any subsequent opposition, revocation or invalidity proceedings.[7]

Regulation 1/58 binds only the 'institutions of the Community' and so there is no 'legal' barrier to the OHIM linguistic framework. But it is at least arguable that the doctrine of linguistic equality in a more generic or 'constitutional' sense is contravened. This claim was expressly rejected by the CFI. Alongside arguments grounded in Article 12 EC and non-discrimination on grounds of nationality, it had been submitted that '[Regulation 1/58] lays down clearly one of the principles of Community law from which no derogation by subsequent regulation of the Council is permitted'.[8] In still more constitutional language, the Greek Government argued that '... the Community legal order does not recognise the superiority of particular official languages in relation to the others and ... the EC Treaty as well as Regulation [1/58] lay down the principle of plurilingualism and language neutrality'.[9] It then asserted that the departure from primary Community law exhibited in the OHIM rules 'is all the more serious because no grounds are given for it'.[10] In contrast, the Council argued that derogation from Regulation 1/58 was not problematic, since it 'contains no fixed principle of Community law'.[11] Taking a very pragmatic view, the Council claimed also that 'there is no Community law principle of absolute equality between the official languages. Otherwise, there would be no [Article 290 EC]'.[12] It continued along these lines, making express reference to 'budgetary considerations' and explaining simply that it had made a choice, one 'based on a balancing of the interests of undertakings on the one hand and the possible drawbacks such as those raised by the applicant on the other'.[13] Perhaps here, we glimpse the real issues at play; and it is unlikely that the impact of (at that time, imminent) EU enlargement was too far from anyone's mind either.

The findings of the CFI are neatly formalist, but lacking any constitutional depth. The Court denied that Regulation 1/58 could establish a principle of equality between languages, since this would be 'tantamount to disregarding its character as secondary law'.[14] On this point, it did not discuss Article 314 EC at all and was equally silent on the legal equality of all language versions of secondary legislation. In situations where the second language indicated on the trade mark application had to be used for opposition, revocation or invalidity proceedings, it was felt that the Council had made 'an appropriate and proportionate choice, even if the official languages of the Community were treated differently'; this reasoning seems to be based primarily on the fact that the OHIM had selected its working languages 'from among the most widely known languages in the Community'.[15]

The decision in *Kik* thus replaces something which has always been assumed—that the equality of the official EC languages is a fundamental principle of the Community legal order—with the fluidity of a doctrinal deficit. The CFI declared that Regulation 1/58 could not amount to the source of this principle, but it never considered the Regulation as, instead, its manifestation or reflection—displaying an interpretative literalism much at odds with jurisprudence on EC general principles more broadly.[16] There is no substantive discussion on legal certainty, and arguments grounded in Article 12 of the EC Treaty and nationality discrimination were given short shrift. Again, this just doesn't quite fit with the marriage of language and non-discrimination more generally, thinking, for example, of case law on the free movement of persons.[17]

The CFI decision cannot be divorced from its political context, a point raised above in the context of finances, linguistic streamlining and EU enlargement. Pragmatism obviously—and properly—has its place in any discussion of EC language arrangements, but the interpretative reasoning applied in *Kik* could have repercussions well beyond the OHIM; the reluctance of the Court even to consider a constitutional basis for EC language policy leaves it open to simple legislative amendment. Only one of the Member States, Greece, seemed remotely troubled in this regard, somewhat ironically given its own domestic record in respect of linguistic minorities. Just one other Member State—Spain—intervened. From a position of some comfort, since Spanish is one of the (five) OHIM languages, Spain's submission was loaded with pragmatism, stressing the fact that the rules allow for 'a choice between the five most common languages in the Community'.[18] But would the Spanish government think quite so pragmatically about things if OHIM employed the *four* most common languages in the Community or, further down the line, if it was proposed that English and French only, for example, should be used for all EC administration?

On appeal, neither Advocate General Jacobs nor the Court of Justice engaged in any constitutional discussion, reaffirming the ethos of the CFI's reasoning.[19] Surely this case could have been better handled by confirming a general principle of respect for linguistic equality, albeit one that is subject to reasonable/legitimate limitation? Such a solution gives scope for both constitutional grounding and pragmatic, where justifiable, restrictions. But instead, by pulling the constitutional carpet from underneath the notion of linguistic equality, EC linguistic action in any domain—minority or otherwise—cannot be rooted in a secure constitutional premise. This, in turn, opens the way for further incoherence across the scale of linguistic protection, thinking of the multitude of different competence fields which involve a linguistic interest, as will become clear below. So while it might seem appropriate that EC language policy be endowed with a considerable degree of flexibility—enabling it to be adapted to various language policy domains more successfully—flexibility, which itself rests on an ephemeral footing, brings distinct problems. The (limited) gap-filling potential of Article 151(4) EC in this context will be discussed separately below.

## MINORITY LANGUAGE 'POLICY'? OUTLINING AND ADVANCING EC ACTION

This section aims briefly to establish whether the EC can be said to have a minority language policy at all, piecing together the various strata of institutional action in the field and assessing whether the 'parts' add up to a distinct sum. Something of an institutional split can be loosely identified at the outset, with the Commission and European Parliament having concentrated largely, though not exclusively, on the cultural side of language policy, and the Court of Justice having to contemplate language within a more rights-based framework and to determine the extent to which (minority) linguistic claims can restrict the trade ideals of the internal market. The institutional split is also reflective of the political/legal thread running throughout this chapter. Political lobbying for improved minority language policy has concentrated traditionally on the European Parliament and Commission, even though the majority of their initiatives had not rested on a legal footing and, indeed, have recently run into legal trouble. Apart from limited procedural rights now tied in with EU citizenship (see Article 21 EC), there is no very striking institutional awareness of language choices as a compelling expression of language rights. EC commitments to minority language policy are usually hinged on fairly inchoate (and often rhetorical) notions of respect for linguistic and cultural diversity,[20] or on the extent to which the linguistic dimension of a given issue might be allowed to prevail over competing, usually market, values. The latter point is balanced initially by the legislative institutions but falls ultimately to be decided by the Court; as will be seen, its skills of appraisal here are, on balance, undeveloped, tending to bolster market orientation rather than cultural interests (Nic Shuibhne, 2004; de Witte, 2004).

It is intended here to provide just enough description of various legislative initiatives and judicial decisions to facilitate a more analytical and (political/legal) comparative discussion of what has happened to date. A distinction can be drawn at the outset between two 'groups' of minority languages in the EC context. First, two languages—Irish and Letzeburgesch—are national languages in their respective Member States but neither language has been accorded (full, see note 1) status as an official Community language. This already slight grouping may, however, be broken down further still. Irish is mentioned in Article 314 EC and so versions of the treaties are required to be made available (and thus also have legal effect) in that language. And this has subsidiary implications. For example, the rights of EU citizens when writing to various EC institutions and bodies (now codified in Article 21 EC) relate to languages 'mentioned in Article 314'—thus including Irish—rather than the twenty 'official' languages or Regulation 1/58. Irish is also a working language of the Community courts, although it has yet to be used in proceedings. Finally, Irish has been included in a number of EC language education programmes. Letzeburgesch—though constitutionally recognised as the national language of Luxembourg—has not been endorsed as a 'Treaty language' to a similar extent, although it has been included in some EC language education programmes.

As regards minority languages more generally, however, they have neither working nor official status in the EC (although, in a very limited and incidental sense, special provision may be made in the course of ECJ or CFI proceedings for those who feel unable to express themselves adequately in any of the 'official' languages).[21] Neither are they included in EC language education programmes. It would simply be impossible fully to include all minority languages in the official EC language regime, though this argument is less clear-cut in respect of, at least, the language education programmes, since success or otherwise here could surely be measured objectively by consumer response. And related to this, it is arguable that the Community's apparent dismissal of minority languages contrasts starkly with its rhetoric on multilingualism. But it would be misleading to conclude that the absence of minority languages from the 'official' EC language policy has implied a corollary absence of Community activity.

The European Parliament is generally considered to be the key player here. The late 1970s saw a renewed commitment to the idea of European integration, but alongside an awareness of cultural and especially minority concerns. Crucially, an Intergroup for Minority Languages—which is still active—was established in 1983. And in a series of renowned Resolutions in the 1980s, the Parliament called for co-operative EC/Member State protection of minority languages, grounded in respect for the diversity of cultural identities and the realisation of free expression. These (non-binding) measures—the Arfé Resolution (1981), a second Arfé Resolution (1983) and the Kuijpers Resolution (1987)[22]—concentrated on the language domains of education, the media/communications and public life, always distinguishing a co-ordinating role for the Community and a more proactive responsibility for the Member States; the need to collect information on (and to co-ordinate and fund research projects in respect of) minority language communities throughout the EC was also stressed. Examples of practical results that can be traced to the work of the Parliament include the founding of the European Bureau for Lesser Used Languages (EBLUL) in 1981 and the report of the Istituto della Enciclopedia Italiana on linguistic minorities in the EC, produced in 1986.[23]

Although, as noted above, resolutions are not legally binding in any case, it is still striking that the European Parliament took any interest in addressing minority languages at all, since it could not draw on any substantive provisions of EC law to bolster its calls for action at that time. The ratification of the TEU is significant on this point. Article 151 EC codified a Community competence in the field of culture for the first time; and Article 6(3) TEU requires the Union to respect the national identities of its Member

States. It is not surprising, then, that the Parliament's 1994 Resolution, while similar in its basic aims and objectives, is bolder in tenor and more comprehensive in ambition than any of its predecessors.[24] The Resolution on Regional and Lesser Used Languages, adopted on 13 December 2001,[25] referred to the continually strengthening corpus of supportive legal instruments—to the Council of Europe's European Charter for Regional or Minority Languages and the 'home-grown' EU Charter of Fundamental Rights (Article 22 of which commits the Union to respecting cultural, religious and linguistic diversity). The financial focus of this Resolution reflects concerns of ongoing importance, discussed in more detail below.

Overall, what can be drawn from the work of the European Parliament is a sense that while the Community has a different function in the field of minority language protection vis-à-vis the Member States, its distinct responsibilities are nonetheless real. The role of the EC in respect of co-ordination and encouragement had taken root. As will become clearer below, even substantive (market) EC law and policy can impact on language issues, and thus on languages and on their speakers. Crucially, the European Parliament wove this consciousness directly into the agenda for Community action.

But it must also be pointed out that while the European Parliament called consistently on the Commission to implement its proposed objectives, little concrete action was taken relative to the scope of the resolutions themselves. What should be borne in mind here is the requirement in Community law generally to ground binding legislative measures in the Treaty—and this presented quite a different challenge for the Commission. Nevertheless, even before the adoption of Article 151 EC, it issued a series of official communications on EC action in the cultural sector.[26] The early versions of these documents were understandably cautious, limited in both scope and intended effect. In light of the absence of an explicit cultural competence at the time, the Commission developed something of a sectoral approach instead, identifying elements of cultural policy that related to more general Community competences (such as free trade in cultural goods, or free movement and establishment for cultural workers). In other words, the Commission did not attempt either to design or implement an autonomous cultural policy; rather, it made more visible a domain-specific application of general trade principles.

With the added incentive of completing the internal market by 1992, *A Fresh Boost for Culture in the European Community* was published in 1987.[27] The role of the Community in the audio-visual and technological sectors was strengthened significantly, but efforts on behalf of the book trade were also intensified and here we find specific reference to minority languages (regarding the translation of significant literary works into and from minority languages). In 1988, the Commission established the Committee on Cultural Affairs, to monitor the implementation of actions decided by the Council. The Commission also established a Commissioner for Cultural Affairs and a Department for Cultural Affairs; following the reorganisation of the Commission in 1999, cultural policy (including minority language policy) is now dealt with by the Education and Culture Directorate General. In its final communication on culture before the ratification of the TEU,[28] the Commission anticipated the effect of Article 151 EC, which commits the Community to contributing to 'the flowering of the cultures of the Member States', although it is arguable that the post-Maastricht cultural programmes are not really substantively different.

The current cultural framework (operative from 1 January 2000 to 31 December 2006) is contained in the Culture 2000 programme.[29] It was devised primarily to channel and co-ordinate the provision of finance for cultural projects and is largely a continuation of the Commission's long established blueprint. Minority languages do feature in the programme; for example, the sixth recital of the preamble provides that 'special attention should be devoted to safeguarding the position of Europe's small cultures and less widely-spoken languages'. Annex 1 ('Activities and Implementing Measures') establishes the types of project that can be supported by Culture 2000; section 1.2 lists subject areas that can form the basis of co-operation agreements, including 'projects aimed at the highlighting of *cultural diversity and of multilingualism*, promoting awareness of the history, roots, common cultural values of the European peoples and their common cultural heritage' (emphasis added). More specific guidelines on how multilingualism should feature in Community cultural policy can be found with respect to the book sector (see, for example, section 1(b) of Annex 2). Significantly, a separate funding programme for minority language projects had existed in addition to the possibilities available under Culture 2000 or any of its predecessors.[30] However, in light of an ECJ decision on Community expenditure more generally (discussed in more detail below), the reinstatement of this budget line has not yet been secured.

The 1996 Euromosaic Report, prepared by selected language centres on behalf of the Commission, should also be noted here.[31] It is one of the few empirical studies to examine the economic dimension of minority language issues in the EC and it concluded that diversity is a source of economic possibility rather than (as is typically assumed) a competitive hindrance. It also identified corollary responsibilities for the EC to take appropriate action in favour of minority language groups. And finally, in a joint EU/Council of Europe project, 2001 was designated European Year of Languages. The rationale behind the mission was presented as a celebration of diversity and multiculturalism, and its objectives were focused on the promotion of language education. Regional and minority languages were included in the scope of the project to a certain, though limited, extent.

From all of the above, it is clear that the Commission has been involved in minority language issues for some time now, as an element of its evolving work on cultural policy, and as an independent concern in terms of the provision of funds and the assignment of research. The Commission might thus be said to deal primarily with the practical—and especially financial—side of things, not necessarily focusing on speakers in terms of minority language rights. To ascertain whether this aspect is addressed at all at Community level, it is necessary now to turn to more 'indirect' minority language policy and to look at relevant Community case law. There are two key divisions in this context: first, case law juxtaposing market and linguistic values in a general sense and, second, cases involving *minority* language ideology specifically.

The use of language in EC institutions represents, in a sense, the primary manifestation of EC language policy. But the way in which language is relevant to almost all other Community spheres must be stressed. For example, freedom of movement for workers within the Community is guaranteed by the Treaty (Article 39 EC); but when someone moves to another Member State, they will probably cross language as well as geographical frontiers. The EC has addressed the linguistic dimension of free movement from two main perspectives. It supports a number of preparatory language education programmes but also tries to anticipate and deal with difficulties that might arise after resettlement in the new state (eg trying to facilitate the education of children of migrant workers in both their native language(s) and in the language(s) of the host state).

The Court of Justice has confirmed that a worker from another Member State may legitimately be subject to language policy requirements in the host state, so long as the basic principles governing free movement—non-discrimination and proportionality—are respected.[32] Conversely, language rights already granted by a Member State to its nationals must be extended to other Community nationals where appropriate.[33] As regards the right of establishment and freedom to provide services—ie Articles 43–48 and 49–55 EC respectively—the same general principle applies: Member States may impose linguistic competence conditions on the exercise of trades and professions but such requirements must apply equally to nationals and non-nationals alike; they must also comply with the principle of proportionality (ie the measures adopted by a Member State must be proportionate to the objectives of the language policy pursued).[34]

Concerning the free movement of goods, the key issue from the linguistic perspective is the regulation of product labelling—to avoid creating barriers to trade, but equally bearing in mind the principle of consumer protection and the right to information on the functions and properties of products on the EC market. The compromise reached legislatively and enforced traditionally by the Court of Justice demands that product labels be 'in a language easily understood' by the consumer, which may not necessarily equate to a Member State's official language(s).[35] This raises a difficult question of competing values, consumer protection 'versus' consumer choice, and their attempted balancing by the Community institutions. But what has never really been considered is the extent to which domestic language policy requirements might override the free movement of goods as an independent policy consideration, not just one enmeshed with the value of consumer protection.

This issue has been complicated still further by (political) developments. In 1997, what is now Article 16(2) of Directive 2000/13 was introduced, providing that:

> [w]ithin its own territory, the Member State in which the product is marketed may, in accordance with the rules of the Treaty, stipulate that those labelling particulars shall be given in one or more languages which it shall determine from among the official languages of the Community.

In reality, this will almost certainly amount to the imposition of each State's own official language(s), allowing for exclusive stipulation of a local language—which is precisely what was rejected judicially in the case law on a 'language easily understood'. Moreover, 'official' here relates to the Community context only—minority languages are thus excluded. It is probable that the Member States acting via the Council wished to codify a (not necessarily correct) presumption that a state's official language(s) will inevitably pass the 'easily understood' test. This could even be framed in cultural terms, reflecting a wish to preserve national diversity in the face of homogenising trade rules. But such a conception of 'diversity' stops firmly at national borders and progresses a version of things which, from the regional and/or minority perspective, is potentially damaging. This example introduces the limitations of regional influence at Community level, given that power lies effectively with the Member States—a point of considerable import for language policy and one raised again below.

Turning now to case law on minority languages more specifically, the circumstances of *Mutsch* related to linguistic arrangements in Belgium for a German-speaking municipality. In a brief but important statement, the Court declared that

> [i]n the context of a Community based on the principles of free movement of persons and freedom of establishment, the protection of the linguistic rights and privileges of individuals is of particular importance.[36]

The scope of the judgment in *Groener* is a bit more problematic. This case examined a precondition attached to certain teaching posts in Ireland, ie demonstration of competence in the Irish language (recognised constitutionally as the national and first official language of Ireland but a *de facto* minority language). It was noted above that linguistic competence requirements are permitted by Article 3(1) of Regulation 1612/68 and that such requirements may be imposed on nationals of other Member States so long as they are justified by reason of the nature of the post to be filled, applied in a non-discriminatory manner and proportionate to the linguistic aim to be achieved. But the Court in *Groener* seemed to rely heavily on the constitutional status of Irish when confirming that '[t]he EEC Treaty does not prohibit the adoption of a policy for the protection and promotion of a language of a Member State which is both the national language and first official language' (*Groener*: para 19). It was not altogether clear, then, whether a language requirement could be justified solely by recourse to minority rights ideology.

Recent ECJ jurisprudence reflects a more confident attitude towards the terminology and ethos of minority languages within the Court, however; and the interim evolution of the Community, both legally and politically, is surely significant here. In *Bickel and Franz*, the Court confirmed what it had implied in *Groener*—that protection of an 'ethno-cultural minority' was *prima facie* a legitimate policy aim, although it did not find that extending to the applicants in the present case the right to use German in the courts for criminal proceedings in Bolzano would undermine the achievement of that aim (*Bickel and Franz*: para 29). Once again, then, we find that a Member State enjoys discretion when determining its internal language policy, but only up to a point. Where relevant, language rights provided for domestically must be extended on a non-discriminatory basis to nationals of other EC Member States; furthermore, the overriding Community test of proportionality is material. What is now beyond question is that this reasoning applies equally for *minority* language rights.

Another feature of the decision in *Bickel and Franz* worth noting here is its manifestation of a truly 'European' citizenship, in that German-speakers—persons residing typically in Bolzano and the two applicants in the case (from Austria and Germany respectively)—were treated similarly and thus formed something of a transnational grouping, quite apart from Italian citizens residing outwith Bolzano. The converse of this, however, is that language arrangements made for a particular geographical area—with the incentive of preserving regional cultural autonomy—were effectively overridden by the Court of Justice. This highlights the anomaly in the constitutional structure of the Community legal order introduced briefly above—on the one hand, EC law has obvious and concrete implications at the regional as well as national level, yet the channels through which subnational authorities may participate in EC policy and decision-making are actually shaped by domestic constitutional structures.

To summarise, it is clear that responsibility for the substantive implementation of minority language rights is considered still to reside at Member State level, at least in the first instance. But equally, the ECJ will review national practices where the principles of free movement have been activated. In a basic sense, the Court will assess a Member State's language policy against the Community benchmarks of non-discrimination and proportionality; this is nothing new, long established since the decisions in *Mutsch* and *Groener*. But there is also an emerging approach less discernible in the early decisions, in that the Court seems more willing now to examine the substantive issues raised—still from an EC perspective on free movement but one which is fused more openly with consideration of minority language rights. To date, the results of this interpretative method have benefited the individuals concerned and have, as a result, promoted the use of the minority languages in question. But it is an underdeveloped interpretative process; and the feeling persists that the results were achieved as much by market-compatibility accident as by language-friendly design. The Court floundered considerably when asked to consider the nature of 'culture' in *Parliament v Council*, for example, discussed below in the context of the cultural policy integration clause.[37]

And so, EC action in respect of minority languages is varied in both scope and effect, and not always readily visible as a coherent policy ambition. Whether initiatives developed by the institutions should be gathered together more rationally, to set down an explicit minority language policy, is obviously something to be considered; this is an exercise performed most recently for 'general' human rights protection via the proclamation of the EU Charter. Equally valid is the question of whether and how Community minority language policy might be developed still further, beyond the boundaries reached to date. Traces of the philosophy of linguistic diversity and the worth of language rights do permeate the substance—and results—of the programmes and judgments outlined above; but the absence of an articulated (constitutional) source for minority language policy and of principled linkages between its various threads greatly inhibit the scope of what could be achieved. This means, then, that 'Community' cultural principles and co-ordinated linguistic standards—which should be clearly discernible and relevant across the spectrum of EC law—are, at best, embryonic. This holds true in respect of both 'direct' (eg cultural policy programmes) and 'indirect' (looking to the application of internal market law in cases with a minority language dimension) EC action.

The potential of the cultural policy integration clause—Article 151(4) EC—should be examined in more detail at this point. It has been in existence for more than a decade now; has it had any effect? The provision stipulates that the Community *and* the Member States are required to take cultural aspects into account in their action under other Treaty provisions. Moreover, an amendment secured via the Amsterdam Treaty effected the insertion here of an express guarantee of respect for cultural pluralism ('in particular in order to respect and to promote the diversity of its cultures'). Could this be a substitute for the type of constitutional underpinning found wanting above? In other words, instead of building a more direct minority language policy on a constitutional foundation, should we focus instead on ensuring minority language sensitivity across the board?

Article 151(4) is, in essence, a political tool, relevant at the conception and implementation of EC legislative action. But ultimately, the Court of Justice will regulate the extent to which more general requirements of Community law can be limited by its application. And here, the absence of a more coherent constitutional understanding of language interests is still likely to prove prejudicial because the Court's thinking on language policy to date is inconsistent, to say the least. Its decisions on the free movement of goods and persons are often disjointed, but its struggle with Article 151(4) and the scope of 'culture' more generally in *Parliament v Council* is especially instructive, if unsettling.[38] The European Parliament was seeking to have a Council decision annulled on the grounds that Article 151 should have been (co)specified as its legal basis; the decision provided for a multiannual programme to promote the linguistic diversity of the Community in the information society, aimed particularly at the needs of small and medium-sized enterprises facing different language markets.[39] The Commission had identified Article 157(3) EC as the legal basis for the measure. When Parliament was consulted by the Council, as required by Article 157(3), it proposed a number of amendments that enhanced the cultural and linguistic aspects of the programme, including that of dual legal basis. The Council did not amend the measure prior to its adoption, leading to Parliament's action for annulment under Article 230 EC. Essentially, the question to be decided was whether the main aim of the programme was the promotion of cultural and linguistic diversity—thereby going beyond cultural 'aspects' per Article 151(4) and triggering the application of Article 151(2) as an additional legal basis—or whether the programme was founded on primarily economic and industrial objectives; in this latter case, as argued by the Commission, there would be cultural and linguistic 'spin-offs' but this would not require Article 151(2) to be employed.

The Court first stated that the objectives of the measure could not be determined solely by reference to the wording of its title; rather, it would consider 'whether, according to its aim and content, as they appear from its actual wording, the contested decision is concerned, *indissociably*, both with industry and culture'.[40] The Court went on to distinguish between the 'essential' and 'incidental' components of a measure, asserting that this approach captured the *raison d'être* of Article 151(4) EC.[41] This is completely sensible. But in going on to find that the cultural aspects of the contested measure *were* incidental, affirming that the Council was right to take the cultural dimension into account under Article 151(4) only, the Court wavered between pragmatism and a potentially restrictive understanding of culture. In particular, it considered that the 'marginalisation of languages that remain excluded from the information society' was not a 'risk of a specifically cultural nature', designating the programme more as 'an object or instrument of economic activity'.[42] Thus, on fairly pallid reasoning, the judgment boiled down to an assessment of intention and emphasis. This is an inevitably subjective exercise—Parliament had argued that the contested decision was intended to safeguard linguistic diversity, the Council and Commission disagreed.

Both the Court and the Advocate General were careful, however, to point to the value of the Article 151(4) mechanism; Advocate General La Pergola considered that '[it] shows that culture is regarded, in the Treaty, as a ..."transversal" value, which potentially touches upon every sector of activity in the Community'.[43] Moreover, the Commission has asserted that Article 151(4) has been taken on board to some extent.[44] Yet the danger that the institutions might sidestep a policy integration clause remains a very real one. How can the cultural aspects of each and every proposed Community measure be assessed in reality? And, without actions such as that initiated in *Parliament v Council*, how can the potentially countless evaluations of the legislative institutions be appraised?

The input of both the Committee of the Regions and the European Parliament, as conceived in Article 151(5) EC, could be valuable here. It might even be viable to establish a body of some sort—involving either the Committee or Parliament, or both—to examine proposed legislation from the cultural perspective. Such a body would be prescriptively attuned to cultural interests and might thus identify potential concerns more readily, securing an operative rather than token execution of the provision. The assignment of a policy integration clause to Article 151 is certainly to be welcomed; as with any such clause, however, its true value comes to be realised more through implementation than ratification. Even so, it is not enough to make up for the constitutional wound inflicted in *Kik*: aside from difficulties identified above, it can, by definition, apply only in respect of 'cultural' aspects of language policy. And so, all of this recalls the need to think seriously about what can actually be expected from the EC outwith the realm of trade.

## FRAMING THE GAP: LAW AND EXPECTATIONS

The basic qualification put forward at the outset now emerges more substantively: the range of EC possibilities in respect of minority languages might well go beyond what is currently in place but, nonetheless, must be tempered by an understanding of the EC legal milieu. Even if a solid foundation for EC minority language policy existed, just what exactly should the Community strive to require and accomplish? Furthermore, a distinct gap has emerged between what the EC has achieved, or could (legally) achieve, and what minority language speakers expect from it. Despite the realisation of minority language rights in many EC Member States and despite the enunciation of standards by international organisations like the Council of

Europe, there remains a clear trend among minority language groups to call for the EC to progress minority language preservation and promotion more proactively. In reality, what is probably hoped is that the EC might somehow secure greater and stronger status for minority language rights 'at home'—*within* the Member States—where the implementation of policy has a more immediate and continuous effect.

As outlined above, the EC institutions have been dealing with minority language issues for some time now, both as a secondary dimension of other Treaty topics and, although less so, as an independent policy concern. Looking in particular at the activities of the Commission, what emerges most strongly is a commitment to the co-ordination and provision of funding for minority language projects with a transnational dimension. It would not simply be 'nice' if this work was consolidated and developed; it is a responsibility. The extent to which language shift throughout the Member States is affected by the dynamics of European integration is often overlooked. Even at a purely economic level, creating and maintaining the internal market has resulted in the distortion of linguistic environments. The relative utility of many languages has been diminished by the spread of the languages of wider (market) communication. Acting individually, the Member States cannot address these influences effectively; and the lack of concern displayed by most of them in *Kik* doesn't bode well. A co-ordinated understanding of cultural and linguistic diversity is lacking within Community law; this must be redressed, yet the power so to do lies primarily, if somewhat ironically, with the Member States.

In the longer term, this hinges on the capacity of the Member States as masters of the Treaty, since they retain the power to set the priorities of the Community. But linguistic and cultural concerns were not high on the agenda at the Convention on the Future of Europe. Even though the constitutional dimension of EC language policy has been argued here to be lacking, it is simply a fact that the political will to take language policy on board, in whatever guise, is just not there. Indirect attempts to cleave open a judicial path have generated inconsistent results, contrasting *Kik*, for example, with *Bickel and Franz*.

Without a more empowering Treaty amendment, and so working with what we have, can the Community go any further and devise a minority language policy that would be more meaningful at state (and regional) level? The most basic starting point here is that the institutions can act only where a legal basis can be derived from a provision or provisions of the EC Treaty. This principle is codified in Article 5 EC, the first line of which provides that '[t]he Community shall act within the limits of the powers conferred on it by this Treaty and of the objectives assigned to it therein'. The principle of non-interference by the EC in the internal affairs of its Member States (ie in areas not covered by the Treaty) is the converse expression of this idea.

The EC may seem at times to have a law-making mind of its own, given the strident power of the integrative engine; but the *Tobacco Advertising* judgment illustrates a judicial rap on EC legislative knuckles when the legislative institutions are felt to be overstepping Treaty boundaries.[45] The division of EC/Member State competence is especially problematic in areas of shared or complementary competence. Article 151 EC on cultural policy is an example of the latter. Few would argue against the bulk of action in the cultural domain being taken by the Member States, acting largely autonomously. But a Community 'contribution' to the 'flowering' of cultures has also been set down in the Treaty. Which level of governance should act, then, when both have *some* power to do so? The resulting uncertainty takes on heightened significance for present purposes, given that cultural policy—even more than education, fundamental rights and EU citizenship—is probably, strategically, the best locus for the development of EC minority language policy.

As a practical tool for determining *capacity* to act when more than one level of authority has the *competence* to act, the principle of subsidiarity should be mentioned. The second paragraph of Article 5 EC provides that:

> [i]n areas which do not fall within its exclusive competence, the Community shall take action, in accordance with the principle of subsidiarity, only if and in so far as the objectives of the proposed action cannot be sufficiently achieved by the Member States and can, therefore, by reason of the scale or effects of the proposed action, be better achieved by the Community.

Guidelines on the application of these criteria are contained in the EC Treaty Protocol on the Application of the Principles of Subsidiarity and Proportionality. But there remains a difficulty in practice when quantifying tests like 'sufficiently achieved' and 'scale or effects', calling for political rather than legal judgment. Subsidiarity can curb the law-making capacity of the EC and infer that action is best taken at a 'lower' level of governance. Equally, however, where the tests set out in Article 5 EC can be satisfied, the Community is not only permitted but required to act; and how this pans out for any given situation can only be determined on an individual basis for each proposed Community measure. The delimitation of competence between the EC and its Member States is therefore, at best, complex; and it is a question that can only be touched upon superficially here. The scrutiny of proposed legislation for compliance with subsidiarity was a key topic at the Convention. And it is a debate worth tracking, given that it is likely to affect fundamentally the development of EC cultural, and thus minority language, policy in the future.

Looking to more immediate possibilities, then, two ways in which the Community can exercise competence in the minority language domain have been identified: action at EC level *per se* and, more tentatively, action as a co-ordinator of Member State policy. Looking first to direct action, there are persuasive ideological arguments for the inclusion of (some) minority languages in (some) official EC language arrangements. In this vein, the seeping inclusion of Irish provides a possible model. But it would not be a particularly wise or sustainable move in terms either of efficiency or of tangible benefit for the speakers concerned. The creaking EC language policy has, on balance, more immediate and urgent concerns: cutting translation delays in the interests of access to justice and coping with EU enlargement being the most acute. This does not mean that minority languages and their speakers should be excluded from EC responsibility; but it does suggest that typically 'domestic' solutions do not bring, indeed cannot bring, the same benefits at the supranational level.

The EC institutions have for some time provided funding for minority language projects; the continuation, consolidation and expansion of this activity is imperative. At present, systematic funding has been suspended for reasons related to legal basis; yet there is no (legal) reason why Article 151 EC cannot be employed here and it is *this* course of action that demands most immediately to be pursued. Budget line B3-1006 was established in 1982 as a direct consequence of the first Arfé Resolution. But it was not authorised by a legislative act and it is difficult to suggest a Treaty provision that the Commission could have used at that time. Here, we see political goodwill notwithstanding the absence of legal grounding. But the security of the arrangement was never taken for granted; the reduction of the budget line for the first time in 1997 highlighted its precarious foundations. The fatal strike against its continued existence was brought about by the ECJ in a case entirely unrelated to language issues, where the Court held that every 'significant' EC expenditure must be grounded in the prior adoption of a legislative act.[46] As a direct consequence of that judgment, minority language funding is now provided on an *ad hoc* basis only—presumably, on the logic that such amounts could not be classed as 'significant'.

Returning this practice to a more secure footing is one of the key priorities of minority language lobbying groups and it was generally assumed to be forthcoming (eg Fronia, 1999: 69–74). But the long-mooted multiannual programme has not yet materialised, and EC funding (for EBLUL, for example) still hangs on a discretionary basis. It had been anticipated that a programme would be presented by the Commission in late 1999; the apparent reason behind the ongoing delay is that the Commission's legal services advised that any such programme must be enacted under Article 151 as well as Article 149 EC (education).[47] The significance of this is that Article 151 requires unanimity of the Member States in decision-making, whereas Article 149 is administered via qualified majority voting. And here lies the irony—now, there is no legal reason why Article 151 EC cannot be deployed; but political unanimity has yet to be achieved. One option—proposed though rejected at Nice, but now back on the agenda following the publication and signing of the still contested Treaty establishing a Constitution for Europe[48]—might be to lobby for the removal of the unanimity requirement in Article 151 EC. The watery focus on co-ordination and express exclusion of harmonisation in that provision might well provide sufficient safeguards. But such a tactic should not be entered into lightly, since it removes each Member State's cultural veto. The unanimity requirement can constitute a protection mechanism for (typically smaller) Member States having special needs in the cultural and linguistic sectors that might otherwise prove vulnerable. It also embalms measures enacted with some political security. An alternative way forward would be to drive home the fact that a dedicated budget line is not, actually, anything new—just a reinstatement of what had quietly existed for over two decades. Ironically, Greece is often seen as a stumbling block here; but surely its diversity-laden submissions in *Kik* generate a degree of political bargaining capital?[49]

Granting financial support, while crucially important, is obviously not sufficient in terms of devising and implementing a successfully holistic language policy. In tandem with this, the Community institutions need urgently to contemplate and effect a more coherent understanding of linguistic and cultural diversity, and to apply this more systematically when the more established economic values of the internal market clash with very real cultural ones. This should not be taken to the extreme of unpicking the internal market; but there must be some room in the scheme of harmonisation, free movement and mutual recognition for values than cannot—and should not—be transcended by a raw efficiency of trade.

Limitations on competence feature more acutely still in respect of the EC as a co-ordinator and supervisor of Member State powers. In any event, this is not necessarily a legitimate objective for the Community to pursue. It is no longer, if it ever was, an organisation concerned solely with economic policy. That is not the decisive point here. What asks again to be recalled is the harder question of power-sharing. The often brittle relationship between the Member States and the Community is characterised by insecurity; Member States baulk at the implications of EC action in many shared or concurrent policy zones, notwithstanding the fact that they themselves have caused Community competence to be incorporated into the Treaty in the first place. But, applying *both* a legal and a political lens, there is simply little evidence to suggest support for a more invasive EC approach to minority language policy just yet.

## CONCLUSION: BRIDGING THE GAP?

Realisation of minority language rights is rooted in considerations of equality and non-discrimination, of effective participation and cultural democracy. This holds true at both national and international levels, and it thus applies equally to the Community. But while there are (rectifiable) shortcomings in the fulfilment of EC minority language support to date, claims for 'more' must always be mitigated by remembering both the purpose and legal limitations of supranational government. A blunting mismatch of political and legal priorities has been evident throughout this chapter; it is truly rare to find a proactive coincidence of ambition and capacity from both of these perspectives. There are serious EC language policy defects needing urgent attention, of which a more effective minority language policy is just one. But political energy seems to be channelled excessively into either avoiding tough issues or chasing legal chimeras. Appropriate legal bases are available for appropriate EC action; but political will needs reorienting if real change is to be achieved. Perhaps we have to be both more forceful and more humble in our expectations here; but we are equally entitled to be more demanding.

## Appendix: EC Treaty Provisions relevant to (Minority) Language Policy

*Article 21*

…

Every citizen of the Union may write to any of the institutions or bodies referred to in this Article or in Article 7 in one of the languages mentioned in Article 314 and have an answer in the same language.

*Article 149*

1. The Community shall contribute to the development of quality education by encouraging cooperation between Member States and, if necessary, by supporting and supplementing their action while fully respecting the responsibility of the Member States for the content of teaching and the organisation of education systems and their cultural and linguistic diversity.

2. Community action shall be aimed at:

– developing the European dimension in education, particularly through the teaching and dissemination of the languages of the Member States …

*Article 151*

1. The Community shall contribute to the flowering of the cultures of the Member States, while respecting their national and regional diversity and at the same time bringing the common cultural heritage to the fore.

2. Action by the Community shall be aimed at encouraging cooperation between Member States and, if necessary, supporting and supplementing their action in the following areas:

– improvement of the knowledge and dissemination of the culture and history of the European peoples;

– conservation and safeguarding of cultural heritage of European significance;

– non-commercial cultural exchanges;

– artistic and literary creation, including in the audiovisual sector.

3. The Community and the Member States shall foster cooperation with third countries and the competent international organisations in the sphere of culture, in particular the Council of Europe.

4. The Community shall take cultural aspects into account in its action under other provisions of this Treaty, in particular in order to respect and to promote the diversity of its cultures.

5. In order to contribute to the achievement of the objectives referred to in this Article, the Council:

– acting in accordance with the procedure referred to in Article 251 and after consulting the Committee of the Regions, shall adopt incentive measures, excluding any harmonisation of the laws and regulations of the Member States. The Council shall act unanimously throughout the procedure referred to in Article 251;

– acting unanimously on a proposal from the Commission, shall adopt recommendations.

*Article 290*

The rules governing the languages of the institutions of the Community shall, without prejudice to the provisions contained in the Statute of the Court of Justice, be determined by the Council, acting unanimously.

*Article 314*

This Treaty, drawn up in a single original in the Dutch, French, German, and Italian languages, all four texts being equally authentic, shall be deposited in the archives of the Government of the Italian Republic, which shall transmit a certified copy to each of the Governments of the other signatory States.

Pursuant to the Accession Treaties, the Danish, English, Finnish, Greek, Irish, Portuguese, Spanish and Swedish versions of this Treaty shall also be authentic.

## Notes

1 From 1 January 2007, Irish will also be an official language, bringing the total to 21. This will, however, be a limited official status than that of the other 20 EU languages: See Council Regulation 920/2005/EC of 13 June 2005, OJ 2005 L156/3.

2 A critical example here is that the twenty language versions of all EC legislation are equally (legally) authentic; this contrasts with the rule that judgments of the Court of Justice are legally authoritative in the language of the case only (see Nic Shuibhne, 2002: 12–21).

[3] Regulation 1/58, OJ 1952–58 Eng Sp Ed 59 (see Nic Shuibhne, 2002: 8–12).

[4] Case T-120/99 *Kik v Office for Harmonisation in the Internal Market (Trade Marks and Designs) (OHIM)* [2001] ECR II-2235.

[5] Case C-361/01P *Estate of Christina Kik deceased v OHIM*, judgment of 9 September 2003, [2003] ECR I–8283.

[6] Case T-107/94 *Kik v Council and Commission* [1995] ECR II-1717; upheld by the ECJ on appeal (Case C-270/95P, [1996] ECR I-1987); these challenges failed on admissibility grounds in respect of the standing of individual applicants in cases of judicial review (see Article 230 EC) and so arguments on the substantive (language) elements were not considered by either Court.

[7] For more detail on the OHIM language rules, see Regulation 40/94, OJ 1994 L11/1.

[8] *Kik* (Case T-120/99), para 39.

[9] *Ibid*, para 42.

[10] *Ibid*, para 45.

[11] *Ibid*, para 51.

[12] *Ibid*, para 52.

[13] *Ibid*, paras 53–54.

[14] *Ibid*, para 58.

[15] *Ibid*, para 63.

[16] The Court of Justice, in particular, has frequently divined general principles of law by piecing together a patchwork of even marginally relevant Treaty provisions, perhaps the classic example being its 'creation' of the primacy of EC law (see Case 26/62 *Van Gend en Loos v Nederlandse Administratie der Belastingen* [1963] ECR 1 and Case 6/64 *Costa v ENEL* [1964] ECR 585); see Usher (1998).

[17] See in particular Case 379/87 *Groener v Minister for Education and the Dublin Vocational Education Committee* [1989] ECR 3967; Case C-274/96 *Criminal Proceedings against Bickel and Franz* [1998] ECR I-7637; and Case C-281/98 *Angonese v Cassa di Risparmio di Bolzano* [2000] ECR I-4139.

[18] *Kik* (Case T-120/99), para 50.

[19] See, for example, *Kik* (Case C-361/01 P), Opinion of Advocate General Jacobs, especially paras 57 *et seq*.

[20] See, for example, Article 6(3) TEU, which states simply that '[t]he Union shall respect the national identities of its Member States'. The contribution to this volume by Miquel Strubell i Trueta explores comprehensively the 'language of language' in official EC documentation.

[21] On the Court of Justice specifically, see Articles 29–31 of the ECJ Rules of Procedure, OJ 2003 C193/1, as amended; see also Articles 35–36 of the CFI Rules of Procedure, OJ 2003 C-193/2, as amended. More generally, however, and since the time of writing, see Council Conclusion of 13 June 2005 on the official use of additional languages within the Council and possibly other institutions and bodies of the European Union, OJ 2005 C148/1.

[22] Arfé Resolution (1981) on a Community Charter of Regional Languages and Cultures and on a Charter of Rights of Ethnic Minorities, OJ 1981 C287/106; Arfé Resolution (2) (1983) on Measures in favour of Minority Languages and Cultures, OJ 1983 C68/103; and Kuijpers Resolution (1987) on the Languages and Cultures of Regional and Ethnic Minorities in the European Community, Doc A 2-150/87.

[23] Istituto della Enciclopedia Italiana (1986).

[24] Killilea Resolution on Linguistic and Cultural Minorities in the European Community (1994), OJ 1994 C61/110.

[25] OJ 2002 C177 E/334.

[26] See, for example, *Community Action in the Cultural Sector*, EC Bulletin Supp 6/77 and *Stronger Community Action in the Cultural Sector*, EC Bulletin Supp 6/82.

[27] EC Bulletin Supp 4/87.

[28] *New Prospects for Community Cultural Action*, COM(92) [1992].

[29] See Decision No 508/2000/EC of the European Parliament and Council, OJ 2000 L063/1. See, for the future, the Commission's 'Culture 2007' proposal, SEC (2004)954. (This proposal is still going through the Community co-decision legislative procedure at the time of writing.)

[30] See, for example, the *Kaleidoscope* (Decision No 719/96/EC, OJ 1996 L99/20), *Ariane* (Decision No 2085/97/EC, OJ 1997 L291/26) and *Raphael* (Decision No 2228/97/EC, OJ

1997 L305/31) programmes, on cultural co-operation in the arts, literature and cultural heritage fields respectively.

31 European Commission (1996).

32 The basic rules on language competence requirements are contained in Article 3(1) of Regulation 1612/68 (OJ 1968 Sp Ed L257/2, p 475), as developed by the Court of Justice in Case 379/87 *Groener v Minister for Education and the Dublin Vocational Education Committee* [1989] ECR 3967 and Case C-281/98 *Angonese v Cassa di Risparmio di Bolzano* [2000] ECR I-4139.

33 See in particular, Case 137/84 *Ministère Public v Mutsch* [1985] ECR 2681 and Case C-274/96 *Criminal Proceedings against Bickel and Franz* [1998] ECR I-7637.

34 See, again, *Bickel and Franz*, on services; on establishment, see Case C-424/97 *Haim v Kassenzahnärztliche Vereinigung Nordrhein* [2000] ECR I-5123.

35 See principally Directive 2000/13, OJ 2000 L109/29 (consolidating in a single text the now redundant Directive 79/112, OJ 1979 L33/1) and eg Case C-33/97 *Colim v Bigg's* [1999] ECR I-3975.

36 *Mutsch*, para 11; a more overt, although inconclusive, discussion of *minority* language rights can be found in the Opinion of Advocate General Lenz; see especially pp 2688–90.

37 Case C-42/97 *European Parliament v Council of the European Union* [1999] ECR I-869; and see Article 151(4) EC.

38 Case C-42/97 *European Parliament v Council of the European Union* [1999] ECR I-869.

39 OJ 1996 L306/40; see especially Articles 1(1) and 2(1), and Annex I.

40 *Parliament v Council*, paras 37–38 (emphasis added), referring to Case C-300/89 *Commission v Council* [1991] ECR I-2867.

41 *Ibid*, paras 39–42.

42 *Ibid*, paras 52–53; the phrase at issue here is contained in the twelfth recital of the preamble to the Council Decision: 'languages that remain excluded from the information society would run the risk of a more or less rapid marginalisation'.

43 *Parliament v Council*, Opinion of Advocate General La Pergola, para 7.

44 1996 (COM) 160 Final.

45 Case C-376/98 *Germany v European Parliament and Council* [2000] ECR I-8419.

46 Case C-106/96 *United Kingdom and others v Commission* [1998] ECR I-2729; see, in particular, para 26.

47 See (2000) vol 16:2 *Contact Bulletin* 1.

48 See the Progress report on IGC 2000 prepared for the Feira European Council (CONFER 4750/00, Brussels, 14 June 2000), Annex 3.1, p 74; and more recently, see OJ 2003 C169/1.

49 France is also considered to be problematically unilingual. There had been considerable optimism among minority language groups when France signed the Charter for Regional or Minority Languages on 7 May 1999, given staunch resistance to the promotion of linguistic diversity encountered traditionally. These hopes were thwarted, however, by a decision of the Constitutional Council declaring that ratification of the Charter would contravene Article 2 of the French Constitution, which states simply that '[t]he language of the Republic is French'. As with Greece, however, these events could provide a basis for some successful political bargaining in the EC context.

## References

de Witte, B (2004) 'Language Law of the European Union: Protecting or Eroding Linguistic Diversity?' in R Craufurd Smith (ed), *EU Law and Cultural Policy* (Oxford, Oxford University Press).

European Commission (1996) *Euromosaic: The Production and Reproduction of the Minority Language Groups in the European Union* (Luxembourg, Office for Official Publications of the European Communities).

Fronia, J (1999) 'The Future Role of the European Commission in Respect of Lesser Used Languages' in Comhdháil Náisiúnta na Gaeilge, *International Conference on Language Legislation: Conference Proceedings* (Dublin, Comhdháil Náisiúnta na Gaeilge), 69–74.

Istituto della Enciclopedia Italiana (1986) *Linguistic Minorities in Countries belonging to the EC* (Luxembourg, Office for Official Publications of the European Communities).

Nic Shuibhne, N (2002) *EC Law and Minority Language Policy: Culture, Citizenship and Fundamental Rights* (The Hague, Kluwer).

Nic Shuibhne, N (2004) 'Labels, Locals and the Free Movement of Goods' in R Craufurd Smith (ed), *EU Law and Cultural Policy* (Oxford, Oxford University Press).

Usher, JA (1998) *General Principles of EC Law* (London, Longman).

**Table of Cases (numerical)**

*ECJ*

Case 26/62 *van Gend en Loos v Nederlandse Administratie der Belastingen* [1963] ECR 1

Case 6/64 *Costa v ENEL* [1964] ECR 585

Case 137/84 *Ministère Public v Mutsch* [1985] ECR 2681

Case 379/87 *Groener v Minister for Education and the Dublin Vocational Education Committee* [1989] ECR 3967

Case C-300/89 *Commission v Council* [1991] ECR I-2867

Case C-270/95P *Kik v Council and Commission* [1996] ECR I-1987

Case C-106/96 *United Kingdom and others v Commission* [1998] ECR I-2729

Case C-274/96 *Criminal Proceedings against Bickel and Franz* [1998] ECR I-7637

Case C-33/97 *Colim v Bigg's* [1999] ECR I-3975

Case C-42/97 *European Parliament v Council of the European Union* [1999] ECR I-869

Case C-424/97 *Haim v Kassenzahnärztliche Vereinigung Nordrhein* [2000] ECR I-5123

Case C-281/98 *Angonese v Cassa di Risparmio di Bolzano* [2000] ECR I-4139

Case C-376/98 *Germany v European Parliament and Council* [2000] ECR I-8419

Case C-361/01P *Estate of Christina Kik deceased v OHIM*, [2003] ECR I-8283.

*CFI*

Case T-107/94 *Kik v Council and Commission* [1995] ECR II-1717

Case T-120/99 *Kik v Office for Harmonisation in the Internal Market (Trade Marks and Designs) (OHIM)* [2001] ECR II-2235

**Table of Legislation**

Directive 79/112, OJ 1979 L33/1

Directive 2000/13, OJ 2000 L109/29

Regulation 1/58, OJ 1952-1958 Eng Sp Ed 59

Regulation 40/94, OJ 1994 L11/1

# 8

# *The Political Discourse on Multilingualism in the European Union*

MIQUEL STRUBELL

EUROPE IS NOT one of the most linguistically diverse of continents. Africa and Asia, in particular, have far greater numbers of languages. What makes Europe unique, perhaps, is the large number of languages that have for centuries been standardised, and have acted as vehicles for a written literary tradition. To put it another way, Europe was the first large region in the world where language played an important role in nation state building (see Wright, 2000). Each European state has, in the main, granted a dominant status to a single, 'national' language, and has reinforced its position in society by a wide variety of measures which in essence makes its use by the citizen indispensable.

This is no banal issue. Languages have in the past been used virtually as weapons. Social attitudes towards immigrants and stateless nations, or autochthonous linguistic minorities, have on occasion been remarkably similar. Here are two examples.

> A law-abiding, thrifty and industrious race (the Scots) is being supplanted by immigrants whose presence tends to lower the social conditions, and to undermine that spirit of independence which has so long been a characteristic of the Scottish people.[1]

For their part, the Scottish highlanders were on the receiving end, alongside Bretons, Basques and Welshmen, when they were likened to 'half savage relics':

> Experience proves that it is possible for one nationality to merge and be absorbed by another; and when it was originally an inferior and more backward portion of the human race, the absorption is greatly to its advantage. Nobody can suppose

> it is not more beneficial to a Breton, or a Basque of the French Navarre, to be brought into the current of the ideas and feelings of a highly civilised and cultivated people—to be members of the French nationality ... than to sulk on its own rocks, the half savage relic of past times, revolving in his own little mental orbit, without participation or interest in the movement of the world. The same remark applies to the Welshman or the Scottish Highlanders, as members of the British nation.[2]

These extracts are a good example of a pecking order: the Scots complain about their Irish immigrants, while the English complain about the 'half savage' Scottish highlanders.

The symbolic and real importance attached to languages in each European country meant that language would naturally play an important role when it came to embarking upon the process of European integration, first through the Council of Europe, and also through the European Economic Community, the European Community and, later, the European Union. Language is not merely a means of identity and identification in social terms: it is the means of communication *par excellence*. Linguistic homogeneity could not therefore be the basis for European integration. As Sue Wright has pointed out (2000: 119):

> The European Union does not replicate the nation state in all domains and in particular there has been no suggestion that there should be the linguistic and cultural homogeneity that was encouraged within or imposed on the nation state. Indeed European Union policy is the very reverse, seeking as it does to promote cultural diversity and linguistic pluralism.

Wright draws attention to the paradoxical fact that 'in much of the writing on European integration the question of language is simply not raised'. Indeed, 'there seems to be a conspiracy of silence on the matter, although it is clearly highly significant in such a plurilingual setting where problems of communication impact on every stage of the process' (Wright, 2000: 120). She speculates (at 121) that 'perhaps the question of language is omitted from the debate because it is too sensitive a question to be aired in the present phase of integration'. I have heard such an opinion expressed on various occasions, in relation, for instance, to the Council itself. Most of the official and working documents that deal with the issue limit themselves to dealing with the technical aspects of increasing the services required to cater for an increasing number of official and working languages. Wright believes that 'discussion would be possibly counter productive for integration and this would account for integrationists' reluctance to address the problem of plurilingualism honestly' (at 121).

Moreover, even where language issues are voiced, the level of debate is fairly superficial. Not all attempts have gone to the depth of several international seminars, and proponents of English as a solution are highly critical, as befits them, of multilingual formulae:

> The language policy in the European Union is both ineffective and hypocritical, and its ideas of linguistic equality and multilingualism are costly and cumbersome illusions. Why have these illusions been kept up for so long? First, because the French ... cannot accept the decline of their own linguistic power. Second, because the politically correct ideologies of some sociolinguists constantly fuel opposition against the idea of English as a European lingua franca. And third, because powerful translators' lobbies fight for their raison d'être.[3]

Nevertheless, the European Union does function, and it is the purpose of this paper to try to delve into the language debate as seen by the Union's institutions. In doing so, a number of key concepts will repeatedly emerge, and it will hopefully become clear that they are used at best with variable meanings and intentions, and at worst as mere rhetorical devices which allow the key issues to avoid being centrally addressed.

I shall firstly discuss the concept (and even 'principle') of 'linguistic diversity', as it is used in a range of EU documents. As we shall see, the verbs variously attached to the concept in these texts reveal highly divergent approaches to the issue, each of which implies a different degree of commitment, and need for action, on the part of the Union.

Following these fairly conceptual considerations, we shall move into three areas of what can be regarded as 'language policy'. To start with, the second section of the paper is devoted to the use of languages by the Union itself, as an organisation. This will entail a discussion of what the relevant Regulation refers to as the 'official and working languages of the Institutions of the Community'. We shall review the move from the highly specific 1958 terminology to a wide variety of similar terms, the implications of which have, to my mind, surpassed the intention of the original Regulation.

The third section looks at another area of policy: the actions and programmes of the Union to influence the language competence and availability, with regard to citizens and to services being offered to them. The title of this section is 'language learning and multilingualism'. Following this comes a section on an issue close to the heart of Catalans (among many others): the position of the institutions of the Union regarding languages other than the official and working languages of the Union. This is where the differences between the Council (that is, the governments of the Member States), the Commission and the Parliament are greatest, and where to my mind the Union's language policies are most at fault. Finally, in the conclusion, a plea is made for an end to linguistic exclusion in EU policies and practice.

## LINGUISTIC DIVERSITY

We find references to diversity of various kinds in a number of important instruments. I have chosen three, at different legal levels. Firstly, a document with no legal status as such, which is an institutional statement of the position of the Member States and also of the Parliament: the Charter of Fundamental Rights. I am starting with this text because it turned out to be one of the starting points for the future Constitution. Article 22 of the Charter, which comes under Chapter 3 (on Equality), refers to three kinds of diversity:

> Article II-22 Cultural, religious and linguistic diversity
> The Union shall respect cultural, religious and linguistic diversity.

This precise text, as Article II-82, appears in the "Treaty establishing a Constitution for Europe"[4], which has not yet come into force. Respect for cultural and linguistic diversity is also laid down in Article I-3(3) of the same Treaty: "[The Union] shall respect its rich cultural and linguistic diversity, and shall ensure that Europe's cultural heritage is safeguarded and enhanced."

The European Bureau for Lesser-Used Languages (EBLUL) had made a call for a reference to cultural and linguistic diversity to be included in the draft of the text of the Charter. It appears that it was at the last moment that a reference to religious diversity was added.

Let us retain the statement that diversity has to be respected, and also the interesting fact that this obligation upon the Union appears in a declaration of citizens' rights and also in the Constitution.

The second document is indeed the most significant existing legal text of the Union, ranking in status with the treaties of Accession: the Treaty of Amsterdam. Similar mandates are fixed in the Treaty of Amsterdam, signed in October 1997. Article 149 (ex-126) is one of the few articles that refers to cultural diversity. Paragraph 1 states that:

> The Community shall contribute to the development of quality education by encouraging cooperation between Member States and, if necessary, by supporting and supplementing their action, while fully respecting the responsibility of the Member States for the content of teaching and the organisation of education systems and their cultural and linguistic diversity.

A second reference appears, two articles later. In the article laying down the powers of the European Community in the field of culture, we read (Article 151, para 1):

> The Community shall contribute to the flowering of the cultures of the Member States, while respecting their national and regional diversity and at the same time bringing the common cultural heritage to the fore.

The third and final document I shall draw upon for a reference to diversity is a policy document, defining a particular Community action, which lasted one year: the Decision 1934/2000 on the European Year of Languages 2001. Diversity is also referred to in the Union's programmes, though in a different sense. Let us quote Recital 5 of the Decision establishing 2001 as the European Year of Languages[5]:

> The languages question is a challenge that must be tackled as part of the European integration process and the European Year of Languages may therefore prove to be highly instructive as far as the formulation of measures to encourage cultural and linguistic diversity is concerned.

Here the Union's institutions speak of 'encouraging' diversity, which, as we shall see, is different from 'respecting' it.

Before moving on, it is worth pointing out that the Council has, on one occasion at least, elevated the status of 'linguistic diversity' to that of a 'principle'. In a 2002 Resolution, following on from the European Year of Languages, the Council invited the Commission to 'take into account, in this context [of supporting the Member States in their implementations of various recommendations], the principle of linguistic diversity in its relations with third and candidate countries'.[6]

In the citations above, we have seen that the verb attached to the word 'diversity' has not always been the same. This is of enormous importance, for the meaning of the word clearly varies in different contexts. Let us now take a look at this issue.

## The 'equality of languages'

The first significant statement allows us to speak of a principle of equality of languages. The earliest references I have tracked down appear in European Parliament documents, which on various occasions have called for assurances that the equality of the official and working languages of the Union within the Parliament will not be broken. In a 1982 Resolution, the Parliament:

> (2) Confirms the rule that there is to be absolute equality between the Community languages, whether used actively or passively, in writing or orally, at all meetings of Parliament and its bodies.[7]

Twelve years later[8] the following was stated:

> (I) having regard to Parliament's previous stances on the use of languages, [the Parliament]

> 1 Confirms that all of the European Union's official languages are also the working languages of the European Parliament;
> 2 Reaffirms that all of the Union's official languages must be used on a strictly equal basis, wherever necessary, for all meetings of the European Parliament, whether they are used actively or passively, orally or in writing.

Note that the Parliament is talking about two separate things: firstly, the equality of legal status ('official languages') is equated with the status of 'working languages'; and secondly, the use of the official languages must be strictly equal within the Parliament. However, the latter grand and solemn proclamation is rather spoilt by the addition of the phrase 'wherever necessary'!

In the same Resolution, another Recital is significant in this regard:

> (E) whereas all Members of Parliament are equal and are entitled to treatment on an equal basis in all respects, including languages.

Here it is not the languages as such, but their speakers, who are 'entitled to treatment on an equal basis'. It is important to bear this in mind: when all is said and done, we are not interested in dictionaries, but in people!

Nevertheless, the equality of languages is not a universal principle. A 1990 EP Resolution on Catalan states that, in its opinion, the principle of equality is limited in its scope:

> (E) whereas ... it is not possible fully to respect the principle of equality for all the languages spoken in the countries of the Community, there are in the case of Catalan, opportunities for its use which could be taken up at the present time.[9]

The Council has also referred to the 'equality of languages'. The 12 June 1995 European Council (General Affairs) meeting in Luxembourg[10] stated its view (in para 6) that citizens will support an integrated Europe only if they are granted 'equal access' in the languages of the Union.

> From the citizen's point of view, support for an integrated Europe will require an assurance that the languages of the Union will be taken into consideration and will require equal access to information, in conformity with Member States' internal law and with Community law.

We shall return to this concept of 'languages of the Union' later on. The same 1995 Council Conclusions state even more clearly the views of the Ministers as regards the languages which, to paraphrase George Orwell's unforgettable expression, are more equal than others:

> (13) The Council would also reiterate the importance it attaches to the equality of the official languages and working languages of the Union's institutions, namely, Danish, Dutch, English, Finnish, French, German, Greek, Italian, Portuguese,

> Spanish and Swedish, in accordance with Regulation No 1/1958, as amended, determining the languages to be used by the institutions of the Union. The Council recalls the particular status of Irish under Article S of the Treaty on European Union and the Treaty of Accession of Denmark, Ireland and the United Kingdom.

Note the reference to Irish: not at that time an official and working language, but a language whose speakers were granted certain rights in the institutions of the Union. We shall return to the special case of Irish below.

Equality is also referred to in a Recital to the European Year of Languages Decision of 2000:

> All the European languages, in their spoken and written forms, are equal in value and dignity from the cultural point of view and form an integral part of European cultures and civilisation.

Note here that it is the 'cultural point of view' that is highlighted, not the political one, or the issue of democratic transparency within the Union. Throughout the Year Commissioner Viviane Reding[11] made constant reference to this Recital, and this is a welcome step: but to bring about practical consequences of this consideration lay beyond her powers.

## The meaning of linguistic (and cultural) diversity

Let us now look, in turn, at the six verbs attached to diversity in various documents. They are the following: maintain, preserve, safeguard, respect, promote, and encourage.

**Maintain:** In dealing with economic, social and monetary questions, the Presidency Conclusions of the Cannes European Council summit (26 and 27 June 1995) emphasise, in the section on 'Employment':

> The development potential of new growth sectors (for example, multi-media) and the potential for job creation in promoting the information society. It calls for work to continue on establishing the regulatory framework that will enable it to develop, while taking care to maintain cultural diversity and bearing in mind the objective of equal access to these new services.[12]

A more recent Council Resolution (16 December 1997)[13] on the early teaching of European Union languages also wants to make it clear that such an objective should 'maintain' diversity, for it aims:

> ... to promote European multilingualism by promoting the early teaching of European Union languages, while maintaining Europe's cultural and linguistic diversity.

**Preserve:** 'Preserving' and 'Maintaining' are used as virtually synonymous, as shown by a recital in the 1989 Decision establishing the Lingua Action programme,[14] which ends by making a qualification that is very similar to the 1997 Council Resolution just quoted:

> Whereas greater foreign language competence will enable the Community's citizens to reap the benefits of completion of the internal market and will enhance understanding and solidarity between the peoples which go to make up the Community, while preserving the linguistic diversity and cultural wealth of Europe …

The Council Conclusions of 12 June 1995 referred to above include a 13-point statement on linguistic diversity and multilingualism in the European Union and refer to linguistic diversity as follows:

> (5) The Council emphasizes that linguistic diversity must be preserved and multilingualism promoted in the Union, with equal respect for the languages of the Union and with due regard to the principle of subsidiarity.

A revealing distinction is made in this statement as to the difference, in the Council's view, between 'linguistic diversity' and 'multilingualism', which we shall find again later.

**Safeguard:** The e-Content Decision of 2000 makes another reference, this time to 'cultural diversity'. Among the strategic objectives of the Programme we find:

> Creating favourable conditions for the reduction of market fragmentation and for the marketing, distribution and use of European digital content on the global networks to stimulate economic activity and enhance employment prospects, safeguarding cultural diversity, optimising the European heritage and facilitating access to knowledge.[15]

**Respect:** Several references have been made above to this treatment of diversity in Community texts—firstly in the Treaty of Amsterdam, where Article 149, para 1 states that 'The Community shall contribute to the development of quality education by encouraging cooperation between Member States and, if necessary, by supporting and supplementing their action, *while fully respecting* the responsibility of the Member States for the content of teaching and the organisation of education systems and *their cultural and linguistic diversity*'.

This article deserves special attention. In the opinion of the legal services of the Commission, respect for linguistic diversity in Article 149 is a negative, qualifying, restrictive mandate. This thwarted the attempt by the

DG for Education and Culture to put forward a multiannual programme, *Archipel*, to support regional or minority languages under this Article.

Article 149 raises a second interesting issue. The text has been misquoted in a number of official documents. It ensures that the Community, in its actions in the field of education, will fully respect 'the responsibility of the Member States for the content of teaching and the organisation of education systems and their cultural and linguistic diversity'. To this author it is perfectly clear that the Community is duty bound to respect two separate items: (i) responsibility of the Member States for their education systems and (ii) their cultural and linguistic diversity. This interpretation is clearly supported, in a number of linguistic versions[16] of the text of the Treaty, by the absence of the preposition 'for' before the final phrase 'their cultural and linguistic diversity'. Nevertheless there are texts that interpret Article 149(1) as if it stated that the Community has to respect the responsibility of Member States in two areas: (i) their education systems and (ii) their cultural and linguistic diversity. A summary overview of the text of the article in various languages does not in the author's view justify this interpretation. An example of the distorted interpretation is given by the Council (Education and Youth Affairs) when, without beginning with the crucial word 'respecting', it speaks of:

> (1a) the responsibility of Member States for the content of teaching and the organisation of education systems and their cultural and linguistic diversity.[17]

A few days earlier, in a written reply to MEP Pere Esteve, the Council had also given this interpretation of Article 149[18]. Shortly afterwards, the Council of the European Union adopted a Resolution of 14 February 2002 on the promotion of linguistic diversity and language learning in the framework of the implementation of the objectives of the European Year of Languages 2001, which likewise 'recalls' exactly the same text in its paragraph 2.

A second reference in the Treaty to respecting diversity appears two articles later. In the article laying down the powers of the European Community in the field of culture, we read (Article 151, para 1):

> The Community shall contribute to the flowering of the cultures of the Member States, while *respecting their national and regional diversity* and at the same time bringing the common cultural heritage to the fore.

The same Article 151, in paragraph 4, stipulates that:

> The Community shall take cultural aspects into account in its action under the provisions of this Treaty, in particular in order *to respect* and to promote the diversity of its cultures.

Thirdly, and perhaps most significantly, we have cited above a more general reference to respect in Article 22 of the Charter of Fundamental Rights, which states that 'The Union shall respect cultural, religious and linguistic diversity'. What we are not told is what this 'respect' amounts to at the end of the day. But the practical consequences of respecting diversity are not uniform in nature. In my view, respecting religious diversity entails non-discrimination and a neutral attitude: in no way should the institutions of the Union be seen as anything other than secular. Respecting cultural diversity may again mean treating people equally, regardless of their cultural traits and identity. However, it is impossible for an institution to be linguistically neutral, unless it is silent! Thus 'respect' in dealing with languages has to mean something different, entailing behaviour which varies according to the linguistic traits of the citizen.

Such a formulation in a document defining 'Fundamental Rights', placed in a section on Equality rights, strikes one as curious, to say the least. Nonetheless the insertion of this article in the Charter, largely at the behest of the European Bureau for Lesser-Used Languages and the lobby it managed to mobilise, may be a big step forward for supporting 'regional or minority languages' as we shall see later; but it will need some translation into more tangible commitments on the part of the institutions, a task facing many organisations, in the context of the Convention, at the time this paper was being drafted.

**Promote:** The 'promotion' of linguistic diversity has been the objective of an important Community action, namely, the MLIS programme. The Council of 21 November 1996 decided to adopt 'a multiannual programme to promote the linguistic diversity of the Community in the information society'.[19] The legal basis of this programme was questioned by the European Parliament, but the Court of Justice upheld the view of the Council of the European Union.[20] What is important here, though, is that the promotion of linguistic diversity of the Community is clearly defined in a particular area ('the information society') which had hitherto been dominated by a single language, English. Note that the e-Content programme that succeeded the MLIS programme continues to have as one of its priorities the creation and use of multilingual digital content.

In the section on 'Respect', Article 151, paragraph 4 was quoted. Note that it also refers to the promotion of diversity:

> The Community shall take cultural aspects into account in its action under the provisions of this Treaty, in particular in order to respect and to promote the diversity of its cultures.

**Encourage:** Of a similar nature to the promotion of diversity, we find the word 'encourage' in the European Year of Languages Decision, specifically in recital 5:

> The language question is a challenge that must be tackled as part of the European integration process and the European Year of Languages may therefore prove to

be highly instructive as far as the formulation of measures to encourage cultural and linguistic diversity is concerned.

Thus an official document refers to 'the language question' as a 'challenge that must be tackled'. This will be taken up below.

To close this section on the various meanings of the concept 'diversity' we have seen that whereas in some circumstances diversity is an attribute or criterion which should be 'respected', in others it should be 'promoted' or 'encouraged', while in still others it should be 'safeguarded'. In short, these verbs reveal very different understandings of the meaning of the term 'diversity'. We have seen that even the term 'respect' demands contextualisation. The 'promotion' of diversity, that is, the transformation of an existing state of affairs, should probably be associated more specifically with the issue of language learning and, in the case of the MLIS programme, with the availability of products in a range of languages. The 12 June 1995 Council Conclusions referred to above provide a useful distinction in this regard, for they do indeed attach different verbs to each concept: 'linguistic diversity must be preserved and multilingualism promoted in the Union'. Finally, it would seem reasonable to argue that 'safeguard' and 'preserve' refer to the maintenance of an existing state of affairs that may be under threat—though this threat is not described in the texts—and that therefore deserves special measures of some kind. Clear support for this view can be gleaned from the many Calls for proposals[21] published up until 2000 by the European Commission to provide support for measures to *promote and safeguard regional or minority languages and cultures*. The object is much less abstract, and therefore much clearer: it is not 'diversity' which is directly being addressed, but rather minority languages and cultures. This now defunct pilot scheme will be referred to later.

Following the success of the European Year of Languages, the DG for Education and Culture, began working, at the request of the Council itself, on an Action Plan for Promoting Language Learning and Linguistic Diversity.[22] The Commission recognises the need for action in the field of regional and minority languages in section 4: 'Building a Language-Friendly Environment'. Its initial reaction is to place the burden for their promotion on others' shoulders:

> National, regional and local communities need to bear in mind, therefore, that some languages require special attention, especially those which are seriously endangered because the number of native speakers continues to decline from generation to generation.

Nevertheless, the Commission paper does accept responsibility for finding ways of continuing to support such languages, as in the past:

> The Union has for many years supported small-scale projects to promote regional and minority languages. This help was mainly made available outside the

> mainstream cooperation programmes in education, training, youth, culture and media. However, policies aimed at such languages cannot be viewed in isolation; in the longer term, all relevant Community funding programmes could include more support for linguistic diversity (including regional and minority languages).

We shall return specifically to the issue of 'regional and minority' languages later on.

## OFFICIAL LANGUAGES AND WORKING LANGUAGES OF THE INSTITUTIONS OF THE EUROPEAN UNION

Let us now look at some of the ins and outs of a supranational (rather than international) body, successively known as the European Economic Community, the European Community and the European Union, which instead of adopting a single language as have some international bodies (such as the Organisation for Security and Co-operation in Europe) or two languages (such as the Council of Europe, which operates through English and French), or even six languages (such as the United Nations), has been trapped by its 'original sin' of stating that the official languages of each of the Member States would be likewise official within the institutions of the organisation. I say 'original sin' only because the criterion presented no special problems at the outset, with six members and only four official languages (Dutch, French, German, Italian); but the number has grown from six to twenty, following the successive enlargements, the latest of which was in 2004. Furthermore, Irish was granted the status of an official and working language of the European Union by the Council (General Affairs) in Luxembourg on 13 June 2005[23], though the amended Regulation will only come into effect on 1 January 2007[24]. Before the end of the decade the number of official and working languages will probably have increased further, with the possible incorporation of Croatia, Bulgaria, Romania and Turkey.

The consequences of this non-decision on the rules governing the use of languages are considerable. The Translation Service is one of the largest departments of the European Commission, while the Joint Interpreting and Conference Service (JICS) is apparently the largest interpreting service in the world.[25] Because of the burgeoning cost and complexity of these services:

> ... it is difficult to see how serious contemplation of both present arrangements and the need for reform can, in real terms, be postponed for much longer.[26]

The growing contact of people of different languages in this European context, most of which developed for at least several centuries in a largely monolingual environment, each language holding supremacy within their national borders, has led to facetious remarks to the effect that *all* European languages are now minority languages.

The language 'regime' of the Union is fixed in a Council Regulation, significantly the very first that was passed, in 1958.[27] At that time, as I have just stated, there were only four official languages in the Member States: Luxembourg shared its official languages with France and Germany (Luxembourgish, or Lëtzeburgesch, was not to attain the status of an official language in its own country until 1984), while Belgium shared its own with France, Germany and the Netherlands. At that time, no other languages had any legal status in the six countries.

We may ask ourselves why the language 'regime' was not fixed by, say, the Parliament, or by each of the institutions separately. The reason is simple: Article 290 (ex-217) of the consolidated versions of the Treaty Establishing the European Community[28] states that:

> The rules governing the languages of the institutions of the Community shall, without prejudice to the provisions contained in the Rules of Procedure of the Court of Justice, be determined by the Council, acting unanimously.

What in English is described as 'The rules governing the languages of the institutions of the Community' in Romance languages is described as 'linguistic regime'. But two important points need to be underlined. Firstly, this article does not speak of 'official' languages, or 'working' languages, nor are such terms to be found anywhere in the Treaties. These concepts emerge in the Council Regulation referred to above, so they cannot be regarded as deriving from primary Community legislation. And secondly, the Regulation limits itself to talking about language use by the institutions, and not to language learning measures or language promotion programmes. Thus to limit the latter merely to languages which are officially used by the institutions would seem hard to justify.

We may now ask on what grounds the Council talks about the 'languages of the Union'. References appear earlier to 'the official languages of the Communities'.[29] Nowhere in the Treaties is this term used. Whilst it is clear that the 'languages spoken in the Community'[30] are not the same as 'the languages of the Union', the latter term alternates with others such as 'Community languages', the 'European Union's official languages' and so on.

Article 1 states that 'The official languages and the working languages of the institutions of the Community shall be Dutch, French, German and Italian'.

The reasoning behind this choice, beyond the reference to Article 290 (ex-217) of the Treaty Establishing the European Community, is given in the solitary recital that precedes the articles: 'each of the four languages in which the Treaty is drafted is recognised as an official language in one or more of the Member States of the Community'. This was, and has remained, true as the Community has expanded; but it is *not* conversely true, as it was in 1958, that the Treaty is drafted in *all* the official languages in one or more of the Member States of the Community: for Welsh, Catalan, Basque, Galician, Breton, Frisian and others have since attained official status in the various Member States. The Treaty is, at the time of writing, currently drafted in only 20 languages, as laid down in Article 314 of the Consolidated Version of the Treaty Establishing the European Community[31]:

> This Treaty, drawn up in a single original in the Dutch, French, German, and Italian languages, all four texts being equally authentic, shall be deposited in the archives of the Government of the Italian Republic, which shall transmit a certified copy to each of the Governments of the other signatory States.
>
> [Pursuant to the Accession Treaties, the Czech, Danish, English, Estonian, Finnish, Greek, Hungarian, Irish, Latvian, Lithuanian, Maltese, Polish, Portuguese, Slovak, Slovenian, Spanish and Swedish versions of this Treaty shall also be authentic.].

Note that until the Council decision of 13 June 2005 referred to above, *Irish* had a particular status. Whereas it was one of the 'Treaty languages', it was not included in the amended Regulation No 1/1958, that is, Irish was not one of the 'official languages' or 'working languages' of the institutions of the Union. The effect upon Irish-speaking citizens of this exclusion was attenuated by the wording of Indent 3 of Article 21 (ex-8d) of the same Consolidated Version of the Treaty Establishing the European Community, which states that:

> Every citizen of the Union may write to any of the institutions or bodies referred to in this Article or in Article 7 in one of the languages mentioned in Article 314 and have an answer in the same language.

Since we have just seen that Article 314 includes Irish, this right was accorded to Irish-speaking citizens as well. Incidentally, a similar statement appears in the Charter of Fundamental Rights.[32]

If and when the Treaty establishing a Constitution for Europe[33] comes into effect, the spirit of this statement will be maintained in indent 4 of Article II-101 (Right to good administration):

> Every person may write to the institutions of the Union in one of the languages of the Constitution and must have an answer in the same language.

What consequences does status as an 'official language' or a 'working language' have? Naturally, and for reasons of legal certainty, all legally binding official texts are currently published in all twenty languages. This affects, first and foremost, the Official Journal, which has twenty editions, in all the official and working languages. Both the EU portal, http://europa.eu, and the European Parliament portal, http://www.europarl.europa.eu are in twenty languages. So too, to be sure, are the main Community websites. But there are European Community websites which are not in all these languages. The Regional Funds website Info*regio* is one (http://ec.europa.eu/regional_policy/), and the Research website is another: http://cordis.europa.eu/. Both offer services only in six languages (including the latest addition, Polish). This has to be seen in the light of the fact that a European Court of Justice Judgment states that Community institutions other than those strictly bound by the wording of the Treaties are not under a commitment to have all twenty languages as working languages. These institutions are five in number: the European Parliament, the Council, the Commission, the Court of Justice[34] and the Court of Auditors.[35] Other agencies are thus apparently exempt from applying the criterion on 'Full multilingualism' which thus, as a legal concept, does not exist in the Union, despite repeated references to it in texts such as the 11 December 1990 European Parliament Resolution. The case, which was unsuccessfully brought by the since-deceased Mrs Kik against the Office for Harmonisation of the Internal Market, was turned down by the Court of First Instance precisely on these grounds.[36]

Moreover, some websites are not adapted so as to allow correspondence in Irish. A good example is a question put in the European Parliament by Seán Ó Neachtain (UEN) to the Commission,[37] in which he pointed out that no provision was made for selecting Irish as either a first or second choice language when filling in the M@ilbox form on the General Information Services page of the Commission; that is, Article 21 had not been complied with by the Commission.[38] Commission President Prodi's reply completely evaded the issue, arguing, to my mind irrelevantly, that 'Gaelic is not mentioned in Regulation No 1/1958'.

What appears from the Regulation to be a clear definition of the legal status of the twenty languages—'The official languages and the working languages of the institutions of the Community'—is not in practice followed in all official texts which refer to them. Far from it, the variety of terms used is bewildering, confusing and, at times, suspicious.

Without any claim whatsoever to exhaustiveness, here is a selection of quotes:

- *'Official languages of the Community'*
  Article 1 of the European Year of Languages Decision states, in indent 2, that measures 'will cover the *official languages of the Community*, together with Irish, Letzeburgesch, and other languages in line with those identified by the Member States for the purposes of implementing this Decision'.
- *'Community languages'*
  A 1995 Commission White Paper, *Education, Training, Research: Teaching and Learning: Towards a Learning Society*, established as its Objective Four proficiency for all *in three Community languages.*

- *'Languages of the Union'*
  In a 1995 Council document[39] we read 'While reaffirming the principle of equal status for each of the languages of the Union …'
- *'European Union languages'*
  The Council Resolution of 16 December 1997 on the early teaching of European Union languages, apart from the term in its title, also speaks of 'languages of the Union' and above all of 'Union languages'.

So it is clear that the terms 'Community languages', '[European] Union languages', 'languages of the Union' and 'official Community languages' popped out of the conjurer's top hat one fine day. In this case, the conjurer was the Council which, of course, brings together the representatives of Member States' governments.

The only correct formula, in my view, for referring to the twenty languages would be to talk of *the official languages and working languages of the Union's institutions*, as used in point 13 of the 12 June 1995 Council conclusions (that, incidentally, also refers, in point 5, to 'the languages of the Union'):

> 13. The Council would also reiterate the importance it attaches to the equality of the *official languages and working languages of the Union's institutions*, namely, Danish, Dutch, English, Finnish, French, German, Greek, Italian, Portuguese, Spanish and Swedish, in accordance with Regulation No 1/1958, as amended, determining the languages to be used by the institutions of the Union …

I stated above that this use of terminology allows the institutions to go well beyond their remit, in my view, when it comes to language-linked policies. Thus the main programme designed to promote languages, Lingua, was and still is limited to the twenty official languages, plus Irish and Luxembourgish. Why the latter two? The reasoning is somewhat tortuous, and the real reason is not mentioned. The Socrates 2 programme[40] states in the Comenius Action that Community financial assistance may be awarded for the following:

> (b) projects aimed specifically at teaching and learning the official languages of the Community, together with Irish (*one of the languages in which the Treaties establishing the European Communities are drawn up*) and Lëtzeburgesch (*a language spoken throughout the territory of Luxembourg*),[41] including in frontier regions of the Member States, the official languages of the Community in neighbouring regions of other Member States. The projects may be bilateral, especially where they target one of the less widely used or less widely taught of these languages and should include exchanges of pupils in addition to the activities referred to in point (a).

In the section on the Lingua Action the same affirmations and justifications are stated.[42]

Thus the inclusion of Irish was based on the fact that it is 'one of the languages in which the Treaties establishing the European Communities are drawn up', and Lëtzeburgesch is 'a language spoken throughout the territory of Luxembourg'. The real explanation must be another: their inclusion allows the 'national' languages of these two Member States access to Community funds. The wording (which dates back to 1989, when the Lingua programme was first introduced) ensures the continued exclusion of other European languages such as Welsh and Catalan. And what can we say about all twenty official languages? The Lingua programme—later Action—could not elegantly have been said to be designed mainly for the 'official and working languages of the institutions of the European Union'. As we have said above, the programme has nothing to do, let us face it, with the use of languages within the institutions. But by referring to the same languages as 'Union languages' (or synonyms) it appears easier to maintain a restrictive criterion.

Yet exclusive criteria are not always applied. The Multilingual Information Society (MLIS; 1996–9) programme, for instance, left the door open to all European languages, and, for instance, several projects involving, among others, Catalan, Welsh and Irish were co-funded. The drafters of the programme were aware (Recital 12) that 'languages that remain excluded from the information society would run the risk of a more or less rapid marginalization'. 'The aim of this action line is to support, for *all European languages*, the construction of a European infrastructure of multilingual resources and to stimulate the creation of electronic language resources.'

I have already made reference to the confusing array of terms that refer to the same concept. Nowhere is confusion more rampant than in the use of the expression 'lesser-used'. Originally coined as a more neutral synonym of 'minority' languages, and used for instance in the name of the European Bureau for Lesser-Used Languages,[43] it later crept into legislation to refer to the smaller of the official languages of the institutions of the EU, namely Danish, Dutch, Finnish, Greek, Portuguese and Swedish, where particular emphasis was able to be placed on the less widely spoken and taught of these languages. As an example of the confusion, let us cite the Council's reply to a question put to it by MEP Michl Ebner in 1999,[44] in which he asked the Council to outline its policy on the safeguarding and promoting of lesser-used languages in the European Union. There is no doubt in my mind that he was referring to languages such as Catalan, Sardinian and Sami. Yet the reply referred solely to the Lingua Action in the Socrates programme, which speaks about the less widely spoken and taught of the Lingua languages: these include only the official languages of the institutions of the EU, plus Irish and Luxembourgish. The Council's only concession to the true intention of the MEP is its almost grudging statement that

'Due consideration would moreover be given by the Council to any future Commission proposals concerning lesser-used languages'.

## LANGUAGE LEARNING AND MULTILINGUALISM

We have seen above that the 'promotion of linguistic diversity' has on occasion been used to refer to the promotion of language learning, that is, of citizens' multilingualism. The institutions of the Union seem to be fairly consistent in using the term 'multilingualism' to refer to the capacity of individuals to speak more than one language. They have become increasingly aware of the pressing need to ensure that as high a proportion of citizens as possible can operate in several languages. This has naturally led to a consensus that primary and secondary schools, as well as universities, should teach more than one 'foreign' language. In its March 1995 Resolution on foreign language teaching, the Council claimed that since 1976 'the Council and the Ministers for Education meeting within the Council have dealt with the promotion of the teaching of the languages of the Union on many occasions'.

The Resolution states (though almost camouflaging the objective within the text) that:

> ... pupils should as a general rule have the opportunity of learning two languages of the Union other than their mother tongue(s).

This timid reference came before the Commission report to the European Parliament, the Council, the Economic and Social Committee and the Committee of the Regions on implementation of the 1995 White Paper on education and training, entitled *Teaching and Learning: Towards the Learning Society*.[45] In its reaction to the White Paper, the Council noted that some Member States, in the context of their national policies, did not wish to rule out the learning of non-Community European languages.[46]

Curiously enough (for reasons to be elucidated shortly) it was while the commissioner for Education and Culture was French, namely Edith Cresson, that a number of official documents, in the form of White Papers and Commission communications, were produced to enhance the role of learning foreign languages. Two paragraphs in the preamble to the 2000 Decision establishing the European Year of Languages make reference to such documents:

> (13) The Commission's 1995 White Paper 'Education, training, research: Teaching and learning: towards a learning society' established as its Objective Four proficiency for all in three Community languages. The Commission's 1996 Green Paper 'Education, Training, Research: The obstacles to transnational

mobility' concluded that 'learning at least two Community languages has become a precondition if citizens of the European Union are to benefit from occupational and personal opportunities open to them in the single market.:

(14) Council Resolution of 31 March 1995 on improving and diversifying language learning and teaching within the education systems of the European Union states that pupils should as a general rule have the opportunity of learning two languages of the European Union other than their mother tongue(s) for a minimum of two consecutive years during compulsory schooling and if possible for a longer period.

The Council also adopted a Resolution on the early teaching of European Union languages, on 16 December 1997, while it is obvious that the issue of learning two foreign languages has gained momentum over the years, and the Council has referred to it at least twice in recent years.[47]

Another document, emanating this time from the DG for Education and Culture, referred, in much clearer terms, to the acquisition of two foreign languages other than the student's own: the White Paper *Teaching and Learning: Towards the Learning Society* (1995) contained as its fourth general objective 'proficiency in three Community languages', and the need for 'everyone, irrespective of training and education routes chosen, to be able to acquire and keep up their ability to communicate in at least two Community languages in addition to their mother tongue'. It advocated a start at pre-school level, with systematic teaching in primary education and a second Community language starting in secondary school, including some subject teaching in a foreign language (Trim, 2002).

The interest of France, a country with a long history of actively pursuing monolingualism among its citizens, a quarter of whom spoke languages other than French (disparagingly called 'patois') little more than a century ago,[48] in promoting the learning of a second foreign language in schools is easily explained. The Commissioner for Education and Culture (and former French prime minister), Mme Edith Cresson, hand in glove with President François Mitterrand, engaged in an offensive purportedly to favour linguistic diversity and multilingualism, but which was in fact a French response to the overwhelming choice of English in, particularly, schools across the Union. Their reasoning was as follows: let us give up the idea of challenging the leadership of English as the first foreign language to be learned, and instead try to secure the place of French as the main second foreign language. To do this, however, it was necessary to break the tradition in many European educational systems of only offering a single foreign language to their pupils. The offensive therefore had to aim for all schools to teach at least two foreign languages. Given that France is a country whose policy has, since even before the 1789 Revolution, been ferociously monolingual, it seems ironic that it should now spearhead a multilingual aim for the citizens of the European Union.

| | Mother tongue | Second language |
|---|---|---|
| English | 16% | 31% |
| German | 24% | 8% |
| French | 16% | 12% |
| Italian | 16% | 2% |
| Spanish | 11% | 4% |
| Dutch | 6% | 4% |
| Swedish | 2% | 1% |
| Greek | 3% | 1% |
| Portuguese | 3% | 0% |
| Danish | 1% | 0% |
| Finnish | 1% | 1% |
| Russian | 0% | 0% |
| 'Others' | 1% | 4% |
| TOTAL | 100% | 68% |

How multilingual are the citizens of the Union? A survey carried out among EU citizens of the 15 member states as a prelude to the European Year of Languages 2001 to find out who speaks what in the Member States (15 at that time), showed that the main international language, English, was the mother tongue of only one in six Europeans.[49]

German, spoken by slightly under a quarter of European Union citizens, was the leading mother tongue, but even that was spoken by a minority. However, let us not confuse the term 'minority', used here in an arithmetical sense, with its use in the term 'minority language'. It is important not to misunderstand (innocently or otherwise) the nature of the relations between languages which have been promoted to the status of 'national' languages, in contrast to other languages which, at best, have been allowed some kind of second-rate status, and at worst have been ignored or even persecuted. Majority-minority is simply a way of referring to dominant-subordinate relationships in which the selected language may or may not have been numerically superior, at least originally. This certainly was not the case with French (Occitan was more widely spoken) or, in another part of the world, Indonesian. It is the association with power that gives a particular way of speaking, in a multilingual context, its 'majority' status. A well-known statement (attributed to various sociolinguists, including Lluís V Aracil, but apparently originally formulated by Max Weinreich)[50] sought to help to discriminate between a dialect and a language, in non-linguistic terms, by giving an original definition to the term language: 'Language is a dialect with an army and a navy.'

What more can be gleaned from the Eurobarometer report? Two basic points as far as personal multilingualism is concerned: (a) 53% of Europeans say that they can speak at least one European language in addition to their mother tongue; and (b) 26% say that they can speak two European foreign languages[51]. Finally, a reference in the text to cases not actually included in the questionnaire itself:

> Countries with the largest number of respondents saying they had 'another' language as mother tongue (possibly reflecting the place of regional languages or the languages of recent migrants) are Spain (4.7%)[52], UK (4.1%) ...

It should be borne in mind that the term 'foreign language' which appears throughout the report does not mean the same to all citizens. Throughout Europe we have examples of language borders not coinciding with political frontiers. Though the language may be the same on both sides, it may well be regarded as a foreign language, or even as a dialect, on the side where it is in a minority, or subordinate, position. Cases in point include German ('Alsatian') in France, as far as a 'foreign' language is concerned, and as far as dialectal problems are concerned, Catalan in Aragon (where it is called 'fragatí', 'lliterà', 'tamarità', 'mequinençà', 'xapurreao' and, more recently, 'Eastern Aragonese' ... *anything* except Catalan!) or in Valencia. In the latter region, and especially its capital, right wing regionalists stirred up such a frenzy over the name of the language and relations, in general, with Catalonia, that bookshops were bombed, intellectuals threatened, etc (Strubell, 1994; Neugaard, 1995). Had their intentions been more laudable, the bizarre spelling systems and speculations about the origin of 'Valencian' that emerged in the region during the seventies and eighties would make interesting reading.

Returning to Community jargon, the clear distinction between safeguarding a pre-existing level of diversity, and using the expression 'promotion of linguistic diversity' to refer to the development of new competences among the citizens, or new products in various languages, is visible in the 1995 Council Resolution cited in this paper:

> The promotion of linguistic diversity thus becomes one of the major issues in education. While reaffirming the principle of equal status for each of the languages of the Union, thought should therefore be given to the tools appropriate for improving and diversifying the teaching and practice of such languages, thereby enabling every citizen to have access to the cultural wealth rooted in the linguistic diversity of the Union.

Other than the Lingua programme and, since 1995, Action within Socrates, by far the best example of a Community policy to promote multilingualism was the European Year of Languages 2001, which makes a special reference to it worthwhile. The idea was the Council of Europe's, and the financial support came from the European Union/Community. The aims of the Year were both generic and specific: basically, to raise awareness of the richness of linguistic and cultural diversity within the European Union, to encourage multilingualism, to bring to the notice of the general public the advantages of knowing several languages, to encourage lifelong learning of languages, and to collect and disseminate information about the teaching and learning of languages.

It is worth looking in a little more detail at the content and aims of this one-year programme, as for the first time the Council and the Parliament agreed on a policy document regarding the use and promotion of languages in Europe, and not merely on the teaching of foreign languages. The objectives therefore express, out in the open, some of the concerns felt by the Member States.

The target groups the EYL was especially designed for were to include, among others, '... pupils and students, parents, workers, job seekers, the speakers of certain languages, the inhabitants of border areas, the peripheral regions, cultural bodies, deprived social groups, migrants, etc'.[53]

Among measures foreseen in the Programme, there were those aimed at 'better defining the expectations of different target groups (*including those in bilingual areas*) with regard to language learning and the way in which the Community could fulfil those expectations'.

Of particular interest is the list of languages eligible for support under the EYL programme:

> 2. During the European Year of Languages, information and promotional measures will be undertaken on the theme of languages, with the aim of encouraging language learning by all persons residing in the Member States. These measures will cover the official languages of the Community, together with Irish, Letzeburgesch, and *other languages in line with those identified by the Member States for the purposes of implementing this Decision.*[54]

References in the programme to both migrant groups and minority languages are to be found, though in the latter case every kind of euphemism is used: the speakers of certain languages, the inhabitants of border areas, the peripheral regions, other languages in line with those identified by the Member States for the purposes of implementing this Decision.

Let us now, for the remainder of this paper, return more specifically to the so-called lesser-used (or 'minority' or 'regional') languages.

## REGIONAL AND MINORITY LANGUAGES

In dealing with policy and discourse regarding these languages and the communities that speak them, a clear distinction can be drawn between the positions of the Parliament, the Commission and the Council. In the report on *The European Union and Lesser-Used Languages* commissioned by the European Parliament and published in 2002,[55] an overview is given of the EP's position on the issue of minority or regional languages. The Report makes it clear that the interest of the Parliament has been fairly constant for over twenty years:

> This interest has led to various reports and to six Resolutions: the Resolution on a Community Charter of Regional Languages and Cultures and on a Charter of Rights of Ethnic Minorities of 16 October 1981 (Rapporteur: Arfé[56]), that of 11 February 1983 on measures in favour of minority languages and cultures (Rapporteur: Arfé[57]), that of 30 October 1987 on the languages and cultures of regional and ethnic minorities in the European Community (Rapporteur: Kuijpers[58]), that of 11 December 1990 on the situation of languages of the Community and the Catalan language (Rapporteur: Reding), that of 9 February 1994 on linguistic minorities in the European Community (Rapporteur: Killilea[59]); that of 13 December 2001, on regional and lesser-used European languages[60]; and more recently, that of 4 September 2003 (Rapporteur: Ebner)[61].

The Parliament has clearly been much more enthusiastic than other institutions in addressing this issue and in calling for action at both the Member State and the Community level. No multiannual programme has yet been put in place, though from 1983 to 2000 there was up to 4m funding annually for subsidies to support initiatives for the promotion of regional or minority languages (to use Council of Europe terminology). As a result of the European Court of Justice Judgment C-106/96 of 12 May 1998, budget line B3-1006 was suspended because of the lack of a legal basis, and 2.5m was allocated annually under budget line B3-1000 to finance preparatory measures for a multi-annual programme in support of regional and minority languages and cultures for 1999–2001. At the same time, the European Bureau for Lesser-Used Languages and the three Mercator Centres[62] were and still are supported under a separate budget line, A-3015, as institutions of European interest.

The Commission web page on support for such languages is relevant, for it relates the promotion of regional and minority languages to Article 22 of the Charter of Fundamental Rights (2000):

> Respect for linguistic and cultural diversity is one of the cornerstones of the European Union, now enshrined in Article 22 of the European Charter of Fundamental Rights, which states '*The Union respects cultural, religious and linguistic diversity.*' On the initiative of the European Parliament, which has adopted a series of resolutions on this subject, the European Union has taken action to safeguard and promote the regional and minority languages of Europe.[63]

The budget was (and still is, however reduced) administered by the Commission. The Commission has been keen to put into place a coherent policy, albeit without legal basis up to now. The need for a clear description of the situation and needs of these lesser-used language communities was detected at an early stage. Special mention should be given to the Euromosaic Report, commissioned by the European Union in 1993 and updated twice since then, in the light of successive enlargements.[64] These reports followed earlier overviews of the situation of minority and regional languages in the Community. They has been succeeded thanks to the fact that the Language Policy Unit of the Directorate General for Education and Culture commissioned the report 'Support for minority languages in Europe' (2003)[65] which analyses the issues surrounding the protection and promotion of regional and minority languages in the EU.

In an address[66] in Helsinki (11 October 2002) on 'The future of regional and minority languages in the European Union', Commissioner Viviane Reding said:

> The European Union has been active in supporting its regional and minority languages since 1983. EU support has taken two forms. From the very beginning we were the main source of funding for the European Bureau for Lesser-Used Languages. In recent years, EBLUL has received some eighty percent of its annual budget from the European Union. The EU has also been the main financial backer of the Mercator information network.
>
> In addition to this, from 1983 to 2000, we awarded grants for projects promoting and safeguarding regional and minority languages. These have covered the full range of actions relevant to language revitalisation. Education has been the main focus of attention, accounting for over half of project funding. The remainder has been shared equally between culture, media, direct language promotion and essential linguistic resources such as grammars and dictionaries.

Until quite recently the Council had never discussed the question of 'regional and minority languages', perhaps on account of the extremely varied positions different Member States have with regard to this subject, with Greece at one extreme. Before the drafting of the Treaty establishing a Constitution for Europe, the only time a minority language other than Irish and Luxembourgish was even indirectly referred to, before the parliamentary question cited above and the 2000 Decision establishing the EYL, was in the following Recital in the 1995–9 Socrates programme:

> Whereas certain languages, without being official languages of the European Union, are recognized at national level and are used to a significant extent as teaching languages in universities; whereas teaching in these languages should offer possibilities for access to parts of the programme concerning higher education.

In consequence, and following pressure by Catalan MEPs, specific mention was made, in a footnote to later editions of the Erasmus I Candidate Handbook, to a recital in the Preamble of the Decision, to the effect that language training for Erasmus students and professors involved in exchanges could cover not just the official languages of the Union, but also other languages used significantly as languages of instruction at university level, such as Welsh, Basque, Catalan, etc. However, the recital was removed in the follow-up Socrates programme.

Things changed, however, when the Treaty establishing a Constitution for Europe was drafted. After the first indent of Article IV-448[67], "Authentic texts and translations", which repeats the same formula used in earlier Treaties regarding the equal authenticity of the Treaty in each of the listed languages, a new, second indent was adopted, at the insistence of the Spanish government, under political pressure from Catalan parties on the domestic front, stating the following:

> 2. This Treaty may also be translated into any other languages as determined by Member States among those which, in accordance with their constitutional order, enjoy official status in all or part of their territory. A certified copy of such translations shall be provided by the Member States concerned to be deposited in the archives of the Council.

The explanation of this inclusion appears in Declaration 29[68] of the Final Act of the Intergovernmental Conference which, in relation to Article IV-448(2) states that it:

> "[...] contributes to fulfilling the objective of respecting the Union's rich cultural and linguistic diversity [and] the Conference confirms the attachment of the Union to the cultural diversity of Europe and the special attention it will continue to pay to these and other languages."

What the Conference understood as "special attention" remains to be clarified.

The indent is the visible outcome of a considerable campaign in Catalonia and other Catalan-speaking regions, which focussed renewed attention on the use of the status of Catalan in the institutions of the Union, during the 2001 European Year of Languages. The issue was covered in the Final Report of the Evaluation process.[69]

> According to survey results, the website was mainly used by people who already had an interest in language learning issues, such as language teachers, or people who were currently learning a language. Other users included specific groups, such as Catalan speakers who were involved in a campaign to have Catalan recognised as an official language of the EU and therefore wished that the site included a Catalan version. (p. 49)

> There are some notable differences between answers from the Catalan group and answers from survey respondents as a whole, which may impact on the overall survey results. These differences needs to be seen in the light of the fact that the European EYL website was used as a discussion forum by various organisations and individuals promoting Catalan during the Year, enabling contributors to lobby for changes in the status of the Catalan language. (p. 58)

Up to now at least the Spanish government has acted in accordance with this provision, accepting the translations made by the regional governments into Basque, Galician and a joint Catalan/Valencian version.

Of potentially greater impact was the request by the Spanish government[70] that Regulation No. 1/1958 be amended to incorporate these languages, for certain functions. In the end, the Council Conclusion of 13 June 2005[71] included a statement about "languages other than the languages referred to in Council Regulation No 1/1958 whose status is recognised by the Constitution of a Member State on all or part of its territory or the use of which as a national language is authorised by law". The uses foreseen are (a) Making public of acts adopted in codecision by the European Parliament and the Council; (b) Speeches to a meeting of the Council and possibly other Union Institutions or bodies; and (c) Written communications to Union Institutions and bodies. The Council invited the other Institutions (principally, the Commission, the Committee of the Regions and the Parliament) to conclude administrative arrangements on this basis. The Conclusion contains many qualifying statements that limit the practical and legal effects of its decision. Though far from the Spanish government's original request, the Spanish government has signed agreements with several of these institutions.

The practical outcome of these agreements is beginning to be observable in practice. The "Debate Europe" website set up by the Commission has 20 language versions. However, its "European Discussion Forum"[72] offers 21: top of the list (in alphabetical order), is the Catalan option. This advance has been greeted with enthusiasm by Catalan-speaking Europeans, whose interventions (on September 11$^{th}$ 2006) totalled 420, behind only English, French and German, and ahead, therefore, of much larger language communities such as the Spanish (312) the Italians (256), the Poles (99) or the Dutch-speakers (194).

## CONCLUSION

Many European States are none too positive about linguistic and cultural diversity, often having done everything within their power (sometimes including genocide and mass expatriations) to eliminate diversity. Many Europeans (some of whom, of course, are now MEPs) were brought up without questioning the "one state, one nation, one language" value system underlying this long-standing policy, while the Member State representatives in the Council have merely said that the present linguistic system in the Union, designed when there were only four official and working languages, has to be extended so as to cater for the official languages of all countries which join the Union.

One feels for the Commission, trapped as it is between the Parliament, which as we have seen has issued a number of calls for a multiannual Community programme to support regional and minority languages, and the Council, which has never discussed the issue ... or dared to discuss it, given the presence of manifestly belligerent Member States. The DG for Education and Culture did attempt to put forward a multiannual programme, Archipel, to support regional or minority languages, under Article 149, but it was thwarted first by the legal service, and then by the maintenance, in the Nice Treaty, of Culture as a competence requiring a unanimous vote in the Council. This came after the announcement made before the European Parliament in 1999 by the then Commissioner-designate responsible for Education and Culture, Viviane Reding:[73]

> I intend to present to the Commission a proposal for a multiannual programme for the development of the European dimension in education through the learning, promotion and dissemination of regional and/or minority languages.

It is in this framework that a group of Catalan specialists in this field, under the umbrella name of 'Europa Diversa', put to the Convention on the future of the European Union a set of 'Proposals for a new EU language regime':[74] a pragmatic proposal, which at the same time would overcome language exclusion and marginalisation. The proposal fell on deaf ears.

What does need mentioning, as significant initiatives on the part of the Commission, is the two-pronged development in the field of "language learning and linguistic diversity". First, an Action Plan (2004-2005)[75]; and more recently, the Communication on Multilingualism[76], which for the first time tries to bring together a discussion of Multilingualism in society, in the economy and in the Commission's relations with citizens. In the context of education, the latter states that:

> The teaching of regional and minority languages should also be taken into account as appropriate, as should opportunities for migrants to learn the language of the host country (and the teaching of migrant languages). (p. 5)

The Commission says that it will "investigate ways of supporting language diversity networks through the new integrated Lifelong Learning programme" in an oblique reference to "minority" and "regional" languages. Indeed, it seems that this new "Action programme in the field of lifelong learning" will open the door to a much more inclusive view of languages. Thus we read[77]:

> "(17) Promoting the teaching and learning of languages and linguistic diversity, including the official languages of the Community and its regional and minority

> languages, should be a priority of Community action in the field of education and training [...].

It would seem, then, that the lack of enthusiasm in the institutions of the Union for issues relating to regional, minority and migrant languages is not as notorious as it was a few years ago. Though the time is not good (the enlargement of the Union brings in a much more widely diverse set of official and working languages), it is true that the Council has moved in the right direction, and the Commission is now paying more than lip service to these issues. Nevertheless, the official approach is still that such languages are the responsibility of the Member States (a perverse reading, as I have said, of the wording of Article 149(1) of the Treaty).

There is an interesting reference, made in passing, which I think is worth quoting in the conclusion of this paper, for it draws attention to another advantage of diversity. We find it in Recital 8 of the EYL Decision, where language learning is seen as beneficial for enhancing awareness of cultural diversity:

> It is important to learn languages as it enhances awareness of cultural diversity and helps eradicate xenophobia, racism, anti-Semitism and intolerance.

At all levels, this realisation is important for Europe: for its present and its future. It remains to be seen whether the Union will be able to include all constituent languages of the peoples of Europe in its definition of cultural diversity, over and above its frequent declarations of good intent.

## Notes

[1] Letter written in 1926 by the Church and Nation Committee of the Church of Scotland to the Secretary of State for Scotland in 1926 on the subject of Irish Immigration. Quoted in Church of Scotland General Assembly Report (2002).

[2] Mill, 1946 [1861]: 65.

[3] House, 2001.

[4] http://europa.eu.int/constitution/en/lstoc1_en.htm

[5] 300D1934. Decision No 1934/2000/EC of the European Parliament and of the Council of 17 July 2000 on the European Year of Languages 2001. *OJ* L 232, 14/9/2000 pp 1–5. http://europa.eu/eur-lex/pri/en/oj/dat/2000/l_232/l_23220000914en00010005.pdf.

[6] Council Resolution of 14 February 2002 on the promotion of linguistic diversity and language learning in the framework of the implementation of the objectives of the European Year of Languages 2001. Ref 2002/C 50/01 (32002G0223(01). *OJ* C 50 23/2/2002 pp 1–2, http://europa.eu.int/smartapi/cgi/sga_doc?smartapi!celexapi!prod!CELEXnumdoc&lg=EN&numdoc=32002G0223(01)&model=guichett; http://europa.eu.int/eur-lex/pri/en/oj/dat/2002/c_050/c_05020020223en00010002.pdf.

[7] EP Resolution on the multilingualism of the European Community, of 14 October 1982, http://www.ciemen.org/mercator/ue23-gb.htm [last accessed 11 September 2006]

[8] EP Resolution on the right to use one's own language, of 25 July 1994, http://www.ciemen.org/mercator/ue23-gb.htm. [last accessed 11 September 2006]

[9] EP Resolution on languages in the Community and the situation of Catalan, of 11 December 1990, http://www.ciemen.org/mercator/ue16-gb.htm . [last accessed 11 September 2006]

[10] European Council (General Affairs). Presidency Statement: Luxembourg, 12/6/1995. Press 174. Nr 7839/95. Item 'Linguistic diversity and multilingualism in the European Union. Council Conclusions'. http://db.consilium.eu.int/newsroom/LoadDoc.asp?MAX=121&BID=71&DID=43589&LANG=1

[11] For example 'The Future of Regional and Minority Languages in the European Union', speech by Viviane Reding, Member of the European Commission responsible for Education, http://europa.eu.int/futurum/documents/offtext/sp111002_en.htm.

[12] http://www.europarl.eu.int/summits/can1_en.htm.

[13] Council Resolution of 16 December 1997 on the early teaching of European Union languages, *OJ* C 1, 3/1/1998, http://europa.eu.int/scadplus/leg/en/cha/c11042.htm; http://europa.eu.int/abc/doc/off/bull/en/9711/p103109.htm.

[14] Council of the European Communities. Decision of 28 July 1989 establishing an action programme to promote foreign language competence in the European Community (Lingua). Ref 89/489/EEC (31989D0489). *OJ* L 239, 16/08/1989, pp 24–32, http://europa.eu.int/smartapi/cgi/sga_doc?smartapi!celexapi!prod!CELEXnumdoc&lg=EN&numdoc=31989D0489&model=guichett.

[15] Council of the European Union. Decision of 22 December 2000 adopting a multiannual Community programme to stimulate the development and use of European digital content on the global networks and to promote linguistic diversity in the information society. Ref 2001/48/EC (301D0048). *OJ* L 14, 18/1/2001, pp 32–40. ('e-Content'), http://europa.eu.int/smartapi/cgi/sga_doc?smartapi!celexapi!prod!CELEXnumdoc&lg=EN&numdoc=301D0048&model=guichett; http://cordis.europa.eu/econtent/.

[16] Article 149(1): 'The Community shall contribute to the development of quality education by encouraging cooperation between Member States and, if necessary, by supporting and supplementing their action, while fully respecting the responsibility of the Member States for the content of teaching and the organisation of education systems and their cultural and linguistic diversity.'

1. La Comunidad contribuirá al desarrollo de una educación de calidad fomentando la cooperación entre los Estados miembros y, si fuere necesario, apoyando y completando la acción de éstos en el pleno respeto de sus responsabilidades en cuanto a los contenidos de la enseñanza y a la organización del sistema educativo, así como de su diversidad cultural y lingüística.

1. La Communauté contribue au développement d'une éducation de qualité en encourageant la coopération entre États membres et, si nécessaire, en appuyant et en complétant leur action tout en respectant pleinement la responsabilité des États membres pour le contenu de l'enseignement et l'organisation du système éducatif ainsi que leur diversité culturelle et linguistique.

1. La Comunità contribuisce allo sviluppo di un'istruzione di qualità incentivando la cooperazione tra Stati membri e, se necessario, sostenendo ed integrando la loro azione nel pieno rispetto della responsabilità degli Stati membri per quanto riguarda il contenuto dell'insegnamento e l'organizzazione del sistema di istruzione, nonché delle loro diversità culturali e linguistiche.

[17] 2391st Council meeting (Education and Youth Affairs), Brussels, 29 November 2001. Education. Linguistic diversity and language learning in the framework of the implementation of the objectives of the European Year of Languages. Resolution. Ref 14388/01 (presse 437), http://register.consilium.eu.int/pdf/en/01/st14/14717-a1en1.pdf.

[18] For further details see Strubell (2003).

[19] Council of the European Union. Decision 96/664/EC of 21 November 1996 on the adoption of a multiannual programme to promote the linguistic diversity of the Community in the information society (MLIS). *OJ* L 306, 28/11/1996, pp 40–48, http://europa.eu.int/smartapi/cgi/sga_doc?smartapi!celexapi!prod!CELEXnumdoc&lg=EN&numdoc=31996D0664&model=guichett.

[20] Judgment of the Court of 23 February 1999. *European Parliament v Council of the European Union*. Council Decision 96/664/EC—Promotion of linguistic diversity of the Community in the information society—Legal basis. Case C-42/97. Ref 61997J0042. European Court Reports 1999 Page I-0869. Notice No 1999/C 100/11. *OJ* C 100, Vol 42, 10 April 1999, http://europa.eu.int/eur-lex/en/archive/1999/c_10019990410en.html. Summary, http://europa.eu.int/cgi-bin/eur-lex/udl.pl?REQUEST=Seek-Deliver&LANGUAGE=en&SERVICE=eurlex&COLLECTION=oj&DOCID=1999c100p00070008.

[21] Ref EAC/19/00 (*OJ* C 266 of 16 September 2000), http://ec.europa.eu/education/policies/lang/funding/index_en.html.
[22] Commission Staff Working Paper: Promoting Language Learning and Linguistic Diversity. Brussels, 13/11/2002, Sec(2002) 1234. http://ec.europa.eu/education/policies/lang/policy/consult/consult_en.pdf; http://www.europa.eu.int/comm/education/policies/lang/policy/consult/consult_en.pdf [last accessed, September 12 2006];. The Working Paper was studied by several bodies, e.g. Opinion of the European Economic and Social Committee on the 'Commission staff working paper Promoting language learning and linguistic diversity', SEC(2002) 1234, *OJ* C 85/126, 8/4/2003, http://europa.eu.int/eur-lex/pri/en/oj/dat/2003/c_085/c_08520030408en01260128.pdf.
[23] Press release (French): http://ue.eu.int/ueDocs/cms_Data/docs/pressdata/en/gena/85437.pdf
[24] For practical reasons, the Council decided that only regulations adopted by the European Parliament and the Council under the co-decision procedure will have to be available in Irish. Other legislative acts will be exempted for a transition period of five years to allow time to train and recruit translators. Source: Translation DG: "Irish becomes the 21st official language of the EU". http://ec.europa.eu/dgs/translation/spotlight/irish_en.htm
[25] InfoBase Europe. Factsheet 48, http://www.ibeurope.com/Database/Factsheets/F048lang.htm.
[26] Shuibne, 2001.
[27] Regulation 1/1958 of the Council, 15 April 1958, in which are established the linguistic rules of the institutions. Ref 31958R0001, *OJ* B 17, 6/10/1958, http://eur-lex.europa.eu/LexUriServ/LexUriServ.do?uri=CELEX:31958R0001:EN:HTML.
[28] http://europa.eu.int/eur-lex/en/treaties/selected/livre2_c.html.
[29] For example, the Lingua Action programme (1989).
[30] European Parliament Resolution on languages in the Community and the situation of Catalan, of 11 December 1990, http://www.ciemen.org/mercator/ue16-gb.htm.
[31] European Community. Treaty Establishing the European Community. Consolidated version.; http://europa.eu.int/eur-lex/en/treaties/dat/C_2002325EN.003301.html; http://europa.eu.int/information_society/activities/eten/library/reference/ec_treaty_en.pdf. Article 314 was formerly Article S in the Maastricht Treaty (1992).
[32] 'Every person may write to the institutions of the Union in one of the languages of the Treaties and must have an answer in the same language.' Charter of Fundamental Rights of the European Union. Article 41.4. Ref 2000/C 364/01, *OJ* C 364, 18/12/2000. p. 18. http://eur-lex.europa.eu/JOHtml.do?uri=OJ:C:2000:364:SOM:EN:HTML.
[33] Treaty establishing a Constitution for Europe. *OJ* C 310 of 16 December 2004. http://europa.eu/constitution/index_en.htm
[34] Irish became a working language of the Court of Justice and of the Court of First Instance, but not of the other institutions, as soon as Ireland acceded to the EEC.
[35] Source: Article 7 (ex-4) of the Consolidated version of the Treaty Establishing the European Community.
[36] *Kik v OHMI*. Ref T-120/99. Judgment 12/7/2001, http://eur-lex.europa.eu/LexUriServ/LexUriServ.do?uri=CELEX:61999A0120:EN:HTML
[37] European Parliament. Written question 0909/03 by MEP Seán Ó Neachtain (UEN) to the Commission (13 March 2003). Subject: Communicating with the European Commission in the Irish Language (Gaeilge), http://www2.europarl.eu.int/omk/OM-Europarl?PROG=WQ&L=EN&PUBREF=-//EP//TEXT+WQ+P-2003-0909+0+DOC+SGML+V0//EN&LEVEL=3&NAV=S. Reply by Commission President Prodi: http://www2.europarl.eu.int/omk/OM-Europarl?PROG=WQA&L=EN&PUBREF=-//EP//TEXT+WQA+P-2003-0909+0+DOC+SGML+V0//EN&LEVEL=3&NAV=S&SAME_LEVEL=1
[38] http://europa.eu.int/geninfo/mailbox/form_en.htm.
[39] Council Resolution of 31 March 1995 on improving and diversifying language learning and teaching within the education systems of the European Union. Ref 31995Y0812(01). *OJ* C 207, 12/8/1995, pp 1–5. http://europa.eu.int/smartapi/cgi/sga_doc?smartapi!celexapi!prod!CELEXnumdoc&lg=en&numdoc=31995Y0812(01)&model=guichett.
[40] Decision No 253/2000/EC of the European Parliament and of the Council of 24 January 2000 establishing the second phase of the Community action programme in the field of education 'Socrates'. Ref 32000D0253. *OJ* L 28 3/2/2000, p 1. Amended by 32003D0451 (*OJ* L 069 13/3/2003, p 6), http://europa.eu.int/smartapi/cgi/sga_doc?smartapi!celexapi!prod!CELEXnumdoc&lg=EN&numdoc=32000D0253&model=guichett.

[41] The reasoning behind the inclusion of Irish and Luxembourgish first appeared in the 1989 Lingua programme: 'Whereas there is a specific need to encourage the teaching as foreign languages of all official languages of the Communities, together with Irish, one of the languages in which the Treaties establishing the European Communities are drafted, and Letzeburgesch, a language spoken throughout the territory of Luxembourg ...' The wording in the Preamble to the 1995 Socrates Programme, in its reference to the Lingua Action, is virtually identical. Reference: Decision No 819/95/EC of the European Parliament and of the Council of 14 March 1995 establishing the Community action programme 'Socrates'. Ref 31995D0819, *OJ* L 87, 20/4/1995, pp 10–24, http://europa.eu.int/smartapi/cgi/sga_doc?smartapi!celexapi!prod!CELEXnumdoc&lg=EN&numdoc=31995D0819&model=guichett.

[42] 'In this context, language teaching covers the teaching and learning as foreign languages of all the official languages of the Community, together with Irish (one of the languages in which the Treaties establishing the European Communities are drawn up) and Lëtzebuergesch (a language spoken throughout the territory of Luxembourg). Special attention shall be paid throughout the programme to promoting the less widely used and less widely taught of these languages.' Lingua Action programme.

[43] http://www.eblul.org.

[44] Written question P-2604 on promoting and safeguarding lesser-used languages (10 December 1999), *OJ* C 219 E, 1/8/2000, p 182, http://www2.europarl.eu.int/omk/OM-Europarl?PROG=WQ&L=EN&PUBREF=-//EP//TEXT+WQ+P-1999-2604+0+DOC+SGML+V0//EN&LEVEL=3&NAV=S. Reply (31 January 2000), *OJ* C 219 E, 1/8/2000, p 182, http://www2.europarl.eu.int/omk/OM-Europarl?PROG=WQA&L=EN&PUBREF=-//EP//TEXT+WQA+P-1999-2604+0+DOC+SGML+V0//EN&LEVEL=4&NAV=S&SAME_LEVEL=1.

[45] Commission communication COM(95) 590 final, November 1995 (Luxembourg: Office for Official Publications of the European Communities, 1996). http://europa.eu.int/en/record/white/edu9511/index.htm.

[46] European Council (Education). Presidency Statement: Brussels (6/5/1996). Press 122 Nr 6802/96. 1. 'The Council meeting on 6 May 1996 discussed the White Paper *Teaching and Learning: Towards the Learning Society* presented by the European Commission on the initiative of Commissioners Edith Cresson and Pádraig Flynn with the agreement of Commissioner Martin Bangemann ... The objectives defined in the White Paper and the measures it proposes raise problems which cannot be ignored ... D. Some Member States take the view that the attention they pay to the languages of the European Union, which are considered important and given priority under the 1995 Resolution to promote multilingualism, cannot of course, in the context of their national policies, rule out that paid to other languages.' http://www.consilium.europa.eu/cms3_applications/Applications/newsRoom/LoadDocument.asp?directory=en/educ/&filename=009a0004.htm.

[47] a. Council Resolution of 14 February 2002 on the promotion of linguistic diversity and language learning in the framework of the implementation of the objectives of the European Year of Languages 2001. Ref 32002G0223(01), *OJ* C 050 , 23/2/2002, pp 1–2. http://europa.eu.int/smartapi/cgi/sga_doc?smartapi!celexapi!prod!CELEXnumdoc&lg=EN&numdoc=32002G0223(01)&model=guichett; http://europa.eu.int/eur-lex/pri/en/oj/dat/2002/c_050/c_05020020223en00010002.pdf.
b. Presidency Conclusions, Barcelona European Council, 15 and 16 March 2002. Ref D/02/8, Brussels, 16 March 2002.

[48] About 27% of those born before 1920, surveyed in 1999, declared that when they were young their parents spoke a regional language with them, either 'habituellement' (17%) or 'occasionnellement' (10%). These figures had declined to just 5% of those born between 1975 and 1980; in only 1% of cases did parents speak this language with them 'habituellement': Clanché (2002).

[49] Special Eurobarometer, 'Europeans and Languages', February 2001. Ref 147. Full report: http://www.ec.europa.eu/public_opinion/archives/ebs/ebs_147.en.pdf Executive summary http://www.ec.europa.eu/public_opinion/archives/eb/ebs_147_summ_en.pdf (6 pp). See also http://www.ibeurope.com/Database/Factsheets/F048lang.htm. Full text quoted as 'Eurobarometer 54 Special'.

[50] 'In 1945 the Yiddisch linguist Max Weinreich formulated the much quoted metaphor (in Yiddisch): 'A shprakh iz a diyalekt mit an armey un a flot' in the article 'Der yivo un di problemen fun undzer tsayt' ('Yivo' and the problems of our time), in the periodical *Yivo-bleter* 25/1/13. Source: http://www.olestig.dk/scotland/weinreich.html.

[51] A more recent Eurobarometer survey, "Europeans and Languages" (Special Eurobarometer 237, published in September 2005) states that "Half of the citizens of the Member States assert that they can speak at least one other language than their mother tongue at the level of being able to have a conversation. This is 3 points more than perceived in 2001 in the EU15 (EB 51.1)" (page 3). http://www.ec.europa.eu/public_opinion/archives/ebs/ebs_237.en.pdf . "Europeans and their languages" is a still more recent survey (Special Eurobarometer 243), published in February 2006: http://ec.europa.eu/public_opinion/archives/ebs/ebs_243_en.pdf

[52] 9% of the Spanish sample in the 2005 Eurobarometer survey mentioned Basque or Catalan as their mother tongue.

[53] Article 2, para c.

[54] Article 1, indent 2. Decision on the European Year of Languages 2001.

[55] The *European Union and Lesser-Used Languages*, Coordinator: Miquel Strubell. Series EDUC 108-EN. European Parliament, Luxembourg, 2002.

[56] Ref A1-965/80. Published *OJ* C 287, 9/11/1981, p 57. http://www.ciemen.org/mercator/UE18-GB.htm . Summaries of each Resolution: http://www.eiop.or.at/eiop/texte/2000-016.htm.

[57] Ref A1-1254/82. Published *OJ* C 68, 14/3/1983, pp 103–4, http://www.ciemen.org/mercator/UE20-GB.htm in Mercator database; and Minority Electronic Resources (MINELRES):. http://arts.uwaterloo.ca/minelres/eu/re830211.htm .

[58] Ref A2-0150/87. Published *OJ* C 318, 30/11/1987, pp 160–4, http://www.ciemen.org/mercator/UE21-GB.htm and http://arts.uwaterloo.ca/minelres/eu/re871030.htm.

[59] Ref A3-0042/94, Report of the Committee on Culture, Youth, Education and the Media on Linguistic and Cultural Minorities in the European Community. Resolution published *OJ* C 61, 28/2/1994, p 110, http://www.ciemen.org/mercator/UE23-GB.htm and http://arts.uwaterloo.ca/minelres/eu/re940209.htm.

[60] European Parliament. Resolution on regional and lesser-used European languages, adopted on 13 December 2001. Ref B5-0770/2001. *OJ* C 177E 25/7/2002, http://europa.eu/eur-lex/pri/en/oj/dat/2002/ce177/ce17720020725en03340336.pdf.

[61] European Parliament. Resolution with recommendations to the Commission on European regional and lesser-used languages—the languages of minorities in the EU—in the context of enlargement and cultural diversity (Rapporteur: Michl Ebner), adopted on 4 September 2003, Ref P5_TA(2003)0372, RR503926EN.doc, A5-0271/2003, http://ec.europa.eu/education/policies/lang/doc/hebner_en.pdf

[62] http://www.mercator-central.org.

[63] http://ec.europa.eu/education/policies/lang/languages/langmin/langmin_en.html.

[64] http://www.uoc.edu/euromosaic/ and 1996 publication: Nelde, Peter; Strubell, Miquel & Williams, Glyn. *Euromosaic. Production and reproduction of minority language groups in the EU*. European Commission, Luxembourg, 1996. ISBN 92-827-5512-6
See also http://ec.europa.eu/education/policies/lang/languages/langmin/euromosaic/index en.html.

[65] http://ec.europa.eu/education/policies/lang/languages/langmin/files/support.pdf

[66] Delivered at the Conference on creating a common structure for promoting historical linguistic minorities within the European Union, http://europa.eu.int/rapid/pressReleasesAction.do?reference=SPEECH/02/474&format=HTML&aged=1&language=EN&guiLanguage=en.

[67] *OJ* C 310, 16.12.2004. Article IV-448 on p. 191. http://eur-lex.europa.eu/LexUriServ/site/en/oj/2004/c_310/c_31020041216en01860202.pdf

[68] http://europa.eu.int/constitution/en/ptoc163_en.htm

[69] ECOTEC Research & Consulting Limited. *Evaluation of the European Year of Languages 2001.*
*A Final Report to the Directorate General Education and Culture*. Contract No. 2001-2394/001-001 LAN LANGUAGE. August 2002. http://europa.eu.int/comm/dgs/education_culture/evalreports/languages/2002/eyl2001/EYL2001xprep_en.pdf

[70] Memorandum del Gobierno Español. Solicitud de Reconocimiento en la Unión Europea de Todas las Lenguas Oficiales en España. 13/12/2004. http://www.es-ue.org/Documents/MemorandumLenguasCCAA10%C2%BA(DEFINITIVA)ES10dic04.DOC

[71] Council conclusion of 13 June 2005 on the official use of additional languages within the Council and possibly other Institutions and bodies of the European Union. *OJ* C 148, 18/06/2005 P. 1–2. http://europa.eu.int/eur-lex/lex/LexUriServ/LexUriServ.do?uri=CELEX:52005XG0618(01):EN:HTML.

Significantly, this was the same meeting at which Irish was recognised as an official language and a working language of the institutions of the Union, by a decision to amend Regulation No. 1/1958.

72 Debate Europe: http://europa.eu/debateeurope/index.htm.
European Discussion Forum: http://ec.europa.eu/comm/coreservices/forum/index.cfm?forum=debateeurope&lang=ca.

73 Viviane Reding, Commissioner-designate for Education and Culture, 2/9/1999. DOC_ENDV380380397EN.doc, PE 230.789/rev.II, pp 20–21, Quoted in http://www.inst.at/studies/s_1006_e.htm.

74 http://europa.eu.int/futurum/forum_convention/documents/contrib/acad/0300_c_en.pdf.

75 Communication from the Commission to the Council, the European Parliament, the Economic and Social Committee and the Committee of the Regions - Promoting language learning and linguistic diversity: an action plan 2004-2006 [COM(2003) 449 final]. Brussels, 24/7/2003. http://europa.eu/scadplus/leg/en/cha/c11068.htm

76 Communication from the Commission to the Council, the European Parliament, the European Economic and Social Committee and the Committee of the Regions. *A New Framework Strategy for Multilingualism.* Brussels, 22 November 2005. COM(2005) 596 final. http://europa.eu/languages/servlets/Doc?id=913.
http://europa.eu/languages/en/document/74

77 Amended proposal for a Decision of the European Parliament and of the Council establishing an integrated action programme in the field of lifelong learning. Adaptation following the agreement of 17 May 2006 on the Financial Framework 2007-2013 (presented by the Commission pursuant to Article 250(2) of the EC Treaty). Brussels, 24.5.2006. COM(2006) 236 final. 2004/0153 (COD). http://eur-lex.europa.eu/LexUriServ/site/en/com/2006/com2006_0236en01.pdf

## References

Andersen, OS (2001) 'A Language is a Dialect with an Army (and a Navy)', http://www.olestig.dk/scotland/weinreich.html.

Church and Nation Committee of the Church of Scotland. Letter sent to the Secretary of State for Scotland in 1926 on the subject of Irish Immigration. Quoted in the Church of Scotland General Assembly 2002 Report, http://www.churchofscotland.org.uk/downloads/churchandnationtext.txt.

Clanché, F (2002) 'Langue régionales, langues étrangères: de l'héritage à la pratique', *INSEE Première*, No 830, February 2002, http://www.insee.fr/fr/ffc/Ipweb/2002/ip830/intro.html.

Coulmas, F (ed) (1991) *A Language Policy for the European Community: Prospects and Quandaries* (Berlin, Mouton de Gruyter).

Europa Diversa (2002) 'Proposals for a New EU Language Regime', *Convention on the Future of the European Union,* http://europa.eu.int/futurum/forum_convention/documents/contrib/acad/0300_c_en.pdf.

European Commission (2000) Co-funded projects for Regional and Minority Languages and Cultures, http://europa.eu.int/comm/education/policies/lang/langmin/language_en.pdf.

European Council. Presidency Conclusions. Cannes European Council summit, 26 and 27 June 1995.

European Cultural Foundation (1999) *Which Languages for Europe?* Report of the Conference held in Oegstgeest, the Netherlands, 9–11 October 1998, Amsterdam.
European Parliament Written question E-3948/00 by MEP Pere Esteve to the Council (20 December 2000). Subject: The Catalan language in the European Union. *OJ* C 235 E, 21/08/2001, 35–36 (Reply: 7 May 2001).
European Union. Treaty of Amsterdam, amending the Treaty on European Union, the Treaties establishing the European Communities and certain related acts, signed on 2 October 1997.
Grin, F and Moring, T (2003) *Support for Minority Languages in Europe*. DG for Education & Culture, European Commission, http://ec.europa.eu/education/policies/lang/languages/langmin/files/support.pdf
House, J (2001) 'The Language Policy in the European Union', *Guardian Weekly*, 19 April 2001.
InfoBase Europe, Factsheet 48, http://www.ibeurope.com/Database/Factsheets/F048lang.htm.
Intergovernmental Conference 2003–2004. Final Act. http://europa.eu.int/constitution/en/ptoc163_en.htm
Luxembourg. Loi du 24 février 1984 sur le régime des langues.
Mill, JS (1946) [1861] *Considerations on Representative Government* (London, Longman).
Nelde, P, Strubell, M and Williams, G (1996) *Euromosaic. Production and Reproduction in the Minority Language Groups in the EU*, European Commission, Luxembourg, 1996.
Neugaard, EJ (1995) 'The Continuing Valencian Language Controversy', *Language Problems and Language Planning*, vol. 19, 60–6.
Reding, V (1999) Address to the Committeee for Education & Culture, European parliament (2/9/1999). DOC_ENDV380380397EN.doc, PE 230.789/rev.II: 20–1.
Reding, V (2002) 'The Future of Regional and Minority Languages in the European Union', address delivered at the Conference on Creating a common structure for promoting historical linguistic minorities within the European Union, Helsinki (11 October 2002).
Shuibhne, N (2001) 'The European Union and Minority Language Rights', 3(2) *MOST Journal on Multicultural Societies*, ISSN 1564-4901.
Spanish Government. Memorandum del Gobierno Español. Solicitud de Reconocimiento en la Unión Europea de Todas las Lenguas Oficiales en España. 13/12/2004. http://www.es-ue.org/Documents/MemorandumLenguasCCAA10%C2%BA(DEFINITIVA)ES10dic04.DOC
Special Eurobarometer 54, 'Europeans and Languages' (February 2001) Ref 147 (Brussels, INRA).
Special Eurobarometer 237, 'Europeans and Languages' (September 2005).

Special Eurobarometer 243, "Europeans and their languages" (February 2006).

Strubell, M (1994) 'Catalan in Valencia: The Story of an Attempted Secession', in Lüdi, Georges (Hrsg.) *Sprach-standardisierung*. Schweizerische Akademie des Geistes- und Sozialwissenschaften/Universitätsverlag Freiburg, 229–254.

Strubell, M (2002) (coord) *The European Union and Lesser-Used Languages*, Series EDUC 108-EN. European Parliament, Luxembourg.

Strubell, M (2003) 'Towards a European Language Policy/Cap a una política lingüística europea' in *Actes del 2n Congrés Europeu sobre Planificació Lingüística. Andorra la Vella, 14, 15 I 16 de novembre de 2001* (Barcelona, Departament de Cultura, Generalitat de Catalunya), 458–72.

Trim, J (2002) 'Foreign Language Policies in Europe, with Special Reference to the Roles of the Council of Europe and the European Union' in SJ Baker (ed), *Language Policy: Lessons from Global Models, Proceedings from Language Policy*, conference held at the Monterey Institute (Monterey, California, September 2001), http://www.miis.edu/docs/lang-policy/ch12.pdf.

Wright, S (2000) *Community and Communication. The Role of Language in Nation State Building and European Integration* (Clevedon, Multilingual Matters Ltd).

# 9

# *English as Lingua Franca: A Challenge to the Doctrine of Multilingualism*

CHRIS LONGMAN

## UNITED IN DIVERSITY: A VISION OF MULTILINGUAL EUROPE

THE EUROPEAN UNION is robust in its defence of the equality of languages. The introduction to the Commission Translation Service's 'A Multilingual Community at Work' spells out this mission:

> Equal status for the official languages, or multilingualism, goes to the heart of what the Union is all about. Language is part of national and personal identity. There can be no question of imposing a sort of artificial 'Euro-identity'-far from it: the languages of Europe are part of its immense and diverse cultural heritage, and they should be cherished. . . . As the European Union grows, the practical difficulties of according equal status to the languages of its constituent nations will also grow; but any approach that failed to respect the languages of the peoples of the Union would betray the very foundations of Union philosophy.[1]

Any attempt to give one language any kind of privileged position within this regime thus becomes entirely contrary to the spirit of European integration. Linguistic diversity, in this view, is a prerequisite for constructing a Europe where all citizens enjoy equal status and equal rights, and where public support is maintained for the European idea (European Commission, 1999: 2). It is the purpose of this chapter to explore the issue of whether the growing use of English as a lingua franca ('language of wider communication' or 'international language') undermines one of the cornerstones of the European project: language status equality.

The chapter will begin with a brief overview of the language regime of the EU, and an analysis of the ways in which the concept of multilingualism is used in EU discourse. The following section introduces the challenge that is posed to the doctrine of multilingualism by the increasing dominance of English as a global language within Europe, and its position within the European institutions. Subsequently an assessment is made of the inequality and privilege that exists behind the ideals of multilingualism in the EU, and how the English language has been perceived as a threat to other languages in Europe. The chapter concludes with an appraisal of the impact of English as a lingua franca on institutional, societal and personal multilingualism.

## The EU Language Regime

The foundation of the European Union language regime is the principle of official multilingualism within the institutions set out in Regulation No 1/58, the first regulation of the Council of the then EEC, which is the basis of what has become known as the EU's language charter.[2] For the original six Member States the four official languages of those states became co-official at EEC level.[3] Each subsequent enlargement added the new official state languages to the Regulation repertoire. Translating and interpreting between four official languages clearly does not amount to an insuperable problem, with only 12 language translation combinations necessary (ie four languages multiplied by translations into three others). The situation has become more complicated as the EC/EU has grown over the years, as Table 1 below shows.[4] The official and working languages of the European institutions, which numbered four at the start of the project, grew in May 2004 to number 20 with the enlargement into central and eastern Europe, plus Cyprus and Malta.

In order to serve the language needs of this complex set of institutions there are language services which deal with day-to-day written and oral communication. These services represent the most extensive (and expensive) translation and interpretation services in the world.[6]

*Table 1: Official Languages of the EU 1958–2004*

| No of languages | From year | Official languages | Language combinations |
|---|---|---|---|
| 4 | 1958 – | French, German, Italian, Dutch | 12 |
| 6 | 1974 – | + English, Danish[5] | 30 |
| 7 | 1982 – | + Greek | 42 |
| 9 | 1986 – | + Spanish, Portuguese | 72 |
| 11 | 1995 – | + Swedish, Finnish | 110 |
| 20 | 2004 – | + Estonian, Latvian, Lithuanian, Polish, Czech, Slovak, Hungarian, Slovene, Maltese | 380 |

## Analysing Multilingualism

There are three very distinct ways in which the term 'multilingualism' is used in EU discourse, and it is worth bearing these in mind in the attempt to assess the challenges that are faced by multilingualism in the EU:

- institutional multilingualism: the notion that there are many languages represented and catered for within the institutional structure;
- societal multilingualism: the notion that more than one language is spoken in a given society;
- personal multilingualism: the notion that a given individual speaks more than one language.

The EU, in its promotion of multilingualism, is therefore aiming for three different objectives:

- institutional multilingualism: the *de jure* equality of the official and working languages of the Union, as stated in Council Regulation No 1/58;
- societal multilingualism: because Europe is a continent in which many languages are spoken, respecting and protecting cultural and linguistic diversity is an objective of the EU;[7]
- personal multilingualism: the avowed objective of the EU that its citizens should be competent in their mother tongue (MT) and two foreign languages (MT + 2).[8]

## The Limitations of Multilingualism

There are many challenges to the different interpretations of multilingualism in the EU. For example, as far as institutional multilingualism is concerned, the multilingualism recognised does not reflect the multilingual reality of Europe which includes not just official state languages but also regional and minority languages (RMLs) (those with official status, such as Catalan, Welsh and Frisian, or those without official status, such as Corsican or Breton), non-territorial languages (such as Romani), and languages of recent immigrant communities (for example Hindi, Urdu, Arabic and Turkish). Furthermore, the EU makes no distinction between 'official' and 'working' languages, though for many people a 'working' language is a dominant language of international communication within institutions. In the EU this would make English and French the *de facto* working languages in most institutional communicative situations. However, strictly speaking, all official languages are working languages according to the EU.[9]

Since the foundations of this linguistic regime were established with the very first Regulation passed by the Council of Ministers in 1958 there has been an enormous change in the character, and an increase in the range of competences, of the Community/Union, but little or no change in the linguistic regime itself. With the exception of certain trifling measures to help protect and promote regional and minority languages, and encourage foreign language learning, there has been no political will to revisit the basis upon which the language regime rests (Phillipson, 2003; Wright, 2000). Part of the problem arises because there is little consensus about the objectives of any changes despite almost universal concern that the present situation is unfair and potentially unsustainable. Mamadouh (1999) outlines three essential criticisms of current EU practices of institutional multilingualism, which all pull in different directions:

- those who would like to see institutional multilingualism extended to include more languages, such as the Catalans, and other users of RMLs;
- those who would like to see the current regime applied more thoroughly, such as the Germans, who are the largest single block of native speakers in the EU, but who see their language receiving very unequal treatment compared with English and French. The other smaller language communities also fit into this category;
- those who believe that the efficient functioning of the EU requires that the number of official and working languages be reduced to two or perhaps three.

Clearly all these positions have some merit, but they are gravely problematic too, and in the absence of any one position becoming more acceptable than the others, the language regime drifts on in an atmosphere of *laissez-faire*, with politicians unwilling to address this contentious issue. But within this political lacuna the position of English as a dominant international language is consolidated.

The language regime of the EU, however, does not simply consist of the principle of institutional multilingualism as set out in Regulation No 1/58. The regime consists of a variety of different regulations, norms, practices and policies which relate to the internal workings and relationships within the EU institutions themselves, and also to the relations of these institutions with Member States, sub-state authorities, civil society and European citizens. Furthermore, there are policies for which the EU has competences which impact, either directly or indirectly, on language use in Europe. Nevertheless, the normative basis for dealing with the issue of language in the EU institutions is encapsulated in Regulation No 1/58 with its insistence on the equality of status and rights between Member State languages as used by the institutions in their internal dealings and in their relations with Member States and citizens. The reasoning behind such an insistence on the multilingual character of the EU can be stated as follows: European integration is much deeper than intergovernmental co-operation and directly affects citizens, who have the right to be able to understand the laws being made in their name; furthermore, citizens have the right to communicate with the institutions of the EU, and cannot be expected to learn a new language, or pay for a translation, in order to do so; and finally, citizens have the right of access to EU documents in a language they can understand, given that these documents refer to policies that are being discussed or enacted that affect their daily lives (Rowe, 2002).[10]

However, the need to guarantee equal access to European public life and political institutions is compromised by the need for people to communicate in the civic and institutional domains, frequently without recourse to language support services. It is therefore unsurprising that a lingua franca is sought to facilitate integration, even though this manifestation of the principle of integration may thus undermine the principle of respecting diversity. The perceived utility of a common international language appears to outweigh the concern of retaining and promoting a multilingual EU, and increasingly the language of choice for Europeans operating within and around the EU institutions is English.

## THE CHALLENGE OF ENGLISH

### English as a Global Language in Europe

Before moving on to analyse the impact of English in the EU, it is appropriate to remind ourselves of the position that English occupies, globally and more specifically in Europe.

The dominance of English as the widest spoken language in the world is widely attested (Phillipson, 1992; Crystal, 1997a; Crystal, 1997b; Graddol, 1997; Julios, 2002; Phillipson, 2003). There are no precedents for a language having the powerful combination of such a large number of speakers (as shown in Table 2 below) with the geographical distribution and reach of English.

For the first time in history we are able to truly speak of a 'global language'. This novelty is compounded by the fact that social, political, economic and cultural change has never been so rapid as in the past half century. There are no precedents for trying to understand what will happen to languages in a global environment that places such emphasis on interdependence and communication. As Crystal remarks,

> [t]here has never been a time when so many nations were needing to talk to each other so much. There has never been a time when so many people wished to

*Table 2: Number of English Speakers Worldwide*[11]

| | |
|---|---|
| Native English speakers | 375 million |
| English as second language speakers | 375 million |
| English as foreign language speakers | 750 million |
| Total | 1.5 billion (more or less $^{1}/_{4}$ of the World's population) |

> travel to so many places. There has never been such a strain placed on the conventional resources of translating and interpreting. Never has the need for more widespread bilingualism been greater, to ease the burden on the professional few. And never has there been a more urgent need for a global language.[12]

Furthermore, English dominates in a variety of specific domains, such as international commerce and banking, scientific publications, international conferences, tertiary education, audio-visual production, international travel safety, and the internet, as well as being the dominant working language of many international organisations (Graddol, 1997).

Within the context of European integration and governance, English occupies an exceptional place as a an intra- and inter-institutional lingua franca, as the most utilised drafting language for the Commission (European Commission Translating Service, 1999; European Commission DG Translation (2002)—see Table 3 below) and as a widely used medium of communication between civil society and the European institutions. It is the most studied first foreign language in the education systems of all non-anglophone Member States (Eurydice, 2001: 96), and 75% of all citizens of the EU agree that it is the most useful language to know (Eurobarometer 54, 2001: 1). Indeed, when researchers for Eurobarometer asked whether 'everyone in the European Union should speak English', 69.4% of the 16,078 people questioned agreed (*ibid*: 6).[13] This startling figure gives us much food for thought. Has the English language really been accepted by such a large proportion of European citizens as being a necessary component of public and private life?[14]

In order to begin to understand the possible reasons behind these beliefs, it is worth considering what has caused English to achieve the dominant role it has within Europe. Phillipson (2003: 64-65) lists a variety of structural and ideological causes, the most salient of which in the context of this chapter are as follows:

- English is an integral part of the globalisation process, especially in the fields of commerce, finance, politics, science and the (electronic) media;
- there is greater economic and political interdependence and labour mobility in Europe as the European Union develops (as well as in the contemporary globalised world) which is facilitated by breaking down language barriers and by using languages of wider communication, such as English;

*Table 3: Original Drafting Language in the European Commission*

| Language | 1992 | 1997 | 2001 | 2004 | % change 1992-2004 |
|---|---|---|---|---|---|
| **English** | **35.1%** | **45.4 %** | **56.8%** | **62%** | **+ 26.9%** |
| French | 46.9% | 40.4 % | 29.8 % | 26% | - 20.9% |
| German | 6.2% | 5.4 % | 4.3 % | 3.1% | - 3.1% |
| Others | 8.8% | 8.7 % | 9.1 % | 8.8% | 0% |

- the US and UK have heavily promoted 'their' language since the 1950s;[15]
- higher education (bringing in much needed finance) is increasingly the province of transnationally mobile students who wish to study in the global language, in the US, Canada, the UK and Australia, and gradually more in continental European universities which offer courses in English to attract foreign students;
- national governments in Europe have switched to English as the first foreign language in their education systems, away from previously taught languages such as French, German and Russian;
- language policy is frequently overlooked or fragmented between ministries at Member State level, leading to no overall co-ordination, allowing English to become the default dominant lingua franca;
- English, as spoken by ever increasing numbers of non-native speakers, is less associated with the interests of a particular state, but is associated with prestige and power in a globalised world.[16]

It could be argued that this rise of English as a global lingua franca has very positive outcomes, increasing cross-cultural communication and promoting transnational understanding. Within the context of increased European interdependence in political, civic and social domains, a lingua franca becomes a profoundly important medium of integration. Without doubt, European economic integration and interdependence is facilitated by a language of Europe-wide communication, and given that English is already by far the most known foreign language, and the most widely taught in schools across Europe, it would seem that English is the ideal candidate for this role. Some commentators, such as Smith (1996) take quite an extreme view on this issue: if there is a single market and a single currency, why not a single language? If the EU lacks a transnational demos, why not facilitate one by encouraging a community of communication that is able to express itself and debate in a lingua franca?[17] Indeed, Jürgen Habermas has argued that the extensive use of English offers the possibility of realising the goal of a common European identity (Habermas, 1995). However, most commentators would agree that the issue is far more complex than this, and this chapter will outline various critiques of, and responses to, the increasing dominance of English as a lingua franca in Europe, and how this dominance challenges the fundamental doctrine of diversity and equality in the EU.

## English in the European Union Institutions

Before moving on to assess the ideals and inequalities bound up in the doctrine and reality of multilingualism in the EU, it is worth outlining the role that English plays in the EU institutions themselves. Despite the doctrine of formal institutional multilingualism and the *de jure* equality of 'official and working' languages, the situation has never been quite so simple. Certain languages have always been predominant as working languages. Until the accession of the UK, Ireland and Denmark in 1973 French dominated the internal workings of the EC (Truchot, 2002). However, from the late 1970s onwards, and especially with the accession of the Nordic countries in 1995, English has informally become the predominant language of internal communication within and between the institutions of the EU, especially within the administrative domain (Truchot, 2002; Phillipson, 2003; Creech, 2005). As Labrie points out in relation to the principle of multilingualism, 'There has always been a discrepancy between ideological recognition of this principle and its pragmatic application. With the enlargement of the European Union, that discrepancy can only grow' (Labrie, 2000: 9). Many commentators have pointed out that the language services, already under considerable strain before the 2004 enlargement, are now unable to cope with the extra nine official languages, though the personnel of the services themselves are much more positive (eg Buck, 2002; McCluskey, 2001).[18]

Thus, a *de facto* system of working languages exists in the EU, with English and French in the dominant position. Even German, the language with most native speakers in the EU, does not have the influence that numbers would seem to dictate. During the Finnish presidency (July to December 1999), after four presidencies in which German had been used alongside English and French as the working language of meetings, the Finns reverted to the custom of only using English and French plus the language of the current presidency, much to the chagrin of the German delegation. English and French are 'the de facto drafting languages inside the Commission' (European Commission Translation Service, 2002: 8) and between these two languages it is clear which language is losing ground. Table 3, for example, shows how the use of English for drafting in the Commission has risen at the expense of French.

Although the Union describes all 20 official languages as 'working languages', this is clearly not the case. In the Commission, for example, the working languages are restricted in most contexts to three. As Brian McCluskey, Director of the Commission Translation Service, remarked in a speech in Lisbon in 1998, 'we have in the Commission the concept of working languages, an arrangement which means that all Commission decisions are prepared in French, English and German for internal discussion and development, and are only put into the other official languages when the document is ripe for adoption by the Commission. Material coming from outside, such as national reports, is generally translated into one of the working languages, usually French or English, and sometimes both, so that the Commission officials can work on it' (McCluskey, 1998: 6). Furthermore, McCluskey describes working on 'documents for the weekly Commission meetings, which have always to be available in the three working languages' (*ibid*).

Thus we ought to make a distinction between 'working languages' at the official/secretariat level (two or three languages), and 'working languages' at the political level where elected representatives interact (all official languages). However, there is evidence that this distinction is breaking down and that there is an increased need or willingness at the political level to use a more restricted language regime for pragmatic reasons.[19] Outside of the European Courts of Justice (which operate with French as the internal working language) there is a progressive move towards English as the dominant working language in the institutions of the EU.

## IDEALS AND INEQUALITIES: ENGLISH IN THE EU

In the previous section, the position of English was discussed in terms of the institutional workings of the EU. It appears that what is at stake is the ideal of institutional multilingualism, which may be challenged by the increasing dominance of English as a lingua franca as a default communicative and drafting medium within the institutions. However, as noted before, the concept of multilingualism has societal and personal aspects which the EU has an interest in promoting. Thus this section looks not just at the impact of English on the institutional multilingualism of the EU, but also at the societal aspect (whether English is a threat to the cultural and linguistic diversity of Europe, leading to the possible decline of other natural languages), and the personal aspect (whether the stated aim of the EU that all citizens should speak their mother tongue plus two other Union languages is not being achieved due to the focus of citizens and Member State education systems on providing mother tongue plus English as the preferred option).

### Assessing the Ideal of Multilingualism

The challenge that the English language poses for the three types of European multilingualism presented in the introduction to this chapter can be expressed as follows, in Table 4:

As far as institutional multilingualism is concerned, the *de facto* use of dominant languages such as English and French as 'unofficial' working languages has undermined the claim of equality of official and working languages since the very beginning of the European integration project, but recently the dominance of one language, English, in the internal workings and some of the external output of the EU has become problematic. The societal multilingualism of linguistic diversity, as interpreted by the EC/EU, has always rested on a rather anachronistic vision of one state, one nation, one language, and does not truly represent the genuine multilingual character of Europe, including regional and minority languages. Given that many

*Table 4: European Multilingualism, the EU Vision and the Challenge of English*

| Types of multilingualism | Definition | EU vision | Challenge of English |
|---|---|---|---|
| **Institutional** | many languages are represented and catered for within the institutional structure | the *de jure* equality of official and working languages of the Union | the increasing dominance of English as a lingua franca and as a drafting medium within the institutions |
| **Societal** | more than one language is spoken in a given society | the protection and promotion of cultural and linguistic diversity | English as a threat to the cultural and linguistic diversity of Europe, leading to the possible decline of other natural languages |
| **Personal** | a given individual speaks more than one language | citizens should be competent in their mother tongue (MT) and two foreign languages (MT + 2) | the focus of citizens and Member State education systems on providing mother tongue plus English as the preferred option |

regional and minority languages are not given the support and promotion necessary to ensure their survival, it can be legitimately asked whether the impact of a dominant language such as English further exacerbates the difficulties faced by these languages. Finally, personal multilingualism is problematic from two points of view: first, the EU has few competences in the realm of primary and secondary education, and can therefore only try to influence policy from the sidelines; and second, the issue of those who are already bilingual with a regional or minority language and state language does not appear to figure in the EU scheme. In other words, the EU vision is already challenged and not well thought through. This confusion is compounded by the existence of a language such as English which now has such a high status as an international language that it is becoming the *de facto* first choice first foreign language for European citizens. The EU appears to be rapidly moving towards what Laitin (1997) has described as a 'two plus or minus one' language regime, where the majority speak their mother tongue + English (two languages), a minority speak their mother tongue (regional language) + the state language + English (three languages), and native English speakers just speak English.

Thus, in the institutional, the societal and the personal spheres, the position of English as an international language appears to challenge the EU's doctrine of multilingualism.

## The Commission's View on English as a Lingua Franca

What, though, are the specific complaints that the European Commission brings to the concept of a European lingua franca, which it identifies with English (European Commission, 2002: 7)? The Commission recognises that a lingua franca might have advantages, in that 'it would mean that for the first time ever the whole of Europe would have a shared medium for basic communication; commerce and travel between Member States would become easier' (*ibid*). However, the Commission argues strongly that there are important limitations, the implication being that multilingualism is a more appropriate way forward. For example, businesses need to speak in the language of the customer in order to sell; a lingua franca is insufficient for mobile labour to integrate into host societies; and real mutual understanding between cultures only comes through direct contact in the language of that culture (*ibid*). On the surface these appear to be potent arguments, yet on reflection their cogency may be questioned. As the single market and globalisation become more entrenched, businesses (the majority of which are small and medium-sized enterprises) have to interact with other businesses in many countries and language communities. To have a workforce with the capacity to speak the languages of so many customers would put an unbearable strain on all but the largest companies. More probable solutions are the use of translators and interpreters, the use of local agents, or direct communication in a lingua franca. As for the mobile labour argument, is it clear that a worker who decides to move from one country to another has previously considered this and acquired the language of that state? Perhaps the Commission is suggesting that skilled and unskilled workers should acquire a repertoire of languages at school just in case they decide to exercise their right of freedom of movement. Surely a more realistic scenario would be that a worker moves and learns the language once he or she has arrived (or maybe attends classes for a limited time before departure). In this case, knowledge of a lingua franca might be extremely useful as a short term measure to enable basic transactions during the period of settling in, whilst the host language is being acquired. The third criticism, relating to cultural awareness, also seems rather limited. People in general only learn one or maybe two foreign languages at school, thereby, in the Commission's view, giving them privileged access to understanding the cultures of those countries. The question arises: what about the other cultures of the EU? Are they not important? And furthermore, does the learning of a state language really provide an insight into the internal diversity of that state? Does the learning of Spanish offer an insight into Catalan, Basque and Galician cultures? Perhaps the more general teaching of cultural awareness, including the exploration of the diversity of European cultures, might be a more appropriate use of classroom time.

I have no quibbles with the Commission's desire to see European citizens speaking two languages other than their mother tongue, but to criticise the use of English as a lingua franca on these grounds is not sufficient. There are more potent arguments surrounding this issue, to which we shall now turn.

## Inequality and Privilege

The notion of inequality needs further analytical distinction. There is the notion of inequality between speakers of a given language, and inequality in the status of languages.

### *(a) (In)equality of Speakers: The Politics of Privilege*

There are three aspects to this argument. The first is simply linguistic: if negotiations, discussions, conversations or whatever form of communication take place in one language, native speakers will be at an advantage over non-native speakers in their dominance of the idiom. The second advantage for native speakers is that they do not have to spend a large proportion of their time in education learning the language to a high level. They can use this time to learn or hone other skills, thereby putting them at an advantage in those domains. The third argument is that a world-view that is associated with that culture is implicit in a language. In the case of English, it may be argued, language carries cultural baggage, and promotes the social, economic and political values of the UK and the USA. The advance of English thereby gives a triple advantage.

However, to play devil's advocate, one could argue that the monolingual native speaker of a lingua franca may also be at a disadvantage. As far as greater linguistic competence is concerned, it could be argued that non-native speakers feel more comfortable speaking to each other, due to their having similar communicative competence and perceived equality of status as non-native speakers of an international lingua franca. A native speaker, in this view, is one who introduces colloquialisms and cultural references into the conversation that do not carry any meaning for the non-native speaker to the detriment of communication, and the reinforcement of a hierarchical relationship of competence. The language used will be more complex, and spoken with greater speed, thereby making communication more, not less, difficult. Native speakers may also react to non-native speakers in a condescending way if communication does not flow in a fashion to which the native speaker is accustomed. In this scenario a native/non-native speaker conversation has more potential pitfalls than a non-native/non-native conversation.[20] Perhaps the price one ought to pay for having one's language as a lingua franca is to learn how to communicate in multilingual situations in a clearly understandable form of English.[21] It is an interesting question of linguistics whether the English language is developing a transnational form, one that is not so attached to UK or US standards. If so, there may, in the future, be a need for native English speakers to become adept in communicating in, and being receptive to, an international English (Inglish?) with newly evolved syntax and phonology.[22]

However, despite these counter arguments, it would appear reasonably incontrovertible that on balance native English speakers are advantaged because their language is the lingua franca.

*(b) (In)equality of Languages: The Politics of Status*

As the European Commission Translation Service notes, 'Equal status for the official languages, or multilingualism, goes to the heart of what the Union is all about. . . . [A]ny approach that failed to respect the languages of the peoples of the Union would betray the very foundations of Union philosophy' (European Commission DG Translation, 1999: 4).[23] This is a very powerful statement of the principle of institutional multilingualism which is supposed to reflect the societal multilingualism of Europe. However, as noted before, this 'philosophy' is full of contradictions.

Despite the EU's insistence on the equal status of official languages, as set out in Council Regulation No 1/58, 'languages are not equal in political or social status, particularly in multilingual contexts' (Graddol, 1997: 5), and the equality of languages in the EU has always been more of an illusion than a reality. This illusion is exposed when it is recognised that the EU ideal of language equality is based on an outdated 19th/20th century image of internally homogenous nation states; the actual complex mosaic of autochthonous languages in Europe is not reflected in the EU's language regime, and equality is only offered to languages of a certain status. The dismissive attitude towards regional languages such as Catalan, Welsh and Breton may be illustrated with a COREPER document from the French Presidency of the EU in 1995: '*Le pluralisme linguistique, un élément essentiel de l'identité européenne, une condition pour l'avenir de l'Europe*' with the footnote: '*ce mémorandum . . . ne concerne pas les langues régionales et minoritaires des Etats Membres*'[24] (European Commission, 1995). The rhetoric of diversity is still extremely state-centric, despite the EU promoting itself as a multi-level polity in such documents as the 2001 Commission White Paper on European Governance.

The illusion is further exposed with the consideration of dominant 'unofficial' working languages amongst the officials of the institutions, and increasingly amongst their political counterparts, as discussed above. Of course this should not surprise us. In a multilingual context the temptation will always be to work in the most convenient manner, and to include all speakers and listeners through the use of working languages or a lingua franca rather than rely on depersonalising or time-consuming interpretation and translation services.[25] Perhaps the only surprise is the speed in which English has been adopted in this role of working language, especially by younger generations. In a forum in which European students debated the future of the European Union in the European Parliament in Strasbourg in April 2002, the responsible MEP, Alain Lamassoure, made the following comment: 'It is worth mentioning that while French and English were the two chosen working languages for the event, eventually 90% of the business ended up being conducted in English, even among the French students, the desire to be understood quickly and to communicate directly prevailing over considerations of eloquence and accuracy of expression.'[26] The two characteristics of English as a lingua franca that are apparently so valued are speed and direct personal contact.

However, the option of officially privileging one or two dominant languages does not exist. As de Swaan notes (2001: 167), 'a persistent immobilism prevails. In fact, no decision to change the language regime of the governing bodies has ever been agreed upon'. Indeed, de Swaan goes on to show that such an agreement would be impossible to achieve under present conditions. Thus the institutional multilingualism of the EU remains central, and is indeed robust in certain institutions such as the Parliament, yet it coexists uneasily with dominant working languages which provide a pragmatic solution to complex communicative needs. Furthermore, this multilingualism is based on a model of national identity that may not be entirely appropriate in a contemporary Europe of identities in transformation, such as those expressed through vibrant and increasingly autonomous stateless nations.

## LANGUAGE, IDENTITY AND THE POLITICS OF DIVERSITY

The arguments in this section are directed less at the institutional multilingualism that the EU purports to uphold, and more towards societal multilingualism, the linguistic and cultural diversity of Europe that must be respected according to EU treaties.[27]

The tight relationship between language and national identity are part of the modernist process of nation state construction, a historically contingent political phenomenon arising out of a medieval world of dialect continua and a lingua franca of Latin-speaking church elites. The hardening of national boundaries coincided in the 16th to 17th centuries with the development of print capitalism and the establishment of language academies, and subsequently the boundaries between languages followed the politics of state-building (Anderson, 1991; Wright, 2000). The emerging modern state, imposing uniformity on its citizens through education, military service and a dominant form of the 'national' language, created the conditions for reifying a language-national identity link that persists to this day. Language still has a symbolic power as a marker of national identity.

Despite the rhetoric of linguistic diversity, the European Union has consolidated this one nation, one state, one language model within its official language doctrine. This reification of a language-identity link may be perceived as a retrogressive step, based more on an outdated modernist discourse than reflection on the current interdependencies of the contemporary social, economic and political world. The conception of an internally homogenous sovereign nation state is challenged by the notion of globalised and Europeanised interdependencies in which multiple identities are held at sub-state, state and supranational levels (Hooghe and Marks, 2001: 51-67), by sub-state nationalism and regionalism which have secured political autonomy for regions with autochthonous languages, and by political allegiances which are becoming more globally fragmented through the rise of new social movements based on networks made possible by information technology. So language use may reflect this complexity through being used in diverse forms at different levels and in a variety of domains. English, in this view, has a particular status and role as the language of supra/inter/transnational communication, operating in distinct domains, and not affecting the underlying native languages of the speakers in question.

## The Denationalisation of English?

For historical and cultural reasons, English has achieved a position and status that no other language has attained. In doing so it may have reached a critical number or critical distribution of speakers (which Crystal (1997a) sees as analogous to the notion of critical mass in nuclear physics) beyond which no single group, state or organisation can stop its growth. In this view, neither the actions of the British government, nor the combined actions of other Member States' governments, can alter the trajectory of increased use of English. Even the United States is powerless to change the use of English across the globe. Individual citizens, if they are engaged in any kind of transnational communication, are increasingly choosing English as the lingua franca, and are prepared to spend large amounts of their time and their own money in reaching a proficient level of English for occupational, educational or personal leisure use. If states decided to restrict learning opportunities, either in the state education system or in the private language school sector, this would be an unwarranted infringement on personal liberty and choice. Given the present need for English in so many domains, any attempt to restrict its use would have major political repercussions.

If one accepts the above arguments that English has become a language that is beyond social control, that political management of the language has become all but impossible, it is a short step to take to argue that it therefore does not 'belong' to any one culture, and that it is truly international. As a language of 'stateless' communication English may operate as a neutral, utilitarian tool. If non-native speakers outnumber native speakers by about 3:1 (see Table 2) the language may be said to have moved beyond being one monolithic 'hegemonic' voice, associated with one specific culture. Although some native speakers may still try to perpetuate old dichotomies of 'proper English' and 'foreigners' English', this has little to do with the English language itself, and has more to do with native speakers' inability to 'let go' of 'their' language. The evolution of the tongue should progress according to the logic of transnational social need, drawing upon the vast diversity of different Englishes that are blooming across the world (House, 2001). As the use of the language between non-native speakers increases, the explicit link with the native-speaking states will decline, the language being used as a utilitarian tool rather than as a carrier of cultural values. This is not to say that English would cease to carry cultural meaning for those whose native language it is; it is merely to say that a distinction needs to be made between language as a marker of identity (in native-speaking countries) and language as a communicative tool for 'denationalised' international use. What needs to be assessed is whether the growth in the English language as a communicative tool threatens other language identities.

## Language Conflict and the Threat of English to Other Languages

The concerns over perceived threats to national, cultural or linguistic identity have led to some scholars, such as Yukio Tsuda and Tove Skutnabb-Kangas, to elaborate ideal case paradigms which present the choice between the increasing dominance of English as a lingua franca on the one hand, and the protection and promotion of language diversity on the other, as opposites in an overarching conceptual framework. Tsuda (1997), in a similar fashion to Robert Phillipson, sees the dominance of English as neo-colonialism resulting in inequality, discrimination and disadvantage. Tsuda moves beyond the arguments about inequality and privilege presented above, proposing that language dominance leads to colonisation of the mind, linked specifically in the case of English with Anglo-American commercialisation which extols shopping as the primary activity of human existence, trapping the human race in a cycle of consumption. In order to counter this pernicious state of affairs, Tsuda proposes an 'ecology of language' paradigm based on a human rights perspective that respects equality in communication, multilingualism and the protection of national sovereignty. This is contrasted to a 'diffusion of English' paradigm which has at its core a globalised, monolingual capitalist project seeking the homogenisation of world culture along Anglo-American lines. Skutnabb-Kangas (2000) elaborates on this idea to produce a differentiated model which paints a black and white picture of the two paradigms, and which uses laden terms such as 'genocide', 'imperialism' and 'polarization' to describe the diffusion of English paradigm.[28]

The two paradigms in both Tsuda and Skutnabb-Kangas are clearly ideal types, and should not be taken too literally. However, the thrust of these arguments is that somehow there is a mutual exclusivity involved, and that multilingualism is not compatible with the diffusion of English as a lingua franca. This appears to be far from proved, as the case of Europe may well testify. The growth of the use of English as a lingua franca has coincided with the reinvigoration of many regional and minority languages. The contradistinction of the ecology of language paradigm with that of the diffusion of English appears as a zero-sum argument that ignores the empirical evidence available from Europe.

There is, within the EU, a political environment in which state languages are supremely well established through national education schemes and vibrant entertainment, communications and news media. Multiculturalism and regionalism have given minority cultures and language communities the confidence to express themselves, often supported by the state and the EU, and consolidated by human rights instruments. In this scenario, diversity and the diffusion of English appear not as contradictory forces, but as potentially complementary facets of evolving multi-level political and sociocultural identities in Europe.

A further point to be made about the ecology of language argument is the implicit claim (or explicit in the case of Skutnabb-Kangas) that linguistic diversity is a good in itself, analogous to the case of biodiversity. But whereas the claim may be made that biodiversity is a natural system of interdependence in which an equilibrium is necessary, and that the destruction of one part will have dire, and scientifically measurable, consequences for the whole, language diversity is composed of socially constructed systems, interdependence among which is not of the same order as biodiversity.[29]

However, there is a further argument that can be brought to bear on the potentially detrimental effect that English may have on other languages, which is based on the classic language conflict argument that is used to explain the decline of many regional languages of Europe. Dominant state languages have been promoted over regional languages through the education system, justice system, bureaucracy and military service, causing a shift from the use of the local language to that of the state. Different degrees of coercion have been applied in Europe, from outright prohibition of the regional language (eg in Spain during the Franco years) to neglect (eg Sardu in Sardinia today). Frequently it is parents themselves who do not pass on their mother tongue (language reproduction) because they have been convinced that the local language is backward, and want their children to 'get on' in life through the use of the dominant state language, as has been the case in Brittany in France (Nelde, Strubell and Williams, 1995). Language conflict arguments apply when there is competition within the same domain, such as using a language to report a crime to the police, speaking to your doctor, or filling in an official form. In bilingual societies, for example in Catalonia, Wales, Friesland and Sardinia, the regional language has to compete in everyday situations with the official state language with all the resources that an official state language has at its disposal. Although there may be every protection in law possible for the regional language, a sense of inferiority might still be attached to the language which manifests itself in a reluctance to use it in official or formal situations. Such a situation of diglossia has been noted in Friesland, where a local expression demonstrates the idea rather neatly: 'Frisian is the jacket worn about the house; Dutch is the best suit.'[30] In this situation, language shift occurs over generations and the language declines in use.[31]

The argument here is concerned with whether the growing dominance of English increases language conflict between English and domestic languages. When individuals and communities are faced with the choice between two languages in a given social context, a situation of language conflict arises which will result in the enhanced social acceptance and increased use of the more prestigious or useful language (in this case English), to the detriment of the weaker one.

To answer the question of whether the current status and role of English as a lingua franca fits this classic language conflict model, it is relevant to distinguish between four ideal types of domain: personal, public, occupational, and educational.[32] Within the personal domain, the use of a lingua franca would be limited to transnational occupational and networking situations. As such it affects a small number of people who have explicitly chosen to work in the type of situation that requires a large degree of foreign language communication. For the vast majority of people the personal domain would be untouched by the need for a lingua franca, so little or no conflict would arise.

The public domain for European citizens is dominated by the necessity to communicate in the official languages of state or region, and debate is conducted through national or regional media in native languages. There is no transnational public sphere in Europe; there is no shared public debate through the media in a lingua franca in Europe. European issues are mediated through more localised means. As Schlesinger and Kevin argue, 'rather than imagine a single European public sphere . . . we should think about the growth of interrelated spheres of European publics', and furthermore, '[i]n reality, any common European public agenda is likely, in the process of media reception, to be diversely "domesticated" within each distinctive national or language context' (Schlesinger and Kevin, 2000: 228). Thus the public domain use of a European lingua franca would be restricted to a socio-political elite working in and around Brussels, either within the European institutions themselves or in the organs of civil society that cluster around these institutions, affecting a small minority of Europeans.

This latter domain use (the working environment of the Brussels/Strasbourg/Luxembourg triangle) shades into the occupational domain, in which English is being increasingly used as the international language of business. In this respect, knowledge of a language is a skill that workers need to a greater or lesser extent depending on the type of work they do, similar to the need for skills such as IT. It is here that the influence of English is making its mark in the increasing use of 'anglicisms', or English loan words, that are colonising the workplace, and also in the growing need for communication in the international economy.[33] This is more noticeable today because of the shift in economic activity to a more globalised knowledge-based economy with its implicit communicative functions geared towards the provision of screen-based services (Graddol, 1997). It is here that language use is perhaps most fluid. The perspective of language since the renaissance has been primarily determined by territorial factors, the rise of the 'nation state' and protectionist economic policies. The contemporary world may be characterised more usefully in terms of flows and networks in an increasingly borderless world (Castells, 2000; Jönsson, Tägil and Törnqvist, 2000). In such a world the role of language becomes central to the smooth and efficient running of globalised economic affairs, and English as the business lingua franca is colonising this domain, with repercussions in terms of being regarded as the language of power, success and prestige.

It is in this business domain, and also in the domain of higher education and research, that the presence of English is most keenly observed. The educational domain at primary and secondary levels is still dominated by the national and regional vehicular languages, but scientific and research communities are becoming increasingly dominated by English (Graddol, 1997; Hoffmann, 2000; Truchot, 2002). English in higher education has two aspects: facilitating the cross-pollination of academic ideas through publications, research papers and conferences, but also being the vehicular language of many courses, even outside the UK and Ireland, which service the growing need for English in the occupations that students aim for after they have finished their studies. Thus it is in these two domains-business and higher education-that the language conflict argument has most resonance, the ethics being balanced between the advantages of greater intercultural communication and understanding and the disadvantages of language dominance and the threat to language use in specific domains for the less widely used languages. The fear here is of language shift occurring, though perhaps a more accurate description of how language is changing in Europe today would be 'domain creep', in that English might increasingly dominate specific fields (through academic and occupational use), squeezing national and regional languages out.

## Language Colonialism

Building on arguments expressed above of inequality and conflict in language relationships and status, it is worth pursuing the notion that the 'home' countries of a lingua franca such as English benefit from such inequality. Specifically it might be asked whether a lingua franca is promoted in order to take advantage of such benefits, in this case by the UK and USA (and other Anglophone countries). If, as argued above, the English language carries cultural baggage, and promotes the social, economic and political values of the UK and the USA, are we entitled to conclude from this that there is an argument that the promotion of English is tied in with an imperialist agenda that seeks global dominance through political, economic and linguistic means.[34]

The linguistic imperialism argument is closely associated with Robert Phillipson and his 1992 book of that name. In it, and in subsequent books and articles, Phillipson argues that the promotion and spread of English are based on an assumption that one language (ie English) is preferable to others, an assumption that is based on the promulgation of a 'myth' that the world needs one language of international communication. The dominance of this one language-English-is structurally entrenched through the allocation of more resources to it, resulting in exploitative Anglo-Americanisation and the homogenisation of world culture. Within European society, Phillipson and Skutnabb-Kangas (1994) argue that we are witnessing the emergence of a diglossic situation of language hierarchy in which English is the dominant language, and other languages are marginalised.

What these arguments imply is that the language is inextricably bound to the language communities from which it originated. As discussed above, this view may be questioned using arguments based on the increasing neutrality of English, pointing out that the language has become a global resource which is not 'owned' by any one community or power (McArthur, 1996; Hayhoe and Parker, 1994), but rather one that is 'owned' by the global community. The argument of cultural homogenisation is certainly one that deserves attention, though it is far from obvious in Europe today that the use of English as a lingua franca has had a detrimental effect on cultural diversity. If anything, the linguistic diversity of Europe is experiencing something of a renaissance with increasing autonomy amongst stateless nations and linguistically distinct regions having greater control over language planning than previously. In fact the greatest threat to linguistic diversity was the ideal, and attempted consolidation, of the homogenous nation state over the past two centuries, an ideal that is reified in linguistic terms by the EU language regime that only recognises state languages, not regional ones, in its official language regime. A more complex picture is now emerging in Europe of a multi-level linguistic environment, with increasing use of a lingua franca, combined with entrenched state languages, and with reinvigorated regional and minority languages protected by international charters, human rights legislation, and EU programmes.

## CONCLUSION: DIVERSITY, MULTILINGUALISM AND THE IMPACT OF ENGLISH

It has been argued in this chapter that the EU's language regime and policies were designed with the best intentions, to respect diversity and to ensure democratic transparency, but that the regime is challenged by socio-linguistic and political developments that have seen regional and minority languages reinvigorated and the English language emerging as a *de facto* lingua franca in certain social, economic and political domains. It is the latter development that principally concerns us here, and we are now in a position to reflect on what this means for the three aspects of multilingualism that the EU is concerned to respect.

### Institutional Multilingualism

There is unlikely to be any change to the present *de jure* language regime in the EU. There will be a continuation of the uneasy tension that exists between the explicit statement of equality of official and working languages and the increasing use of English as a lingua franca. Language services will still be central, but pragmatic solutions will also be increasingly accepted in terms of official internal institutional use.

### Societal Multilingualism

If anything, linguistic and cultural diversity is healthier today than twenty years ago. Just as Europeanisation has been complemented by regionalisation and the re-emergence of autonomous minority nations, so the growth in the use of English as a lingua franca in Europe has coincided with greater awareness of regional and minority languages. Old nation state identities and interests are being transformed into multi-layered identities with global, European, national, regional and local aspects. Language use reflects this transformation.

## Personal Multilingualism

With increased economic, political and social interdependence in Europe as the EU is consolidated and expands, there is a greater need for cross-national communication. This is bound to lead to greater use of foreign languages, most significantly English. Both the quantity and quality of intra-European communication is likely to increase, meaning that individual bilingualism[35] will become the norm (with the probable exception of native Anglophones), facilitating cross-cultural, transnational communication. If the EU persists in promoting a mother-tongue + 2 foreign languages policy which implicitly rejects the idea of English as the default first foreign language, yet again there will be a tension between the EU ideal and the European reality, just as there is with the working languages issue raised above. Citizens and their state education systems will plough resources into the language that is perceived to be most useful. Which language Europeans learn will be their democratic choice, not the choice of European bureaucrats, however well-intentioned they may be. That language is perceived to be English by 75.2% of Europeans (Eurobarometer 54, 2001). Furthermore, the majority of citizens also reject the idea of learning two foreign languages if the Eurobarometer survey on Europeans and languages is representative:

*Table 5: Special Eurobarometer 54 (2001) Europeans and Languages: Questions*

| | Agree | Disagree | Don't know |
|---|---|---|---|
| Everyone in the EU should speak **one** EU language in addition to their mother tongue | **71.1%** | 20.2% | 8.7% |
| Everyone in the EU should speak **two** EU languages in addition to their mother tongue | 32.4% | **53.4%** | 14.1% |
| Everyone in the EU should be able to speak English | **69.4%** | 22.5% | 8.1% |

Given the above, it is highly improbable that a situation will arise in the near future that will challenge the continued growth of English as a lingua franca or as a dominant language in certain domains of human communication. If this is accepted, then the focus ought to shift to the compensatory political and social mechanisms by which other languages are empowered and enriched. It is not within the scope of this chapter to delve too deeply into these matters. However, a few points would not go amiss with regard to the three different aspects of multilingualism.

As far as the institutional perspective is concerned, the tension between the ideal of full multilingualism and the *de facto* restricted language regime that is apparent in the EU institutions is likely to continue within official circles. This in itself may not be considered problematic. However, it is the 'leakage' of this restricted regime into the political domain and into the public sphere through the provision of information in a limited number of languages that is of most concern. The democratic principles that underlie representation, participation and access to information need to be respected, and can only be so with financial investment in, and respect for, the work of the language services of the Union. Such investment should be seen as a priority to ensure that political representatives and the public are not linguistically disenfranchised (Ginsberg and Weber, 2005). Democracies do not baulk at the cost of elections, so why should they resist paying for the equally democratic rights associated with deliberation, participation and access to information?

With regard to societal multilingualism, if the EU is serious about the value of linguistic diversity in Europe then greater support should be given to all language communities to reflect the true diversity that exists in European society. It may not be pragmatically possible to include **all** languages, including regional and minority languages, in the institutional language regime of the EU, but greater acknowledgement of, and support for, RML communities would help towards compensating them for such a policy.

As for individual multilingualism it might be promoted effectively by complementing the learning of the popular choice of first foreign language, English, with the option of a second foreign language and/or education devoted to cultural awareness and linguistic diversity in Europe. Only when European citizens are aware of the wealth of European culture and heritage as a whole will a sense of European identity that reflects the EU's ideal of being united in its diversity become achievable. I see no necessary contradiction between this and the use of English as a lingua franca. English will certainly be no panacea to Europe's problems, leading inevitably to better transnational communication and understanding, but neither should it be seen as principally a threat to the essential diversity and richness of European culture.

## Notes

[1] European Commission DG Translation, 1999: 4.

[2] The use of this expression may be found, for example, in the European Commission translation service's 1999 document, A *Multilingual Community at Work* (p 5), where the Council Regulation is displayed in full under this title.

[3] Though French was dominant within the administration of the institutions until the mid to late 1970s. See below.

[4] On 13 June 2005 it was agreed to make Irish an official language from 1 January 2007, bringing the total to 21 languages. Future enlargements will stretch the capacity of the language services of the EU even further. Bulgarian and Romanian entry will push the number of official languages up to 23 (506 language combinations), Croatian to 24 (552 combinations), and Turkish membership (if it happens) up to 25 (600 language combinations).

[5] Irish also exists at present as a 'Treaty Language', but is not an 'official and working' language as set out in Article 1 of Regulation No 1/58 requiring daily translation and interpretation. (See note 4 above for the status of Irish from 2007.)

[6] The cost of the language services of the EU was running at approximately 800m per year before the 2004 enlargement. Although this is a large sum of money, the EU pointed out that this was only slightly more than EE €2 per citizen per year (source: Commission DG Interpretation) http://europa.eu.int/comm/scic/thescic/multilingualism_en.htm. With the 2004 enlargement it was estimated that this figure might rise to €3 per citizen per year (Assembleé Nationale Française, 2003: 63). However, in a press release of 13 January 2005, the Commission stated that, '[a]fter enlargement, with a population of 453 million, the cost of translation at all (EU) institutions, once they are operating at full speed, is estimated at 807 M€ (per year ... This represents a cost to each citizen of €1.78 ' (Europa, 2005). Creech (2005: 30) makes the point that this figure is as low as it is because many documents are left untranslated from their original English and French versions.

[7] The Treaty on European Union is not specific about respect for linguistic diversity; there is simply the respect for cultural diversity, at both national and regional levels (Title XII, Article 151, Consolidated Version). However, there have been many Parliament and Council Resolutions that have mentioned the respect for linguistic diversity and the need for the EU to co-ordinate Member State policy since then. (See EBLUL, 2003.) The Charter of Fundamental Rights expressly states in Article 22 that '[t]he Union shall respect cultural, religious and linguistic diversity'. This is reiterated in the Constitutional Treaty of 2004, in both Part II (The Charter) and Part I (The Objectives of the Union), though it appears after the French and Dutch referenda of May 2005 that this document may never be ratified. Despite this rhetoric of respect, the Union has always been at pains to emphasise that language policy is a competence of Member States, and that the role of the EU is one of co-ordination of coherent pan-EU strategies. (See, for example, Council Resolution of 14 February 2002 on the promotion of linguistic diversity and language learning.)

[8] This priority is clearly stated, for example, in the 1995 European Commission White Paper on education and training, p 69, and reiterated in Council Resolution of 14 February 2002 on the promotion of linguistic diversity and language learning.

[9] See Council Regulation No 1/58. For further discussion of the issue of working languages in the EU, and the distinction between the administrative and political domains, see the section below on English in the EU institutions.

[10] Obviously, any restriction on the provision of all documents in all official languages has implications for the democratic legitimacy of the EU. If democracy requires openness and transparency, the provision of public access to documents is necessary, and if this is not provided in a language that a member of the public can understand, the polity's democratic credentials are undermined. This is clearly an issue that the EU ought to take seriously given the 'democratic deficit' and 'legitimacy gap' that it is accused of having.

[11] Sources: Graddol, 1997; Crystal, 1997a. It should be pointed out that the figures for second language and foreign language speakers are contentious in that they rely to a degree on self-assessment of ability, especially the latter category. The crux of the matter is the level of competence at which one is able to say that one is a speaker of a given language. For further discussion see Graddol (1997) and Crystal (1997a). This 3-way split in terms of English as a native, second and foreign language owes much to the work of Braj Kachru, and his model of inner, outer and expanding circles of world Englishes, where the inner circle represents states where English is the primary mother tongue, the next ('outer') circle represents states where English has official status but is not the mother tongue of citizens, and the last ('expanding') circle where English is a foreign language learnt for international use (Kachru, 1985, 1992). For further discussion in relation to the EU, see Berns (1995).

[12] Crystal, 1997a: 12.

[13] 69.4% agreed, 22.5% disagreed, 8.1% didn't know. See Eurobarometer 54, 2001: Executive summary, p 6.

[14] Perhaps the point worth raising here is that there is a difference between believing that something is necessary and actually liking it or approving of it. For example, if the question had been about everybody paying taxes, the response would have been positive, yet no-one actively enjoys paying taxes!

[15] The idea that the British and US governments explicitly and extensively promoted English to bolster Cold War interests and the security of UK and US worldwide investments is a centerpiece of Phillipson's analysis. Although I believe that there is an element of truth in this argument, I do not agree with Phillipson's theoretical stance that crude colonialism as seen

in the 19th and 20th centuries has been replaced by a subtler form of cultural and linguistic imperialism which is still based on simple 'centre-periphery' relations. I discuss Phillipson and the idea of linguistic colonialism later in this chapter. For further views, see Holborow (1999), especially pp 73–80.

[16] Van Parijs (this volume) also points out that the dominance of a lingua franca is due to 'probability-sensitive learning' (the motivation to learn the most useful language, spoken by most people) and 'maximin communication' (the principle of minimal exclusion). There is thus a variety of structural and ideological reasons why English has achieved the dominant position it has in Europe, and globally.

[17] For a discussion of the ideas and debates surrounding the role of language in nation state building and European integration, especially connected with democracy and 'communities of communication', see Wright, 1999 and 2000.

[18] Brussels-focused internet news providers have reported that there is a crisis in the translation service with headlines such as: 'Commission cracks down on verbiage in response to translation crisis' (EurActiv.com 27/05/04), and 'EU translation service on the brink of collapse' (EUobserver.com 26/05/04). The Commission in a press release of 13 January 2005 was much more bullish ('Translation in the Commission: where do we stand eight months after enlargement?'). However, they only managed to provide this press release in two languages, English and German. http://europa.eu.int/rapid/pressReleasesAction.do?reference=MEMO/05/10&format=HTML&aged=1&language=EN&guiLanguage=en.

[19] The workings of the European Convention 2002-3 are a good example of this, where the plenary sessions were conducted in the 11 official languages, but the 11 working groups used very restricted language regimes, none working in more than four languages, English and French being the default languages and others being provided only in the case of real need. Hence, the majority of political actors were having to work in a language other than their native tongue. (See Longman (2004) for further details.) There is evidence that this practice is becoming more common even in the Council of the European Union and in the European Parliament. For details of proposals with regard to the future language regime of the EP outside the plenary sessions, see European Parliament (2004).

[20] This topic is one worthy of socio-linguistic research. Do non-native speakers tend to avoid communicating with native speakers due to implicit hierarchical relations being involved? Do non-native speakers prefer to communicate with each other to avoid being in a perceived inferior position?

[21] Attempts are being made to increase clarity of expression for English speakers in the European institutions. The European Commission's translation service is running a campaign called 'Fight the FOG' to encourage authors and translators to write more clearly.

[22] As Jenkins notes in relation to the phonology of English as an international language, 'There is really no justification for doggedly persisting in referring to an item as "an error" if the vast majority of the world's L2 English speakers understand it. Instead, it is for L1 speakers to move their own receptive goal posts and adjust their own expectations as far as international (but not intranational) uses of English are concerned' (cited in Seidlhofer, 2001: 151). For further discussion of the case for describing English as a lingua franca as distinct from English as a native language, see Seidlhofer (2001).

[23] Interestingly, the 2005 version of this DGT brochure introduces a reference to the restricted language regime in the internal workings of the EU-English, French and German (European Commission DG Translation 2004, p 3).

[24] 'Linguistic pluralism, an essential element of European identity, a condition of the future of Europe.' Footnote: 'This memorandum does not concern the regional and minority languages of the Member States.'

[25] I do not wish to denigrate the highly professional interpreting services of the EU. I merely wish to point out that any simultaneous interpretation creates a kind of barrier to interpersonal relations, and that written translation may not appear quickly enough for time-pressed politicians and officials.

[26] The debate and Lamassoure's comment may be found at: http://europa.eu.int/futurum/documents/other/oth280401_en.htm.

[27] For example the Treaty on European Union (Nice consolidated version) Articles 149(1) and 151; and the Treaty Establishing a Constitution for Europe (2004) I-3.3 and II-82.

[28] For a table showing the elements of the opposing paradigms, see also Phillipson, 2003: 161.

[29] Furthermore, it could be argued that linguistic diversity, considered as a good in itself, is a value-theoretic judgement which may guide normative judgements in language planning, but which does not allow us to conclude that languages should be protected at all costs. I am not claiming that diversity is not a valuable asset to be cherished; rather, it is possible for language diversity to coexist with a lingua franca.

[30] Quoted in Stephens (1976: 574).

[31] With regard to regional languages it is apparent that in some regions, notably Catalonia and Wales, such languages have entered into a new phase of growth, having been supported by language planning measures, and with greater public respect accorded to the languages. The same cannot be said of Breton or Sardu, however. For further details of language production and reproduction in western Europe, see the Euromosaic Report (Nelde, Strubell and Williams, 1995).

[32] This distinction is one that the Council of Europe describes in its 'Common European Framework of Reference for Languages', available at http://www.coe.int/t/dg4/linguistic/Source/Framework_EN.pdf (synopsis available at http://www.coe.int/t/dg4/linguistic/Synopsise_EN.asp#TopOfPage).

[33] There is evidence that loan words are often short lived, however (Loonen, 1996: 6).

[34] It is a matter of historical interest that the world's most powerful and extensive empire in the 19th century and early 20th century was the Anglophone British Empire, and that since the Second World War the world has become increasingly dominated by the Anglophone USA (which is increasingly being described in imperial terms).

[35] I do not wish to imply that Europeans will not only speak their mother tongue but will also speak English to native-like fluency. The term 'bilingual' may apply to a wide variety of proficiencies. As Crystal explains: 'scholars now tend to think of bilingual ability as a continuum: bilingual people will find themselves at different points along this continuum, with a minority approaching the theoretical ideal of perfect, balanced control of both languages, but most being some way from it, and some having very limited ability indeed' (Crystal, 1997b: 364). Thus when I propose that most Europeans will be bilingual with English, I mean that most Europeans will be able to communicate in some way in English as their first foreign language.

## References

Ammon, U (1994) 'The Present Dominance of English in Europe with an Outlook on Possible Solutions to the European Language Problems' *Sociolinguistica* 8: 1–14.

Andersen, CH, Christensen, L and Troest, MO (1997) 'An Administrative Lingua Franca within the EU', http://earth.subetha.dk/~eek/museum/auc/marvin/www/library/uni/projects/adlfineu.htm

Anderson, B (1991) *Imagined Communities: Reflections on the Origin and Spread of Nationalism* (London, Verso).

Assembleé Nationale Française (2003) *Rapport d'information sur la diversité linguistique dans l'Union Européenne* (Herbillon Report), 11 June 2003, http://www.assemblee-nationale.fr/12/pdf/europe/rap-info/i0902.pdf (accessed August 2006).

Aziz, M and Van Parijs, P (forthcoming) 'Linguistic Legislation for XXIst Century Europe' in B De Witte (ed), *European Law and Language Diversity* (Oxford, Oxford University Press).

Barbour, S (2002) *Language, Nationalism and Globalisation: Educational Consequences of Changing Patterns of Language Use* (Clevedon, Multilingual Matters).

Berns, M (1995) 'English in the European Union' *English Today* 12(3): 3–11.

Buck, V (2002) 'One World, One Language', www.aiic.net/ViewPage.cfm/page732 (accessed August 2006).

Castells, M (2000) *The Information Age: Economy, Society and Culture: Vol 1, The Rise of the Network Society* (Oxford, Blackwell).

Cenoz, J and Jessner, U (2000) *English in Europe: The Acquisition of a 3rd Language* (Clevedon, Multilingual Matters).

Cheshire, J (2002) 'Who We Are and Where We're Going: Language and Identities in the New Europe' in M Holt and P Gubbins (eds), *Beyond Boundaries: Language and Identity in Contemporary Europe* (Clevedon, Multilingual Matters).

Clyne, M (2000) 'Lingua Franca and Ethnolects in Europe and Beyond' *Sociolinguistica* 14: 83–9.

Creech, RL (2005) *Law and Language in the European Union: The Paradox of a Babel 'United in Diversity'* (Groningen, Europa Law Publishing).

Crystal, D (1997a) *English as a Global Language* (Cambridge, Cambridge University Press).

Crystal, D (1997b) *The Cambridge Encyclopedia of Language* (Cambridge, Cambridge University Press).

De Swaan, A (2001) *Words of the World* (Cambridge, Polity).

Dollerup, C (1996) 'English in the European Union' in R Hartmann (ed), *The English Language in Europe* (Exeter, Intellect).

Dürmüller, U (1994) 'Multilingual Talk or English Only? The Swiss Experience' *Sociolinguistica* 8: 44–64.

EBLUL (European Bureau of Lesser-Used Languages) (2003) *Vade Mecum: A Guide to International Documents on Lesser-Used Languages of Europe*, 3rd edn (Brussels, EBLUL).

Eurobarometer 54 (2001) 'Special Report: Europeans and Languages' (Brussels, INRA).

Europa (2005) 'Translation in the Commission: Where do we Stand Eight Months after Enlargement?' Press release, 13 January 2005 Memo/05/10, http://europa.eu.int/rapid/pressReleasesAction.do?reference=MEMO/05/10&format=HTML&aged=1&language=EN&guiLanguage=en (accessed August 2006).

European Commission (1995) *Mémorandum de la présidence sur la pluralisme linguistique dans l'Union Européenne*, SI (95) 46-4034/95 (Brussels, Office for Official Publications of the European Communities).

European Commission (1999) *Proposal for a Decision of the European Parliament and of the Council: European Year of Languages 2001*, Brussels, COM (1999) 485 final.

European Commission (2002) Commission Staff Working Paper, *Promoting Language Learning and Linguistic Diversity-Consultation*, SEC (2002) 1234.

European Commission DG Translation (1999) *A Multilingual Community at Work* (Luxembourg, Office for Official Publications of the European Communities).

European Commission DG Translation (2004) *Translating for a Multilingual Community,* http://europa.eu.int/comm/dgs/translation/bookshelf/brochure_en.pdf (accessed August 2006).

European Parliament (2004) *Committee of Constitutional Affairs: Working Document on precautionary measures for the application of general arrangements on multilingualism provided for in Rules 117 and 139 of the Rules of Procedure* (2003/2227(REG)). Rapporteur: Gianfranco Dell'Alba, http://www.europarl.eu.int/meetdocs/committees/afco/20040119/513315EN.pdf (accessed August 2006).

Eurydice (2001) *Foreign Language Teaching in Schools in Europe*, Eurydice European Unit, http://www.eurydice.org/Documents/FLT/En/FrameSet.htm (accessed August 2006).

Ginsberg, V and Weber, S (2005) 'Language Disenfranchisement in the European Union' *Journal of Common Market Studies* 43(2): 273–86.

Graddol, D (1997) *The Future of English?* British Council, http://www.britishcouncil.org/english/pdf/future.pdf) (accessed August 2006).

Habermas, J (1995) 'Remarks on Dieter Grimm's "Does Europe Need a Constitution?"' *European Law Journal* 303: 307.

Hartmann, R (ed) (1996) *The English Language in Europe* (Exeter, Intellect).

Hayhoe, M and Parker, S (eds) (1994) *Who Owns English?* (Milton Keynes, Open University Press).

Hobsbawm, E (1996) 'Are All Tongues Equal? Language, Culture and National Identity' in P Barker (ed), *Living as Equals* (Oxford, Oxford University Press).

Hoffmann, C (1996) 'Societal and Individual Bilingualism with English in Europe' in R Hartmann (ed), *The English Language in Europe* (Exeter, Intellect).

Hoffmann, C (2000) 'The Spread of English and the Growth of Multilingualism with English in Europe' in J Cenoz and U Jessner (eds), *English in Europe: The Acquisition of a 3rd Language* (Clevedon, Multilingual Matters).

Holborow, M (1999) *The Politics of English: A Marxist View of Language* (London, Sage).

Holt, M and Gubbins, P (2002) *Beyond Boundaries: Language and Identity in Contemporary Europe* (Clevedon, Multilingual Matters).

Hooghe, L and Marks, G (2001) *Multi-level Governance and European Integration* (Oxford, Rowman and Littlefield).

House, J (2001) 'A Stateless Language that Europe Must Embrace', conference speech, IATEFL, 2001, http://www.guardian.co.uk/GWeekly/Story/0,3939,475288,00.html (accessed August 2006).

Jönsson, C, Tägil, S and Törnqvist, G (2000) *Organizing European Space* (London, Sage).

Julios, C (2002) 'Towards a European Language Policy' in M Farrell, S Fella and M Newman (eds), *European Integration in the 21st Century: Unity in Diversity?* (London, Sage).

Kachru, B (1985) 'Standards, Codification and Sociolinguistic Realism: The English Language in the Outer Circle' in R Quirk and H Widdowson (eds), *English in the World: Teaching and Learning the Language and Literatures* (Cambridge, Cambridge University Press).

Kachru, B (ed) (1992) *The Other Tongue: English Across Cultures,* 2nd edn (Urbana, University of Illinois Press).

Kraus, P (2000) 'Political Unity and Linguistic Diversity in Europe' *European Journal of Sociology* XLI(1): 138–63.

Labrie, N (2000) 'Globalisation and Management of Linguistic Pluralism in Europe', unpublished paper given at the symposium 'Cultural Diversity and the Construction of Europe', UOC, Barcelona, 14–16 December 2000.

Labrie, N and Quell, C (1997) 'Your Language, My Language, Or English? The potential language choice in communication among nationals of the EU' *World Englishes* 16: 3-26.

Laitin, D (1997) 'The Cultural Identities of a European State'*Politics and Society* 25(3): 277–302.

Longman, C (2004) 'The Convention as Communicative Environment: the challenge of multilingual deliberation', paper delivered at the CIDEL Workshop 'One EU, Many Publics', Stirling University, 5–6 February 2004, http://www.arena.uio.no/cidel/WorkshopStirling/PaperLongman.pdf (accessed August 2006).

Loonen, P (1996) 'English in Europe: from timid to tyrannical?' *English Today* 12(2): 3–9.

Mackey, WF (2001) 'Conflicting Languages in a United Europe' *Sociolinguistica* 15: 1–17.

Mamadouh, V (1999) 'Beyond Nationalism: three visions of the European Union and their implications for the linguistic regime of its institutions' *GeoJournal* 48: 133–44.

McArthur, T (1996) 'English in the World and in Europe' in R Hartmann (ed), *The English Language in Europe* (Exeter, Intellect).

McCluskey, B (1998) 'A Different Kettle of Fish: the challenge of multilingual translation in specialist fields', speech at the 1998 Lisbon Expo.

McCluskey, B (2001) 'Respecting Multilingualism in the Enlargement of the European Union-The Organisational Challenge' *Terminologie et Traduction* 2: 7-21 (Luxembourg, OOPEC), http://europa.eu.int/comm/translation/reading/articles/pdf/2001_06_07_vienna_mccluskey.pdf (accessed August 2006).

Nelde, P, Strubell, M and Williams, G (1995) *Euromosaic: The Production and Reproduction of the Minority Language Groups of the European Union* (Brussels, Office for Official Publications of the European Communities).

Phillipson, R (1992) *Linguistic Imperialism* (Oxford, Oxford University Press).

Phillipson, R (2003) *English-Only Europe? Challenging Language Policy* (London, Routledge).

Phillipson, R and Skutnabb-Kangas, T (1994) 'English, Panacea or Pandemic?' *Sociolinguistica* 8: 73–87.

Rowe, R (2002) 'The Use of Languages by the EU Institutions' *Terminologie et Traduction* 2: 5–10 (Luxembourg, OOPEC).

Schlesinger, P and Kevin, D (2000) 'Can the European Union Become a Sphere of Publics?' in EO Eriksen and JE Fossum (eds), *Democracy in the European Union: Integration through Deliberation* (London, Routledge).

Seidlhofer, B (2001) 'Closing the Conceptual Gap: the case for a description of English as a lingua franca' *International Journal of Applied Linguistics* 11: 133–58.

Siguan, M (1995) *L'Europa de les Llengües* (Barcelona, Edicions 62).

Skutnabb-Kangas, T (2000) *Linguistic Genocide in Education—or Worldwide Diversity and Human Rights?* (Mahwah, NJ, Lawrence Erlbaum).

Smith, R (1996) 'Single Market, Single Currency, Single Language' *English Today* 12: 10–14.

Stephens, M (1976) *Linguistic Minorities in Western Europe* (Llandysul, Gomer Press).

Truchot, C (2002) 'Key Aspects of the Use of English in Europe', text commissioned for the Language Policy Division of the Council of Europe, http://www.coe.int/t/dg4/linguistic/Source/TruchotEN.pdf#search=%22Key%20Aspects%20of%20the%20Use%20of%20English%20in%20Europe%E2%80%99%22 (accessed August 2006)

Tsuda, Y (1997) 'The Hegemony of English and Strategies for Linguistic Pluralism: Proposing the Ecology of Language Paradigm', http://www.toda.org/conferences/hugg_hon/hugg_hon_papers/y_tsuda.html accessed January 2004)

Van Parijs, P (2000a) 'Must Europe be Belgian? On democratic citizenship and multilingual polities' in C McKinnon and I Hampsher-Monk (eds), *The Demands of Citizenship* (London, Continuum).

Van Parijs, P (2000b) 'The Ground Floor of the World: on the socio-economic consequences of linguistic globalisation' *International Political Science Review* 21(2): 217–33.

Wallraff, B (2000) 'What Global Language?' *The Atlantic Online*, November, http://www.theatlantic.com/issues/2000/11/Wallraff.htm.

Wright, S (1999) 'A Community that Can Communicate? The linguistic factor in European integration' in D Smith and S Wright (eds), *Whose Europe? The Turn Towards Democracy* (Oxford, Blackwell).
Wright, S (2000) *Community and Communication: the role of language in nation state building and European integration* (Clevedon, Multilingual Matters).

# 10

# *Europe's Linguistic Challenge*[1]

PHILIPPE VAN PARIJS

ON 7 MARCH 2001, Romano Prodi-President of the European Commission, Goeran Persson, (then) current Chairman of the European Council and Swedish Prime Minister, and Guy Verhofstadt, (then) future Chairman of the European Council and Belgian Prime Minister, met hundreds of pupils from the three Brussels-based European schools in the canteen of one of these schools. Many pupils from the eleven language sections (corresponding to the EU's eleven official languages of the time) queued to ask a question, including a Greek girl, who asked President Prodi about the EU's policy as regards languages. 'From its very beginning,' Prodi replied in substance, 'equality between official languages has been a fundamental principle of the European institutions, and it must remain so.' And they moved on to the next pupil in the queue.[2] As the meeting was taking place in a school canteen, and hence without the interpreting boxes and other equipment that routinely facilitate multilingual exchanges in European institutions, you may wonder how hundreds of children from fifteen European countries and eleven distinct language sections managed to communicate with their distinguished guests. From the first to the last minute (except for a brief intervention in French by the French commissioner Michel Barnier, who had come along with Prodi) the meeting was conducted exclusively in English, including a speech forcefully asserting the principle of linguistic equality.

For reasons to be explained below, Prodi was right in both choice of medium and content of message. But the discrepancy between blatant inequality at the level of facts and fundamental equality at the level of declarations nevertheless raises a number of serious questions, at least four of which can be formulated as issues of fairness. In this article, I shall consider these in turn, and indicate what I believe to be the best way of handling each of them. But before doing so, I need to spell out the nature of the fundamental mechanism that explains what happened in the canteen and which underlies, far more broadly, the core of the dynamics of secondary language learning and multilingual interaction, not only in today's Europe, but throughout history and throughout the world.

WHY WE ARE MOVING TOWARDS ONE LINGUA FRANCA

Most of the trends in linguistic competence that we can observe can be understood as the product of the (sometimes explosive) interaction of two micro-mechanisms.

**Probability-sensitive Learning**

What I shall call *probability-sensitive learning* simply captures the following two-dimensional fact. The extent to which people maintain and improve their linguistic competence in some particular language is strongly affected by the probability of expecting to have to function in that language. This is in the first place a matter of motivation: the more likely it is that competence in a particular language will be useful to communication, the greater the effort one will decide, individually or institutionally, to invest in learning it. But this differential learning is also in the second place a matter of opportunity: the more often one finds oneself in a context in which a particular language is actually being used, the smaller the effort required to learn it. Moreover, these two dimensions of the mechanism feed into each other: the motivation easily induces the creation of more opportunities than those that offer themselves spontaneously, and the actual enjoyment of the opportunities (over and above the expectation of further opportunities) may nurture the motivation to learn by enabling people to experience what difference it makes to possess the linguistic competence required to understand what is being said and to take an active part in the conversation.

I am of course not denying that other factors-for example, how aesthetically attractive one finds the language one considers learning, or how close it is to one's native tongue, or how large a literary corpus it gives access to-may significantly affect either the motivation to learn a language or the ease with which one will learn it, or both. All I am asserting is that, through these two channels of motivation and opportunity to learn (and retain), the probability of having to interact in a particular language will be a massively important determinant of the extent to which average competence in a particular non-native language tends to expand or shrink in a particular population. A greater probability means both a larger expected benefit from any given level of linguistic proficiency in the language concerned and a lower cost of acquiring or preserving it. More sophisticated measures of the communicative value of a language have been offered, for example Abram de Swaan's (2001) stimulating notion of Q-value. But none of them offers the promise of improving much, if at all, upon the simple probability of interaction in that language as a predictor of differential learning and retention.

**Maximin Communication**

What I shall call the *maximin law of communication* captures a distinct, somewhat less obvious but hardly less general mechanism, which can be sketched as follows. Suppose you have to address simultaneously a set of people who each know to various extents a number of languages and by all of whom you want to be understood. When deciding which language among those you know you should pick, the question you will spontaneously tend to ask yourself will not be which is your own best language, or which language is the best language of the majority, or which language is best known on average by your audience, but rather which language is best known by the member of your audience who knows it least. In other words, you will systematically tend to ask yourself whether there is any language that is known to some extent by all. If, to the best of your knowledge, there is one and only one, you will choose it. If there is none, you will tend to choose the language that is known to some extent by most. And if there is more than one, you will make a guess for each of them about the level of competence achieved by the person least competent in it, and you will choose the language for which this level of competence is highest.

This 'maximin' criterion amounts to maximising the minimum competence. It can also be described as a criterion of minimal exclusion. It has a number of direct corollaries, such as the systematic victory, in linguistically mixed marriages, of the language of the 'worst linguist', ie of the partner who knows least well the language of the other and systematically tends to be the speaker of the more widely spread of the two languages.

Again, I am not claiming that this maximin law operates without exception. To start with, deviation from it happens on a massive scale for pedagogical reasons. In foreign language classes, for example, teachers often know the mother tongue of their pupils (which may well be their own) far better that the pupils know the language they are learning, but the mutually accepted rules of the teaching game will frequently entail the partial or total banning of the maximin language. For analogous reasons, some people choose (as I did) to speak their mother tongue with their children, even though their children have been all along and they have themselves become significantly more fluent in at least one other shared language.

On a less massive scale but often in a highly sensitive way, deviation may also occur, even in informal contexts, for what could be called expressive reasons. This may happen in negative fashion, for example when post-1989 East Europeans struggle to communicate with one another in English, even when it would be (linguistically) far easier for them to do so in Russian. It may also happen in positive fashion. For example, on several occasions I have addressed a Brussels audience in Dutch rather than French, despite the fact that all would have understood me adequately in French, while some did not in Dutch, perhaps because the organisers felt that some fair time sharing between French and Dutch needed to be kept. At least in part for an analogous reason, a *vade mecum* dispatched by the French foreign ministry insistently instructs France's representatives in all European institutions that, even at informal meetings or after the interpreters have gone home, 'les Français parlent leur langue' (Ministère des affaires étrangères, 2002).[3] Provided the number of mother tongues involved does not exceed two or three, this sort of consideration may also lead one to operate, as often done at interpretation-free federal-level meetings in Belgium and Switzerland, according to the rule 'Each speaks his/her own language'.[4]

However, as soon as efficiency in communication prevails over pedagogical or expressive concerns, perceptible inequalities in the minimum knowledge of the various languages involved will generate a hardly resistible pressure for all to adopt the maximin language: What's the point of uttering beautiful sentences with carefully chosen words if my audience would understand me far better were I to express myself more clumsily in a language far more familiar to them. Hence, although didactic effectiveness and symbolic impact may sometimes strongly constrain language choice, this will not prevent the maximin criterion from running the show whenever communication is the prime concern, ie in the bulk of spoken and written language use.

## An Explosive Interaction

Needless to say, these two mechanisms interact powerfully with each other. The more a particular language is being learned in some section of the world population, the more likely that language is to be the maximin language in contexts of interaction involving members of that section of the population. And the more often a particular language is picked as the language of interaction, the stronger the motivation for learning it and the more frequent the opportunity to learn it. It is worth noting that this positive feedback loop would also exist if the speech partners systematically tended to pick the language for which the average knowledge is greater (call it the maxi-mean language), or even the best language of the majority, but it would then operate at a considerably slower pace.

To illustrate this difference, take the situation that used to prevail before the Swedes and the Finns joined the EU. Both the maxi-mean and the maximin language in contexts of informal interaction between multilinguals within and around the European institutions then tended to be English and French in varying proportions (with German far more often maxi-mean than maximin). Given how small a percentage of the total population of speech partners they represented, the arrival of the Scandinavians did not change much in terms of maxi-mean. But it made a big difference in terms of maximin. For while the second best language for most British and Irish people was and is French, the Scandinavians' average competence in French was far poorer, and therefore tended to make English a clear winner in terms of maximin (though only marginally better than before in terms of maxi-mean) in any context in which they turned up. It is obviously far easier for newcomers to upset the prevailing choice of a language under maximin than under maxi-mean: it suffices for them to be almost completely ignorant of the prevailing language, while everyone else knows at least some more of at least one of the languages they know better. And once the switch is done, language learning is accordingly redirected for both incentive and opportunity reasons, leading further contexts to do the switch, and so on.

Undoubtedly, this analysis is very rough. Its basic assumptions need to be qualified and its implications should be modelled out in detail to provide precise answers to questions such as the following. Under what conditions does this twofold mechanism lead to a convergence to a single lingua franca? Under what conditions is it on the contrary consistent with the lasting coexistence of two or more linking languages? Under what conditions does it imply the decline of multilingualism (as opposed to bilingualism), and indeed of any bilingualism that does not consist in combining a mother tongue and the lingua franca? Under what conditions is it consistent with stable universal diglossia-competence of all members of a community in both their mother tongue and the lingua franca-or does it imply a long-term threat to the very survival of linguistic diversity? I do not know the answers to these questions (and would be interested in finding them out). But I have been, from the day of my birth, a participant observer in enough thousands of situations of multilingual interaction, and seen enough figures, tables and graphs depicting existing trends, to feel confident about the nature and power of the twofold mechanism outlined above.

## WHY WE NEED ONE LINGUA FRANCA

Whatever the power of the mechanism just described, one may want to pause to ask whether we really need the one lingua franca which it tends to bring about. Given the values to which I am committed, there is not the slightest doubt in my mind that we need a way of communicating directly and intensively across the borders drawn by the differences of our mother tongues, without the extremely expensive and constraining mediation of competent interpreters. We need it in particular if we do not want Europeanisation, and beyond it globalisation, to be the exclusive preserve of the wealthy and the powerful who can afford quality interpretation. If we want all sorts of workers', women's, young people's, old people's, sick people's, poor people's associations to organise on the ever higher scale required for effective action, we must equip them with the means of talking to one another without interpreting boxes and highly skilled and paid professionals in them. One way of putting this is to say that we need to meet the linguistic preconditions for turning Europe, and ultimately the world, into one *demos*, without this needing to mean that Europe, or the world, is thereby turned into a single *ethnos*: a forum can be shared thanks to a common language without the culture, including the language, becoming one. It cannot be taken for granted, however, that the linguistic preconditions for the existence of a single demos involve the adoption of one lingua franca.

## Clever Softwares?

Firstly, one can try to imagine a situation in which technological development will have made informal communication possible between different language groups without requiring the learning of a single common language. It suffices to combine the best of voice recognition and translation softwares to convey instantaneously through earphones in any chosen language what is being said in any other. Both kinds of software, we are told, are making fast progress. But those who have experienced some of the oddities generated by translation software even when having to cope with only slightly casual style, and by voice recognition software even under favourable acoustic conditions, can imagine how stilted and contrived a spontaneous interchange would need to become in order for its participants to feel reasonably confident of being understood.[5]

Moreover, any interacting group soon develops a small culture of its own, with words being used between inverted commas, as it were, or proper names turned into nouns, or short-lived imports from another language. Even very imperfect mastery of a common language would provide for a far better medium than beautiful mastery of one's own language constantly threatened by ridiculous stiffness on one side (if one bears the technology in mind) and the risk of ridiculous misunderstandings on the other (if one does not). Techno-freaks can keep dreaming about it. But there is no salvation to be gained from these quarters in my view.

## Esperanto?

If technology does not enable us to dispense with a common language, why not opt for a neutral one? This second solution is less fanciful. It is vigorously defended on grounds of neutrality and simplicity. But these two advantages look far greater than they really are. And in addition, the spreading of Esperanto faces a prohibitive hurdle.

Take neutrality first. Esperanto is of course far from being neutral in the sense of equidistant from all existing languages. It belongs unambiguously to the Western group of Indo-European languages, with identifiable Latin,

Slavic and Germanic ingredients. Even within Europe with Finnish, Estonian, Hungarian, Basque and Maltese as part of the picture, it cannot make any claim to 'neutrality'. Moreover, it does not stand a chance as a European lingua franca if in addition English needs to be learned as a worldwide lingua franca. But when offered on a world scale, it must lose all hope of being sold on grounds of fairness, especially to the millions in India, Nigeria, South Africa or even now Japan and China who have already invested massively in the learning of another Western language and will understandably show little patience for this new Eurocentric gimmick which they are enthusiastically invited to absorb.

It is true that, unlike English, Esperanto would be a learned language for everyone, and hence its adoption as a lingua franca would definitely be more egalitarian than that of English or French. This advantage, however, would only be transitional. Just assume that Esperanto successfully spreads and starts being used in a growing number of contexts, including by mixed couples in the upbringing of their children. Nothing would then prevent it, after some generations, from thickening from a lingua franca into the mother tongue of some-as happened to Swahili, for example-with the consequence that once again neutrality would be lost and the whole process of designing a neutral language, in the modest sense of being the mother tongue of no one, would need to be relaunched from scratch.

Secondly, consider the ease of learning. Syntactic and morphological rules are exceptionless in Esperanto, and therefore undoubtedly far simpler to learn from a grammar book than are those of natural languages. Moreover, compared to languages like English and French whose spelling was established long ago and very conservatively managed, Esperanto offers a sensible relationship between oral and written forms. However (usually shorter) irregular forms are rarely, if ever, sheer irrational nuisance. Natural languages operate complex trade offs between least effort in memorising and least effort in pronouncing, and the more intensively a language is used, the more the latter matters relative to the former. Esperanto turned into a real, living language would soon be subjected to such pressures. Moreover, Esperanto made relevant for all contexts would need to beef up its lexical stock massively through imports from other languages. Like all other languages today, it would import massively from English, and probably more than others because of its smaller initial stock. Hence, it would not take long for it to start looking like a bulky language, with a slim Esperanto component that can be learned in a couple of days and a huge English vocabulary with subtle nuances which could take years to master. Most fundamentally, however, the notion that Esperanto unambiguously has the upper hand over English in terms of learning rests on a very schoolish picture of language learning. As pointed out earlier, the learning of a language is essentially a matter of having the opportunity to play, whisper and quarrel, listen to music, watch TV and scan the web in that language, and a matter of being motivated to do all these things, especially at an early stage in one's life. If this more realistic picture of large-scale language learning replaces that of enthusiastic but lonely xenophiles confined to grammar books and vocabulary lists, it is no longer so clear that Esperanto is, in the relevant sense, easier to learn.

With its claims to neutrality and simplicity thus drastically qualified, Esperanto is hardly in a strong position to face the formidable hurdle it faces, precisely as long as it is not the mother tongue of a significant group. Investing in the learning of such a language is definitely cheapened by the exceptional simplicity of its morphological and syntactic rules. But as long as speech partners, films, music and TV broadcasts in that language are not all over the place, it still comes at a significant cost for someone with average learning skills. In the case of widespread natural languages, there is a secure minimum return on the learning investment, thanks to the tens or even hundreds of millions of people with whom one can be sure one acquires the capacity to communicate. Even in the case of Esperanto, the most widespread among the artificial languages currently advocated, this minimum return is not guaranteed, as all depends on whether a sufficient number of people will be willing to make and keep making the deliberate effort of learning the language, which is itself dependent on which language learning choices they expect others to make (see Selten and Pool, 1991).

The size of this handicap, relative to English, keeps growing as English keeps expanding in terms of native speakers, mainly thanks to continued net migration into English-speaking countries, and, at a much faster rate, in terms of the total number of people competent in it: English is probably the only natural language today, and certainly the only major language, with (far) fewer native speakers than people who learned it as a second language.[6] Given the twofold mechanism sketched at the start-probability-sensitive learning and maximin-dislodging it from this position will become an ever more impossible task. Esperanto is a wonderful way of linking up a fantastic bunch of generous and hospitable people around the world, but it is no more hopeful than clever software as an alternative Europe-wide or world-wide medium of communication.

## Lingua Franca Pluralism?

Having granted that we need a natural language, perhaps we should not rush into asserting that we need only one. To avoid the drawbacks and dangers of the dominance of a single language, many (especially, but not exclusively, among those whose language stands a chance of being picked as one of the lingua francas in the event that the proposed formula is implemented) have proposed that there should be two or three lingua francas side by side, with identical status.

A first way of understanding this lingua franca pluralism consists in viewing the selected lingua francas as alternatives to one another: each person learns one of them and only one. But reflection on some very modest arithmetic exercises should suffice to make us quickly discard this version of the idea. In a population of six people with three distinct mother tongues, a balanced choice between two lingua francas provides a common medium to randomly grouped people far more frequently than a random choice of a second language, but with a decreasing frequency as the size of the grouping rises. And this frequency decreases sharply as the number of distinct mother tongues increases. By contrast, the learning by all of the same lingua franca provides a common medium in 100% of cases, whatever the size of the groupings and whatever the number of mother tongues. Moreover this can be achieved with a sizeable discount, as those whose mother tongue is being learned can be exempted from the learning of any second language (see Appendix).

There is, however, another interpretation of lingua franca pluralism which performs just as well as the single-lingua-franca option in ensuring inter-communication in all groupings. It consists in viewing the two or more languages granted lingua franca status not as alternatives but as complements. In other words, the rule is no longer that each individual is supposed to learn one of the lingua francas, but that he must know them all. At first sight this may seem to be wasteful overkill: two or three times more learning without any gain in inter-communication, as one lingua franca is sufficient. It is, however, reasonable to conjecture that the passive knowledge of a language is easier to acquire (and even easier to be believed to be acquired) than an active knowledge of it. Therefore, the cost reduction that flows from the fact that natives of a language promoted to lingua franca status no longer need to acquire an active knowledge of the original lingua franca must be matched against the cost increase flowing from the fact that others need to acquire a passive knowledge of that language. In Belgium or Canada, therefore, quite apart from being perceived as fairer (an issue to which I return shortly), an 'each his own language' regime may compete reasonably well, in terms of cost-effectiveness, with a single-lingua-franca regime.

The trouble comes again when the number of native languages increases. In the European context, French is keen to share lingua franca status with English. But this would mean that Germans, for example, still need to acquire an active knowledge of either French or English, while in addition having to acquire a passive knowledge of the other. As they form the largest native language group, they find this understandably hard to accept. If francophones are to have a chance of winning their case, they therefore realise that they need to broaden their alliance by proposing to further share this lingua franca status with German.[7] But how will the Spanish, the Italians, and all the rest feel? Making life more comfortable for the Germans and the French by exempting them from acquiring an active knowledge of English makes things considerably worse for all others, now forced to acquire a passive knowledge of two more languages without being exempted from acquiring an active knowledge of one of them.

What may make sense in the presence of two native tongues, possibly even three, does not make the slightest sense when there are many. Any attempt to press for the adoption of one's native tongue as a second lingua franca in this supplementary sense will immediately be seen for what it is: trying to get greater comfort for oneself at the expense of increasing the burden on those who enjoy the privilege of having had their native tongue picked as the only lingua franca so far-which is defensible enough-but also on all other language groups who are not better situated than oneself-which is indefensible. Any attempt to assuage some of these by offering to extend the lingua franca status to them at the same time risks turning the net benefit to oneself into a net cost, unavoidably further increases the burden on any group still left out, and further boosts the global cost of the whole scheme.

Hence, for quite a different reason, lingua franca pluralism is no more promising in the supplementary sense than in the alternative sense. Whatever the language historical fate happens to have picked, we definitely need convergence to a single lingua franca. Those saddened by the fact that it is not the one they learned as infants will have to come to terms with it. Their narcissism should not jeopardise the satisfaction of our urgent communicative needs, in Europe and in the world.

## UNFAIRNESS AS UNEQUAL ACCESS TO LINGUISTIC ADVANTAGE

The twofold mechanism sketched above and the feedback loop between its two components enable us to understand what is now leading to the dominance of English. No hidden conspiracy by the Brits, let alone the Americans, but the spontaneous outcome of a huge set of decentralised decisions, mainly by non-anglophones, about which language to learn and which language to use. Our exploration of imaginable alternatives then led to the conclusion that the increasing dominance of one natural language as the single lingua franca simply makes a lot of sense: to communicate with one another, we need one and only one idiom, and it will need to be a natural language. Both unavoidable and wise then? Undoubtedly. Fair too? Certainly not. I now turn to four possible characterisations of the nature of the unfairness involved and briefly indicate in each case how I believe it is best to respond to the problem, as characterised.

### Undeserved Linguistic Rents

First, convergence towards a lingua franca that is the mother tongue of a subset of the population concerned unavoidably provides the members of this subset with undeserved advantages over the rest. They can express themselves with more ease and therefore tend to be more active and more persuasive in discussions conducted in the lingua franca, whether of a business, political or social nature. In addition, some jobs restricted to native speakers of the lingua franca-such as a far more than proportionate number of language teachers and language editors paid for by non-natives, a more than proportionate number of translators and interpreters into that language paid for by international organisations-would not exist without the privileged status enjoyed by that language. Moreover, a large number of jobs that are not specifically linguistic in content are explicitly or implicitly restricted, or far more easily accessible, to native speakers of that language, because of the central importance of being able to communicate in that language.[8] This booming demand for people proficient in the lingua franca unavoidably tends to boost the relative pay of people with native competence in that language, whether, for example, through being able to ask for high fees for private language tuition or through faster promotion in inter- or supra-national organisations.

The undeserved inequalities thus created are by no means restricted to inequalities between natives and non-natives of the lingua franca. Among non-natives, there are also huge and increasingly consequential social inequalities in terms of the extent to which the family environment provides children and adolescents with both the opportunity and the motivation to learn the lingua franca. There is a big difference between children whose parents have both a rich set of foreign connections with people who commonly speak the lingua franca and a purse large enough to fund Summer courses in Oxford, and those who have never taken part in any English conversation and whose parents would not know how to start to give them the chance of however modest an immersion.

## Stepping Back

Thus, growing unfairness there appears to be. Before considering what can and must be done about it, it is worth pausing briefly to get a sense of perspective.

First, the problem thus characterised is far from being unprecedented. In most nation states, the majority of the population had a mother tongue, usually labelled a 'dialect', that differed notably from the national language, as used in the media and the educational system, in high culture and political life, and in business transactions beyond the local level. Indeed, in many places, there is still a big discrepancy between the home language of many families, especially rural ones, and the nationally imposed lingua franca. In most cases, linguistic distance was not as great as between most European languages and English, but in some cases it was, and in all cases it involved forms of disadvantage in economic and political life, often even forms of blatant discrimination, closely parallel to those now encountered as English becomes just as much of a trans-national must as the dialect of the capital was a national must.

In the national context, the task of drastically reducing the resulting inequality of opportunities was (regarded as) accomplished through compulsory schooling in the national language. In the case of a trans-national lingua franca that no one would dare to try to impose as the main language of the various national populations concerned (and rightly so, as I shall argue later), the job looks far trickier. But let us bear in mind that the average number of years spent at school and the resources devoted to education in today's European context are enormous from both a historical and a comparative perspective. For example, when we are demanding that a country like the Congo, whose educational system is in shambles and whose formal political life is entirely conducted in an alien language mastered by no more than an estimated 7% of the population, should operate democratically, and hence at the very least enable a majority of its citizens to more or less follow what is going on, we are demanding something incomparably more utopian, in terms of its linguistic preconditions, than universal competence in English throughout Europe.

Moreover, as reflected in recent surveys, the process is well underway. In Belgium, for example, where there are two national languages on the same footing, average competence in English for the younger cohorts of adults is considerably higher than average competence in the second national language has ever been in the history of the country.[9] It is true, however, that even in these younger cohorts it remains a minority feature, and on average still a very long distance from the competence of native speakers. But there is one simple and cheap measure which, if taken vigorously throughout Europe, can be expected to have a dramatic impact both in reducing this distance and in spreading competence in English at all layers of the population.

## Ban Dubbing!

To see what this could be, just reflect for a while on the distribution of competence in English across European countries, as revealed by Eurobarometer (see Table 1). If we leave out the UK and Ireland because they are essentially anglophone, and Belgium and Luxembourg because they are multilingual, we are left with eleven countries, five with a Germanic language, four with a Latin language and two others. To no one's surprise, the five Germanic countries score better in terms of self-assessed knowledge of English (with an unweighted average of 65%), than the four Latin countries (with an unweighted average of 38%). This seems to provide strong support for the common wisdom that this sizeable inequality is rooted in the fact that

*Table 1: Percentage who say they 'know' English (EU 15)*[10]

| Age group | Up to 15 | 15 to 39 |
|---|---|---|
| United Kingdom | 99 | 98 |
| Ireland | 95 | 96 |
| Sweden | 79 | 94 |
| Denmark | 75 | 84 |
| Netherlands | 70 | 80 |
| Finland | 61 | 87 |
| Germany | 54 | 74 |
| Greece | 47 | 71 |
| Austria | 46 | 66 |
| France | 42 | 63 |
| Belgium | 40 | 55 |
| Italy | 39 | 63 |
| Spain | 36 | 61 |
| Portugal | 35 | 59 |
| Luxembourg | 19 | 27 |

English is an (admittedly quite latinised) Germanic language, and hence intrinsically easier to learn for the average citizen of the former set of countries than for the average citizen of the latter.

There is however, a second conjecture that turns out to be far more consistent with the data as soon as some attention is paid to the two remaining countries. Greek and more so Finnish are uncontroversially far more remote from English than either the Latin or the Germanic languages. As one moves from Finnish to Greek and next to the Latin and the Germanic group, one would therefore expect competence in English to rise monotonically. Yet for the population as a whole, the profile yielded by the data is 61% for Finland, 47% for Greece, 38% for the average Latin country and 65% for the average Germanic country. Even worse, for the younger generation (under 40), we find 87% for Finland, 71% for Greece, 61.5% for the average Latin country and 79.5% for the average Germanic country. On closer inspection, therefore, linguistic distance looks like a very bad—and worsening—predictor of competence in English.

To find a better predictor, let us partition our eleven countries according to the number of native speakers of their official language worldwide: fewer than 10 million (Denmark, Finland, Sweden), between 10 and 50 million (Greece, the Netherlands), between 50 and 100 million (Italy, France, Germany, Austria) and over 100 million (Portugal, Spain). The average proportion of people who say they know English now drops quite sharply and consistently from one category to the next: 72%, 58.5%, 45% and 35.5%, respectively, for all age groups together; 88%, 75.5%, 66.5% and 60%, respectively, for those under 40. Why?

My conjecture is that the key intermediate variable is the relative frequency of dubbing versus subtitling in the broadcasting of English-language series, films and other programmes. It is estimated that the average cost of one hour of dubbing is about fifteen times the cost of one hour of subtitling (Luyken *et al*, 1991). Hence, the threshold, in terms of number of viewers, at which it starts making sense to incur the cost of translation is far lower in the case of subtitling than it is in the case of dubbing, which a majority of viewers seem to prefer.[11] Consequently, the extent to which English-language productions are dubbed, rather than subtitled, can safely be expected to rise steadily as one moves from countries whose language is spoken by comparatively few people, such as Denmark, Sweden, Finland, Greece and the Netherlands, to countries populated by the members of larger linguistic groups.[12] As revealed by incipient research, the watching of undubbed foreign programmes provides, under appropriate conditions, a powerful way for children to learn foreign languages.[13] No wonder, therefore, that we should find a strong negative correlation between size of the language group and competence in English.

In order to motivate the proposal I am about to make, I do not need to assert that no other factor plays a significant role. It is sufficient for me to be able to assume, as the available evidence strongly suggests I can, that the learning mechanism in question is a powerful one. We cannot do much about linguistic distance between languages, or about the numbers of native speakers of the various languages, or therefore about the relative profitability of subtitling and dubbing. But we can outlaw dubbing. And if we do so, while providing supportive language teaching and letting MTV music, web chats and other less virtual trans-national contacts do the rest of the job, competence in English will become, in the space of one generation, even less of a problem than it now is in the most English-literate parts of the European continent.[14]

Refusing to ban dubbing in those countries in which it is currently common practice amounts to unnecessarily inflicting a linguistic handicap on the most disadvantaged layers of the populations concerned and therefore strengthening the privilege enjoyed by the elite whose access to competence in English is far easier through quality schooling and foreign contacts. It also amounts to perpetuating an increasingly costly disadvantage for many members of their populations who are at all likely to be involved in the global economy, in supra-national organisations or in the trans-national civil society. If we want to be serious about fighting linguistic injustice in the sense of unequal access to linguistic advantage, therefore, my recipe is simple and inexpensive: *Ban dubbing!*[15]

## Three Objections

One possible objection is that such a ban would violate the fundamental freedom of expression. Note, however, that it applies indiscriminately to all languages, that it involves no restriction whatsoever on the content of that which is being subtitled or dubbed, and that it does not prevent anyone from addressing directly through the media an audience with whom it has no language in common.[16] This objection is therefore bound to be regarded as ludicrously formalistic, especially if the ban it incriminates can persuasively be shown, along the lines sketched above, to better equip a large proportion of the population to express themselves in a language in which it will be increasingly crucial for them to be able to express themselves in order to be heard by those who they will need to be heard by.

A second objection is that the ban would directly harm the interests of professional actors, who use dubbing as a way of securing more regular income than film or theatre contracts can provide. There will undoubtedly be an effect of this kind, but it will be buffered, if not offset, by a significant increase in the demand for local production if it remains the case, beyond the transition period, that a majority of people prefer dubbing to subtitling. A residual net negative effect on professional actors taken as a whole cannot be ruled out. But the vested interest of a tiny minority cannot legitimately block a move that would massively benefit a large, comparatively disadvantaged majority.

Finally, there is the risk that the ban would be bypassed as a result of people going to the cinema or watching videos and DVDs not subjected to the same ban. While the ban seems easy enough to extend to cinemas, it seems more difficult for videos and DVDs. But the fall in demand from TV channels and cinema distribution may in itself be sufficient to make quality dubbing unprofitable for videos and DVDs alone, even if some boosting of the demand for dubbed videos is triggered by the ban. Needless to say, if the effect of the ban were that people would shift entirely to programmes in the native language, or to cartoons with a sound track in the native language, or to dubbed videos, or to a combination of these, the intended effect would not be achieved. But although some shift in each of these three directions can be expected, it is most doubtful that it would inhibit a lasting and expanding impact, especially as tolerance for subtitling develops through practice and as teletext technology makes it possible to offer a wide range of individual choices for subtitle languages and to optionally get rid of subtitling altogether as competence in English (or any other non-native language) makes it superfluous for a growing number of non-native people for an ever wider range of programmes.

## UNFAIRNESS AS THE UNEQUAL SHARING OF THE BURDEN OF LANGUAGE LEARNING

### Free Riding

To phrase as sharply as possible our second problem of linguistic injustice, let us next assume that competence in English has spread massively to the non-native speakers, and pretty equally among them, so that the adoption of English as a lingua franca no longer gives a great advantage in discussion or competition to English natives or to non-natives with a privileged access to English. Language-related injustice has not disappeared. For unlike the community of natives, the non-natives have had to devote a considerable amount of time and resources to the learning of a foreign language.[17] It is estimated that the average time required to master a foreign language is 10,000 hours-compared to a standard school year totalling less than 1,000 hours in the classroom.[18] However speculative such estimates, it is clear that the cost in time and resources of acquiring proficiency in a foreign language is huge. This heavy effort obviously benefits the community that performs it-otherwise it would not bother-but also, in some cases possibly to an even larger extent, the community whose language is being learned.

In other words, there is a public good-the creation of a lingua franca-being enjoyed by all linguistic groups throughout the world involved in global communication, but produced only by those groups whose language has not been picked as the lingua franca, with the lucky ones whose native language happens to have been picked enjoying a free ride. This is the second sense in which 'linguistic injustice' can be said to be involved. What can be done about it?

## Cost Sharing

Scandinavians, who speak some of the least widely spread of the EU's official languages, have tended to be pretty blunt in admitting the dominance of English, whilst being quite imaginative in suggesting how the induced fairness could be reduced. Thus, the first Danish delegation to the European Parliament is said to have made the following proposal. They conceded upfront that they could not expect others to understand Danish and agreed to speak English, but only on condition that the others, including the French, did the same with the sole exception of the British, who would have to speak French. The British were no doubt quick to point out that this would be grossly unfair to them as they would be forced to express themselves in a language that only a minority would grasp, while everyone else could be understood by all. As they were still allowed to speak in English at that stage, the others must have understood that they had a point, and the idea was dropped.[19]

More recently, the Swedish Prime Minister, somewhat scared at the prospect of a near doubling of the number of official EU languages, made a distinct proposal. Instead of having all countries paying jointly (roughly according to their wealth) for the translating of everything into every language, why not have a system in which the cost of language services would be systematically shared equally between the countries whose language is being used and the countries into whose language the translation is being made. As an ever greater majority of texts is being produced in English and as the Swedes are competent enough in English not to need a translation for most documents, the rule would end up practically exempting the Swedes from any contribution. Fairly, it might be said, as this counts as a compensation for their investment in the learning of English. Efficiently too, it may be added, as this would provide other countries with an incentive to follow suit, thereby facilitating massive savings in translation costs. At the limit, all translation costs would be eliminated as a result of all countries conforming to the Swedish pattern. However, while translation costs may then be down to zero, unfairness would not, as one linguistic community would still get away with not learning a foreign language.

## Proportionality between Cost and Benefit

As argued persuasively by Jonathan Pool (1991), the only real solution to this problem, the only real way of reconciling communicative efficiency and linguistic fairness in this second sense, consists of introducing a subsidy from the linguistic group whose language is being learned to those who do the learning. How high should this subsidy be? Various criteria are worth discussing. For example, Pool (1991) proposes that each language group should contribute to the cost of the learning of the lingua franca according to its numerical size, while David Gauthier's (1986) general conception of co-operative justice as maximin relative benefit would amount, in this case, to requiring equality among the per capita benefits derived from the existence of the lingua franca by the various language groups.[20]

I argue elsewhere (Van Parijs, 2002) that neither of these *prima facie* attractive criteria is defensible and that a distinct one is to be preferred: the equalisation of cost-benefit ratios across language groups or, put differently, proportionality between (total or per capita) contribution of each group to the cost of the existence of the lingua franca and (total or per capita) benefit derived from it. Suppose we measure roughly the benefit to a language group of the existence of the lingua franca by the number of people with whom the latter enables members of the group to communicate. And suppose we measure the contribution of a language group by the amount (in money and time) its members spent acquiring the lingua franca, if any, plus the taxes paid in this connection to other language groups, if any, minus the subsidies received in this connection from other language groups, if any. What the proposed criterion requires is that, across all language groups involved, the total cost (taking taxes and subsidies into account) be proportionate to the number of people the language group can communicate with thanks to the lingua franca.

In all circumstances, this criterion will require a net transfer from the linguistic group whose language is being learned to the groups who do the learning, and the per capita size of this language tax will grow, other things being equal, as more and more people learn the language. The size of the transfer will never exceed the benefit to lingua franca natives, as the criterion requires the ratio of cost to benefit to be the same for all, and the learning only makes sense if the benefit exceeds the cost. Yet, it is clear that the criterion justifies massive transfers from those countries in which the bulk of the English natives live—in particular the United States, home to 70% of them-towards the rest of the world.

## Four Qualifications

This conclusion needs to be qualified in four ways. Firstly, as the biggest language groups in the world-the mandarinophones and the hispanophones-fully join the global game, the English natives will not be the only ones from whom fairness will require a contribution. For as one moves from a larger to a smaller language group that learns the lingua franca, it is not just that the total amount of the subsidy justified by our criterion shrinks, but also its per capita level, because smaller groups unavoidably gain more speech partners than large ones thanks to the lingua franca. So much so that for small language groups learning the lingua franca alongside far bigger ones, this subsidy may be negative. Thus, overall equality of cost-benefit ratios may require small learners such as the Danes, the Dutch and even the French, to pay, along with the Americans and the Brits, for part of the learning of English by such potential big learners as native speakers of Mandarin, Castillan, Hindi and Bengali.[21]

Secondly, as English spreads as a world lingua franca, the quantity of learning may be rising, but its per-unit cost is bound to fall at some point, for two reasons. One is that there are more and more opportunities to speak English as the number of (non-native) English speech partners expands, and the expansion of costless opportunities to speak is the surest way of cheapening language learning. The second reason is that the local spread of competence in English makes it possible to provide prospective learners with the competent teachers they need at much less cost—it is no longer necessary to import natives at high cost or to send children on immersion courses in native territory. For this reason the swelling of the global cost of lingua franca learning is bound to be far less than proportional to the swelling of its quantity. At the limit, if it ever became as easy and natural to learn the lingua franca as it is to learns one's mother tongue, ie if our first problem of linguistic unfairness had become solvable at no cost, our second problem of linguistic unfairness would vanish altogether.[22]

Thirdly, one has to draw the full implications of the fact that talking to some willing native speakers of a language in a context in which it is natural to speak that language is one of the most widespread and most effective ways of improving one's knowledge of a language-this is precisely the opportunity side of the probability-sensitive learning mechanism at the core of the language dynamics sketched towards the beginning of this paper. But it is its reverse side that I now want to draw attention to. As competence in English spreads worldwide, there are ever fewer circumstances, because of the maximin dynamics sketched earlier, in which English natives will have a natural opportunity to speak another language and improve their knowledge of it. The advantage of being able to use one's own language in an ever growing number of contexts therefore has the side effect of making it increasingly difficult to learn other languages. Even though the importance of knowing other languages for communication purposes decreases accordingly, this is a genuine disadvantage. One way of putting it is that language learning is to a large extent made up of free-riding on patient speech partners. As English spreads, interaction between English natives and others occurs more and more—soon nearly exclusively-in English. Consequently, this type of free-riding of English natives on others will reduce to very little, relative to the symmetric free-riding of these others on English natives (even though an ever growing majority of the people to whom non-English natives will be talking English will be other non-English natives).[23] This growing asymmetry in learning assistance may be far from offsetting the growing asymmetry in exemption from learning, but it does qualify the assessment of the size of the unfairness involved.

## Poach the Web!

Finally, one must be aware of the fact that both the incentive and opportunity to learn any foreign language but English will decrease as English increasingly suffices to get by wherever one is. As a consequence, English will become more and more a globally public language, while other languages will remain or increasingly become globally private languages. Having no private language means being far more liable to give away information to any outsider who cares to listen or read. This may take some minor forms: whatever your mother tongue, you may benefit from overhearing two American tourists telling each other, in the queue to the museum, that the door to the toilet is locked. Had they been Finnish, you would have lost your position in the queue. Trivial asymmetric benefiting of this sort may seem hardly worth mentioning. But as more and more information gets loaded onto the web, easy to access, copy and use worldwide, this asymmetry is assuming gigantic proportions. Whatever is being made available in this way to the 350 million English natives is being made available simultaneously to the 700 million or so non-natives who bothered to learn English (and are massively over-represented among web users from their respective countries). By contrast, practically none of the information that these 700 million put on the web in their native languages can be 'overheard' by English natives, because so few of these know other languages. Of course, more and more of the material put on the web by non-English natives will be in English (far from exclusively, or even mainly, to communicate with English natives). But as long as a significant proportion is produced and made available in other languages,[24] a deep asymmetry remains, which, again, partly cancels the advantage derived from one's language having become the lingua franca. Indeed, it provides the only realistic chance of ever cancelling that advantage to a significant extent. Let me explain.

My point of departure was that English natives derive a massive advantage as a result of their language having been picked as the lingua franca and that this unfairness needs to be corrected through a fair sharing of the burden of producing the public good, ie of the learning of the lingua franca by those with a different mother tongue. But it is hard to imagine the US and the UK gathering huge amounts of cash to compensate countries whose populations spontaneously crave to learn English anyway, and do so. But it is not exactly crazy to believe that the web can be poached, ie taken advantage of without a compensatory payment. The difficulty of protecting property rights effectively on the web means that poaching, tolerated or not, will assume ever growing proportions. In actual practice, by far the most effective (though selective) lock may well be language-for those who do not understand it. But as English spreads, all English material gets unlocked for the world, and poaching becomes increasingly asymmetric. No vigorous efforts should be made to repress it, to enforce intellectual property rights over English-language content accessible in this way-or indeed in (increasingly obsolete) printed form. No collaboration can be legitimately expected for the sake of redressing the massive resulting (net) free riding by non-English natives. For this is nothing but compensatory free riding. My slogan-like response to linguistic unfairness in the second sense is therefore as simple as was my response to unfairness in the first sense: *Poach the web!*

## UNFAIRNESS AS UNEQUAL INFLUENCE

### Americanisation

Suppose 'Ban dubbing!' works as a way of equalising language-based inequalities, and suppose 'Poach the web!' works as a way of offsetting the unequal distribution of language-learning burdens. The outcome will undoubtedly be an acceleration of the very process to which these two strategies are meant to respond: as the consumption of undubbed TV programmes and the use of English-language websites expand, competence in English keeps increasing, but, as a by-product, so does the absorption of intellectual products conceived and produced in English-speaking countries, above all the United States.

This is the case not only directly because ever more is heard or read directly in English by non-English natives relative to what is heard or read by English natives in languages other than English. This primary bias is further amplified by a derived bias in the flow of translations. This can be seen in two ways: firstly, far more is being translated from English into other languages than from other languages into English; and secondly, for any given language, an ever greater proportion of what is produced in English is translated into that language than is translated from any other language. This must hardly come as a surprise: the very spread of competence in English among those who have to make decisions about what to adapt or translate gives a far greater chance of discovery and translation, for a given quality and interest, to anything that is available in English. And once the process is underway, marketing strategies focusing on known names will further amplify the process (see Melitz, 1999). Might this not lead to unfairness in a third sense, as unfair inequality in the ability to spread one's ideas and, tightly linked to this, to a worrying worldwide ideological domination by the United States? (See eg Wilmet, 2003.)

Let us first clarify a confusion. Whatever you may hear said in English, there is of course nothing intrinsically 'pro-capitalist', or 'anti-poor', or 'market-imperialist' about the English language, just as it is not because Marx wrote in German that there is something intrinsically 'anti-capitalist' or 'pro-proletarian' or 'state-fetishist' about the German language. Like all other languages in the world, English and German have the means of expressing negation, so that whatever Marx wrote in German you can also deny in German and whatever Bush said in English you can also deny in English. Similarly, contrary to what is occasionally asserted, there is nothing intrinsic to English that makes it more suitable for expressing things rigorously and succinctly. (Mathematical economics, let us remember, was born in French, and analytic philosophy in German.) Which is not to say that there are no distinct national intellectual traditions, shaped by educational practices and cultural fashions, nor therefore significant statistical differences between average levels of rigour or long-windedness in speeches and writings in the various languages.

## Seize the Loudspeaker!

Hence, the real problem is not the use of English as such, but rather the fact that the political content of English-language discourse, as reflected for example in academic textbooks, newspaper articles, TV series and web content, tends to differ in ways which many regard as undesirable from what the discourse would be in non-anglophone countries if these were sheltered from anglophone influence. What 'makes sense' in terms of public policy in the United States is strongly shaped by the heavy dependence of political candidates at the highest levels on the collection of private contributions to the funding of their electoral campaigns. As a result of the worldwide spread of competence in English and hence of English-language publications (in the original or in translation), this situation unnecessarily skews the realm of the politically thinkable and feasible worldwide. For this contingent reason, not because of any intrinsic feature of the English language, there is a real danger of 'Americanisation' that the ban on dubbing and the poaching of the web, as such, would admittedly rather reinforce than contain.

The solution, however, cannot be defensive retreat. It consists in appropriating that medium in order to spread through it whatever content we see fit. Not shrill whispering in provincial dialects, but the uninhibited grabbing of the global loudspeaker provides the way forward. Throughout the world we must become able to say:

English is our language, even when it is, as for many of us, only one of our languages. And we will use it to say what we want to say in it, and not what the government of the country that houses 70% of its native speakers would like us to say.

But to make this strategy effective, the worst would be to hold back and obstruct in all sorts of ways the learning of English by our people, our students, our children, especially the less advantaged among them. They should rather acquire as soon as possible the competence needed to talk and write in English, indeed to feed the web with English material and produce English-language works. If people from all over the world want to be read or heard all over the world, they must not proudly or shyly withdraw into their tiny linguistic world but use the language that will enable them to reach as far as possible, albeit with distinctive accents and in distinctive styles. If ideological domination is to be avoided and, by the same token, if the distribution of worldwide influence is to be made less unfair, one must not resist, but accelerate the competent appropriation of the lingua franca. All the better, therefore, if the ban on dubbing and the poaching of the web takes us in that direction more quickly.

## UNFAIRNESS AS UNEQUAL RESPECT

There is, however, a distinct objection that is sometimes confused with the risk of ideological domination. Conceding, indeed accelerating, the de facto prevalence of one language over all others can be perceived as showing a lack of respect towards these other languages and the people whose identities are closely tied to them. Even if second-language competence is widely and thoroughly spread, even if the burden of learning the lingua franca as a second language is fairly shared by the people who have the lingua franca as their mother tongue, there remains the fact that the language of one subset is being given a privileged status above all the others. The most fundamental injustice, the form of injustice that is hardest to fix, may well turn out to be the associated inequality of respect, of honour, of pride. What can be done about it?

## Demystification

There need not be anything obnoxious, or ridiculous, or insulting for others, in taking pride in one's mother tongue having been picked as a world's lingua franca-not more, at any rate, than in being proud about the fact that a boy from one's village has been picked as a page to the King. It may nonetheless be wise to reassert now and then that the choice was not based on any intrinsic quality. English is just the dialect of some Germanic Barbarians who settled across the Channel, messily bastardised as a result of subsequent French colonisation and gradually enriched, through the centuries, from the top down by sophisticated scholars shamelessly plundering Latin and Greek lexicons and from the bottom up through the reluctant incorporation into grammar books and dictionaries of the unspeakable slang of defiant youth. It may also be of some use to reiterate, whenever an opportunity arises, that the choice is not rooted either in any ethnic superiority of its native population-by now anyway a pretty mixed bunch of people which owes its large size far (and ever) less to the reproductive drive of the Angles than to the assimilating power of the US educational machine.

## Ritual Affirmation

All this may be worth rehearsing whenever arrogance shows up, but equal respect can hardly be expected to be achieved as a result. More significant is the ritual, sometimes ceremonial, affirmation of the equality of all recognised languages. For example, the authors of the Charter of the Fundamental Rights of the European Union (2000) were right in stating, in its article 22, that 'the Union shall respect cultural, religious and linguistic diversity'. And so was Valéry Giscard d'Estaing when he opened the European Convention in February 2002 by saying 'Mesdames et Messieurs' in the EU's eleven official languages of the time, just as it has great significance for the language groups concerned that the Pope should mumble publicly a brief Happy New Year in their own language, however modest the latter's range. However, the lip service thus ceremoniously paid to linguistic equality has obvious limits, not only because of its growing awkwardness as the number of official languages increases from the initial four (in the first two decades of the 'European community') to twenty after the 2004 enlargement and twenty-one from January 2007 with the inclusion of Irish. The number of cases in which oral and written communication will be allowed to transgress the equality rule will keep increasing.[25] More fundamentally, if equality of respect boils down to ceremony, it is hard to dispel the suspicion of hypocrisy.

## Grab a Territory!

In addition to demystification and ceremonial affirmation, however, there is a third, and in my view far more significant way of expressing equality of respect for the various languages concerned. It consists in allowing each of them to be 'the King' in some part, large or small, of the EU's territory, thereby making its own survival secure and bestowing a privilege, within the limits of that territory, on the people who have as a mother tongue the language to which that territory has been ascribed. The message from the EU to its citizens is then simply:

> Free movement within the European Union is one of our great achievements. But if you move for more than a short time to any part of the EU's territory whose official language happens to be different from your mother tongue, you must have the courage *and* the humility to learn that language if you do not know it already.[26]

The symmetry involved in this linguistic territoriality principle, as I shall call it, is the only really significant way in which equality of respect can be shown to be meant seriously, consistent with the full acceptance of systematic asymmetric bilingualism at EU level.[27]

In concrete terms, what the linguistic territoriality principle amounts to is a set of enforceable rules about the public use of language that will systematically frustrate the powerful pro-dominant-language bias incorporated in the interaction between probability-sensitive learning and maximin communication. The territoriality principle will typically impose public education in the local language even on those who would prefer to have their children taught straight in the lingua franca. It will impose administrative or judicial procedures in the local language even in cases where the local public officers master the foreign language better than the foreign person they have to deal with masters the local language. And it will impose the use of the local language in the political realm, even if more residents could be enabled to participate to some extent if another language were used. As a result, more people will learn the local language, or will learn it more thoroughly, than if probability-sensitive learning had been left unconstrained. More interactions will also occur in the local language than if maximin were given free rein, thereby creating both a stronger incentive and a wider opportunity to learn the local language.[28]

If the local language is a powerful language, which most immigrants spontaneously have a strong incentive to learn, the territoriality principle will hardly be felt, as only a very light constraint may be enough for the spontaneous interaction of differential learning and maximin communication to take over and keep that language firmly in place. But when this is not the case, when the 'natural' incentive to learn is weak, the enforcement of the territoriality principle will not only be felt, but more often than not bitterly resented by non-native speakers of the official language, unless it is credibly framed as a fair way of showing equal respect. After 'Ban dubbing!', 'Poach the web!' and 'Seize the loudspeaker!', this is, then, my fourth recipe for linguistic justice in Europe and in the world: *Grab a territory!*

## Arbitrary Borders

Which are the languages that should be given a territory, and how should their borders be determined? There is no neat answer to this question. I propose two (fuzzy) conditions as necessary and sufficient. One is that there must be a sufficiently vigorous movement asking for it-otherwise, the energy needed to bear the cost of forgoing large economies of scale and other expenses related to the setting up of institutions in one's own language will not be forthcoming. The second condition is that the presence of the linguistic group must not be the product of recent immigration, whether from inside or outside the country. Fairness is respected to the extent that it can credibly be said: 'You need to learn our local language here just as we would need to learn yours if we settled in your own place.' Your place may be small, and the probability of my ever settling there close to zero, but the symmetry needed for equal respect does not require equal sizes or equal probabilities. For those allophone immigrants who do not have a protected linguistic homeland-the Kurds, the Arameans, the Baluba-the solution cannot consist in allowing them to grab a territory wherever they decide to migrate, but where they are traditionally settled.

Thus, if and only if the two conditions mentioned are satisfied-vigorous movement, ancient roots-with no doubt some grey area in each case, a territory can be associated with the language. The borders are bound to be contentious, and some compromise will need to be made between geographical neatness and linguistic homogeneity. People stuck on the wrong side of the border will need to have their vested rights protected through special measures that will be phased out with their generation. And of course languages other than the official one can thrive and even get official support, provided the protective measures are powerful enough to keep promoting the official language into maximin position in a sufficient number of contexts for all permanent residents to have both the desire and the opportunity to learn the official language properly.

## Strengthening the 'Natural' Grip

A second difficulty is precisely that for three distinct reasons—one general, two more restricted in scope, though of special importance for the European

Union—the mechanisms of linguistic integration, essential for facilitating the implementation of the territoriality principle, are losing their grip. The first reason is the spread of satellite and cable TV, which considerably reduces the exposure of immigrants of all ages and their children, grandchildren, etc, even born in the new country, to the local language. Quickly reinforced by all types of sorting mechanisms (if the café's TV broadcasts nothing but Turkish programmes, what are the chances of it attracting or retaining non-Turkish customers?), this makes it considerably more difficult for linguistic competence in the local language to spread through the immigrant population, including through the school system, as children are far more likely to keep speaking the immigrant language to each other than used to be the case.

A second reason applies more specifically to those cases where immigrants, in addition to their mother tongue, have some knowledge of English and soon find that they can get away with hardly any knowledge of the local language, as most local people also have some knowledge of English. Especially when the local language is not widely spread and when the immigrants are not sure how long they will stay, probability-sensitive learning will never be sufficient for the local language to take over from English in most everyday circumstances. Worries about this new phenomenon are now commonly aired in such countries as Sweden and the Netherlands.

The third reason applies more specifically to those countries with a developed welfare state that makes it possible for a significant proportion of the immigrant population of working age to live for long periods without entering a work community. The fact that many of the less skilled jobs in the service sector are quite demanding linguistically makes it particularly difficult for immigrants to find jobs, even in the absence of discrimination.[29] And the outcome is that the work sphere is less effective than earlier and elsewhere in providing immigrants with both the opportunity and the motivation to learn the local language. Effective language learning for all therefore arguably requires tougher measures, such as compulsory language courses, sanctioned by proficiency tests, for new immigrants, the prohibition of the immigrant language in class and in the playground, and/or the constrained mixing of children of various origins in schools which are in danger of becoming ethnically homogeneous.

### Stabilising Diglossia

The third difficulty concerns the possibility of stable diglossia. Suppose the process has gone so far that practically everyone in a particular country knows the lingua franca in addition to the country's main mother tongue.[30] Will there then not be a growing number of contexts in which the local language will no longer unambiguously be the maximin language even among natives? Think of the spread of English-language courses in continental

European universities (see Ammon, 2001a; Maiworm and Wächter, 2002). As this trend extends downward from postgraduate to undergraduate levels, there will be a number of domains in which natives of a particular language will find it easier to communicate with one another in English than in their own common mother tongue, or in a variant of their mother tongue perforated by strings of lexical borrowings and occasional full sentences in English. Can some territorial community's universal bilingualism really be more than a transient stage between universal competence in the local language only and the withering away of that language? (see Salverda, 2001; Willems, 2002) Here too, the only safeguard is a toughening of the territoriality principle. But is this sustainable when it is not only the newcomers or some local linguistic minority, but the whole of the native population that is made to feel its pinch so keenly?

## Ground Floor Attraction

The final and potentially most formidable difficulty stems from the asymmetric migration of highly skilled people that the implementation of the territoriality principle will tend to generate.[31] Once the highly skilled of a particular country and their families are about as competent in English as in their mother tongue, the obstacle to moving to the English-language part of the world will shrink to about the same size as the cost of moving to a place where their native language is being spoken, and become far less prohibitive than the obstacle to moving to a country whose language they would need to learn from scratch in order to fully participate in social life, or even sometimes to manage barely comfortable survival. This transforms the part of the world in which the lingua franca is being spoken-what I call 'the ground floor of the world' (Van Parijs, 2000)-into a powerful attractor of high skills, which other countries will have the greatest difficulty counteracting.

Of course, the loss of a number of highly skilled people trained at great expense at home may be partly offset by remittances sent home, through the creation of networks from which the home country will benefit and above all through the return, after a number of years, of better trained and better connected highly skilled workers. Indeed, one might wish to argue that this process is not fundamentally different from the sort of systematically asymmetric migration of high skills that has always existed between cities and their rural hinterland. There is a similarity, but there is also a deep difference. It is not just that remittances are not quite of the same relative magnitude as the daily pay which commuting workers take to their villages when returning home every evening. The solidarity relationship between a city and its hinterland is also far tighter, as a result of all sorts of explicit and implicit transfers organised by a state that encompasses them both. The concentrated use of high skills in cities can therefore be routinely regarded as serving everyone's interest far more easily than asymmetric trans-national migration.

Because of these differences, the global brain drain cannot be observed with the same equanimity as the exodus of the rural intelligentsia. Countries which inflict on prospective settlers the cost of learning a lesser used language put themselves at a competitive disadvantage relative to ground floor countries. They can only compensate for it, at first sight at any rate, by making conditions more attractive for the people they need to attract back or retain. And this must mean, one way or another, that they must shrink the degree of solidarity expected from the more talented, the more skilled, the more mobile, towards the less qualified, the less able, the less mobile.

What can be done about this final problem short of giving up the territoriality principle? The cost to be paid in terms of prosperity and/or solidarity would no doubt be considerably decreased if all countries were linked by a solidarity system that would automatically spread across borders whatever the ground floor produces thanks to the fruitful collaboration of brains drained from all over the planet. As this is still far off on any significant scale, inventiveness is in order. What about a combination of poaching-again-and ground floor enclaves?

As a growing part of what is being produced, especially with a large high-skill input, consists of knowledge, maximal worldwide leakage of the knowledge produced on the ground floor is part of what is needed to offset the free riding of the ground floor on the education, training and (self-)selection of the human capital it attracts. It is the very accessibility of whatever is done in English and the very fact that the spread of English makes the ground floor a receptacle of bright brains from all over the world that also makes it particularly vulnerable to the poaching of whatever (informational) wealth is thereby produced.

Over and above this poaching, other countries might also think of organising carefully circumscribed 'linguistically free zones', ie small areas in which the linguistic territoriality principle is relaxed. The highly skilled and their families who settle in these zones, selected because of their high-tech vocation, would be relieved of the heavy 'tax' of having to learn the local language. As a consequence, the lingua franca would gradually rule within these enclaves about as imperially as it does on the real ground floor.

After having quickly gone through these four difficulties, my answer to the fourth interpretation of linguistic injustice—unequal respect—remains: *Grab a territory!* But there will be many cases in which this grabbing will need to be done in a very sensitive way (first difficulty), require more strenuous effort than used to be the case (second and third difficulties), and come at a cost that will not be easily offset (fourth difficulty).

## CONCLUSION

To conclude: Yes, there is unfairness involved in the fact that one of the native languages is being picked, through countless unco-ordinated choices, as the sole lingua franca. But this unfairness can, to a large extent, be compensated. Firstly, inequalities in competence in the lingua franca can be massively reduced through an effective ban on dubbing and other ways of facilitating early learning. Secondly, inequalities in the shouldering of the burden of learning the lingua franca can be compensated by poaching the web and free riding in other ways on the intellectual production of the natives of the lingua franca. Thirdly, language-based inequalities in influence, and the associated ideological dominance of the United States, can and must be reduced through appropriating the common medium and using it as a loudspeaker. Fourthly and finally, inequality in the respect expressed towards the various languages can be alleviated to some extent through demystification and ceremonial recognition, but above all through allowing each recognised community to effectively give top status to its language within some home territory.

Provided fairness is vigorously pursued along each of these four dimensions, we can accept without rancour or resentment the increasing reliance on English as a lingua franca. We need one, and only one, if we are to be able to work out and implement efficient and fair solutions to our common problems on both European and world scales, and indeed if we are to be able to discuss, characterise and achieve, again Europe- and world-wide, linguistic justice.

## APPENDIX: WHY LEAVING THE CHOICE BETWEEN TWO LINGUA FRANCAS WILL NOT DO

To start with, imagine six people with three mother tongues—two Brits, two French and two Germans-and consider the following three regimes:

(1) No lingua franca: Let them choose their second language at random (each language is chosen with equal frequency).
(2) Double lingua franca: Constrain the choice of a second language by demanding that it is English in half the cases, and French in the other half.
(3) Single lingua franca: Impose English on all non-anglophones, while the Brits learn nothing.

As regards the communicative efficiency of these various regimes, the key question is how frequently the six people will have at least one language in common when gathering at random in groups of various sizes (from 2 to 6). The outcomes, under some simplifying assumptions, are given in Table I.

*Table I: Percentage of groupings with at least one language in common (6 people, 3 mother tongues)*

| Size of the groupings | 2 | 3 | 4 | 5 | 6 |
|---|---|---|---|---|---|
| Number of possible combinations | 15 | 20 | 15 | 6 | 1 |
| (1) No lingua franca | 100 | 60 | 20 | 0 | 0 |
| (2) Double lingua franca | 100 | 80 | 60 | 33 | 0 |
| (3) Single lingua franca | 100 | 100 | 100 | 100 | 100 |

Under the No-LF regime (1), the 6 people will always have a common language when 2 of them meet; in 60% of the cases when 3 meet; in 25% of the cases when 4 meet; and never when more than 4 meet. Under the double-LF regime (2), the percentage of cases in which they have a common language rises, thanks to the constraint on their choice, from 60 to 80% when 3 of them meet; from 25 to 66% when 4 of them meet; and from 0 to 33% when 5 of them meet. It remains 0 when all of them meet. Under the single-LF regime (3), the percentage of cases in which there is a common language rises to 100% whatever the size of the grouping. Moreover, this is achieved with a one-third global discount on the learning involved, since the Brits need to do none of it.

In this simple three-language case, the cost-benefit advantage of opting for a single lingua franca is strong enough. But it becomes overwhelming as the number of mother tongues increases. Take the same example, but with six mother tongues instead of three and re-interpret the three regimes accordingly (Table II). The no-LF, as interpreted, leads to less than half of the two-by-two groupings and to no larger grouping having a common language, while the double-LF regime now performs worse than the random option did in the three-language case. The single-LF, by contrast, still scores 100% for all sizes of groupings and does so at a discount, now reduced from 1/3 to 1/6 of the learning cost.

*Table II: Percentage of groupings with at least one language in common (6 people, 6 mother tongues)*

| Size of the groupings | 2 | 3 | 4 | 5 | 6 |
|---|---|---|---|---|---|
| Number of possible combinations | 15 | 20 | 15 | 6 | 1 |
| (1) No lingua franca | 40 | 0 | 0 | 0 | 0 |
| (2) Double lingua franca | 73.3 | 40 | 13.3 | 0 | 0 |
| (3) Single lingua franca | 100 | 100 | 100 | 100 | 100 |

## Notes

[1] This essay is based on talks given at the University of British Columbia (11 September 2001), at the Université de Paris IV-Sorbonne (16 March 2002), at the Universitat Pompeu Fabra, Barcelona (24 April 2003), at Oxford University (1 May 2003), at the Università degli Studi di Siena (6 July 2003), at the Australian National University in Canberra (15 July 2003), at the Cursos de Verano of the Universidad Complutense in San Lorenzo del Escorial (18 July 2003) and at the Law School of New York University (6 November 2003). It also benefited greatly from three workshops respectively held at the European University Institute (Linguistic Diversity and European Law, Florence, 12-13 November 2001), the International Institute for the Sociology of Law ('The Public Discourse of Law and Politics in Multilingual Societies', Oñati, 5-8 June 2002), and the Hoover Chair of Economic and Social Ethics ('Language Dynamics and Linguistic Justice', Louvain-la-Neuve, 27 June 2002). A somewhat different version of this chapter appears in *Archives européennes de sociologies* (Paris) XLV (1), 2004. I am particularly grateful to Miriam Aziz, Dario Castiglione, Abram de Swaan, Bruno de Witte, Ronald Dworkin, Gilles Gantelet, François Grin, Victor Ginsburgh, Christian List, Tom Nagel, Adam Swift, and Michel Van den Abeele for useful comments and insights.

[2] Based on a witness account by two of my children, and later checked in broad outline with the main actor in the scene.

[3] 'At least in part', because another reason may be the correct anticipation of the dynamics of maximin and differential learning to be sketched shortly: to prevent French from being ever less often the maximin language (chosen even when no one French is around), one must voluntaristically preserve the incentive and opportunity to learn it by using French even when it is not the maximin choice. Not exactly appreciated by those (non-French) who are thereby forced to listen to a language they do not understand, nor indeed by those (French) who are thereby forced to speak French at the risk of being ignored.

[4] The unwritten rule may even sometimes be (for example for a time, I am told, at the regular meetings of the European Commissioners' chiefs of cabinet) 'Each speaks one of the others' languages', as a supreme expression of respect for the other languages, or perhaps as a proud display of one's linguistic competence, or both.

[5] David Crystal (1997: 22) describes what is going on in this respect as a race between global English and the Babel Fish–the ear insert for oral translation in Douglas Adams's (1979: 52) *Hitchhiker's Guide to the Galaxy*–with the spread of the former and the development of the latter each inhibiting investment in the other. English will win effortlessly in the case of all small languages, as the competence in English already achieved further shrinks the market for the very expensive fine-tuning of the sophisticated software required (see Maurais, 2003: 19). But even in the case of language combinations that provide for large Babel Fish markets, English in the brain is far more promising than technology in the ear as a reliable and cost-efficient way of securing understanding (and much besides) in a wide variety of contexts.

[6] Hebrew may provide a second case, but to a fast decreasing extent, whereas for English the gap keeps increasing.

[7] See for example the recent English-French-German proposal by the French national deputy Michel Herbillon, reported by Kovacs (2003), and the even more demanding four-language variant (Spanish included) proposed by the Belgian linguist Marc Wilmet (2003). In these proposals, the natives of the three privileged languages are allowed to speak their own language. In other variants, out of fairness, they are not: see eg Chaudenson (2001: 152), Ammon (2001b: 73), and the proposal by the Flemish deputy Danny Pieters, also reported by Kovacs (2003). I return to the fairness issue below. As long as the only concern is communicative efficiency, a scheme that prevents a native from speaking his own language even when understood by all others is obviously absurd.

[8] Esperantists are particularly active in documenting discrimination in favour of English native speakers in and around the EU's institutions by collecting hundreds of job offers of the following type (www.lingvo.org): 'The Union of Independent Retail Traders in Europe is currently in search of a Jurist. You are English native speaker and fluent in French. Knowledge of the German language is an asset' (*The Bulletin* 8/03/01). 'European Association of Co-operative Banks is looking for an English mother tongue Junior Adviser' (*The European Voice* 1/03/01). 'Delegation of the European Commission in Russia. Press and Information Section

seeks: A Stagiaire. The candidate must have excellent drafting skills in English (preferably of English mother tongue)' (internet, 30/03/03).

9 The percentage of people who regard themselves as speaking 'completely correctly' or 'more or less correctly' the second national language versus English is 17% versus 11% for Belgian residents who attended school in Belgium aged 55 or more, 23% versus 25% for those aged 35 to 54, and 21% versus 36% for those aged 15 to 34 (source: survey by INRA Marketing unit conducted in February 1999 on behalf of TIBEM. For a more detailed analysis of these data and what they reveal, see Van Parijs (1999).

10 Source: Eurobarometer 54. Table 1 uses the data of the Eurobarometer Report prepared at the request of the Directorate Education and Culture of the European Commission, on the occasion of the European Year of Languages (INRA, 2001). It has been computed on the basis of tables 2 and 2a in Ginsburgh and Weber (2003), who had access to the data set, and not just to the (rather clumsy) published report. Table 1 indicates the proportion of residents who either have English as their mother tongue or mention English among the first two languages they 'know' in addition to their mother tongue (if any), first in the whole of the country's population aged 15 or over, and next in the fraction of that population under the age of 40.

11 According to INRA (2001, Summary §6), 29.8% of the European population say they prefer subtitling, and 59.6% that they do not. (Had the question been phrased the other way round, the difference would no doubt have looked less striking.) As pointed out by Koolstra and Beentjes (1999), however, these preferences correlate strongly and positively with prevailing practices in the country, which suggests that preferences tend to adjust.

12 It has been estimated that Dutch children spend about half their TV time watching programmes with English-language sound (Koolstra and Beentjes, 1999: 16).

13 See, especially, van de Poel and d'Ydewalle (1996) and Koolstra and Beentjes (1999) for some experimental evidence on learning English through watching subtitled programmes. Chaudenson (2001: 145, 155–6) also mentions the competence in Italian acquired by Tunisian and Albanian children with no exposure to it other than the watching of Italian TV channels. (A TV once exploded in Tunis, I am told, and the kids rushed out screaming 'Aiuto!'.)

14 I am clearly not the only one to have realised the handicapping effects of dubbing. At European level, the EU's Council of Ministers, in 1990, decided to promote indiscriminately dubbing, subtitling and multilingual broadcasting as ways of overcoming the 'language barrier' (Luyken *et al*, 1991: 208), but a more recent document, drafted by the European Commission's DG Education and Culture in connection with a consultation on linguistic diversity, contains the following passage: 'In some member states, TV programmes and films in foreign languages seldom get onto our screens, or if they do they are often dubbed rather than subtitled because the local market prefers dubbing; yet research shows that films and TV can encourage and facilitate language learning if they are made available in their original language, with subtitles instead of dubbing; subtitling provides an economical and effective way of making our environment more language-friendly.' (European Commission, 2002: 16). Similarly, in the debate about the learning of languages in the Parliament of Belgium's Francophone Community, one deputy briefly suggested: 'I shall content myself with one proposal, simple but far more important than one might think at first sight: abolishing the dubbing of spoken texts on the radio, on TV and in cinemas' (Henry, 2003: section 2).

15 At the end of the process, it may be argued that the advantage of the anglophones has not only been removed, but inverted: it may be more valuable to be fluent in English than in any other language, but it is more valuable to be fluent in two languages, including English, than in English alone. One cannot simply object to this argument that anglophones are no less well equipped to acquire another language than natives of other languages are, and hence that the unfair advantage has not been turned into an unequal advantage. For the ability to learn a language is a matter not only of mental capacity but also of socio-linguistic opportunity, and as the maximin rule drives languages other than English out of 'natural' interaction, the cost of learning English for non-anglophones keeps falling while the cost of learning other languages for anglophones (and everyone else) keeps increasing. One consequence of the universal spread of the lingua franca would then be that anglophones would face competition in their home labour markets from everyone else in the world, while having no real access to those labour markets in which another language remains a requirement. I return to this issue below.

16 The prohibition of subtitling might have been more problematic in this last respect, as dubbing does not offer the same potential as subtitling for checking that the words of a person are not being distorted.

[17] In the United States, over half of secondary school pupils no longer study any foreign language and the cost of foreign language learning per capita can be estimated to be about forty times less than in Switzerland (Maurais, 2003: 24, 32). See Grin (2004) for more useful estimates of the costs involved.

[18] See Piron (2001: 95). Admittedly, this sort of estimate is pretty arbitrary. In the first place, the notion of 'mastering' a foreign language is extremely fuzzy, and once the basic syntax and morphology are learned, hundreds of hours may be needed for tiny improvements in pronunciation, fluency, use of idiomatic expressions and respect for grammatical exceptions, as well as for expanding one's lexical repertoire. Secondly, the number of hours required through a classroom method for any given level of competence is highly dependent on linguistic distance between the mother tongue (and other languages previously learned) and the language to be learned. Thirdly and most importantly, as emphasised above, what happens inside the classroom cannot be dissociated from the motivation and opportunity dimensions of what is going on outside. The 'average' time needed is therefore crucially dependent on the way in which the various combinations of native language background, language to be learned and context are weighted—a rather tricky matter, both conceptually and empirically.

[19] As I have heard this story in several versions, I would not bet on its accuracy. See eg Ammon (2001b: 73). In the same vein, see the multiple-lingua-franca proposals mentioned above, which, in both 'fair' and 'unfair' versions, all face the same decisive difficulty.

[20] In other words, the difference between the average benefit derived from the existence of the lingua franca by the members of a language group and their average contribution to the cost of its learning must be the same for all language groups, whether or not they do the learning themselves.

[21] See de Briey and Van Parijs (2002) for a generalisation to n language groups of the criterion proposed and defended in Van Parijs (2002) in the case of just two.

[22] Moreover, the native lingua franca countries may plausibly argue that the cost they can be expected to share is not the actual cost of learning, but the cost of using the cheapest effective method. If some countries deliberately fail to use such inexpensive and powerful tools as the ban on dubbing advocated earlier, they cannot reasonably expect other countries to foot a portion of the resulting extra bill.

[23] How many times does it happen that some nice Americans or Brits (not of the 'If English was good enough for Jesus Christ, it is good enough for them' type), after managing some painstaking but much appreciated sentences in the local language, are rewarded with a 'Now, let's get down to business' in an English so competent that carrying on in the local language would be felt to be pointless masochism?

[24] Nunberg (2002: 322–4) provides persuasive evidence to the effect that the proportion of web content in languages other than English is increasing and will continue to do so.

[25] The myth of the three working languages (French, German, English) will gradually be recognised as such (fundamentally for the reasons explained above). But it makes plenty of sense, in the many circumstances in which even a mere symbolic use of all official languages will prove far too much, to express the recognition of and respect for linguistic pluralism by using only French and German in addition to English. German and French are the two main languages with the majority of their native speakers inside the EU, and the EU would never have existed had France and Germany not found the strength to take the original initiative and to keep supporting it ever since. It is of course important that this symbolic use of less widely known languages should not alienate European citizens. For reasons spelt out elsewhere (Aziz and Van Parijs, 2002), it seems a particularly bad idea, for example, to maintain the prevalence of French in the European Court of Justice.

[26] Not an advice unanimously given to European authorities, least of all by those who care about nothing but business: 'It is worthwhile to consider whether the EU should answer the call for uniformity on the issue of language business transactions and further protect itself against the potential onslaught of language regulation by each individual Member State. One potential action the EU might take would be to declare a common language in the EU market' (Feld, 1998: 199, quoted by Phillipson, 2001: 113-14). As rightly pointed out for example by Phillipson (2003: 193–8), there is an inherent tension between the EU's ritual assertion that it wants both to encourage contact and mobility in all sorts of ways, and hence multilingualism, on the one hand, and on the other hand the preservation (if not the promotion) of linguistic diversity.

[27] The common distinction, in the area of language rights, between the territorial principle and the personality principle, is often misleadingly formulated (see Réaume, 2003 and Patten, 2003 for some useful discussion). Which language(s) one is allowed to learn at public expense, to speak and write while expecting to be heard, or to receive information and services in, is obviously dependent on the legislation of the territorially circumscribed political entity in which one might wish to do theses various things. In this sense, all language rights regimes instantiate a territoriality principle, just as they instantiate a personality principle in the sense that the rights are ascribed to individual persons. The relevant distinction should rather be phrased in terms of how accommodating the regime is to the linguistic wishes of the people who happen or settle within given borders. This is obviously a matter of degree, with at one extreme even public schools, public services and public life adjusting swiftly to people's desires under the sole constraint of a cost-conscious use of resources (threshold levels, etc), and at the other extreme even private language use and acquisition coercively constrained. Once it is understood that, in a high-mobility, high-communication context, the unconstrained dynamics of differential learning and maximin puts weaker languages under permanent pressure, a serious concern for linguistic diversity and equal respect requires this dynamic to be constrained, though in a way that cannot be rejected as unacceptably coercive. This entails a restriction of the constraints on particular contexts, all in the 'public' sphere. But once the contexts are defined, the linguistic constraint needed to protect the weaker language can be linked either to where one is (what is the local official language) or to who one is (what is one's native language). The first option-which corresponds to the territoriality principle—has the decisive advantage of being both less coercive (one can change one's residence, not one's mother tongue) and cheaper to implement (because of the locally-bound nature of many of the services concerned). Whether it offers a stronger guarantee of survival to a threatened language depends on the relative probabilities of the homeland running empty on the one hand and the race no longer procreating (or intermarrying heavily or spreading thinly) on the other.

[28] The much earlier firm application of the territoriality principle is the secret of Switzerland's relative linguistic peace, compared to Belgium and Canada. There has never been a Germanisation of Geneva analogous to the Frenchisation of Brussels or the Englishisation of Montréal. The solution here advocated for Europe can therefore be said to have had an early formulation by the European Commission's first President: 'The fact that the Europeans do not speak the same language cannot disturb us. Switzerland provides us with the classical example showing that linguistic variety does not constrain, but rather enriches, and we wish for our Belgian friends that they can soon be cited as another example' (Hallstein, 1973: 112, quoted by Kraus, 2004).

[29] In the Region of Brussels, for example, the rate of employment in the working-age population is 64% among Belgian citizens (including naturalised immigrants), but only 33% among non-EU citizens (Decker *et al*, 2000: 15).

[30] Table 1 above suggests that English is known by 94% of Sweden's young adults, for example.

[31] This paragraph summarises the argument developed in Van Parijs (2000).

## References

Adams, D (1979) *The Hitchhiker's Guide to the Galaxy* (London, Heinemann).

Ammon, U (2001a) *The Dominance of English as a Language of Science. Effects on Other Languages and Language Communities* (Berlin/New York, de Gruyter).

Ammon, U (2001b) 'Die Stellung der deutschen Sprache in Europa und in der Welt' in R Chaudenson (ed), *L'Europe parlera-t-elle anglais demain?* (Paris, Institut de la francophonie & L'Harmattan).

Aziz, M and Van Parijs, P (2002) 'Language Legislation for XXIst century Europe' (Université catholique de Louvain, Chaire Hoover, DOCH 87), http://www.etes.ucl.ac.be/Publications/dochs.htm.

Chaudenson, R (2001) 'Rapport de synthèse' in R Chaudenson (ed), *L'Europe parlera-t-elle anglais demain?* (Paris, Institut de la francophonie & L'Harmattan).

Church, J and King, I (1993) 'Bilingualism and Network Externalities', 26 *Canadian Journal of Economics* 337–45.

Crystal, D (1997) *English as a Global Language* (Cambridge, Cambridge University Press).

De Briey, L and Van Parijs, P (2002) 'La justice linguistique comme justice coopérative', 5 *Revue de philosophie économique* 5–37.

de Swaan, A (1993) 'The Evolving European Language System: A Theory of Communication Potential and Language Competition', 14 *International Political Science Review* 241–55.

de Swaan, A (2001) *Words of the World* (Cambridge, Polity Press).

Decker, B, de Villers, M and Thys, S (2000) *Populations issues de l'immigration, marché de l'emploi et discrimination: situation en Région de Bruxelles-Capitale* (Brussels, Observatoire bruxellois du marché du travail et des qualifications).

European Commission (2002) *Promoting Language Learning and Linguistic Diversity—Consultation*, Commission Staff Working paper SEC 1234.

Feld, SA (1998) 'Language and the Globalization of the Economic Market: The Regulation of Language as a Barrier to Free Trade', 31 *Vanderbilt Journal of Transnational Law* 153–202.

Gauthier, D (1986) *Morals by Agreement* (Oxford, Oxford University Press).

Ginsburgh, V and Weber, S (2003) 'Language Disenfranchisement in the European Union' (Université libre de Bruxelles: ECARE & Université catholique de Louvain, CORE).

Grin, F and Vaillancourt, F (1997) 'The Economics of Multilingualism', 17 *Annual Review of Applied Linguistics* 43–65.

Grin, F (1999) *Compétences et récompenses. La valeur des langues en Suisse* (Fribourg, Editions universitaires).

Grin, F (2004) 'On the Costs of Cultural Diversity' in P Van Parijs (ed), *Cultural Diversity versus Economic Solidarity* (Brussels, De Boeck Université).

Hallstein, W (1973) *Die Europäische Gemeinschaft* (Düsseldorf, Econ).

Henry, P (2003) 'L'apprentissage des langues étrangères dans le système scolaire', Parlement de la Communauté française de Belgique, Brussels, 8 January 2003.

Herbillon, M (2003) *Les langues dans l'Union élargie: pour une Europe en VO*, Délégation de l'Assemblée nationale pour l'Union européenne, June 2003. Available in English: Assembleé Nationale Française (2003) *Rapport d'information sur la diversité linguistique dans l'Union européenne* (Herbillon Report), 11 June 2003, http://www.assemblee-nationale.fr/12/pdf/europe/rap-info/i0902.pdf.

Hessky, R (1995) 'Die Rolle der grossen Verkehrsprachen in Ostmitteleuropa am Beispiel Ungarn' in R Wodak and R de Cillia (eds), *Sprachenpolitik in Mittel- und Osteuropa* (Vienna, Passagen Verlag).

INRA (2001) Eurobaromètre 54 Spécial. *Les Européens et les langues. Rapport rédigé pour la Commission européenne*, Direction générale de l'Education et de la Culture, Brussels, February 2001.

Koolstra, CM and Beentjes, JWJ (1999) 'Children's Vocabulary Acquisition in a Foreign Language through Watching Subtitled TV Programmes at Home', 47 *Educational Technology Research and Development* 51–60.

Kovacs, S (2003) 'Le français lutte pour sa survie en Europe', *Le Figaro*, 26 June.

Kraus, PA (2004) 'Between Mill and Hallstein. Cultural Diversity as a Challenge to European Integration' in P Van Parijs (ed), *Cultural Diversity versus Economic Solidarity* (Brussels, De Boeck Université).

Luyken, G, Herbst, T, Langham-Brown, J, Reid, H and Spinhof, H (1991) *Overcoming Language Barriers in Television: Dubbing and Subtitling for the European Audience* (Manchester, European Institute for the Media).

Maiworm, F and Wächter, B (2002) *English-language-taught Degree Programmes in European Higher Education. Trends and Success Factors* (Bonn, Lemmens).

Maurais, J (2003) 'Towards a New Global Linguistic Order?' in J Maurais and MA Morris (eds), *Languages in a Globalising World* (Cambridge, Cambridge University Press).

Meier, M (1995) 'Die Sprachsituation in Tschechien am Ende des 20. Jahrhunderts' in R Wodak and R de Cillia (eds), *Sprachenpolitik in Mittel- und Osteuropa* (Vienna, Passagen Verlag).

Melitz, J (1999) 'English-language Dominance, Literature and Welfare' CEPR Discussion Paper 2055.

Ministère des affaires étrangères (2002) 'La politique européenne de la France. Le français dans les institutions européennes'. Préface by Lionel Jospin, March 2002, 14pp.

Nunberg, G (2002) 'Langues et communautés linguistiques à l'époque du discours électronique' in D Lacorne and T Judt (eds), *La Politique de Babel. Du monolinguisme d'état au plurilinguisme des peuples* (Paris, Karthala).

Patten, A (2003) 'What Kind of Bilingualism?' in W Kymlicka and A Patten (eds), *Language Rights and Political Theory* (Oxford, Oxford University Press).

Phillipson, R (2001) 'Principles for a Supra-National EU Language Policy' in R Chaudenson (ed), *L'Europe parlera-t-elle anglais demain?* (Paris, Institut de la francophonie & L'Harmattan).

Phillipson, R (2003) *English-Only Europe? Challenging Language Policy* (London, Routledge).

Piron, C (2001) 'L'Européen trilingue: un espoir réaliste?' in R Chaudenson (ed), *L'Europe parlera-t-elle anglais demain?* (Paris, Institut de la francophonie & L'Harmattan).

Pool, J (1991) 'The Official Language Problem', 85 *American Political Science Review* 495–514.

Réaume, DG (2003) 'Beyond *Personality*: The Territorial and Personal Principles of Language Policy Reconsidered' in W Kymlicka and A Patten (eds), *Language Rights and Political Theory* (Oxford, Oxford University Press).

Salverda, R (2001) 'De lokroep van het Engels. Taalbeleid op z'n Nederlands', 44 *Ons Erfdeel* 3–10.

Selten, R and Pool, J (1991) 'The Distribution of Foreign Language Skills as a Game Equilibrium' in R Selten (ed), *Game Equilibrium Models* Vol 4, 64–87 (Berlin, Springer).

Van de Poel, M and d'Ydewalle, G (1999) 'Incidental Foreign-language Acquisition by Children Watching Subtitled Television Programmes', 28 *Journal of Psycholinguistic Research* 227–44.

Van den Abeele, M (2004) 'Les langues dans l'Union européenne: au delà des combats d'arrière-garde', Université libre de Bruxelles, Seminar 'Economie de la culture', 9 February 2004.

Van Parijs, P (1999) 'Lingua franca', 9 *La Revue nouvelle* 114–19.

Van Parijs, P (2000) 'The Ground Floor of the World. On the Socio-Economic Consequences of Linguistic Globalisation', 21 *International Political Science Review* 217–33.

Van Parijs, P (2002) 'Linguistic Justice', 1 *Politics, Philosophy and Economics* 59-74. Also in W Kymlicka and A Patten (eds), *Language Rights and Political Theory* (Oxford, Oxford University Press).

Willems, J (2002) 'De euro in de brieventas, een Engelstalig diploma in de boekentas?' 100 *Deus ex Machina* March, 24–28.

Wilmet, M (2003) 'L'anglais, Esperanto des auditoires?' *La Libre Belgique*, 15 October 2003.

# 11

# *The Babel of Europe? Networks and Communicative Spaces*

PHILIP SCHLESINGER[1]

ONE POWERFUL NARRATIVE of the European future goes like this: we can project a process of economic and political integration that, over the *longue durée,* will knit together the diverse communicative spaces within which the continent's identities and cultures are articulated. The driving force will be the European Union, which—at the time of writing—is still in the midst of discussing a future constitution for itself. To the extent that a European public sphere consolidates itself, the role of national languages within the emergent formation will be gradually redefined, in part due to the growing dominance of a lingua franca among European populations, namely English. This process will certainly not be linear; nor will it be free of internal conflicts concerning the relationships between state sovereignty and federal or confederate powers. Nevertheless, it does seem to be a path likely to be taken, even though there are many obstacles on the way. However, we could hardly imagine this scenario of a New European Communicative Space to be an endogenously generated process, or some sort of immanent unfolding of potential. Indeed, just how much the EU growth-story depends for its success on the benevolent support of the United States—its highly conditional endogeny, as it were—was made rudely apparent on 23 January 2003. In a supposedly off-the-cuff remark, the US Secretary of Defense, Donald Rumsfeld, challenged opposition from the French and German governments to the Bush administration's handling of the Iraq crisis. He said, dismissively:

> You're thinking of Europe as Germany and France. I don't. That's old Europe. If you look into the entire NATO Europe today, the centre of gravity is shifting to the east. Germany has been a problem, and France has been a problem. But if you look at vast numbers of other countries in Europe, they're not with France and Germany on this, they're with the United States. (Cited in Harnden and Delves Broughton, 2003)

Thus was coined the pregnant distinction between 'old' and 'new' Europe—one instantly translated into political discourse to become the everyday coinage of pundits of various ideological persuasions (see eg Baker, 2003; Fuller, 2003; *Guardian Unlimited*, 2003; Krauthammer, 2003; Mönninger, 2003). Rumsfeld's formula was rapidly used by analysts to describe the 'New European' backing for the US position on Iraq orchestrated by the British Prime Minister, Tony Blair, and his Spanish counterpart, José Maria Aznar, in an open letter published by the *Wall Street Journal*. This manoeuvre divided member states, as well as drawing in EU candidate members. A second pro-US letter was signed by a bevy of post-communist candidate members (BBC News, 2003).

The consequences of the European fracture named by Rumsfeld are still playing out at the time of writing, and they have had ramifications for the UN and NATO as well as the EU. My purpose here is neither to trace the consequences nor to apportion blame, but simply to note how the power of a profound conjunctural crisis may challenge settled assumptions. The *prises de position* in the late winter and early spring of 2003 raised major questions as to whether the EU could achieve sufficient cohesion to be a counterweight to the USA. A precondition for such a role—arguably—would be not just intergovernmental co-ordination but the formation of a European public that supported a particular projection of the EU's role in the world.

As a thought experiment, let us assume that the EU cannot again reach agreement on how to deal with the USA and that it fractures into (simplistically put) pro- and anti-American camps. Then the EU's further integration—certainly in respect of a common foreign or defence policy, but perhaps in other far-reaching respects too—could be set back for the foreseeable future. An even more far-reaching scenario would be to project the gradual disintegration of the Euro-polity itself, an effective throwing into reverse of the post-World War Two unifying trend under the pressure of new international alignments that once again divide the continent, but in ways different from the Cold War. This could engender the atrophying of the capital that the EU institutional complex has built up, namely the politico-cultural *acquis communautaire*.

Would this have specific communicative consequences? There is a twofold answer. On a linguistic level, a putative Anglo-American hegemony of the so-called 'new' Europe would appreciably speed up the progress of learning English as a European lingua franca. At the level of Euro-networking, and the communicative practices that go along with this, we could see a certain amount of rewiring along the fault lines of 'old' and 'new' Europe, should that division become increasingly fixed. If we entertain such thoughts, however implausible, we throw into relief the present bedrock of integrationist assumptions.

From *that* point of view, the EU is implicitly conceived as a machine for generating wider—and deeper—social communication, for interconnecting discrete spheres of publics. But the limitations of that process were dramatised by the crisis over Iraq and the divergent interests that emerged from it. Due to its present diffuseness as a political formation, the EU could not respond to the Iraq crisis as a *union*. It proved to be governmentally much divided, polarised between France and Germany on the one side and the UK and Spain on the other. But, some argued, at least according to the opinion polls and in terms of demonstrations on the streets, many of the European Union's *nations*, responding as singular national publics, had proved to be substantially united in their opposition to war. For those who looked optimistically into the glass, such as the philosophers Jacques Derrida (2003) and Jürgen Habermas (2003), the birth of a European public space could be discerned, at least on questions of war and peace. For some europtimists it seemed that linguistic differences and national loyalty were not matters of decisive importance (Toynbee, 2003). But the Iraq crisis, however profoundly motivating it may have been for its opponents, did not constitute a sufficient condition for *sustaining* a common public across frontiers. For instance, as the UK became a warring power, the majority initially opposed to an invasion—however questionably measured by the polls—became a supporting majority.

Perhaps the damage-limitation squads will succeed in effecting a new balance between Atlanticism and Europeanism and my crisis scenarios will be seen as utterly irrelevant musings. If so, I might as well revert to what I *was* going to say *ante bellum,* and which might still be possible, after extensive post-Iraq repair work and compromise between different visions of the EU's future.

## THE EU AS A COMMUNICATIVE SPACE

If we assume the continued politico-economic integration of the European Union, as well as its continued expansion, its sheer complexity as a communicative space also necessarily grows. Can we sensibly think of it as *a* space at all? It is rather an increasingly interconnected grouping of overlapping communicative communities with the *potential* to become a loosely integrated communicative space, not just for elites but also for entire peoples. And from there—who knows? The number of official languages spoken inside the Union grows with each wave of accession states. In 2002, there were eleven such languages, whereas in 1957 there were only four. (Let me stress that these are *official* languages, not actual language communities.) With a further ten accessions in 2004, the official language count increased to twenty. And there are yet more candidates in the wings. On the face of it, therefore, we could be forgiven for thinking the EU to be a self-generating Babel. To invoke 'Babel' is to use a shorthand way of talking about the cultural differences embodied in language.

Why *self*-generating? Because at one level, it is EU policy to promote linguistic diversity and language learning. In spring 2002, EU member states were invited by a range of EU bodies to pursue just that line. The acquisition of linguistic skills was linked to the fashionable rhetoric of the 'knowledge economy'. We encounter once more that all too recognisable mix of low and high politics: let's improve competitiveness, and yes, by the way, let's also celebrate cultural difference. In such linguistic pluralism there is an underlying aspiration to fashion a European communicative space out of linguistic diversity so that 'citizens have the skills necessary to understand and communicate with their neighbours' (Commission of the European Communities (CEC), 2002: 5). Good Euro-neighbours should speak several languages and not build fences—with due apologies to Robert Frost. This line is consistent with more than two decades of official thinking about the EU as a cultural and communicative space.

Published at the end of 2002, the Commission's consultation paper based its picture of the distribution of language skills on a special Eurobarometer survey published in 2001 (European Commission, 2001). Over half the population of the Union speaks a language in addition to its mother tongue. In some member states almost everyone is bilingual. English is the first foreign language for one-third of all citizens; one quarter, however, can speak two other languages (with French and English leading the pack, though for rather less than 10 per cent of the EU's citizens in either case). It is plain that language skills are unevenly spread, with younger people displaying the greatest competence, alongside managers. Two-thirds of the British cannot speak another language.

The Commission observes that English has become a 'world lingua franca' and in Europe that 'it is rapidly gaining ground as the first foreign language chosen by parents for their children. It is displacing the languages traditionally taught in European schools, such as German, French, Spanish and Italian, even in areas in which the most "logical" first foreign language would be the language of a neighbouring state' (CEC, 2002: 7). But a lingua franca has its limitations: the Commission therefore argues that over and beyond any common tongue, European citizens require at least 'meaningful communicative competence' in other languages (CEC, 2002: 7).

The sociologist Abram de Swaan has argued that English is becoming the 'supercentral' language of communication at the civic level inside the EU. Plausibly, he also maintains that this supercentrality will co-exist with the continuing importance of national languages (which have been state-supported and closely connected with official national identity for at least two centuries in some cases): here the 'robustness' of languages and their political protection is a key factor. De Swaan (2001: 173–4) has schematised the likely hierarchy of language uses in the EU as follows:

A. national languages are used within the domestic sphere of member states, allowing for diglossia with the supercentral language;

B. civil Europe's first language for 'transnational communication' will be English, followed by German/French;
C. all official languages will continue to be used ceremonially, for public law etc—as part of the EU's founding principles;
D. the languages of the bureaucratic corridor are, and will be, English and French—although according to *The Economist,* English is now rapidly becoming the dominant working language (Charlemagne, 2003a: 42).

As the Commission's surveys show, the advantages of English have steadily grown. Its prominence is being reinforced by the growing second-language competence of younger generations—sustained by most, if not all, national educational systems. 'Over 92% of secondary-school students in the EU's non-English speaking countries are studying English, compared with 33% learning French and 13% studying German' (Charlemagne, 2003a: 42). But, as has been widely noted, many factors prevent the formal adoption of a single Union language, not least the strong connection between languages, states and collective identities. What seems clear—largely due to the global cultural, economic and political dominance of the United States—is that the irresistible pull of English language competence will become an important part of the derived European citizenship possessed by citizens of the Union's member states.[2] Although the picture sketched out above shows that we do not have conditions of linguistic equality in the EU, or in Europe generally, the continent is less of a Babel than might be supposed, due to the multilingual capacity of many Europeans and the growing ascendancy of English. This will continue to be so, whether the process of European union continues or whether it is disrupted.

## SOCIAL COMMUNICATION

Language is a key aspect of the broader process of social communication—that is, the gamut of distinctive signifying practices that defines and delimits a communicative community operating within the framework of a broad, anthropological idea of a culture as a 'distinct whole way of life' (Williams, 1981: 13). We might try to understand the EU's communicative dimension by developing a social communication theory capable of entertaining the Union's emergent complexity, in particular in respect of the challenges it poses for states, nations and collective identities (Schlesinger, 2000). By complexity, I refer to 'the number of elements in interaction and the number of different states that those interactions can give rise to' (Boisot, 1999: 5).

A social communication approach to the theory of nationalism was first explicitly attempted by Karl Deutsch half a century ago (1966 [1953]). However, its origins probably lie further in the past. Fifty years before

Deutsch, the Austro-Marxist theorist Otto Bauer wrote his seminal account of the 'national question' (Bauer, 1907). This is the likely precursor of Deutsch's theory. Bauer and Deutsch have together exercised a remarkable—and virtually unacknowledged—influence over some of the most significant recent theorising about the communicative dimension of the nation. Their central contention continues to have a bearing on how we might understand the contemporary, multinational EU. The present relevance of now venerable Austro-Marxist thinking is more than some passing coincidence. Finding a pluralistic solution to communicative complexity inside the European Union has a strong family resemblance to Bauer's wish to give due recognition to national cultural autonomy in a multinational empire. The intimate connection between language and nationality was central to his analysis—and not least the passions and emotions that linguistic claims could—and did—generate within what Robert Musil made famous as *Kakania*.

Bauer (2000 [1907]: 34) contended that a modern democratic nation should be seen as a 'community of culture'. In contemporary conditions that are more sensitive to multiculturalism, it is more apt to think in terms of a community of *cultures*. He also famously observed that the nation was a 'community of fate' (*eine Schicksalsgemeinschaft*), which was engaged in 'general reciprocal interaction' (Bauer, 2000: 100), thereby sharing a common language. He remarked:

> The culture's sphere of influence extends only as far as the communicative possibilities of the language. The community of interaction is limited by the scope of the linguistic community. Community of interaction and language reciprocally condition each other ... (Bauer, 2000: 102)

The nation *qua* linguistic community, then, is conceived as self-contained, or at the very least, as tending towards communicative closure. This is an early statement of a social communication theory of the nation. This effort to address the *Kulturkämpfe* of the declining years of the Austro-Hungarian Empire has left its conceptual imprint on contemporary theorising about the public sphere in the European Union. Karl Deutsch (1966 [1953]: 19–20)—an early theorist of European union—seems not to have recognised his own debt to Bauer's conception of the nation as a cultural community. Central to Deutsch's argument is the view that nations and nation-states are strongly bound by their patterns of interaction: 'People are held together "from within" by this communicative efficiency, the complementarity of the communicative facilities acquired by their members' (Deutsch, 1966 [1953]: 98). Social communication, in other words, produces collective cohesion—and invites us to share in a common fate. Bauer and Deutsch have a fundamentally similar approach to how communicative and cultural practices and institutions (to which language is central) may strengthen the collective identity of a national group by creating boundaries.

This simple—but compelling—idea is reproduced in a number of influential theories of nationalism. Ernest Gellner's (1983) view that culture is 'the distinctive style of conduct and communication of a given community' and that it is 'now the necessary shared medium' of the nation is likewise at root a theory of cohesion.[3] Cultural boundaries become defined by national cultures, which diffuse a literate 'high culture', in which the key agency is the national education system. Media are seen as sustaining that political community, providing it with its deep codes for distinguishing between self and other. Relatedly, Benedict Anderson (1991) contended that mechanically reproduced print-languages unified fields of linguistic exchange, fixed national languages and created idiolects of power. So, by going to Gellner's schools, cultured nationals acquire the competence to read Anderson's novels and newspapers. For each of these writers, the collective consumption of mediated communication (based on a common national language) creates and sustains a sense of national belonging. Michael Billig (1995) both endorses and extends this broad argument. As nationals, he suggests, we live less in a state of perpetual mobilisation than one of the banal assimilation of everyday symbolism and categorisation: flags, anthems, distinctions between home and foreign news, national histories and languages, a particular sense of political geography. National identity is unremarkably reproduced. Culture holds us together: it both conditions and informs our conceptions of national identity. Social communication theorists may differ on the key mechanisms or processes that produce such cultural cohesion, yet all agree that some or other dimension of communication is central to how the nation should be conceived.

Of course, no culture is an island. All ostensibly national systems of communication are influenced by what lies outside. National cultures are usually permeable, however much they are censored and controlled, and in the age of the internet and satellite broadcasting that relative openness is necessarily greater than ever before. I have argued elsewhere (Schlesinger, 2000) that the main thrust of classical social communications theory concerns itself with the *interior* of the national culture and communication, with what makes us what we are, and that which draws boundaries around us. Look at Bauer's problematic and such interiority is not surprising: it is utterly congruent with the assertion of national communicative space within a wider constitutional framework of competing national cultures. Such a neatly demarcationist theory of social communication and public space is not tenable. It is especially the case, in a 'globalised' world, that its limitations are thrown into relief, although that does not mean we should now regard the shaping role of the state in social communications as irrelevant (Street, 2001).

## BORDERS AND NETWORKS

The evolution of the European Union poses Otto Bauer's century-old problem afresh: how may many diverse national, ethnic, linguistic and other cultural communities achieve autonomy within a single, overarching political framework? The old Habsburg Empire had to adjust to nationalist claims from below. By contrast, the EU is an importer of already-formed nations shaped by (more or less well) established states.[4] The gradual emergence of such a supranational formation modifies how we conceive of established communicative relations between national publics and state-centred systems of power. It makes us aware of the diverse *levels* at which publics might form and how our communicative competence (to which language is indeed central) needs to make appropriate adjustments. However, the analysis cannot stop at the level of the member state, treating this as the simple expression of the nation. Amongst other things, it is made more complicated by the continuing vitality of regional or minority languages, operating at a sub-state level, most potently perhaps in regions that are also stateless nations.

That said, the role played by the state is central to the argument. The EU, after all, is a union of states and a unique political formation. How we now conceive of the key political component or building block is crucial. David Held has argued that we can no longer think of the political community as bounded by the sovereign nation-state. Political communities, he suggests, are 'better thought as multiple overlapping *networks* of interaction ... [that] crystallize around different sites and forms of power, producing patterns of activity which do not correspond in any straightforward way to territorial boundaries' (Held, 1995: 225; my emphasis). Political communities, in short, are part of an interdependent world and are limited by this in their decisions. In consequence, 'The cultural space of nation-states is being rearticulated by forces over which states have, at best, only limited leverage' (Held, 1995: 126). This view leads Held (1995: 227) to argue that the regulative ideal for the world is to establish a cosmopolitan democratic public law that is 'entrenched within and across borders'. It is precisely that aspiration which has been placed in jeopardy by the US-led invasion of Iraq (Held, 2003).

Held's invocation of the metaphor of the network is no accident. It reflects the shift away from thinking of the state as a firmly bounded container of politics, economics and culture, and is increasingly being used to rethink European communicative space. Consider the illustrative movement in Jürgen Habermas's approach: his early theory took the European *nation-state* addressed as a political community as its framework (Habermas, 1989). That was the classic space of *Öffentlichkeit*, of a publicness contained within firm borders. But how are we to think of the multi-level complexity of the EU in Habermasian terms? Both national and European discourses co-exist. 'Europe' is inside the nation-state as part of the domestic political agenda and also as a constitutive part of the broader politico-economic framework; yet, it is also still another place, a different political level and locus of decision-making that is outside. In the EU, given this ambiguity, the national, state-bounded context no longer completely defines the political scope of communicative communities. To analyse emergent European communicative spaces, the focus needs to shift to the new, supranational arenas and their constituent publics. It must take account of how publics may also emerge at the sub-state level, on the basis of a linguistic or cultural distinctiveness that may be reinforced by media of communication (Cormack, 2000; Moragas Spà *et al*, 1999).

Habermas (1997: 373–4) now argues that communicative space is to be understood in terms of 'a *highly complex network* ... [that] branches out into a multitude of overlapping international, national, regional, local and subcultural arenas' (emphasis added). Yet, an underlying conception of a *single* public sphere does remain. It is within this logically presupposed integrative frame that so-called 'hermeneutic bridge-building' between different discourses occurs. To put it plainly, a European communicative space conceived in network terms has become the new political playground (Habermas, 1997: 171).

Habermas portrays the public sphere as potentially unbounded, as having shifted from specific locales (such as the nation) to the virtual co-presence of citizens and consumers linked by public media. A European public sphere would therefore be open-ended, with communicative connections extending well beyond the continent. Certainly, contemporary communication flows and networks ensure that no—or hardly any—political community can remain an island. But how does the suggestion that we all really belong to a *global* village sit alongside the postulate of a *European* identity? Which are the communicative boundaries most relevant for the development of a distinctive political identity and political culture inside the EU? In other words, how might communicative processes contribute to the Union's social cohesion? Or, indeed, disrupt it, in line with divergent political interests, as happened during the Iraq war of 2003.

Habermas (2001: 7, 18) has emphasised the key importance of a European constitution as a means of demarcating a distinctive political space and providing 'a common value orientation'. Habermas stresses the key role of a 'Europe-wide public sphere of political communication' and 'the creation of a political culture that can be shared by all EU citizens'. From this standpoint, the 'constitutive process is itself a unique instrument of cross-border communication'. In fact, *whether* we may regard this process as an effective form of transnational communication is precisely a matter to be empirically investigated.

Constitutional development is therefore of key importance for the articulation of the EU's political identity because it acts as a distinctive boundary-marker. It defines the limits within which distinctive patterns of political culture and communication may be encouraged to emerge. This view broadly accords with that of political geographers such as Jönsson *et al* (2000), who suggest that although the territorial basis of statehood is being modified by the evolution of networks that transcend sovereign boundaries, bounded relations remain important. For them—like Held—the contemporary European state is now a 'negotiating state' that participates in transnational networks.

However, although the emergent but still contested European constitution may eventually designate a grand politico-communicative space, it remains important to recognise that the 'technical range' of information and communication technologies that are used within it has not totally transformed our 'human reach', central to which is the capacity to communicate face to face. As Jönssen *et al* (2000: 184–5) argue: 'social communication is most effective between individuals whose mental worlds have been "formatted" analogously over lengthy periods of time.' This formulation is strikingly congruent with Deutsch's principle of communicative complementarity. Jönssen *et al* hold that 'human thought requires boundaries', based in proximity, likeness and linkage, which means that 'place, neighbourhood and region will continue to play important roles as realms of experience and epistemic communities'. This, in turn, 'fosters local anchorage and regional identity' so that 'In the age of electronic networking, conversation therefore continues to have a major role, as does the face to face meeting' (2000: 185). To rethink 'Europe' as a geo-political space, then, does not dispense with the territorial state but rather complements it, taking account of the emergence of networks (such as business associations, NGOs, regional governments) operating and lobbying alongside the national state. For Jönsson *et al*, the network metaphor encapsulates 'the three simultaneous processes of globalization, regionalization and state adaptation' which relate to what they characterise as the 'archipelago' that is the new European political space (2000: 186).

The concept of the network is also central to the work of Manuel Castells (1996, 1997, 1998), for whom the new communication technologies contribute to the formation of an altogether new kind of society, the 'informational'. From the present standpoint, most significant is the argument that this is the precursor to a new political order, to new forms of association and loyalty: the emerging Euro-polity epitomises what Castells terms 'the network state'. Because of its purported network character the EU is imagined not just as a political-economic zone but also as a specific kind of communicative space.

As Garnham (2000a: 61) has rightly reminded us, we should treat this version of the idea of a new information society with scepticism.[5] His critique of Castells' account of the network is rooted in a political economy of communication that underlines how relations of power are embedded in networks and their uses. Networks of various kinds, we are reminded, are at the heart of a range of communicative processes, whether a postal service, a broadcasting system or telecommunications links. Garnham's focus is mainly on the economic roles of such communications networks rather than their political aspects, although by bringing to the fore questions of access and equity he puts into play how these may be addressed by the politics of regulation. 'A network,' he argues, 'needs to be seen as a club rather than a market.' To understand networks from the standpoint of social communication, it is certainly helpful to stress that they operate as 'systems of collaboration and not of competition' (Garnham, 2000b: 70). But that is to focus on their *internal* workings from a principally economic point of view. Looked at from the standpoint of a political system, competition *between* networks also becomes a key matter of interest and for analysis. In this regard, Castells' analysis of contemporary political dynamics remains suggestive.

The boundaries of the putative European communicative space invoked by Castells are produced by the nexus of political institutions that constitute Union Europe, the dealings between them, and the growing 'subsidiary' horizontal links across the member states (Castells, 1998: 330–1).[6] For instance, he argues that the EU has different 'nodes' of varying importance that together make up a network. Regions and nations, nation-states, European Union institutions, constitute a framework of shared authority. Castells (1997: 51) considers the 'stateless nation' to be a prototype of potentially innovative forms of post-nation-state affiliation—an exemplar of flexible networking that offers multiple identities and allegiances to its inhabitants. Nations (as distinct from states) are characterised as 'cultural communes constructed in people's minds by the sharing of history and political projects'.

In short, Castells' approach implies that complex interconnected Deutschian 'communicative complementarities' emerge out of the informal processes of making the union. The potentially globalising pull of communications technologies is countered by emergent patterns of social interaction in the European Union's space. These are polyvalent: simultaneously, they knit together diverse actors economically, politically and communicatively. In the terms proposed by Eriksen and Fossum (2002: 405), it could be argued that the EU has produced some 'strong publics' that are characterised by deliberation and decision-making. The European Parliament and the constitution-making Charter Convention are two such institutional frameworks, which are crucial to the development of a democratic culture by holding power accountable. Interconnected with such publics are 'weak or general publics' in which public opinion is formed. These less institutionalised formations may operate as networks of a variety of social and political actors, often focused on particular issues (Eriksen and Fossum, 2002: 420).

Arguably, then, the EU is developing a special interactive intensity that favours internal communication and creates an internally differentiated referential boundary with stronger and weaker forms of institutionalisation. This may co-exist with global networking. However, a new constitution, if eventually ratified and actively embraced, is likely to reinforce the internal framework of reference and identification.

Although a 'Europeanised', relatively weak, supranational public space has indeed evolved around the policy-making actors in the various institutions, much activity still ultimately derives from national or regional interests. To be a Castellsian Euro-networker does not mean that one has completely forgotten how to wave Billig's national flag. Networks don't abolish prior national identities, though they may extend and reconstitute them for some purposes.

## EU INSTITUTIONS AND EURO-NETWORKS

Arguably, the wider 'Europeanising' process may be conceived as based in interaction between Euro-institutions and Euro-networks. Not *all* institutions have the same centrality and not *all* networks have the same intensity of interaction. The importance of language may also be of varying importance in the evolution of networks.

If we schematise by way of examples, at one end of the chain are relatively loose and weakly constraining processes of 'Europeanisation' with a network dimension. Maurice Roche (2001: 83) suggests that shopping and tourism are constructing a new Europe 'as both a transnational region and also as a meta-cultural space containing a rich variety of cultures ... [with] a massive potential for creative cultural hybridization'. One might raise a sceptical eyebrow about the cultural effects of shopping *tout court*. However, travel might indeed broaden the mind and such mobility can be identity-transforming. The drive towards a common European airspace redraws both new managerial and geographic boundaries for air traffic. Eurostar has changed the experience of travel between London, Brussels and Paris. The bridge over the Øresund has had a similar role for southern Sweden and Copenhagen (*The Economist*, 2003). The new connections between European 'destinations' created during the past decade by budget airlines may well have wider cultural implications that remain to be researched.

Roche emphasises the importance of Europe-wide sport, notably soccer, for the imagined space of Europe (although this is dominated by male fans). The EU has recognised the role of sport in identity-formation, and the market conditions for both media sport and consumer sport have changed. Roche suggests that spectators' consumption has been Europeanised and that could result in a 'European-oriented cosmopolitanism'. (Quite how this coexists with well-documented instances of sporting xenophobia is another complicated question.) *The Economist* has also taken this line, noting that 'over the past decade European football teams have turned into a living, breathing embodiment of European integration' (Charlemagne, 2003b: 42). Administratively, the European space of football is shaped in line with the multi-level governance of the EU, and lobbies such as G14 and UEFA operate accordingly (Banks, 2002: chapter 7). There are tensions and contradictions between each of these levels: the European elite of the Champions' League shaped by UEFA still has to contend with loyalties centred on the national league level. The supranational still depends heavily on the national, in a word (Boyle and Haynes, 2004).

Moving along the chain, more directly central to discussion of the public sphere is how the European Union is mediated through journalism. A distinct, complex Euro-polity has emerged that generates multi-level forms of political communication encompassing lobbying, official information campaigns, and news reporting. As EU policy making and political direction impinge increasingly on member states, the European dimension increasingly shapes both the content and the agenda of the mediated political discourse of national polities. There is some evidence—at least in elite media—that similar themes are being addressed at the same time, though not necessarily from a shared perspective (Van de Steeg, 2003).

In member states, however, *national* editorial values influence coverage and *national* governmental sources are still of key importance for journalists covering European Union issues (Morgan, 1999). Elements of a European civil society have begun to emerge, organised through the mobilisation of diverse and often competing interests, and orientated towards the political institutions of the EU. National and regional political actors mediate political communication about the Euro-polity. Information about, and the interpretation of, EU activities is disseminated outwards from the Union's administrative heartland through established national and regional networks of communication. Multi-level governance, and the continuing tensions and divergences between the supranational level and those of the member states and regions, require us to think in terms of overlapping spheres of publics.

Inasmuch as a media-sustained, *supranational* communicative space is emerging because of EU integration, this is class-inflected and predominantly the domain of political and economic elites, not that of a wider European public (Schlesinger, 1999; Schlesinger and Kevin, 2000). The skew of the news market in favour of the powerful and influential is congruent with the EU's widely acknowledged 'democratic deficit'. This derives from the predominantly executive and bureaucratic style of its governing institutions (the European Commission and the Council of Ministers) and The Commission's weak accountability to the legislature (the European Parliament). The new constitutional provisions mooted by Giscard d'Estaing's Convention, and agreed by Heads of State and Government in October 2004, were intended to address this problem.

In the European communicative space today some news media are, in effect, creating specialised audiences and readerships by way of seeking markets. An incipient change is taking place in the collectivities to be addressed, ultimately due to the EU's development as a novel political form. We may think of such emergent media publics as pre-eminently occupying a highly restricted transnational space, served by such print media as *The Economist*, the *Financial Times*, the *International Herald Tribune* and, perhaps, in the audiovisual sphere by Euronews and Arte.

The mediated public sphere in the EU remains first, overwhelmingly national; second, where it is not national it is transnational and anglophone but elitist in class terms; third, where it is ostensibly transnational but *not* anglophone, it still decants principally into national modes of address. The continuing national pull of journalistic practice and frameworks of reference explains the sheer difficulty of developing journalism for either a Europe-wide readership or indeed a readership oriented to the European Union contained within a particular nation-state. In this regard, the short life of *The European* (London) and the much briefer one of *l'Européen* (Paris) are instructive cases in point (E Neveu, 2002; Schlesinger, 1999).

Field research in Brussels during the past decade suggests that some weakly transnational forms of exchange have emerged at the EU level between journalists and their sources. Meyer (2000) has argued that there is an increasing tendency for transnational investigative journalism to emerge inside the EU, thereby contributing to the accountability of the institutions. Occasionally, but not so far systematically, this can have political effects, particularly in the exposure of scandal and corruption. This appears to be a transient rather than a systemic feature of the Euro-political scene. Baisnée (2002) also refers to the co-operative context of Brussels reporting, but contrariwise does not argue that a transnational context has emerged, except in a specific sense. For him, journalists have been socialised into being 'European people', indeed—because of their real expertise—he contends they have become 'Europe's only real public' (Baisnée, 2002: 112, 115). Multinational relations and negotiations have become part of the everyday reporting experience—even if there is often editorial hostility to the EU project (so patently the case with several titles in the UK). That said, the Euro-journalism network remains riven by diverse national ideas of professionalism and domestic markets still hold the key to career success.[7]

There are other emergent areas of exchange that require a more direct level of linguistic engagement, a growing depth of cross-cultural knowledge, and the creation of active micro-publics. A prime example is that of European research networks which are increasingly subject to the growing impact of European research funding. The EU integration process brings cohorts of diverse nationals together to deal with matters both of national and wider Community interest. In less than two decades, what once was obligatory Anglo-French bilingualism has given way to the increasingly hegemonic position of English as the prime language of academic discussion and administration, much in line with the supercentralising trend noted above. What goes on in such meetings, how the conversation is conducted, and what might happen to the identities of participants as a result is largely unexplored. Academics, and the programmes of 'framework research' that dance to the European Commission's tune, exemplify such encounters.

The attraction of such programmes lies in access to additional resources, adding to prestige, extending the range of contacts, and in raising the game. We need not assume any cosmopolitan intentions at the outset, but at the same time, we should not discount the effects of prolonged exposure to international co-operation in a framework that defines itself as 'European'. As Van der Meulen (2002: 347) notes:

> The Europeanization of university research can have at least three different meanings: the development of European research networks between university researchers, the participation of university researchers in the European Framework Programme, and the growing importance of the EU as a funding body in the research system with its specific practices of evaluation and priority setting.

There is some evidence—as, for instance, in the case of Finland—that states acceding to EU membership have adapted their networking to what the EU offers, even before joining. Hakala *et al* (2002: 357) liken this process to a 'mobilisation'. Whilst for Finnish researchers 'Europeanisation' has not dislodged existing patterns of international research co-operation (notably with the USA), it has evidently 'strengthened, intensified and formalized' those with EU partners (2002: 375). Frustration with bureaucratic obstacles has led to a more selective approach by those with greatest experience on the European scene. One conclusion is that 'EU initiatives *have supported exchanges and networks* more than the performance of high-quality research itself' (2002: 378; emphasis added).

The anthropologist Catherine Neveu (2000) has explored the internal dynamics of Euro-networking and has sketched out a *processual* approach to 'becoming European', asking what happens when European institutions invite various categories of people to participate in transnational activities. She suggests that the resulting acculturation may have a 'return effect' once those who participate go back to their places of origin. It is involvement in networks and exchanges that she sees as constituting an important path to the formation of a European public sphere.

Interaction with European institutions constitutes a kind of 'training process' that may impact on people's notions of citizenship and identity. An anthropological approach, Neveu (2000) argues, makes one see this as a 'self-producing process', in which background models and representations come into play and are modified. Is it to this kind of encounter that we should look if we are to imagine the emergence of a common *sentimental* basis for diverse nationals thinking themselves to be European? Such a community emerges through activity rather than by virtue of having any prior identity. In Raymond Williams' terms, we might ask whether a common 'structure of feeling' could emerge in this way. (Whatever it might be, however, it would not have the depth and range of national sentiments.)

Neveu (2002) observed meetings of a three-nation urban regeneration network supported by the EU's Euro-Cities programme, hypothesising that a common culture would emerge. It did, facilitated by the accentuation of the individual and professional aspects of participants' identities and by the downplaying of their institutional and national affiliations. However, language remained an irreducibly difficult matter, and debates about the meanings of key terms such as 'community' were enmeshed in prior understandings rooted in national political cultures. There were limits to the translatability of these models due to diverse 'republican' and 'communitarian' assumptions. At points of difficulty, the invocation of national stereotypes became unavoidable. That said, Neveu underlines the potential of such encounters to accentuate reflexivity and extend the range of available representations, which she sees as preconditions for the emergence of a European citizenship.[8]

## CONCLUSIONS

To think about the EU as a potential sphere of publics requires us to look beyond the nation-state to emergent networks that establish their own communicative complementarities. The institutional development of the European Union has clearly provided both an incentive and, in some domains, an active framework of support for such networking. For present purposes, I have left aside any discussion of how Euro-networks embody diverse power relations but that question should be at the core of empirical research. Second, European integration can only partly be understood though top-down policy making; the working out of processes at the base—and their interactions with the institutions—also requires study. Third, the EU's central institutions were instructively shaken during the Iraq war 2003 and will be challenged by the enlargements of 2004 and beyond. As new diplomatic alliances within and beyond the EU space emerge, this is likely to affect the pattern of existing networking over the medium and long terms, a process that warrants study. Fourth, the continuing tenacity of models of thinking rooted in the national (whilst co-existing with an emergent common space) remains impressive. And here, the issue of language differences and the inherent limits of translatability are very important. This also relates to something else, namely how collective sentiments are still linked to national identities and loyalties to states (and often to regional identities within these polities). Along with cultural factors, there are real political determinants of the extent to which, over time, emergent conceptions of Europeanness will articulate with other identities and weigh significantly in the balance of loyalties. As the crisis over Iraq demonstrated in spring 2003, there can be Babel in Europe, even if most of the key players choose to argue about their divisions in English.

## Notes

[1] Versions and parts of this essay were presented at conferences and seminars during 2002/3. My thanks to those who commented at Goldsmiths College in London, the Oñati International Institute of the Sociology of Law in the Basque Country, the University of Ulster in Belfast, the Institut d'Études Politiques in Rennes, the University of Stirling, and the London School of Economics. The University of Stirling awarded me a sabbatical in 2002 during which I began to rethink my views on European communicative space. Thanks to Mike Cormack, John Erik Fossum, Simon Frith and François Foret for their helpful remarks.

[2] There is much else to be said, not least about the questions raised by languages that are not regarded as officially 'national' within several European states as well as those that are termed 'lesser-used'. In the latter case, we approach the issues concerning linguistic survival addressed by Joshua Fishman and his colleagues (2002) in their work on 'reversing language shift'. I simply wish to note these concerns, rather than to discuss them. There remain outstanding questions of claims to linguistic recognition that are deeply connected to questions of identity and sentiment, and these are certainly not going to disappear, whatever the fate of the EU.

[3] A similar broad working assumption is to be found in the work of Louis Wirth, a key exponent of the Chicago School's approach (Rothenbuhler, 2003).

[4] This is an oversimplification, of course. It is certainly not the case that all EU states are to be regarded as homogeneous, as the politics of devolution and/or separatism in, for instance, Belgium, France, Italy, Spain and the UK shows.

[5] Mattelart (2000) has given us a detailed intellectual history and has situated Castells in relation to his key precursor, Daniel Bell.

[6] Castells' more recent work has moved beyond this position. However, the utopian vision of an 'Internet Galaxy' as a zone of citizen freedom still has to contend with a world of states that combine to regulate threats to their control over information (2001: 178–85).

[7] Journalistic production in the EU is overwhelmingly oriented to national consumption. In the case of fiction production in the five main media markets, the latest research also suggests that this is overwhelmingly nationally produced and consumed—unless it comes from the USA. Cross-border circulation of films and TV programmes is very low to non-existent (Lange, 2003).

[8] This has considerable parallels to Baisnée's findings: there is an area of commonality among Euro-journalists but the needs—and models—of different political systems also presently impose insuperable limits.

## References

Anderson, B (1991) *Imagined Communities, Reflections on the Origin and Spread of Nationalism*, 2nd edn (London, Verso).

Baisnée, O (2002) 'Can Political Journalism Exist at the European Level?' in R Kuhn and E Neveu (eds), *Political Journalism* (London, Routledge).

Baker, M (2003) 'US, Rumsfeld's "Old" And "New" Europe Touches on Uneasy Divide', Radio Free Europe Radio Liberty, 24 January.

Banks, S (2002) *Going Down, Football in Crisis* (Edinburgh, Mainstream Publishing).

Bauer, O (2000) [1907] *The Question of Nationalities and Social Democracy* (tr O'Donnell) (Minneapolis, University of Minnesota Press).

BBC News (2003) '"New Europe" backs EU on Iraq', http://newsvote.bbc.co.uk/mpapps/pagetools/print/news.bbc.co.uk/2/hi/europe/2775579.stm, 19 February.

Billig, M (1995) *Banal Nationalism* (London, Sage Publications).

Boisot, M (1999) *Knowledge Assets, Securing Competitive Advantage in the Knowledge Economy* (Oxford, Oxford University Press).

Boyle, R and Haynes, R (2004) *Football in the New Media Age* (London, Routledge).

Castells, M (1996) *The Rise of the Network Society* (Malden, MA, Blackwell).

Castells, M (1997) *The Power of Identity* (Malden, MA, Blackwell).

Castells, M (1998) *End of Millennium* (Malden, MA, Blackwell).

Castells, M (2001) *The Internet Galaxy, Reflections on the Internet, Business and Society* (Oxford, Oxford University Press).

Charlemagne (2003a) 'The Galling Rise of English' *The Economist*, 1 March, p 42.

Charlemagne (2003b) 'How Football Unites Europe' *The Economist*, 31 May, p 42.

Commission of the European Communities (2002) Commission Staff Working Paper *Promoting Language Learning and Linguistic Diversity—Consultation*. Brussels 13/11/2002 SEC (2002) 1234.

Cormack, M (2000) 'Minority Languages, Nationalism and Broadcasting, the British and Irish Examples', 6 *Nations and Nationalism* 383–98.

De Swaan, A (2001) *Words of the World, The Global Language System* (Cambridge, Polity Press).

Derrida, J (2003) 'Pourquoi je cosigne cet appel', *Libération 6857*, 1 June, p 44.

Deutsch, KW (1966) [1953] *Nationalism and Social Communication, An Inquiry into the Foundations of Nationality* (Cambridge, MA, MIT Press).

*Economist, The* (2003) 'Borderless. Dancing to a New Tune, A Survey of the Nordic Region', 24 June, p 6.

Eriksen, EO and Fossum, JE (2002) 'Democracy through Strong Publics in the European Union?', 40 *Journal of Common Market Studies* 401–24.

European Commission (2001) 'Europeans and Languages, a Eurobarometer Special Survey', http://ec.europa.eu/public_opinion/archives/ebs/ebs_147_en.pdf.

Fishman, JA (2002) *Can Threatened Languages Be Saved?* (Clevedon, Multilingual Matters Ltd).

Fuller, GE (2003) 'Old Europe—or Old America?' *International Herald Tribune online*, http://WWW.iht.com/cgi-bin/generic.cgi?/template=articleprint.tmplh&ArticleID=83670, 12 February.

Garnham, N (2000a) *Emancipation, the Media and Modernity, Arguments about the Media and Social Theory* (Oxford, Oxford University Press).

Garnham, N (2000b) 'La théorie de la société de l'information en tant qu'idéologie, une critique', 101 *Réseaux* 53–91.

Gellner, E (1983) *Nations and Nationalism* (Oxford, Basil Blackwell).

*Guardian Unlimited* (2003) 'Europe Old and New, Divisions Hamper Response to Iraq Crisis', http://www.guardian.co.uk/eu/story/0,7369,886166,00.html, 31 January.

Habermas, J (1989) [1962] *The Structural Transformation of the Public Sphere* (tr Burger) (Cambridge, Polity Press).

Habermas, J (1997) *Between Facts and Norms* (Cambridge, Polity Press).

Habermas, J (2001) *So, Why does Europe Need a Constitution?* (European University Institute, Florence).

Habermas, J (2003) 'Europe, plaidoyer pour une politique extérieure commune', *Libération* 6857, 1 June, 44–46.

Hakala, J, Kutinlahti, P and Kaukonen, E (2002) 'Becoming International, Becoming European, EU Research Collaboration at Finnish Universities', 15 *Innovation* 357–79.

Harnden, T and Delves Broughton, P (2003) 'French give Rumsfeld Cambronne Treatment', http://www.telegraph.co.uk/news/main.jhtml?xml=/news/2003/01/24/wrow24.xml, 24 January.

Held, D (1995) *Democracy and the Global Order, From the Modern State to Cosmopolitan Governance* (Cambridge, Polity Press).

Held, D (2003) 'Return to the State of Nature' *openDemocracy*, http://www.opendemocracy.net/content/articles/PDF/1065.pdf.

Jönssen, C, Tägil, S and Törnqvist, G (2000) *Organizing European Space* (London, Sage Publications).

Krauthammer, C (2003) 'Old vs New Europe Isn't New', http://www.townhall.com/columnists/CharlesKrauthammer/2003/02/21/old_vs_new_europe_isnt_new. 21 February.

Lange, A (2003) 'Amenaza a la diversidad cultural europea, La circulación europea de programas de televisión sigue siendo baja', 55 *Telos* 17–22.

Mattelart, A (2000) 'L'âge de l'information, genèse d'une appelation non contrôlée', 18 *Réseaux* 19–52.

Meyer, CO (2000) 'Towards a European Public Sphere? Transnational Investigative Journalism and the European Commission's Resignation' in B Baerns and J Raupp (eds), *Information and Transnational Communication in Europe, Practice and Research* (Berlin, Vistas).

Mönninger, M (2003) Interview, Emmanuel Todd, *Prospect*, June, 24–25.

Moragas Spà, M, Garitaonandía, C and López, B (1999) *Television on Your Doorstep, Decentralization Experiences in the European Union* (Luton, University of Luton Press).

Morgan, D (1999) *The European Parliament, Mass Media and the Search for Power and Influence* (Aldershot, Ashgate Publishing).

Neveu, C (2000) 'Citizens of Europe and European Citizens, Exploring European Citizenship' in I Bellier and T Wilson (eds), *An Anthropology of the European Union, Building, Imagining and Experiencing the New Europe* (Oxford, Berg).

Neveu, C (2002) 'Devenir Européen, entre individualisme et emprise des cadres', 26 *Anthropologie et Sociétés* 127–38.

Neveu, E (2002) 'Europe as an "Un-imaginable Community"? The Failure of the French News-Magazine *L'Européen*', 10 *Journal of European Area Studies* 283–300.

Roche, M (2001) *Citizenship, Popular Culture and Europe* in N Stevenson (ed), *Culture and Citzenship* (London, Sage Publications).

Rothenbuhler, E (2003) 'Community and Pluralism in Wirth's "Consensus and Mass Communication"' in E Katz *et al* (eds), *Canonic Texts in Media Research* (Cambridge, Polity Press).

Schlesinger, P (1999) 'Changing Spaces of Political Communication, The Case of the European Union', 16 *Political Communication* 263–79.

Schlesinger, P (2000) 'The Nation and Communicative Space' in H Tumber (ed), *Media Power, Professionals and Politics* (London, Routledge).

Schlesinger, P and Kevin, D (2000) 'Can the European Union Become a Sphere of Publics?' in EO Eriksen and JE Fossum (eds), *Democracy in the European Union, Integration Through Deliberation?* (London, Routledge).

Street, J (2001) *Mass Media, Politics and Democracy* (Houndsmills, Palgrave).

Toynbee, P (2003) 'A Continent Betrayed', *The Guardian*, 21 March, http://www.guardian.co.uk/Iraq/Story/0.3604,918791,00.html

Van de Steeg, M (2003) 'Rethinking the Conditions for a Public Sphere in the European Union', 5 *European Journal of Social Theory* 499–519.

Van der Meulen, B (2002) 'Europeanization of Research and the Role of Universities, An Organizational-Cultural Perspective', 15 *Innovation* 341–55.

Williams, R (1981) *Culture* (London, Fontana Paperbacks).

# Index

www.ingramcontent.com/pod-product-compliance
Ingram Content Group UK Ltd.
Pitfield, Milton Keynes, MK11 3LW, UK
UKHW020245290926
15470UKWH00002B/742

9 781841 136677